THE LIFE AND LETTERS OF
JOHN BURROUGHS

IN TWO VOLUMES

VOLUME I

THE LIFE AND LETTERS
OF
JOHN BURROUGHS

BY
CLARA BARRUS

*Author of 'Our Friend John Burroughs,' 'John
Burroughs, Boy and Man,' etc.*

With Illustrations

VOLUME I

BOSTON AND NEW YORK
HOUGHTON MIFFLIN COMPANY
𝕿𝖍𝖊 𝕽𝖎𝖛𝖊𝖗𝖘𝖎𝖉𝖊 𝕻𝖗𝖊𝖘𝖘 𝕮𝖆𝖒𝖇𝖗𝖎𝖉𝖌𝖊
1925

925
B

The Riverside Press
CAMBRIDGE · MASSACHUSETTS
PRINTED IN THE U.S.A.

6036

74214

Men in general are neither very good nor very bad. . . . I have never examined even the best without discovering faults and frailties invisible at first. . . . There are two men in every man; it is childish to see only one; it is sad and unjust to look only at the other. . . . Man, with all his vices, his weaknesses, and his virtues, this strange mixture of good and bad, of low and lofty, of sincere and depraved, is, after all, the object most deserving of study, interest, pity, affection, and admiration to be found upon the earth; and since we have no angels, we cannot attach ourselves to anything greater or worthier than our fellow creatures.

— De Tocqueville

CONTENTS

CONTENTS

ILLUSTRATIONS

INTRODUCTION

'Where is the tremendous outdoors of these States?' asked Whitman in 1855. An answer to this question is found in the long life and work of John Burroughs, for by his life, no less than by his books, he lured the throng into the open, away from the artificial, to the beauty of the natural. The attempt to record his life has been about what a friend prophesied it would be — like trying to squeeze all outdoors between the covers of a book.

Once, when cautioning me against the biographer's tendency to undue enthusiasm, Mr. Burroughs said, 'Remember, my books are not the corner-stone of American literature.' Though mindful of this warning, is it too much to say that, coming as they did when so much of artificiality prevailed, his writings and his sane, simple living supplied the needed something to restore saner standards both to literature and life?

Rich in inner vicissitudes, his life challenges interest as a record of what he thought and felt. One becomes deeply concerned with his aspirations and disillusionments; his reactions to the irrevocable; his struggles, defeats, progress.

His life presents few notable dates and events, such as characterize the lives of men of action. Not so much in its contact with great men do we find its chief meaning, as in its wholesome relations with a multitude of everyday folk, and especially with the youth of the Nation. He quickly established frank and cordial relations with persons, regardless of their obscurity or prominence. Accordingly, the names of many an unknown person will be found in these pages, since with such the greater part of his life was passed — fathers and mothers with their children, teachers and pupils, young men and maidens whose nebulous aspirations he divined and helped toward concrete realization.

Early in our acquaintance Mr. Burroughs said: 'Maybe you will write my life some day. It ought to be more worth while than writing histories of those abnormal patients.' (For I was then a physician in a hospital for the insane.)

Soon he began acquainting me with matters of biographic interest, and sending on his diaries and a mass of early correspondence. 'No one else cares about all this,' he wrote — 'you may make something of it some day.' Still he emphasized that with so few picturesque and telling features, his was but 'a humdrum life, with a few honest books to its credit.' On a later occasion he wrote:

Of course you would not make a great book, as you have not a great subject. I have been too much in the background of the life of my times for you or any one to make a striking book about me. But you could make a sympathetic and interesting volume.

My association with Mr. Burroughs extended over twenty years. Previous to meeting him, I had been an enthusiastic reader of his books for a dozen or more years, and had deduced so much of his real self that the actual meeting with him, in his sixty-fifth year, was rather the continuance and deepening of a friendship than the beginning of an acquaintance. By reason of having learned to use the typewriter shortly before, it was my good fortune to be of some service to him at the outset. He was then having a touch of writer's cramp, and, the machine coming to his aid, he could henceforth use a pencil, thus easing his 'balky hand.' Soon he began sending on everything he wrote; so for the next decade my work in a hospital with abnormal personalities was enlivened by the sane, refreshing essays he continually sent for typing. Thenceforth it was my privilege to type, and help see through the press, all his magazine essays (with perhaps three exceptions), and the last fourteen of his books, beginning with 'Literary Values.' In addition to an active correspondence with him extending over some dozen years, I had the further advantage, during vacations, of living in his summer home at Roxbury; and in the spring of 1914, on establishing my home at Riverby, he and Mrs. Burroughs became members of my household.

They who know a man in the homely intercourse of daily life are not always the ones who know him best. One who sees in perspective may see more truly than one at his elbow. However, having first seen him in perspective, I have tried in limning my subject to keep in mind both that and the nearer view.

'The humblest pool,' Carlyle wrote Goethe, 'so it be at rest within itself, may faithfully reflect the image of the sun.' *So it be at rest within itself* — there's the rub! For with the continuance of medical work in one's home, and the upbringing of two, sometimes three, young nieces and nephews; with lectures to medical students; with a genius, and the wife of a genius, in the household; and with many delightful guests coming and going, there were throughout the years but few moments when, like the placid pool, I was sufficiently at rest within myself to attempt a reflection of the image I aspired to portray. Still, as the years passed, in frequent jottings, and in a journal fitfully kept, much was gathered which might serve when the pool should be less troubled.

'You will be sorry some day if you don't keep a journal,' Mr. Burroughs would say, and never said truer words; but when life was too full to admit of it, I caught on countless scraps of paper bits of his talk, and significant incidents, doing this the more easily when several persons were about. Sometimes, apparently busy at the desk, I was really noting his talk. Again, when he was engaged with others, seated out of range of his vision, I set down, unknown to him, what he was saying. Not that he would have objected, but, aware of it, he might have been less spontaneous.

Several chapters in Volume I, and certain ones in Volume II, received the benefit of his criticism. From time to time, during the years, he would lay a few sheets upon my desk saying, 'Something for your book.' Or, 'When you write your book, say this' — often a pertinent suggestion, again a ludicrous one, perhaps in ridicule of some foible. We had a standing joke of accumulating absurdities for 'the book you *could* write.' Nor were all absurdities, but, for one reason or another, were things better left unsaid.

However, all along, I urged him to write his own life. He did make a beginning in a series of letters to me which covered his ancestry and family life, his childhood and youth, and many pages of self-analysis; but as he was never moved to carry these further, in 1914, with his approval, I incorporated them in 'Our Friend John Burrroughs.' With the years the biographical material piled higher and higher, and again, extracting from it enough to make a Boy's Life, in 1920 I published 'John Burroughs, Boy and Man.'

Besides the Autobiographical Sketches written for me, other autobiographic fragments are to be found in his 'Egotistical Chapter' ('Indoor Studies'), and in 'An Outlook upon Life' ('Leaf and Tendril'); also in sketches written for his son, which Mr. Julian Burroughs published after the death of his father in a book called 'My Boyhood.'

Herein I have aimed to trace the pilgrimage of John Burroughs through life; and, believing that one's life is best told by him who has lived it (if he be candid and capable of self-analysis), I have, so far as possible, let Mr. Burroughs portray himself through Journal and letters; while I have traced his exterior life, after I knew him, in day-by-day conduct and conversation. When presuming to quote him, I have really quoted him. Since his death, certain published talks attributed to him are vitiated by the commingling of spurious talk with much that is genuine. Genuine quotations are their own guarantee, but, unfortunately, garbled ones can sometimes deceive those unacquainted with the one they purport to quote. Other books about him, and certain magazine articles and booklets published since his passing, show unwarrantable carelessness in matters of fact; they reprint false newspaper reports and abound in other misrepresentations and distortions; and, in some instances, while laying stress on presenting the real man, make glaringly untruthful (if unwitting) statements in matters connected with his life and character.

Against the shortcomings of this work of mine, I can make one claim: I have striven for accuracy in matters of fact, and have taken pains to authenticate my statements. My sources are first-hand.

In deciding just what use he will make of intimate records and confidences, the biographer is confronted by no enviable task, more especially as, in the case in hand, Mr. Burroughs met vexed questions with such remarks as, 'You will have to do as seems best at the time — *only I want the truth told.*' To tell the whole truth, the many-faceted truth, so often involves grave questions of taste, of expediency, of justice to those who are gone and to those still living, that one is almost tempted to renounce it all; but, on reflecting that in so doing the same problems would fall to others less informed, one carries on, intent upon picturing his subject as faithfully as he may.

If, 'for reasons,' I have not always told the whole truth, I have told nothing but the truth. The reticences observed have been chiefly in deference to the living. Mr. Burroughs himself frequently charged me, 'Paint the critter as you know him, with all his sins upon him.' Again, 'Now don't take your shoes from off your feet as if you were on holy ground.' With the epithet, 'Saint John the Divine,' whimsically applied by a clerical friend, he had scant patience, and was only a bit mollified on its change to 'Saint John the Human,' querying pertinently, 'But why lug in the "saint"?'

It is no saint that I have pictured here — just a natural man (whatever his gifts), with the usual run of strength and weakness inextricably blended; with limitations as well as capacities, with flaws — crudities, if you will — along with gifts and graces.

An ultra-conventional friend, fearing I would make Mr. Burroughs too human, urged, 'He is regarded as somewhat of an apostolic character.' To paint him realistically would, he argued, 'have a deplorable effect upon those who so regard him.' How little he knew John Burroughs! and, in passing, how little of the tolerance of human sympathy! It was just that glossing over that Mr. Burroughs feared; and, knowing this, I have every reason to think he would approve my effort to present the actual man instead of an emasculated figure; to relate the outstanding facts of his life as fully as may be, together with the complexities of his character; to set forth the hampering, as well as favoring, conditions under which he did his work, with his reactions to those conditions.

It is his personality in its entirety that his friends cherish. Out of this grew the books his readers love, and the life unostentatiously and worthily lived. Knowing him well, revering him, and believing him worthy of immortal regard, I have pictured him as I knew him, content to leave the just estimate of him to the understanding minds and hearts of his readers and friends.

My sincere thanks are due all who have helped in the furtherance of this work, whether by encouragement, counsel, personal recollection, anecdote, or the loan of letters to themselves or to others whom they represent. Several who have thus aided have passed on while the work was in progress. For permission to quote from letters previously published, and for the loan of special letters, acknowledgment is made in the body of the work.

To Mr. Charles E. Benton, probably the oldest living friend of Mr. Burroughs, I am deeply grateful for the gift of the Burroughs side of the Burroughs–Benton correspondence, the chief source of continuous biographic data for some forty years. I am also indebted to Mr. Julian Burroughs, to whose opinions and suggestions in matters relating to his father's family life I have naturally deferred. My warm thanks are due Mr. Ferris Greenslet, Mr. Francis H. Allen, and Mr. and Mrs. H. A. Haring for critical reading of the manuscript, and valued suggestions and counsel. And I am under very special obligation to Mr. and Mrs. John Shea, whose encouragement and constructive criticism have continued from almost the inception to the completion of the work. To Dr. Clyde Fisher, and others elsewhere named, I tender sincere thanks for the use of photographs; and I heartily appreciate the help of Dr. Fisher in the verification of certain scientific data. I also make grateful acknowledgment for accommodations and courtesies extended by officials and attendants in the Library of Congress, the New York Public Library, and the American Academy of Arts and Letters.

C. B.

WOODCHUCK LODGE
ROXBURY-IN-THE-CATSKILLS
April, 1925

THE LIFE AND LETTERS OF
JOHN BURROUGHS

THE LIFE AND LETTERS OF
JOHN BURROUGHS

. .

CHAPTER I

ANCESTRY AND ENVIRONMENT

The history of a man's childhood is the description of his parents and environment;
this is his inarticulate but highly important history, in those first times, while of
articulate history he has yet none.

CARLYLE

JOHN BURROUGHS was born in an unpainted, weather-worn
farmhouse nestling in the lap of the hills above the village of
Roxbury, Delaware County, New York, on April 3, 1837. He
was the seventh child of Chauncey A. Burroughs, whose parents and grandparents moved into that locality from Connecticut about 1776, and of Amy Kelly Burroughs, whose
father was a soldier of the Revolution.

He came of a long line of farmers and country dwellers,
mostly humble folk, so that his love of the soil and of all rural
things had a background of many generations. His works are
probably the most noteworthy gift to literature that ever
sprang from a line of farmers in this country. Scores of American farm-boys have risen to eminence in the professions and in
politics, but what other has attained equal rank in the field of
literature? His parents and brothers and sisters were nowise
distinguished from the ordinary run of farming people. There
are almost no traditions of culture or learning, to say nothing
of literary achievement, in either branch of his descent for
many generations. 'I come of a race of plain, unlettered
farmer-folk,' he wrote in an early letter, 'and the world that
you and I know is a sealed book to them.' But while freely
acknowledging his debt to the humble stock from which he
sprang, he said it would have been of signal advantage had
there been a few trained and intellectual men in his line of
descent. However, the qualities of mind and heart which his

parents and grandparents possessed — veracity, humility, religious seriousness, and an ingrained love of the country — were, considering his chosen work, probably about the best ancestral inheritance he could have had.

It is difficult to estimate just how much a man owes to his ancestry and youthful environment, but in John Burroughs both are unmistakably reflected in his intellectual output: his writings have a savor of the soil and a joy in rural things as vital as the red corpuscles of his blood; and they have an effortless beauty and simplicity, like the landscape of which his father's acres form a part. To him it was given to transmute the plain, homely, inarticulate industry of his yeoman ancestry into inimitable interpretations of rural life. His ancestors tilled the fields and tended the kine; while he, grazing where the kine grazed, translated the grass and herbage and all country scenes and sounds into enduring pastorals.

The Burroughs Homestead farm of three hundred and twenty acres lies in the watershed of the east branch of the Delaware — the Pepacton — and at an altitude of some two thousand feet, with an eastern and southern exposure. From this elevation one looks upon the long flowing lines and into the broad cradle-like valleys of the western Catskills, 'with their farms tilted against the sides of the mountains, or lapping over the long sweeping hills.' It is like the goodly land described in Deuteronomy — 'a land of brooks of water, of fountains and depths that spring out of valleys and hills.' Mr. Burroughs used to say that the hand of Time, through incalculable ages, had so moulded and shaped the old Devonian hills as to rub all harshness and angularity from them. The heights, broad-backed and gentle, the slopes, smooth and flowing, give an impression of singular restfulness and simplicity.

It is the look of youth supervening upon a region of vast geological antiquity [he once wrote me]. The slow, gentle forces of air and water, and not the sudden, violent, and disruptive forces that rule in earthquakes and volcanoes, have shaped this landscape. The farms, striped or checked with stone walls, bend over the rounded hills or lean restfully upon their vast slopes, or stretch serenely in the deep, level valley-bottoms; many-colored, with various crops and grasses, and squares of beech and maple woods; always giving the beholder a delightful sense of freedom and repose as the eye dwells upon these green pastoral vistas. It is not a picturesque country, as that

BIRTHPLACE OF JOHN BURROUGHS, NEAR ROXBURY IN THE CATSKILLS

term is generally used, but a country of open green spaces and long sweeping lines in which the eye delights. It is a land of crystal springs and purling trout-brooks, with cattle upon a thousand hills.

It is important in estimating the man and his works to realize how thorough his affiliations with the home scenes have always been, how deep-seated his longings when separated from them. When, at the age of seventeen, he left the old scenes behind, he left his heart there also — every summer throughout his life returning to the Old Home to spend some part of it amid the hills. From the home-farm he gathered most of the harvest of his earlier books, and there, in his steadily productive later years, the greater part of his last eight volumes was written. A true autochthon, this very gentle Antæus knew that he derived his strength from Mother Earth; his instinct for self-preservation kept him close to her sustaining breast.

To his humble origin is due the fact that he looked out upon the universe with fresh, eager eyes. From virgin soil his rich and copious crops were gathered, and while inaptitude for scholarly things necessitated much experimenting and literary fumbling, most of this, being ploughed under, served only to enrich the soil.

His environment clothed him as a mantle. It stamped itself upon his soul. Peculiarly fluid and impressionable, his psychology, and consequently his style, seem literally to have been shaped by the long flowing lines of the hills upon which he looked as a child, by the wide valleys, the wooded heights, the mountain streams. Their counterpart is found upon his page. Nothing in his writing is broken or abrupt; his sentences flow with the same large simplicity as do the lines of his native landscape; seem as spontaneous as the springs; yield the quiet and privacy of the woods; and are as limpid, musical, and varied as a mountain brook — loitering here, hurrying there, 'full but not turbid, sparkling but not frothy, every shallow quickly compensated for by a deep reach of thought.' His page offers freshness, variety, lucidity, power.

One midsummer day many years ago, while walking across the fields of the old home-farm, he halted and gazed yearningly at the slope behind the homestead, saying, after a pause, 'Oh, my native hills! Will they ever mean to any one else what they have meant to me? Once in a hundred years, perhaps, one might come to whom they would mean as much.' And, continuing, 'Others have loved them, of course, but not as I have loved them and yearned over them, and drawn my inspiration from them.' Yet when a boy upon this farm he never thought of the landscape as beautiful; the breezy upland heights over which he roamed were taken as a matter of course. Not until he had gone away from them, and then returned, did he know them as beautiful. 'These hills are like Father and Mother to me,' he often said; and, oftener still, at sundown, climbed to a height overlooking the homestead, there in the waning light listening to the plaintive strain of the vesper sparrow, or catching, as it floated down from the mountain, the chant of the hermit thrush.

In his Autobiographical Sketches [1] he has said that his descent on his paternal side is largely English,[2] on the maternal, largely Irish; and that he knows no break in the line of farmers in his ancestry back to the seventeenth century. Up to this time but three men in the United States by the name of Burroughs were conspicuously connected with other than rural pursuits — the Reverend George Burroughs (collateral line), who in 1692 was hanged as a wizard at Salem; one Stephen Burroughs (lineal descent), born in 1729, who achieved distinction as mathematician and astronomer, and who devised the system of Federal money adopted by the Congress of the United States in 1790; and a cousin of his father's, Dr. John C. Burroughs, a graduate of Yale, who became the first president of the first Chicago University.

His earliest lineal ancestor in the United States of whom we have any record was named John. Coming from the West Indies and settling in Stratford, Connecticut, about 1690, he

[1] See *Our Friend John Burroughs.* This book is the source of most of the quotations from J. B. found in this chapter. The sketches themselves were written to me in the form of letters, in 1903, and later, up to 1912.

[2] Two entries in his Journal ascribe also a Welsh origin on the paternal side, although he usually emphasized his Celtic strain as chiefly Irish, and derived from his maternal forbears. He says in the Journal, 'I am quite persuaded that my family [paternal] is Welsh and pure Celtic.'

One who has written of him and his ancestry has labored to prove, despite Burroughs's own statements, that his Celtic traits are chiefly Scottish; and, though not proving his case, contends for this opinion with an obstinacy that betrays his own Scottish origin. Apparently because, back in 1897, in a felicitous bit of criticism, he had, without the support of facts, made Burroughs wear the Scottish thistle in his cap, as well as the English rose upon his breast, he still strives to maintain the statement, instead of substituting the shamrock for the thistle, and the Welsh emblem (whatever it be), as the facts demand. Mr. Burroughs's love of the Scottish people was so strong that, had he been able to trace the least strain of Scottish blood in his veins, he would have been eager to claim it.

there married Patience Hinman in 1694. Their eldest son, Stephen, born in 1695, married Ruth Nichols in 1719. The third child of this union, also Stephen, became the noted astronomer already mentioned; the seventh child, Ephraim, born in 1740, was the great-grandfather of our author.

Ephraim Burroughs reared a large family and, about the beginning of the Revolution, left Connecticut for New York State, settling in the county of Delaware, near Stamford, where he died in 1818. He was buried in an unmarked grave, in a field now under cultivation. His great-grandson often expressed regret that he did not know the spot where his body lay.

In 1795 the grandparents of John Burroughs, Eden Burroughs and Rachel Avery, moved over the mountain from Stamford to Roxbury, cutting a road through the woods and bringing all their goods and chattels on a sled drawn by oxen. Here, only a few minutes' walk from the place where John Burroughs himself was to be born, they cleared the land, built a log house with a bark roof of black ash, and a floor of hewn logs. The day on which she began housekeeping in that little hut in the woods, his grandmother declared, was the happiest of her life. (The same love of the chimney-corner and of domesticity was conspicuous in her gifted grandson.) Subsequently her mother, 'Granny Avery,' lived with them — a sensitive, petulant woman who one day, when reproved for something, went and hid in the bushes and sulked. 'It is a family trait — I'm a little that way myself,' confessed her great-grandson. In truth, it was his custom during adult life, when harassed or perturbed by the friction of domestic life, or by annoying contact with fellow mortals, to retreat to the woods, finding in the seclusion of nature serenity and healing. One of his maternal uncles, something of a hermit, lived by himself in a hut in the woods.

Eden Burroughs, the paternal grandfather, was a quiet, exemplary man, spare of build, thrifty, domestic, gentle in manner, and religiously inclined — an Old School Baptist. He died at seventy-two.

From the Burroughs branch John Burroughs said he derived his love of peace and solitude and his intellectual impetus. They were of serious trend; 'not strongly sketched in on the canvas of life; not self-assertive, never roistering or uproarious.' While the most of them were farmers, a few in collateral branches became preachers, teachers, and physicians.

From the paternal grandmother, Rachel Avery (as well as from his mother's side), he derived a Celtic strain. Of Welsh origin, her complexion was sandy, as was his father's, a coloring which prevails in many nieces and nephews. (Mr. Burroughs himself had chestnut hair before it began, in his fortieth year, to whiten.) Rachel Avery reared a large family; helped in the fields and at sugar-making; and rode a long distance to mill on horseback, with the meal-bags and a baby.

Edmund Kelly,[1] the maternal grandfather, of Irish descent, was born in Frederickstown, Dutchess County, New York, in 1767. He served under Washington as a boy of fourteen in the Revolutionary War, at first in some humbler capacity, later carrying a musket; and 'doing justice to his country and honor to himself,' as Jay Gould records in his 'History of Delaware County.' In the War of 1812, Edmund Kelly went in the place of a drafted son, preferring the life of adventure to the humdrum life of the farm.

His grandson vividly recollected the little old man with big head and pronounced Irish features, with his blue, brass-buttoned army-coat and red-top boots, who used to tell of the winter at Valley Forge, and who was always ready to go a-fishing. 'Gran'ther was a dreamer, and not a good provider. He would get the trout, but I suspect Granny was sometimes at her wit's end to find the fat to fry them in.' A believer in spooks and witches, he regaled his grandchildren with creepy tales that, in the telling, frightened him anew.

There was doubtless something in Gran'ther Kelly which foreshadowed the nature-lover and writer, although in him it took the form of a love of angling and of the Bible.

He went from the Book to the stream, and from the stream to the Book with great regularity; and when past eighty would woo the trout-streams with all his early fervor. From him I get my dreamy, shirking ways [confessed the grandson]; from him, too, I get that almost feminine sensibility and tinge of melancholy that shows in my books. That emotional Celt, ineffectual in some ways, full of longings and impossible dreams — temporizing, revolutionary, mystical — surely that man is in me, and surely he comes from my Revolutionary ancestor, Gran'ther Kelly.[2]

[1] 'Kelley' is the spelling used by some branches of the family.
[2] Condensed from Autobiographical Sketches in *Our Friend John Burroughs*.

Edmund Kelly lived to be near eighty-eight years of age. Jay Gould is authority for the statement that, besides 'the aged partner of his bosom,' he left 'nine children, eighty-four grandchildren, one hundred and two great-grandchildren, together with a large circle of friends.'

The maternal grandmother, Lovina Liscom,[1] was a big woman, thrifty and domestic, who reared ten children, 'and made every one of them toe the mark.' She bore the brunt of the care of the family, not, however, without on occasion taking her shiftless husband to task. 'She was big enough,' her grandson used to say, 'to take Gran'ther across her knees and spank him. I don't know that she ever did it, but he probably deserved it.' She lived to be past eighty.

Chauncey A. Burroughs, the father of John Burroughs, one of nine children, was born in 1803, in a log house built by his parents on settling in Roxbury. He had sandy hair, a face ruddy and freckled; was quick and blustering in his ways; with a voice harsh and strident. As transparent as a child, with no art to conceal anything, he did not dream that others might sometimes have things to conceal. When a boy he had been mean, saucy, and quarrelsome; given to card-playing, swearing, horse-racing, and Sabbath-breaking. In early manhood he experienced religion, joined the church, and became an exemplary member of the community. His schooling was that of the rural districts. For a time he taught a district school. His reading was confined to Bible and hymn-book, his weekly secular paper, and his monthly religious paper ('The Signs of the Times'). (Among the keepsakes of John Burroughs were time-stained copies of this paper of his father's which he had so often seen him read with fervor — a fervor like unto the son's pursuit of Nature.)

Father was a man of unimpeachable veracity [says the son].[2] He was bigoted and intolerant in his religious and political views. A fond husband, a kind father, a good neighbor, a worthy citizen, and a consistent member of the church. He improved his farm, paid his debts, and kept his faith. He had no æsthetic sensibility and no

---

[1] In *Our Friend John Burroughs*, J. B. gives the name as Lavinia Minot. I remember his hesitancy when giving this: 'Good gracious! have I forgotten my grandmother's name — Minot? — I *think* it was Minot.' And so it was recorded; but later, on being shown Jay Gould's record, which gives 'Lovina Liscom,' he said that was probably correct. Hence the latter name appears in *John Burroughs, Boy and Man*.

[2] Condensed from *Our Friend John Burroughs*.

manners. The primrose by the river's brim would not have been
seen by him at all. His disregard of the ordinary civilities often distressed Mother, but, when she would accuse him of having no manners, he would retort, 'I've got all I ever had, for I never used any of
them.' I doubt if he ever said 'Thank you' in his life — I certainly
never heard him.

However lacking in delicacy his father was, he did not lack
candor; and, however brusque, he was really affectionate and
tender-hearted. Refusing requests for holidays with strong
emphasis, he would yield to coaxing; he almost never gave the
punishment he threatened; would tell a joke on himself with
the same gusto as on another; and ask most embarrassing
questions without dreaming of giving offense.

In size and physical make-up the son was much like the
father. He detected in himself many of his father's ways: 'My
loud and harmless barking when angered, I get from him —
the Kellys are more apt to bite.' The ingenuousness and un-
selfconsciousness which he described in his father were, in
a measure, common to him also; likewise his unimpeachable
veracity, his consistency, his candor, and his ever-ready defense of the faith within him.

Chauncey Burroughs, with no comprehension of his son's
aspirations, felt uneasy at his pronounced taste for books. This
plucking of fruit from the Tree of Knowledge was dangerous
business. Arithmetic was all very well, but when a boy
wanted an algebra, it boded no good; and when he wanted to
go to the village academy — clearly there was something
wrong a-brewing; no telling what he would come to; he might
even become a Methodist minister — a degradation below
which, in the eyes of the Old School Baptist, he could scarcely
fall.

John's mother interceded when the lad pleaded for more
schooling than the district school afforded. Because John was
always coaxing to go away to school, his father concluded he
would never amount to anything — in short, never become a
successful farmer. He had less faith in him than in any of his
other sons, and helped him but little in his struggles, either
toward an education or toward getting established in life, and
yet, in later years, when the pinch came, he was helped by him
far more than by any of his other children — 'a curious retri-
bution,' said the son, 'which gave me pleasure, and him no

CHAUNCEY A. BURROUGHS

AMY KELLY BURROUGHS

pain.' When the son began to receive conspicuous recognition as a writer, the father remained strangely silent; however, when his daughter Abigail once showed him a magazine article about his son, accompanied by his photograph, the father looked at it a long time, and, though he made no comment, his eyes filled with tears. 'My aspirations were a sealed book to him. I was better unhelped, and better for all I could help him,' said the son understandingly; 'and he was a loving father all the same.'

Once, at a time of marked religious excitement in the community, the boy John came upon his father praying in an outbuilding and ran away, knowing it was not for him to hear. His father used to say that he had been so carried away by the preaching of Elder Jim Mead as not to know whether he was in the body or out of the body — a capacity for exalted emotionalism which can be traced in the son's life as well; one instance being when, as a small boy, on reading aloud a passage in the 'Life of Washington,' he became oblivious to everything around him. 'I was lifted out of myself,' he said, 'caught up in a cloud of feeling and wafted I know not whither.' Another similar exalted state he thus described:

I recall one summer morning when walking on the top of a stone wall that ran across the summit of one of those broad-backed hills which you yourself know. I had in my hand a bit of a root of a tree, shaped much like a pistol. As I walked along on the toppling stones, I flourished this and called and shouted and exulted, and let my enthusiasm have full swing. It was a moment of supreme happiness. I was literally intoxicated — with what, I do not know; I only remember that life seemed amazingly beautiful. I was on the crest of some curious wave of emotion, and my soul sparkled and flashed in the sunlight.[1]

In the first chapter of 'The Light of Day,' he pictures a scene in his mother's kitchen: his father and a Methodist neighbor, Jerry Bouton, disputing over their respective religious tenets, predestination, and free salvation. Jerry would come sauntering in after supper, whittling a short stick, always whittling toward him. Having arranged his arguments as he came over the hill, he would give scant heed to preliminaries, but would quickly launch text after text at Neighbor Burroughs in support of his own doctrines. With Bible on

[1] From *Our Friend John Burroughs.*

knees and tallow-dip in hand, the latter would, in turn, loudly
hurl Scripture texts at Jerry, whose cheap and easy terms of
salvation made the lip of Chauncey Burroughs to curl con-
temptuously and his nostrils to dilate. In the description of
the homely scene one glimpses the point of view of the reverent
searcher after truth who, though born forty years too late to
accept the beliefs of his father, had yet an understanding
tolerance of dogmas that to him seemed so vital. Of his father's
religious zeal, and his own zeal in having given his heart to
Nature, he used to say: ' I reckon it is the same leaven working
in us both — Father experienced religion, I experienced Nature.' Worshiping the Creator, the one remained blind to all
created things, accepting the finite judgments of men rather
than the revelations all about him; worshiping the Creator in
his works, the other reverently accepted these as the expression of the inscrutable Power in which he lived and moved and
had his being.

In the account of his ancestry previously referred to, John
Burroughs pays this filial tribute:

Father and Mother! I think of them with inexpressible love and
yearning, wrapped in their last eternal sleep. They had for them the
true religion, the religion of serious, simple, hard-working, God-
fearing lives. To believe as they did, to sit in their pews, is impossible for me — the Time-Spirit has decreed otherwise — but all I
am — all I can do — is to emulate their virtues; my soul can only be
saved by a like truthfulness and sincerity.

Amy Kelly, the mother of John Burroughs, was born near
Albany, in 1808. Her son thus acknowledges his debt to her:

Whatever is most valuable in my books comes from her; the background of feeling, of pity, of love comes from her. . . . I owe to
Mother my temperament, my love of nature, my brooding, intro-
spective habit of mind — all those things which in a literary man
help to give atmosphere to his work. In her line were dreamers and
fishermen and hunters. . . . The Celtic element, which I get mostly
from her side, has no doubt played an important part in my life. My
idealism, my romantic tendencies, are largely her gift. . . . The religion of the Kellys was for the most part of the silent, meditative
kind; but there were preachers, teachers, and scholars on Father's
side.[1]

The upbringing of his mother was similar to that of his

[1] From *Our Friend John Burroughs.*

father: In her childhood the family drove with an ox-team
from Rensselaer County to Delaware County. She was the
tenth and last child of her mother. At school, though she
made but meager progress in the three R's, she became so apt
a pupil in certain other lessons as to marry her teacher,
Chauncey Burroughs, in her nineteenth year. The young
couple went to live with the husband's parents, who were then
dwelling in a frame house, in a clearing near the spot where
Eden Burroughs had built his log hut on settling in Roxbury.
There Hiram, their eldest child, was born. This first home of
his parents John Burroughs described as a picturesque old
house with a low roof; adding, savagely, 'Jim Bartram, who
bought the farm later, pulled it down — I'd like to horsewhip
him!' In later years, during his summers on the homestead
farm, he would walk over to the site of 'Grandfather's house,'
roam about the tumbled stone foundation, and muse and
dream of the grandparents and parents who had started their
lives together there.

In 1826 Chauncey Burroughs bought a neighboring farm
(the present Burroughs Homestead), where he and Amy
Kelly lived the rest of their lives, rearing their family of ten
children.

The house in which John Burroughs was born is no longer
standing, having been replaced in 1850 by the present one,
which he fondly called the Old Home.[1]

One is reminded on looking at this low, spreading, unpainted farmhouse, with its humble barns and out-buildings,
of what the author wrote in 'Phases of Farm Life' ('Signs and
Seasons'):

The wise human eye loves modesty; loves plain, simple structures,
loves the unpainted barn that took no thought of itself, and the
dwelling that looks inward and not outward.

He liked a house to have the look of covering its inmates, as
a hen covers her brood — a sheltering look which the Old
Home assuredly has.

Amy Kelly is described by her son as of medium height,
stout of habit, with brown hair, blue-gray eyes, a fine, strong

[1] A Roxbury neighbor, Martin Caswell, a nonagenarian, who helped work on
the 'new house,' said he remembered John Burroughs as a boy of thirteen, helping
the stone-masons and carpenters in the building of the house.

brow, and a straight nose with a strong bridge to it; a woman
of great emotional capacity, who felt more than she thought;
whose spirit was always a little in shadow; and who was given
to brooding and dwelling upon the more serious aspects of
life.

How little she knew of all that has been thought and done in the
world! [he said] and yet the burden of it all was, in a way, laid upon
her. The seriousness of Revolutionary times, out of which came her
father and mother, was no doubt reflected in her own serious disposition.

A self-conscious, yearning, inarticulate nature, she was
withal a woman of strong natural traits and wholesome instincts, devoted to her children, a faithful and provident help-
meet, an heroic worker, and a helpful neighbor.

When giving his family history, Mr. Burroughs told of two
aunts, a paternal and a maternal, who overstepped the conventional limits — threw their caps over the windmill — and
ordered their lives to suit themselves instead of society. Never
in written or verbal accounts of family or personal history did
he gloss over weaknesses or shortcomings, but spoke of all with
engaging candor. If he mentioned the Reverend George Burroughs — sturdy, exemplary, and dying for conscience' sake
(who was hanged as a wizard in Salem in 1692) — as an ancestral figure, he likewise acknowledged the notorious Stephen
Burroughs, of Massachusetts (born 1765), as probably also
collateral kin — that naïve hypocrite and adventurer who confesses in his memoirs to an astounding amount and diversity
of rascality, yet who apparently reformed and conducted himself well for prolonged periods, especially in the closing years
of his life.

John Burroughs was the fifth son and seventh child of his
parents. His mother was in her twenty-ninth year when carrying him. The size of his head nearly cost her her life. When he
was a small boy, a traveling phrenologist, commenting on the
size and unusualness of his head, predicted for the lad great
renown and riches — the truth of which prediction one con-
cedes, if permitted to put his own interpretation upon the
'riches.'

Recounting the unremitting toil of his mother, the son said
sympathetically:

Her thrift and industry were of the first order. The amount of work she did as a farmer's wife with ten children — spinning, knitting, sewing, weaving, milking, butter-making, sugar-making — and often without the aid of a hired girl, makes my heart ache to think of. The patching and mending of the trousers of us five boys, and the knitting and darning of our socks and mittens, were more than enough for one pair of hands. Then she made her own candles by the slow process of dipping; dried apples and pumpkins; made pickles and preserves; wove rag-carpets; boiled soap, and made cheese; pieced bed-quilts and wove coverlids; and spun flax and wool, and wove them into cloth for shirts and trousers, towels and sheets.

Yet, with all these tasks, she found time to roam the hill-meadows for wild strawberries and the bushy bark-peelings for raspberries. 'How she would work to get the churning out of the way so she could get out to the berry-lot! It seemed to heal and refresh her.'

She, who made her son a writer by transmitting to him what Carlyle would call the aroma of his nature, never read one of his books, although his first book on Whitman and four of his nature books were published during her lifetime. She prized a crude early poem which he wrote — 'My Brother's Farm' — and had it framed and hung in her parlor. If she was unable to appreciate his literary work, she believed in him; her instinct divined in him, the odd one of the family, something which led her to treat him with decided preference and tenderness, and later to take up the cudgels for him; thus securing the few educational privileges he obtained at the hands of his unwilling father.

As Mrs. Orr said of Robert Browning, so was Burroughs, the most important fact in his family history. His brothers became farmers; his sisters, farmers' wives. One brother died in infancy, a sister in early childhood, and a sister and brother in early adult life. Aside from his mother's divination concerning him, only one other in the family, his sister Abigail, appreciated his aspirations, or had any acquaintance with his work. The family letters to him, from father, brothers, and sisters, are homely country letters full of warm-hearted affection. They deal with the price of butter, how many firkins have been sold; how many hundredweight of maple sugar; how the hay-crop turned out; what cows have come in; when the calves will be ready to kill; how much the hogs weigh, and what prices they bring. Financial worries and difficulties

abound in Hiram's letters. Eden's are concerned chiefly with
fox-hunting and his hounds. One announces that his mother
has got her geese all picked; another asks 'John' to help in
marketing their butter and turkeys. They mention sending
him dried apples, lard, and sugar, and receiving from him shad
and herring, peaches, and grapes. The father's letters usually
begin, 'Through the goodness of God I am still alive,' then
proceed to details of his health, with news of the family, and
the farm. In a letter to his son, in 1875, he says:

I am a poor wore out old man I dont expect to stay long in this
country I feel as though I was going to a city whose builder and
maker is God my hope is strong in Jesus the fount of every blessing
John the Old School Baptist doctrine is near and dear to me as I
grow old I am a failable creature. . . .

Abigail writes that she is going to fix over her drab silk
dress and wishes John to get her some poplin to match. She
will pay him in the fall, when she sells her butter. In one letter
she mentions having finished reading one of his books.

He once sent me the following description of another sister:

Jane is a tender-hearted, melancholy woman whose interests
center in home and a large family. She used to admonish me not to
write so much, since 'writing is bad for the head.' She is two years
my senior. In a way she prepared the way for me — very emotional
and plaintive — a soft, pulpy woman who dissolves in tears on the
slightest provocation. I can see myself in her perpetually. She has
had great burdens to bear, and bears them with far more fortitude
than I could.

Hiram, the eldest, cared more for learning than any of the
others except John. He studied grammar, and even learned to
parse, but could hardly write a grammatical sentence, though
he had a fine bold chirography. He and John corresponded
faithfully all their lives, though he had no interest whatever
in the latter's intellectual life. An unpractical man and a
dreamer, but skilled in the use of tools, he had a knack and a
readiness about many things connected with farm life; yet
could not make farming pay; could not elbow his way in a
crowd; was always pushed to the wall.

'There's a tree that Hiram grafted in 1885'; 'This stone-wall
Hiram and I helped build in 1853'; 'Here's the mark of Hiram's
drill — it's been there since I was a boy' — thus Mr. Burroughs

would comment while going about the home-farm in later years.

The poetry of rural life — bee-culture, any fancy strain in sheep or poultry — appealed to both Hiram and John. As boys they used to hang around a certain neighbor's yard where some chickens with specially large top-knots filled their eyes: 'If I had not taken this tendency out in running after wild Nature and writing about her,' said Mr. Burroughs, 'I should probably have been a bee-man, or a fancy-stock farmer. . . . The top-knot was the extra touch — the touch of poetry — that I have always looked for in things, and that Hiram, in his way, craved and sought for, too.'

Very real the gifted brother makes the obscure brother as he tells of his thwarted day-dreams — of his always wanting some plaything, such as fancy sheep or bees; of being so curious about strange lands — keeping his valise packed for years, hoping to go West; once even starting, but losing heart as soon as he got beyond sight of his native hills, the end of life's journey coming before he was again ready to go West.

'He never gazed on Carcassonne!'

One's interest deepens in this humble dreamer as his brother says: 'I see myself in Hiram . . . I have at times his vagueness, his irresolution, and want of spirit when imposed upon. My wife tells me I don't know enough to know when I am insulted.'

Eden had a cheery disposition, was methodical and industrious, and, compared to the others, punctilious in dress. 'Come and see how neat Eden keeps his barn and tool-house, and see his fine garden,' Mr. Burroughs once said to me, adding, with a twinkle in his eyes, 'You see all the family are not so slipshod as I am.' And truly the garden of Eden was a delight to behold.

In the following record, given me early in our acquaintance, Mr. Burroughs brought to the summing-up of facts concerning his family the same straight-seeing and candor that characterized his natural-history observations:

Of my family I can truly say, 'How little they knew of what is best worth knowing in the world!' How little I myself know, but how much less they knew! My brothers read no books; hardly ever looked into a newspaper, unless it were a mere local sheet, though Curtis in his old age did read the 'Signs of the Times.' They did not read in the Book of Nature which always lay open before them, except so far as their needs and duties compelled them to read. Curtis read the weather signs remarkably well. He was habitually glancing up at the sky, and could forecast the weather better than I could. He did not see well, but seemed to carry a barometer in his sense of feeling. Hiram had some bee-lore, and an eye for sled-crooks in trees, yes, and for cradle-fingers. He knew the ways of foxes, as did Eden, he had hunted them so much. None of them were good anglers, or very good farmers, though Father was a first-rate farmer.

Mother, I think, never read a page of anything. Olly Ann had some schooling, but I do not know that she ever read a book; the same with Jane. Abigail was better informed, still she read but little.

Father always took a weekly Albany paper, and would read the Governor's message and comment upon it. Later he took the N.Y. Journal of Commerce. This gave him the markets. He also read his religious paper diligently.

Learning did not come easy to any of us, though Father used to tell his friends, 'John takes to larnin'.' I 'took' fairly well to mathematics (but I never conquered the higher mathematics), and to the ordinary country-school courses; but languages came hard to me, and the feeble attempts I made at Latin and French, during my two terms in the seminaries, resulted in little. I always read the best books of English literature eagerly, but I could never acquire any of the marks or accomplishments of a scholar. Learned names and references and bookish airs would not stick to me. I got much out of books, but not what the schools and colleges give. I lack the pride of scholarly accomplishments. My farmer ancestry rules me in this respect. I am my father and brothers with more culture, but with the same awkwardness and fumbling incompetence in all bookish matters. Perhaps I should say that it is the technical part of literature and science that I fail in. My natural-history knowledge is more like that of the hunter and trapper than like that of the real scientist. I know our birds well, but not as the professional ornithologist knows them. I know them through my heart more than through my head. It is hard for me to remember arbitrary names and technical facts. Those full and ready men who can talk as if out of an encyclopædia — how I envy them! Edison, for instance, can talk chemistry as if out of a text-book. . . .

We are weak as men. We do not make ourselves felt in the community; we are below the average in those qualities and powers which make for worldly success; but this very weakness is a help to me as a writer upon Nature . . . that which hinders me with men, makes me strong with impersonal Nature.

Among these brothers and sisters, in these humble scenes, John Burroughs grew up and reached out for the things his spirit craved, finding them in Nature and in books. His family's lack of interest, and, for the most part, of comprehension, in what made up his real life, accounts for his habitual reluctance to mention his writings at home. 'It was not natural,' he said with unconscious pathos, 'to speak of them among my kinsfolk.' Still, instead of blaming his kin for lack of sympathy, he excused them, saying, 'I sometimes have a half-guilty feeling that I unwittingly robbed them of part of their heritage — Nature gave the lion's share to me.' Or, to quote his brother Eden, 'They give John all the brains — there wa'n't none left for the rest of us.' Intellectual isolation from them, however, seemed only to deepen his yearning:

They can value in me only what I have in common with them, which is, no doubt, the larger part of me. But I love them just the same. They are a part of Father and Mother, of the Old Home, and of my youthful days.

His upbringing amid rural scenes, and with unlettered persons, accounts for John Burroughs better than one might at first think. To the fact that he had few books and plenty of real things is due that sense of reality and unbookishness in his work. The homely life of the farm seems to have been best calculated to develop that kinship with Nature which enabled him to translate her language into the language of human thought and affection. And yet his father was a farm-boy, and his father before him, likewise his brothers, and they all remained humdrum toilers, callous to beauty, devoid of interest either in Nature or in books. Clearly one must seek further to account for the writer we know. True, his maternal grandfather, and his mother, inarticulate as they were, had the stuff of poetry in their souls. Nature drew them as she did him. Still it requires something more than the factors of his ancestry and environment, favorable as was the latter in natural things, to account for him; for, as George Eliot says, the selfish instincts are not subdued by the sight of buttercups, nor is integrity established by the classical rural occupation, sheep-washing; and to make men moral something more is requisite than to turn them out to grass. Something more than turning them out to grass is likewise required to make them devotees of Nature, and literary artists as well; a something more, which, in the case of John Burroughs, was the gift of genius. Deep into his native soil he struck his roots; he drew his breath from the clear mountain air, and drank at perennial springs; and much of soil, air, and water entered into him, causing him to an unusual degree to think with and from his environment; causing, too, his heart to throb with ancestral emotion; but 'the little more — and how much it is!' — rooted him deep in the life of the universe, and gave him insight into the great elemental truths. Thus, linked as he was to the common, homely life about him, and hampered by its limitations, this 'something more' linked him also to the cosmic and the universal.

CHAPTER II

THE FARM–BOY

1837–1854

There was a child went forth every day,
And the first object he looked upon, that object he became,
And that object became part of him for the day or a certain part of the day,
Or for many years. . . .
The early lilacs became part of the child,
And grass, and white and red morning-glories, and white and red clover, and the
    song of the phœbe-bird,
And the Third month's lambs, and the sow's pink-faint litter, and the mare's foal,
    and the cow's calf,
And the noisy brood of the barnyard or by the mire of the pond-side,
And the fish suspending themselves so curiously below here, and the beautiful
    curious liquid,
And the water-plants with their graceful flat heads — all became a part of him.

                             WHITMAN

THE pastoral region where John Burroughs spent the first seventeen years of his life invites to further acquaintance as one learns how deep a hold it had upon his affections, how much it shaped his character and influenced his work. 'I was the Child that went forth,' he once wrote me, 'and every object I looked upon, with pity or love or dread, that object I became, and that object became a part of me; and it is still true in a measure.' This susceptibility and plasticity which characterized boy and man account for the degree to which he became so fused and blended with nature that rural things were bone of his bone and flesh of his flesh. 'Take that farm-boy out of my books,' he has said, 'and you have robbed them of something vital and fundamental.'

The rural district around Roxbury has been from its earliest settlement a dairy country — milk and butter being its chief marketable products. In the absence of railroads, the fifty miles from the Hudson River made a concentrated product necessary. Only the cream of the land, so to speak, could be sent to market; hence butter was the one dependable commodity. All the energies of the farm were turned to its production, and the cow and her needs became the ruling factor in country life. She was, in truth, the 'rural divinity.' The soft, cold, delicious water flowing from every dimple in the hills, and the broad areas of grass land, made dairying the natural and profitable specialty of the farmer.

The landscape in this locality suggests the cow; it has her tranquillity and easy ways, and looks, as Mr. Burroughs said, as if it might have been licked into shape by her tongue. In no other part of the country does one see such large herds dotting the hills and slopes, cropping the grass and the red-thorn, or resting in contented rumination under the trees; and in few other regions is so much hay stored in great barns for winter use. Haying is the one strenuous and hustling time in the whole year, and the care of the cattle the one ur-gent occupation during the rigorous winter months.

The mother of John Burroughs was a famous butter-maker, and he and his brothers and sisters early became expert milk-ers. Although I have recently been told by an old man who knew him in his boyhood that 'John didn't like to get up early — he just as lieve lay till after they'd done milking' — I'm thinking he seldom had the inclination gratified. To drive the cows to and from the pastures in summer, to salt them on Sunday, to clean the stables in winter, to feed the calves their milk in the spring, was a part of his daily routine from the age of eight to sixteen. In one of his early manuscripts, which, when rewritten, became 'Our Rural Divinity' ('Birds and Poets'), is the following passage not found in the published essay:

I have a sort of filial regard for the cow. She seems in a remote kind of way like the old family nurse. . . .

My memory is fragrant with the breath of cattle. I come of a race of drivers of oxen, and milkers of cows. I first opened my eyes, and hope to close them, upon a pastoral country — a country of good green grass, where the cow and her products were the chief wealth of the people.

While paying homage to the rural divinity in his humble tasks, he was taking in through keen senses that which enabled him to write of the cow with a reality and charm that restored her to the dignity she once held in classic literature. On beginning to write, he had, as he said, only to unpack the memories of the farm-boy within him, and bird and animal, and all phases of country life, lived upon his page.

In one of his early, unreclaimed essays ('Butter-Making')

is this appetizing bit of literature extracted from his mother's butter-tray:

There lie the rich masses, fold upon fold, leaf upon leaf, fresh, sweet, odorous, just as the ladle of the dairy-maid dipped it from the churn, sweating great drops of buttermilk, and looking like some rare and precious ore. The cool spring water is the only clarifier needed to remove all dross and impurities and bring out all the virtues and beauties of the cream-evolved element. How firm and bright it becomes! how delicious the odor it emits! what vegetarian ever found it in his heart, or his palate either, to repudiate butter? The essence of clover and grass and dandelions and beechen woods is here. How wonderful the chemistry that from elements so common and near at hand produces a result so beautiful and useful!

His homely occupations furnished the background for this picture of the cow:

Behold her grazing in the pastures and on the hillsides, or along the banks of streams, or ruminating under wide-spreading trees, or standing belly-deep in the creek or pond, or lying upon the smooth places in the quiet summer afternoon, the day's grazing done, and waiting to be summoned home to be milked; and again at twilight lying upon the level summit of the hill . . . or in winter a herd of them filing along toward the spring to drink, or being 'foddered' from the stack in the field upon the new snow.[1]

One can fairly see the barefoot boy sitting on the stone fence enjoying the sight which in after years he thus describes:

The cow . . . is the true grazing animal. That smooth, broad, always dewy nose of hers is just the suggestion of greensward. She caresses the grass; she sweeps off the ends of the leaves; she reaps it with the soft sickle of her tongue. She crops close, but she does not bruise or devour the turf like a horse. She is the sward's best friend, and will make it smooth and thick as a carpet.[2]

Memories of the farm-boy, dating farther back than these, one gathers while roaming with him about the old place and getting glimpses of the child he was.[3]

Picture the farm as it bends over the hills and dips into the valleys, with its streams and springs, its stony pastures, its lush meadows, its sheep-lot, its bush-lot, the clover-meadow, the tansy-bordered road winding around the hill by the little

---

[1] *Birds and Poets.*   [2] *Ibid.*

[3] The source of this chapter is in walks and talks with Mr. Burroughs on the home-farm during the last twenty years of his life.

graveyard, the old sugar-bush in the groin of the hill a little above and to the east of the house, the orchard behind and to the west, the beechwoods just beyond 'the turn 'n the road,' and the woods high up on Old Clump [1] — the mountain on the thigh of which the homestead rests. This long, broad hill, or lower slope of the mountain, is one of the striking features of the Burroughs farm. Steep and smooth, broad-backed and fertile, its soil mainly composed of the old red sandstone, it is the scene of the earliest of our farm-boy's recollections:

How many times I have seen that slope grow ruddy with the plow! [he would say, in glancing up at the great hillside with its long, gently sloping sky-line.] How often at early nightfall, the west yet glowing, have I seen the grazing cattle silhouetted against the sky! In winter the snow gathers in huge piles on the breast of the old hill, the drifts often lasting till May. I have seen them linger there in dirty, dwindling masses and stop the plow.

John's first years were, as with all normal children, a piling-up of sense-impressions — the starting-point of all knowledge. He was perhaps no more highly endowed as to special sense-organs than many another, but his senses were always on duty, his interest always keen in natural things. From the richness and permanence of his early memories, it appears that he began at an earlier age than common to gain control of the sense-material. Memory and imagination seem to have begun their work precociously. Comparatively few persons recollect so vividly the experiences of their third and fourth years. [2]

It is interesting to note the character of things recalled: When he was three and a half years old, the Presidential campaign was on for the election of Harrison and Tyler. As an octogenarian he recalled clearly having seen the men go by the house in a lumber-wagon, with lighted torches, and with a coon — the campaign emblem — hoisted high on a pole. He recalled a vivid bit of scarlet — a dead tanager — brought into the house by a maid, in his third or fourth year; also his terror at seeing a great hawk circling above, then swooping to the earth, he crouching behind a stone wall till the hawk disappeared. (One is moved to ask whether this was fear of

[1] On this mountain J. B. wrote the first essay of his which came to print, in the *Bloomville Mirror*, 1856.
[2] 'Early Memories' (*John Burroughs, Boy and Man*).

bodily harm, or, rather an indication of his instinctive sympathy with Nature. Did he identify himself with the defenseless bird, or mouse, pursued by the hawk, in the way wild creatures of various species scent danger from a common enemy? However this may be, it was by means of the 'fluid and attaching character' that he was enabled to become one with bird and beast and flower — a gift which, lying about us in infancy, deserts most of us when we cease to become as a little child.) He recalled the caps on the shoulder-seams of his first suit, and how they flopped as he ran along the road; his first day at school (before he was five years old); his happiness as he sniffed the April odors; his eager questions put to Olly Ann; recalled his difficulty in learning to distinguish *b* from *d* and *c* from *e*, and his pride in mastering them before a bigger boy did; recalled his angry chagrin at being betrayed by an older boy who had bribed him with a fine long slate-pencil into a humiliating confession, and then failed to keep his side of the bargain; recalled the monotonous hum of his mother's spinning-wheel as he sat on the little low cradle and rocked his baby sister to sleep, till he would finally fall asleep there, too. With peculiar vividness he recalled a day spent at Neighbor Bartram's, when he went with his father on the stone-boat, probably when five or six years old. As he and Eleanor played on a mound of hay, she pretended to be a hen. He could always visualize the shining wisps of hay which she tried to pinch into the shape of an egg before hovering it in the nest. Quite as vivid was the recollection of his forlorn feeling when, riding home behind the oxen, he looked back and saw the little pink sunbonnet, a mere speck in the valley, till finally lost to view. He recalled his grief, as a lad of eight perhaps, when a boy cousin's visit ended, leaving him for a time inconsolable — a forecast of his life-long love of comrades.

Besides the already-noted incidents in which fear was predominant emotion, he recounted others: Gran'ther Ke who fed him and his brothers on tales of spooks and h goblins, had so imbued him with the dread of darkness th he suffered acutely, even when well on in his teens. One pai ful recollection is of his terror one night in the old kitch when his parents were away, and he and the other childre huddled in a corner in the dim candlelight, peopled the bla doorway to the bedroom with fearsome creatures. Whenever he had to pass the graveyard at dusk, he would tiptoe round the bend of the road, afraid to run lest a gang of ghosts should be at his heels. To go alone along the edge of the woods at nightfall, even in the later teens, was a frightful experience — darkness held such nameless terrors. He even dreaded cleaning the stables in the big barn, because of the great black hole beneath.

I was tortured with the thought of what might lurk there in that black abyss [he said], and would hustle through my task, working like Hercules, and sending Cuff in often to scare 'em out.

There seems a fine compensation for his boyish fears in that in advancing age he sat in that same barn — the Hay-Barn Study — with its black hole underneath, and wrote of 'The Phantoms Behind Us' ('Time and Change'). There was still something Herculean in the task, but, tackling it, not without some shrinking, it is true, he looked boldly down the black abyss of Time; saw the 'huge First Nothing'; faced the specters as they rose, and wrestled with them; and came at last to recognize in each a friendly power upon whose shoulders one might rise higher and higher. Out of the blackness peopled with uncouth, gigantic forms, he saw man emerge triumphant; and, proudly admitting his lowly origin, gloried in having put the phantoms forever behind him.

The fear of darkness did not leave him until another primitive instinct, the sexual, began to assert itself. With the dawning of this, and the social instinct, the fear subsided. Not, however, at once. For at an apple-cut, when he wanted to 'see home' his little sweetheart of the pink sunbonnet, although he tried to screw his courage to the sticking-point, he failed, admitting the next day, when teased about his diffidence, that the thought of the long walk home alone, in the dark, had held him back. However, not many months later, the attractions of a maiden in the village helped him to conquer the fear; so that, after paying bashful court till two in the morning, as custom decreed, he walked home over the hills and through the fearsome beechwoods.

Many early recollections are indicative of his eager curiosity concerning natural objects, a curiosity which developed into the absorbing passion that led him tirelessly to investigate the lives of the wild creatures, while his thoughts and fancies played around the observed facts till he understood their causes and relations. It was the same curiosity which in maturer years led him to explore the mystery of life, its origin, evolution, transmutations — which kept him ever concerned about the unanswerable Whence, and Whither.

The birds, he said, stuck to him from the first; their coming in the spring thrilled him, giving a new color to his day. The little red bird, already mentioned, awakened his interest and pity when he was a mere fledgling himself; the calls and songs of the common birds attracted him long before he knew the singers' names. Thus when, at the age of seven or eight, his attention was arrested by a strange bird in the Deacon woods, the experience proved of signal importance: Only a small bluish warbler [1] with a white spot on its wing, but it challenged him as had no other bird before. Through it he got a glimpse of a world of birds of which he knew nothing; a glimpse which so fired his imagination that he half-resolved to know more about the birds some day. [2]

All sorts of sensuous experiences were now pouring in upon him, but chores and pastimes filled the hours, and many years were still to pass before he began the systematic study of the birds. However, long before he knew the birds as the ornithologist knows them, he knew them by heart, the intimate knowledge then and always preceding and superseding the merely technical, making him an interpreter of the birds, rather than a feather-splitting ornithologist. The exacting field of the ornithologist held little attraction for him. Hence, when he wrote his first book about the birds, Helen Hunt, reviewing it, pertinently said that it was not an ornithology; that its author *could* have written an ornithology, but that many who could write an ornithology could not have written 'Wake-Robin.'

One more bird incident left an indelible impression upon the lad. In his youth the passenger pigeons passed over his father's farm in vast armies, coming and going like the summer clouds, especially during good beechnut years, sometimes actually darkening the sky. One spring morning, as he sat

[1] The black-throated blue warbler.
[2] Years later, when he did study the birds, he found the nest and eggs of this particular warbler, and, curiously enough, was the first to describe it in print. (Baird, Brewer, and Ridgway's *History of North American Birds.*)

watching a host passing over, he saw them pour down into the beechwoods. Seizing the musket, he ran up the road, and crept along the stone wall till within a few rods of them. There they whirled and rushed and fluttered and cooed, as they fed on the sprouting nuts. Air and woods and earth were blue with them. The ground seemed a yard deep with them. The whole world seemed turned to pigeons. The lad sat motionless, his gun pointed at the surging mass, his eye traveling along the barrel. Why did he not shoot? Still they came pouring down, and still, spellbound, he waited. For what? Suddenly, with a rush and a roar, they were off! Only then did the dazed dreamer realize what a chance he had let slip. There was no pigeon pot-pie that day in the Burroughs home, but what went on in the lad's soul, as he watched the fluttering birds and listened to their childlike calls, was an earnest of what was yet to be — 'John o' Birds' was perhaps born that eventful day.

Other forms of wild life attracted him. The shrill, cheery calls from the swamps in early spring aroused his eager questioning. To his inquiries as to what made those sounds, he could get no answer. So one evening while it was yet light, determining to find out for himself, he crept in among the rushes, scrooching down and keeping so still he seemed a part of the swamp itself. Soon came a tiny frog climbing a bulrush, hand over hand, as a sailor climbs a mast. The boy held his breath, and soon, the little creature tuning up, John saw him in the very act of piping. Cautiously stretching forth his hand, he captured the elf, which, on becoming accustomed to its new perch, inflated its throat and piped from his hand! Not till many years later did he learn the name of the little hyla.

Similarly he studied the ways of the bumblebees, learning to distinguish three varieties, and where they were wont to build, one season collecting two pounds of bumblebee honey.

In late June, John and his mother would go strawberrying together. The only one of her boys who was a first-class berry-picker, he got the biggest berries and the most of them, divining where they lurked under the leaves. There in the sunny uplands mother and son stooped low, parting away the timothy and daisies, while the warm breath of the meadow came up in their faces, and bobolinks rollicked overhead. As they returned home in silent companionship, the lad, at least, brought back a good deal more than berries. And in the years to come, far from those scenes, he still wandered in those mountain meadows, knee-deep in timothy, the breath of the clover mingling with his breath, the jocund song of bobolinks in his ears, while from out the recollections he distilled the very essence of June in his delectable 'Strawberries.' In truth, many of his best-known essays may be traced to his farm-boy activities; for example, 'Phases of Farm Life,' 'The Idyl of the Honey-Bee,' the Apple essay, 'Our Rural Divinity,' 'Springs,' 'Foot-Paths.'

Among his homely duties were hoeing corn, digging potatoes, picking up stone, cleaning stables, burning stumps, knocking 'Juno's cushions'[1] in the spring pastures, salting the young cattle on the mountain, hunting lost sheep, driving the oxen behind the stone-boat, and turning grindstone to sharpen the mowers' scythes.

A one-time neighbor, Martin Caswell, said on being interviewed: 'Yes, yes, I've worked in the hay-fields with John — he used to rake after. He'd walk along and carry the rake on his shoulder, and his father would call out, " John, why don't you rake?" and John would say, "There ain't enough there yet." But Chauncey would shout, "By Phagus! you rake what there *is* there!"' In time the lad took a hand at haying and learned to hold his swath against any mower of his size and age, sometimes even crowding his elders.

He spent long hours pounding with a flail — threshing out the oats and rye on the barn floor — and pleasanter ones threshing buckwheat in the open. In the sugar season his cup was full to the brim: the sunlight white, the trees nude, the fields brown and sere; the blue smoke rising on the air, robins laughing and running about, nuthatches calling, squirrels snickering, and that musical tinkle of the sap in the pans!

Many an adventure he had as he drove the cows to pasture. It might be a wild chase for a woodchuck that whistled defiantly on taking to the stone wall; or might only be to climb to the big rock by the spring — his Boyhood Rock — and muse and dream, while harkening to the highholes in the woods, or the bobolinks in the meadows. Sometimes, sitting upon the big rock, he would speculate as to where he came from, what the

[1] This poetical term for the cows' droppings he found in Washington Irving.

world was made of, and on other mysteries that occupy the reveries of youth. Half-closing his eyes, and observing the tiny chains of bubbles floating before them, he concluded that this was the stuff of which the world was made; and in later years, he admitted that all his philosophizing had hardly brought a more satisfactory explanation.

After two summers at the stone school-house[1] on the Hardscrabble road, he went to school in the West Settlement — in the summer till he was twelve, after which his schooling was confined to the winter months. The foot-paths he traversed to that school, over hills, through woods and meadows, his reader has since traversed with him.

In school he was a restless lad, unless seated where he could look out of the windows, his frequent requests to go out and wash his slate not wholly due, one suspects, to concern for a clean slate. There came a time, however, when he began to care about his lessons; when he looked longingly at the algebras owned by his school-fellows Jay Gould and Andrew Corbin; and when, after coaxing in vain for an algebra, he resolved to earn the wherewithal himself.

Soon he was taking home the few books in the school library — chiefly a book on Arabia, one about Murphy, the Indian-killer, and a Life of Washington. These he read again and again. Sensitiveness to words developed early; at a new word, or a word newly applied, he pricked up his ears. Overhearing a caller who noticed his rude attempt at drawing say, 'What taste that boy has!' he was all interest and marveled, 'Then there is a kind of taste besides that of things to eat!' He heard a man, at work on the road, use the word 'antiquities' as he unearthed a queer-looking stone, and, on asking what the word meant, glimpsed a new world in the man's explanation. He was given to repeating words and high-sounding phrases met in books. The term 'Encyclopædia Britannica,' heard at a lecture in the village, captivated him. 'What a fine mouthful it was!' he said. Such words he copied in a notebook, thus insensibly collecting the tools for his future work.

Strange to say, he got out of writing compositions whenever he could. On one occasion, rather than stay after school, he

---

[1] This structure, built in 1813, is the only building now standing, of the several buildings where J. B. attended school.

shamelessly accepted the aid of Jay Gould, and passed off
Gould's rhymed effort as his own.[1] Young Burroughs once read
a composition which the teacher himself, to maintain discipline,
had written for him; but the sheepish feeling he had while reading it cured him of wanting ever again to sail under false colors.

At a lecture in the village to agitate the building of an
academy there, John, the only lad in the audience, was much
moved by the speaker's eloquence; but when the man urged
the needs of the village youths, and, pointing to John, said,
'I am speaking for boys like that one yonder,' John blushed
painfully and hung his head. However, as he picked his way
over the hills in the darkness, he was all aglow with the vision
of learning that accompanied him.

Fired by accounts from the boys who returned from Harpersfield Seminary, John dreamed of going there. Finally his
pleading, supplemented by persuasive measures from his
mother, wrung from the father the promise that after he had
done the fall ploughing he might go for the winter to Harpersfield. Day after day, on the side-hill lot, he cross-ploughed
the ground for rye, the plough-handles jerking him about, but
his head high in the clouds — visions of books and classmates
and academic halls hovering over the heads of Prince and Pete,
with Harpersfield at the end of every furrow.

When winter came, however, the expense looked too big for
Farmer Burroughs. The other boys had not gone away to
school; why should John want to go? No, it could not be
— times were too hard — the West Settlement school was
good enough for any one. None but the mother realized what
this refusal meant to the lad, as, gulping down his disappointment, he went for his last term to the district school, resolved to get away the next year on money of his own earning.
This he would do by teaching school.

Accordingly, in the spring, shortly before his seventeenth
birthday, with the black oilcloth traveling-bag, and a few
dollars in his pocket, he started out over the saddle of the
mountain in a snow-squall — the mountain that was the barrier between him and the outside world. Walking eight miles
to an uncle's, he was driven the next day to a tavern on the

---

[1] See *Our Friend John Burroughs*. It was a curious reciprocal aid that Burroughs
and Gould gave each other in their schooldays, the future financier helping with
his pen the future writer, and the future writer, once when Gould was hard up,
buying two books of him, thus helping the future financier with his coins.

turnpike, thence journeying by stage-coach to Olive, in the county of Ulster.

In painful embarrassment, not knowing what was expected of him, the youth awaited the arrival of the old Concord coach; but when, his fare paid, and his name entered on the waybill, he heard the driver say, 'Climb to the top, boy!' he obeyed nimbly, his heart beating tumultuously.

Dr. Abram Hull, a friend of his parents, drove him about the country, and after a few days he found a school in need of a teacher. Obtaining from the trustee a half-promise, he returned home to await his decision, which came in a week's time. He was to come immediately: wages eleven dollars a month and 'board round.' (In advanced age he could still visualize the handwriting of that momentous summons.)

Now came the real leave-taking. Up before daylight, a hurried, silent breakfast, the lunch put up, the good-byes said (the mother concealing as best she could her anxiety — her boy John was going out into the world alone —), the agitated youth, with a wistful look at the group on the door-stone, climbed to the spring-seat beside his father, and away they drove to Dimmick's Corners [1] to meet the 'stage.' More confident now, he mounted the old coach, being set down in time at Shokan, whence he walked the few miles to Tongore, in the town of Olive.

Already homesick for his native hills, the familiar sound of the peepers, piping in the April twilight, made him forlorn. When, a child of four on his first journey from the hearth-stone, he had looked back on reaching the turn in the road, and had seen how far he was from home, he had run back as fast as his legs could carry him. Now there could be no turning back. He must push on, wherever the road led.

Far into the night, awake, amid the strange surroundings, his brain teemed with plans. There came a new conception of himself, a more positive self-feeling, as he thought of his responsibilities as a teacher. Day-dreams must yield to actualities. With the unusual stirring of mental powers came a vague prescience of the place he would one day make for himself. Finally, wearied, he fell asleep, the shrill, insistent voices of the peepers sounding through his dreams.

He awoke in a different world. Wistfully he thought of the home amid the hills, but the Future beckoned.

[1] Now Arkville.

CHAPTER III
THE WRITER IN EMBRYO
1854–1863

There is a time in every man's education when he arrives at the conviction that envy is ignorance, that imitation is suicide; that he must take himself for better, for worse, as his portion; that though the wide universe is full of good, no kernel of nourishing corn can come to him but through his toil bestowed upon that plot of ground which is given him to till. The power which resides in him is new in nature, and none but he knows what that is which he can do, nor does he know it until he has tried.

EMERSON

Of the next epoch in the life of John Burroughs, the period from 1854 till the close of 1863, he declared that little need be said: 'I could say very little myself. I was reading and thinking and trying to get hold of myself. I suppose I was growing all the time.'

Of his growth one may be assured; it may even seem, as one learns more of this obscure decade, that it was one of the most significant in his career — not so much in outward events, although some of these, since they influenced the whole course of his life, were of great import; but more especially in things which contributed to his mental and spiritual development. It was a period during which the main lines of his character were formed and his tendencies fixed. From his books one can gather the manner of man he was after beginning to take his place in literature, but to learn how he reached that place, it is needful to trace his development in later adolescence, when, through deepening emotions, and surer mental grasp, he linked his earlier experiences (the farm-boy's precious mine of sense-impressions) with dawning powers, and began consciously to realize the unity of thought, feeling, and will which enabled him to pursue unremittingly the somewhat rough path that led to his goal.

1. SCHOOL-KEEPING AND EARLY STRUGGLES

A crude, callow youth, obtuse, with no social aptitude; given to stuttering when embarrassed; undisciplined, uninformed, yet full of vague and tremulous aspirations and awakenings — is his description of himself at this period.

It was natural that any boy in Delaware county who was ambitious should go down to Ulster county and teach school. It had been the custom for years. The Ulster trustees looked to the Delaware boys to apply. It was the obvious way to earn money, if you did not want to stay on the farm. Some of our boys went to New Jersey to teach. I followed their example in both cases, going first to Tongore.

He read but little that year, and had then no conscious interest in Nature. Years later he was unable to recall how he had spent his leisure — the alternate Saturdays when no school was kept, which, a year later, he spent in roaming the woods. He could recall the names and faces of his pupils, and certain experiences in boarding 'round, and said in looking back upon the time he seemed to see sunshine over all.

As to my teaching, I had a good faculty for imparting knowledge; but I was not a good disciplinarian. I couldn't be rigid enough. Still, I always got the good will of the children and governed in that way. . . . There I spent the first days away from the parental roof. It seems as if some beloved son of mine had taught that school so long ago.

An eclipse of the sun in May, at corn-planting time, is one of his outstanding recollections; another, the purchase from a peddler of a 'Complete Letter-Writer,' which he used in framing a letter of condolence to his parents when Gran'ther Kelly died (in after years he fairly cringed at the thought of it); and his first letter to Mary Taft, his Roxbury sweetheart, — 'a preposterous letter,' — the first sentence of which was:

DEAR MADAM,
It was a question among the Stoics whether the whole of human life afforded more pleasure, or more pain.

Mary's answer, written on a tiny embossed sheet, addressed to her 'absent but not forgotten friend,' began:

I at last find myself in the attitude to address a few scattered thoughts to you through the medium of the pen.

It would be interesting to know what the attitude was in which Mary found herself just after reading that Stoical beginning by her correspondent.

That summer, coming upon a book on Phrenology, by Fowler and Wells, our youth regarded it as highly scientific because of its initial statement that everything springs from an egg. The book engendered an interest in phrenology and physiognomy which lasted many years. In fact, even in advanced age, although his later knowledge precluded adherence to those early-held theories, his estimate of new acquaintances was considerably influenced by rules laid down by those pseudo-scientists. Subsequently buying Gall and Spruzheim, and subscribing to a phrenological journal, he also expended a dollar and a half of his scanty savings for a chart of his head; and when he began to write, one of his earliest efforts, as seen in a note-book dated 1853-54, was a defense of phrenology.

Partly my own, I suppose, and partly from the Phrenological Journal. I must have been trying to string those sentences together — poor, high-flown stuff! I had no ideas, and was just playing with words, you see. I suppose that is the way many begin to write.

Jealously hoarding the most of his earnings, he carried home fifty dollars that October, which, with what he earned on the farm, paid his way for five months at the Ashland Collegiate Institute, Greene County, New York. It was the first year of the school's life. Two hundred students were in attendance. Algebra, geometry, chemistry, French, logic, composition-writing, and declamation were the requirements. His teacher in logic was a delicate, wide-eyed young man who later became prominent in the Methodist Church as Bishop Hearst.

Our student chose logic because he had never heard of it before. The girl classmates elected Wayland's Moral Philosophy instead; and something of the youth's unflattering opinion of girls' minds, and moral philosophy as well, lingered in tone and expression when telling of it. They parsed from 'Paradise Lost.' Astonished at the celestial warfare there described, the youth announced to a classmate that he credited no word of it — a confession which gave the maiden pause, and to which she referred in later years when corresponding about his essays on science *versus* theology.

At Ashland, only one other in the class excelled him in composition. In a debate on the Crimean War, he took the side of England and France against Russia, and came off with flying colors, having got his ammunition from 'Harper's

Magazine'; but his co-debater found himself up a stump when his turn came, having levied on the same source.

After the term at Ashland the student had to earn more money before indulging in another educational orgy, so, with ten dollars advanced by his father, he started for New Jersey in quest of a school, taking his first ride on a steamboat from Kingston to Jersey City, and his first on the steam cars from there to Plainfield, wondering, as he boarded the train, if the engine would start so suddenly as to jerk off his hat!

After walking twelve miles to apply for a school, and being pronounced by the trustees 'too young and inexperienced,' crestfallen, he reluctantly engaged lodgings at the little inn; gazed long and long at the occultation of Venus by the moon, and in the morning tramped back again.

In New York, he hung wistfully around the office of Fowler and Wells, but could not summon courage to enter; but he browsed half a day among the second-hand book-stalls on William Street, oblivious to all other attractions of the city. His return ticket on the boat secure, and allowing for the stage-fare to Dimmick's Corners, he decided he could walk the twelve remaining miles, and so use the rest of his money for several enticing volumes he had selected. Supper and breakfast? Yes, but see what he would have after his hunger was forgotten! So, thrusting the money into the vendor's ready hand, he packed Saint-Pierre, Locke, Johnson, and Thomas Dick into his oilcloth bag, and sought the steamer bound for Kingston.

The grass was green that twentieth day of May when he crossed Batavia Mountain with his heavy load of books, but 'the air was full of the great goose-feather snowflakes which sometimes fall in late May' — always, always, he remembers the face of the day and the mood of Nature, in connection with significant experiences.

In one of his note-books, the fly-leaf of which bears the date 1855, is a list of seventy-nine books (or, in some cases, an author's entire works), with the heading, 'Books I *will* read.' Some of these have the prices affixed. Some names have a line drawn through them, the first, with the date 1854, presumably indicating that he had already read that. But this can hardly be the case with the Encyclopædia Britannica, so marked.

Some of the titles are marked by a cross. One can only conjecture that he may have so marked them as he read them, or
possibly that he was reading, or had read such, when he made
the list. A remarkable grouping for a youth of eighteen, it
perhaps shows better than can anything else his early thirst
for knowledge. He knew what he wanted to read long before
he could spell correctly the titles of certain books, or the names
of certain authors. [1]

Books I will read:

~~Rottocks's History of the World~~ 3.50   1854
~~Chambers Information for the People~~ 5.00
~~Heroic Women of History~~ 2.50
Vicar of Wakefield .50
~~Pollock's Course of Time~~ .50
Plato by E. Pond .38
Byron Complete 5.00
Manual of Classic Literature
English Literature of Nineteenth Century
Compendium of American Literature
American Oratory
E. A. Poe's Works
Letters from Italy   J. T. Headly .50
~~Philosophy by Channing~~ .40
Psychology .25
The Celebrated Poets
Ancient Philosophy
Modern Philosophy
Hume's Essays
Positive Philosophy
× Macaulay's History of England 3
Gibbon on Rome
Books of Travel
Irving's Works
Prescott's Works
~~Saxton's Works~~
History of Spanish Literature 6.00
~~Josephus Complete~~
Plutarch's Lives
Progress of Civilization
History of Reformation
~~A. J. Davis's Works~~
Tupper's Philosophy

[1] The misspelled words found more particularly in early letters and note-books,
and occasional faulty grammar, have been allowed to stand as significant of J. B.'s
early aims toward self-culture despite his meager educational advantages. Furthermore, he was naturally a poor speller. Misspellings noted are, then, to be interpreted as faults in J. B.'s orthography instead of oversights in typography.

Romance
Butler's Analogy
Bacon's Works
Vattell's Laws of Nations
X ~~Encyclopoedia Brittanica~~
~~Library of Mesmerism and Psychology~~
Theological, etc.
~~Medical and Psychological~~
Percies Anecdotes
Orators of the American Revolution   1.25
~~Tempest and Sunshine or Life in Kentucky~~
The Lady of the Lake
~~City and Country Life~~
X English Traits by Emerson
Sears on India and China
X Select London Lectures
Kossuth's Life and Speaches
Cyclopoedia of Biography
Don Quixote
Essays Biographical and Critical by H. L. Tuckerman
Religious Truth by Professor Hitchcock
Essays on the Formation of Opinions and the persuit of truth
True stories from History and Biography by N. Hawthorn
X Washington and the Revolution by E. P. W.
X Henry Giles'es Writings
Woman's Record by S. J. Hale
Miller's Philosophy of History
Bancroft's History of the U.S.
Hume's England
~~J. T. Headlie's Writings~~
~~Rolin's Ancient History~~   4.00
Russell's Modern Europe   6.00
Hallam's Middle Ages   2.00
Allison's Europe
Lamartine's French Revolution   2.50
Curran and his Cotemporaries $1.25
Dugald Stuart's Philos. of Man's Powers $1.25
Thomas Reid's Essay on Man $1.25
Life, Genius and Beauties of Shakespeare   1.25
Poets and Poetry of Greece   2.25
Boyhood of Great Men by J. E. Edgar   .60
Webster's Speeches
Select British Eloquence   3.50
History of the Crusades   3 vol.   3.75
Evarett's Orations and Speeches   5.00
Star Paper   1.25

Once, when commenting upon his early serious reading, Mr.
Burroughs said, 'I diligently held my mind down to the grind-

stone of Locke's philosophy, and no doubt it was made brighter
and sharper by the process.'

At this period of emotional and intellectual expansion, one
pictures him idling and philosophizing, sauntering the woods
with Locke and Johnson, yet sitting up one whole night to
finish reading his first novel, 'Charlotte Temple.' His reactions
to each were natural: Locke and Johnson set his mental machinery going, and 'Charlotte Temple' let loose such a flood of
emotion that he held himself with difficulty to the homely
farm tasks.

In the autumn he again set out for New Jersey in quest of a
school, but stopping in Olive by the way, and there finding the
Tongore school in need of a teacher, he again engaged himself,
but at double the former wages. How much his decision was
influenced by the glimpse he got of the handsome, bright-eyed
niece of the trustee, with her red cheeks, her trim, compact
figure, and forceful personality, is a question. She was certainly the chief attraction that winter at donation parties and
other neighborhood festivities; and when in April (1856) he
returned home, there was something of an 'understanding' between him and Ursula North. Later, when new scenes and
interests were encountered, and when he had to decide between her and at least two other charmers, propinquity tipped
the scales, and the attraction held.

An early letter from Miss North, in the spring of 1856, which
shows that the course of their love had met an impediment,
shows also her acute, decisive turn of mind. When disclaiming
a rumor which she avers had been maliciously circulated, she
makes this picturesque statement:

But there is so many people that are constantly looking over the
affairs of others and overlooking their own, and I think whoever it
was that told you that yarn what you spoke of, must have a principal so small that you could blow it through a Hummingbird's quill
into a little Red Ant's eye and they would only wink at it. . . .

Continuing, she hopes they will meet in the summer for a re-
newal of their pleasant times; but if anything occurs to prevent
their meeting again on earth, hopes they will so live that they
may 'meet in that far better world whare parting is no more,
and whare trouble never comes.' Such a contingency, however,
was evidently not to the liking of the ardent youth, to whom

this seemed a pretty good world, and that particular maiden too captivating to admit of a postponement of meeting till their arrival in a 'better world.' He evidently arranged a meeting in Olive during the summer, for, despite certain veerings of both contracting parties, the 'understanding' held.

During that second term at Tongore, young Burroughs began writing essays, modeling them after the pompous Johnson. A few years later, however, Jack began to take the measure of his giant, and, finding him dwindling to an almost contemptuous degree, observed acutely that 'Doctor Johnson's periods act like a lever of the third-class — the power applied always exceeding the weight raised.' What had first attracted him to Johnson, Dick, and other essayists, during that unformed period, was the enunciation of some general truth. He had bought Dick's Works on the strength of the opening sentence, 'Man is a compound being'; later to declare, 'What twaddle it all was!' Writing reminiscently of that beginning of Dick's essay, he said:

I liked to see a thing start with a brief, bold generalization like that. It at once launched it into the great philosophical currents. If that sentence had begun with the pronoun I, the works of Thomas Dick had never gone home with me that day. But they dropped out after a few years. I think it was their excess of what was called 'Christian Philosophy' that finally sickened me. I began to want my philosophy and my science straight, without any of the sugar and water of an over-ripe religious sentiment.

The daughter of one of his old school-fellows at Cooperstown Seminary kindly submits a letter[1] written by John Burroughs at the age of nineteen — a stilted schoolboy letter, which yet reveals certain characteristics of the man — love of comrades, a pronounced leaning toward feminine society, distaste for drudgery, a wholesome commingling of physical and intellectual interests, concern for good health, love of nature, a tendency to reminiscence, and a strong vein of sentiment counterbalanced by practicality. Two paragraphs of the letter, written from Roxbury, August 4, 1856, run thus:

[*J. B. to L. B. Paine*]
I have been exercising my physical powers since I left Coopers-

---

[1] The letter is published in full in *John Burroughs, Boy and Man*. Excerpts from this, and from other letters in that volume, are used by the courtesy of Doubleday, Page & Co.

town, wielding the scythe more than the 'old grey quill.' You know
the body must work as well as the mind in order to preserve the
equilibrium and fit the man for accomplishing 'big things.' No one
can have a strong mind without a healthy body, and no one can have
a healthy body without physical labor — work, therefore, if you
would be somebody. . . .

We had grand times at the 'Sem.,' did we not, Paine? Do you
remember the morning we went to see 'Old Dame Nature'? She is a
kind old lady! In her lap are pearls of the richest hue, treasures
richer than Pluto's mines, and she deals them out with a bountiful
hand to all who are pure enough to appreciate them. Think you we
will ever have any more such times, Paine? 'Life is but a flower that
blossoms and is gone.' And its leaves may fall ere we meet again,
but I hope not. I hear the rain-drops spattering against my window.
It makes me rejoice, for it has not rained here in a long time. . . .

In 1909, accompanying the little sheet to which he refers,
Mr. Burroughs wrote:

I am sending you a copy of the paper in which I first saw myself in
print — The Bloomville Mirror — of May 13, 1856. Can you see
anything in it that sounds like me? It may foreshadow my controversial spirit of later years, or my hostility to 'fakirs' of all kinds.

The article, 'Vagaries *viz.* Spiritualism,' signed 'Philomath,'
is a stilted, mildly derisive attack upon a too credulous writer
of a previous issue. It abounds in big words, makes its points
with clearness and force, and scorns the 'proofs' gullibly accepted by the 'spiritual' correspondent. However, nothing in
this essay, written at nineteen, would justify one in saying of
Burroughs, as Godwin said of Bryant, (anent 'Thanatopsis'),
that 'he had a national fame before he had a vote.' Its chief
merit lies in its honest-mindedness. His fame lay far in the
future. The essay closes thus:

And how consistent it is with every notion we ought to entertain
of those celestial beings, to suppose they would leave the bright
shores of immortality and descend to this obscure corner of creation
for the mere purpose of satisfying the idle curiosity of particular
individuals! And why not make their visits in the *light of day* as
well as under the cover of night? But the diabolical schemes of the
'mediums' cannot stand the open sunshine, hence they 'choose darkness rather than light because their deeds are evil.'

Significant, that in his first printed utterance he comes
out boldly as a searcher after truth, an uncompromising hater
of shams. The youth is father to the man whose writings for

five and sixty years have stood for clear seeing, straight thinking, and an engaging manner of presenting the truth as ap-
prehended by him. Significant, too, that even then he pleaded
for things to be tested in the common 'light of day'; just as,
some forty years later, he gave that title to his first volume of
religious discussions.

That article in the 'Bloomville Mirror,' written soon after
closing school at Tongore, came out while he was in the first
flush of student-days at Cooperstown Seminary, whither he
went in mid-April, 1856, with enough money to last till the
close of the summer term.

During those three months he began Latin and English
literature, and continued French and mathematics. He out-
ranked his fellows in composition, and debated in the Web-
sterian Society. In his reminiscences, he recalled giving a
Fourth-of-July oration, in spread-eagle style, on the shores of
Lake Otsego; and contending in a debate in which he affirmed,
with satisfaction to himself and his fellows, that the career of
Mahomet was, on the whole, beneficial to the world.

Passages from his earliest extant autograph essay are here
appended. Written in July, 1856, and originally named
'Work and Wait,' when read at the Students' Exhibition the
essay was renamed by the teacher 'Goodness Essential to
Greatness.' Ornate in handwriting and style, the gist of it is
that the whole duty of man is to fan the spark of divinity within; that only step by step can man reach the highest moral and
intellectual excellence; and that this is not a 'monoply' of the
'privaleged' few, but a common boon bestowed upon all. In
its platitudes, its grandiloquence, its moralizing, solemnly set
forth, one can fairly hear the youthful orator's voice ring
through the academic halls. The poor spelling is not in-
frequently due to carelessness, as a given word is sometimes
correctly and incorrectly spelled on the same page. (Here, and
always, many of his orthographic errors must be set down to
the heat of composition.) A characteristic adolescent essay,
its sincerity and moral earnestness are likewise characteristic
of his later years. One can see, even in this crude effort, the
germ of a later, well-known composition; for the devout spirit,
the grasp upon real values, and the reliance upon the divinity
within one's soul, no less than in the material universe, are the
beginnings of what flowered later in the poem 'Waiting.'

Work and Wait.

"Secure not nature she has done her part,
Do thou but thine."
And be not different of wisdom."— Bulwer.

This world is a vast theatre, created for [...] [...]

BEGINNING AND END OF A SCHOOL-BOY ESSAY

The nebulous state of his mind at this time was happily acted upon by the good library at the seminary, which furnished the elements to help define and solidify his character. At first taken by the rhetorical and stilted, he soon gravitated to the simpler style. From the sententiousness of Johnson he swung away, to come under the spell of Addison and Lamb. From Pope and Young, greatly admired at first, he came to prefer Shakespeare and Wordsworth. Saint-Pierre's 'Studies of Nature' set ajar a door that Emerson flung wide open — Emerson who had at first 'tasted like green apples,' but who was soon keenly relished and assimilated:

I read him [Emerson] in a sort of ecstasy. I got him in my blood, and he colored my whole intellectual outlook. He appealed to my spiritual side; his boldness and unconventionality took a deep hold upon me.

Already keenly alive to the sensuous enjoyment of nature, under Emerson's guidance he went out of doors with a consciousness awakened to the subtler shades of beauty, and to the deeper meanings behind facts — their ideal and spiritual values. This awareness of his unity with nature, which Emerson helped to bring about, grew with his growth, and strengthened with his strength. In this awakened, but still chaotic, state of mind and soul, he left Cooperstown Seminary. His school-days were at an end.

Urged by friends who had migrated to Polo, Illinois, he went there to seek a school, and for the next six months he taught at Buffalo Grove, near Polo. The money for the journey was advanced by his brother Curtis.

A period of rapid mental growth followed. Congenial friends, the kindling of interest in Emerson, improving lectures, access to a good library, a growing impulse toward self-expression, an increased appetite for philosophical subjects — all had a steadying, maturing effect. He did not have to wait for 'the years that bring the philosophic mind.' To him this came unusually early — witness the character of the books he elected to read while in his teens. He gained, in those groping years, a breadth of view, a depth of insight, a steadiness of aim, and a loftiness of purpose looked for only in maturity.

During that winter he wrote a florid, declamatory essay called 'Revolutions,' his second article to appear in print; an assistant teacher, who had a press of his own, printed it for him. 'It is chaff — chaff — no wheat there,' was the author's verdict years later. 'All second-hand truths — nothing that I had thought out for myself.' [1]

'Revolutions' shows considerable advance in craftsmanship over the Cooperstown essay. The Johnsonian influence is still in evidence. The few excerpts here given help to trace the evolution of the writer from the outset:

Progress works changes. Growth is attended by decay. One existing order of things is the stage on which is developed the materials of a higher life. Each declining age gives birth to the spirit of a nobler and better era, and announces the opening of a new act in the great drama of progressive movements. . . .

The ark of civilization has ever been floating towards its premeditated Ararat. The sun of science, like the natural luminary, sinks at one place but to rise at another. When it set to the oriental nations, its prolific rays concentrated on Greece, and she sprang into beauty and refinement. When it declined behind the Athenian hills, its effulgent light burst upon Rome, and she became the mistress of the world. When Rome saw it lowering in her heavens, the West was being illumined by its inflowing tide and growing into power and dominion under its genial warmth. . . .

Revolutions are the natural result of its [the race's] progressive spirit, and the legitimate offspring of its vigorous and healthful growth. They are but shocks from the car of progress which, so far from indicating the slackening of its speed, are the sure evidence of its increasing velocity. . . .

Every revolution that has been enacted upon the world's stage has first commenced in men's thoughts, and gradually worked its way out until the external condition of society has been wrought upon and modified by the inward promptings. . . .

But when the elements of a revolution are opening, you must expect the faint-hearted and soft-headed will cry against it, and cower down under the coming storm like 'supple dogs'; but all who have a sound mind and active faith in the essential validity of the race will hail the advancing change as prolific of valuable results. . . .

In the spring the young man's fancy lightly turned to a maiden in his native state. Often in advanced years he used to say, 'One girl drew me West, but the girl I left behind me drew me back again.' He stopped in Chicago on his return and had a daguerreotype taken.[2] A youthful idealist, one thinks

[1] He had been stimulated to the writing of this essay by *Westward Empire; or, The Great Drama of Human Progress*, by Elias Lyman Magoon; Harper & Bros., 1856.

[2] See frontispiece — the earliest picture of John Burroughs.

on looking at the refined features, the gentle mien, the dreaming eyes, the noble brow, and the long, slightly curling brown hair which frames the sensitive, serious face. Those flowing locks did not, however, find favor with the maiden who had lured him back to the East. None of the youths of Olive wore their hair thus. It must be shorn if he would marry her. So shorn it was — a regrettable concession to the Ulster County Philistines, from an æsthetic point of view, while his too ready compliance divested him at the outset of an assertiveness that would doubtless have been salutary (perhaps even unconsciously welcome) to the more positive character of his betrothed.

He had stopped over in Olive on returning from Illinois, and, on Sunday evening, had attended the little Methodist church, hoping to see Ursula North. There she sat, toward the front of the congregation, while he, from a rear seat, cast many a shy glance in her direction, and waited impatiently for the services to close.

To his surprise, shortly before the Doxology, up arose Miss North, dressed in her best, and walked proudly down the aisle to the vestibule. 'Whether she wanted to make sure I was there, and so would go home with her, or what — I couldn't tell. I know I felt a little ashamed for her, and the higher she carried her head, as she stepped along, the lower I wanted to hang mine.'

The following description of Miss Ursula North was written in 1921, by her sister, Amanda North, then aged eighty-four:

My sister was a very interesting and attractive girl; had a wealth of dark curly hair, was endowed with a strong will power; generally accomplished whatever she undertook. Very industrious, never afraid of work; had no lack of suitors; could have married three excellent young men, if she had given her consent. She spent one winter in New York, became acquainted with a member of the Seventh regiment and they were engaged; but after she returned home realized she did not love him well enough to marry him, so wrote and broke the engagement. I think it was about a year after that she became acquainted with John; he was teaching at Tongore. They were married in about a year and a half. [Here follow details of their parents] . . . I think John was willing to admit my sister had better business qualities than he.

While the young school-teacher was at home haying that summer, he received a letter from a former school-fellow at

Cooperstown, who, in discussing the heart affairs of the students, said:

But neither you nor I have any time to spare for match-making. We have that celebrated hill of science to climb, and want no woman clinging to our nether garments to pull us down or retard our course as we ascend the rugged steep.

The youthful Burroughs, however, was not of like mind, and, though he began in late July to teach at High Falls, a little village near Kingston, he interrupted his teaching over a week-end (September 12th), to take unto himself a wife.

As he walked along the country road from Kingston to Olive, on the day of his marriage, beset by many misgivings, he stopped suddenly and sat down to think it over. He had wanted to postpone the marriage till a more convenient season, but had been overruled. Still, it was not too late to draw back. Wavering and disquieted, he was strongly inclined to turn about; but at the thought of the charms of his betrothed, he threw all other considerations to the wind and pushed on.

A list of expenses for the modest wedding outfit, including new clothes, kid gloves, a gold pin, horse and carriage, the minister's fee, and incidentals, totals thirty-one dollars. The journey was made in a buggy to Shandaken; the Reverend Harry Longyear, pastor of the bride's mother, married them. The bride remained in her father's house; the groom resumed teaching on Monday.

Burroughs, not yet twenty-one, had nothing ahead, as the prudent country folk at Olive would have said, when he married Ursula North — a self-complacent, thrifty, and forceful young woman, thirteen months his senior.

Miss North was of English and Dutch ancestry, sturdy Ulster County farming-folk, provident and prosperous. (John North, the paternal grandfather, had given each of his sons a farm when they married.) Her maternal grandmother, Catherine Robinson, whom she resembled, is said, by Amanda North, to have been a woman of exceptionally strong character, energetic, and industrious. Uriah North, the father of Ursula North, 'had the best farm in the town of Olive, and kept it in good order. He died at eighty-seven — a sturdy Christian, a Methodist.' The mother, Lydia Schutt, was daughter of Josiah Schutt. She bore and reared seven children;

URSULA NORTH
(Mrs. John Burroughs)

she is described by her youngest-born, Amanda, as 'a pretty woman, a good helpmate, a good housekeeper and cook; and a very devoted follower of her Savior — a cross-bearing Christian, who never ate anything on Sunday. She was a Baptist, and died at the age of fifty-one,' shortly before the marriage of her daughter Ursula.

Nature evidently sought to preserve the balance by uniting John Burroughs in marriage to a woman who had preëminently certain traits in which he was deficient, notably pride, self-confidence, and aggressiveness.

A week after marriage, the young husband writes to his bride in Olive the following letter, which one hesitates to print, yet which seems needful to the understanding of much that followed:

My Ursula,

I am not going to be as formal in my letter as you was in yours. I am not going to call you my wife; that sounds too cold and business-like. It is not half so sweet, romantic and lovely to my ear as 'My Own Dear Ursula.' I don't feel towards you as men usually feel toward their wives and I can't bare to call you such. My feeling for you has all the passion, devotion, and romance of a youthful lover. 'Wife' sounds too matronly; it don't express half the sentiment of my heart. I suppose it will do one of these days when the poetry of our early love has given place to prose, when the tide that now floods our souls has ebbed, and this rosy twilight in which we see each other has vanished before the rising sun of life. But, Ursula, is this ever to be so? Can we not always be lovers? Will time and care take all of this poetry and romance out of us?

Do you think it will, Ursula? or can you always love me with the same fond devotion that you do now. You know generally, one or two years after marriage, love degenerates into coldness or indifference; the parties regard one another perhaps with respect or esteem, but that warm, full, gushing love which marks their early attachment, is gone. Ursula, I think it need not be so with us. I can always have the same feeling for you as long as you are the same kind, affectionate and noble-hearted girl that won my love. And I shall always strive to merit the affection that you now bare me.

I sometimes think I will not make the kind of husband that will always suit you. If I live, I shall be an author. My life will be one of study. It may be a weakness in me to cherish the thoughts I do, but I can't help it. I know not why I should not try to realize my aspirations; why I should not strive to rise to that sphere toward which my soul continually aspires. I know I must struggle hard to realize my end, to have my name recorded with the great and good. But if God spares my life, the great world shall know that I am in it. The good, the beautiful, and the true my soul worships; and the more your spirit assimilates to mine in this respect, Ursula, the more I can love you. Open your heart to the good and the beautiful in Nature and in life, and my soul will go out to yours as naturally as the magnet turns to the Pole. But I must talk about something else.

Then you was afraid to have me go to that Cave, was you? Bless your heart! I am glad you are so anxious for my safety, but I would not have you have any unnecessary trouble. I did not go to the cave because it rained, and I guess I should not have gone had it been a fair day, simply because you pleaded so earnestly for me not to. *I will try and do as you want me to, and will come up in two or three weeks — if not before.* You may expect me next Friday night if nothing happens. . . . So here is a kiss until I come. Your

JOHN

Later, from High Falls, October 7th:

MY DEAR URSULA,

I intend to invert the golden rule this time and do unto others as they do unto me. Your letter to me was short and business-like, so mine to you shall be short and business-like. Here is all I have to say at present: I think I shall probably be up to Olive Friday or Saturday. You did not ask me to come in your letter, but I want to come very much, and I hope you will be glad to see me. If I don't come then I shall be oblige[d] to wait four weeks, and it would be very painful to me to be absent from you that long. Oh, how glad I shall be when you can be with me all the time!

Adieu. Yours while life lasts,

JOHN BURROUGHS

Toward spring his wife came and boarded with him in the home of the trustee, returning to her father before the term ended. At close of school the teacher was chagrined that the trustee did not offer to hire him again. Commenting on this, he said:

I suppose I was thinking too much, and not attending to business. I believe they complained that I read in school. But there were other reasons — things over which I had no control — squabbles among the women-folks — some silly quarrel about apple-sauce started it. I shall never forget the shock I got on coming home and hearing my wife's voice raised in altercation and violent denunciation of the woman where we boarded. . . . This probably had something to do with my not getting the school again.

Attempts to get a business position in New York, to which his wife was urging him, were unsuccessful, and the summer of 1858 found him teaching at Rosendale on the Rondout, whence he writes in a cheery vein, wishing she were there keeping house and sailing with him on the river in the balmy evenings:

> ... I think they will raise my wages after the first quarter, so that we could live nice and comfortable, and at the same time I could be pursuing my studies and preparing myself for something else. You must not expect too much of me at first, Ursula; I am very young yet and must study and grow, *work and wait*, before I can take the position in the world that I am capable of taking. My Ursula must have patience and all will be right one of these days. I think I will come up and see you next week. If you could come and meet me with one of your father's horses, write so that I can get it by Thursday, and I will not try to get a horse here.... Be a good girl and make up your mind that we had better go to keeping house....

That fall he became interested in a new kind of harness-buckle invented by the village harness-maker — a buckle with a direct draft on the tongue, instead of the movable tongue of the kind then in use. The inventor had inveigled him into making a drawing of the buckle for the Patent Office, while doing which he had waxed enthusiastic. He dreamed of buckles, and talked of buckles to everybody. The village doctor caught the enthusiasm, and together they bought the inventor out. Buoyant with hope, and basking in the sunshine of his wife's approval, he resigned his school and went to Newark, New Jersey, to superintend the making of the buckles. Months of disillusionment followed.[1] He realized only loss and humiliation; and, after futile attempts to obtain other employment, resumed teaching. Having engaged himself to teach near Newark, he wrote his wife that on his wages of one hundred dollars for sixty days, they could live together as cheaply as she was living at Olive:

> You may ask what we will go to housekeeping with. Well, you know you have some things; our folks will send us some things; I will hire some money, so we can get along till 'our ship comes home from sea.' There is no use to mourn and repine over misfortune, but the way is to 'up and at it again' with a cheerful countenance, and a bold, resolute heart. 'There's a good time coming, boys, wait a little longer.' ...

---

[1] For a detailed story of his adventures with the buckle, see *John Burroughs, Boy and Man*.

Write without delay. . . . Newark is only seven miles from New York, so we can occasionally go to hear Chapin and Beecher.[1]

In a January letter he confessed to his wife: 'It grinds to take up the old occupation after indulging for three months in visions of wealth and independence.' A month later, still urging her to come and keep house, he writes of hearing Edward Everett lecture, but, lonely and depressed, and grievously disappointed at her decision to defer housekeeping, he adds:

The news from B—— about our affairs has distressed me much; the bad news from you, and my own depressed feelings occasioned by the labors of school-teaching and almost incessant study, have quite broken me down, and I feel sad, sad indeed. I never felt the need of your society, or of some congenial companion who can sympathize with me, and come in close communion with my heart and feelings, as I do at present. In a city of strangers, with poverty and misfortune and hard toil; with a mind full of tender recollections of the past, and darkened with uncertainties as to the future; with a heart yearning for old friends and companions, and a spirit racked with thoughts and inward struggles; I more than ever need the assurance of your love, and the presence of your kind, cheerful heart.

Oh, why is it that trouble and disappointment are the inevitable result of our earthly condition. I look at the stars, I look at the setting sun, I look toward the blue horizon, I ramble through the busy city, I delve into the sea of books, I struggle with the mysteries of eternity, and nothing satisfactory can I find. All is a sliding sandbank beneath me. Peace, Beauty, Satisfaction, Rest — where, oh, where can ye be found? Ah! my dearest girl, this poor life cannot be all! this inward longing and struggling point to something beyond the stars!

I received a letter from Father the other day; they were all well, but very much grieved that I had got so far from home. Home! Home! — would that my future days might be as happy as those spent within thy sacred precincts! . . .

The mood then changes; sentiment is abandoned; taking a more masterful tone, he sweeps aside the trivial excuses for delaying housekeeping; tells what he expects of her; gives practical directions for coming — for shipping their belongings; discusses all details, then adds vigorously:

Get your things to the river, put your clothes in your trunk, put my clothes in my trunk, together with my manuscripts, Shake-

[1] Years later he said that in those days he was so eager to hear Beecher, then in the heyday of his fame and power, that he used to run to get there. He couldn't bear to miss a word, and it was lively hustling after getting off the ferry.

speare's works, and my two big dictionaries; get aboard the stage; go
to Rondout; stay overnight with your cousin; and the next day take
the cars for New York, and I will meet you at the depot.

... I shall certainly expect you to come, and if you have my
happiness and your own at heart, you will let nothing detain you.
We can live nicely and happily here. . . .

Our folks are going to send me some apples and butter soon. . . .

In the course of this long letter he declares that if she will
not come, he will give up the school, and travel with the buckle
and a book-agency in the West; but, pushing aside this al-
ternative, he outlines the more desirable plan so irresistibly
as to produce the desired effect. The feminine heart loves a
wooer, but above all else loves a master.

They set up housekeeping in East Orange (February, 1859)
in a modest way. For the first time since marriage the strong
domestic nature of the young husband was satisfied in the
possession of a home; reverses counted for little; he was at
last under his own roof-tree.

2. THE APPRENTICESHIP

The only way to learn to write is to write, Mr. Burroughs
used to say, just as one learns to swim by plunging in and
striking out till he masters the new element. 'The formal
rules,' he declared, 'are so much dead wood unless you have
the root of the matter within yourself.' In 1859 and 1860,
while teaching in East Orange, he plunged in and floundered
about a good deal, and, indeed, it was several years before
he became a bold swimmer. He began writing for the 'Saturday Press,' under the general caption 'Fragments from the
Table of an Intellectual Epicure,' by 'All Souls.' ('Ugh!
the title sets my teeth on edge now,' he said in later years.)
He offered his wares for a dollar an article, and when they
could not pay even that sum, he still wrote for them. Howells
said of the 'Saturday Press,' which had been started in 1858,
that it was nearly as well for one to be accepted by it as by the
'Atlantic Monthly,' since there was no other literary comparison at the time.

A few crumbs from the 'intellectual epicure's' table are
gathered here:

Every book and every sermon ought to be a pair of magnetic
slippers that shall make us dance to a new tune, and feel as if we

were walking on thunderbolts. . . . There is nothing so healthy as a freshet in the soul. A man needs to be elated and depressed; to be lifted up until he feels he could grasp the big dipper and . . . sunk down till one foot breaks through Hades.

Some of the essays which young Burroughs subsequently sent to the 'Press' were named 'Deep,' 'A Thought on Culture,' and 'Poetry.' Between 1860 and 1862, among those he sent to the New York 'Leader' were 'World Growth,' 'New Ideas,' 'Theory and Practice,' 'On Indirections,' and 'Some of the Ways of Power.' All were experimental. He was struggling to attain clearness of expression. Of his early efforts he said:

The two feet upon which they go is analogy. It looks as if, in each case, I had my physical fact in mind first, and then hunted around till I found its mate in some moral or intellectual principle.

In the latter part of April (1860), he wrote to his wife, in Roxbury:

The prospects for a situation of any kind are very poor. The supply of help so much exceeds the demand. They advertised yesterday for twenty men to canvas for the Brooklyn Register. I went precisely at the hour, but the room was so full that I could hardly get in. I suppose there were two hundred applied, and, as many of them had worked at it before, of course my chance was poor. I shall advertize in the Tribune to-morrow.

I am very anxious to get a place, more on your account than my own. It would suit me best to go home, and I believe would be better in the long run. I know you have an idea that it is a very easy matter to get a place, but your ideas would change if you were to try it awhile here in New York. It is the most disheartening business I ever undertook. . . .

Well, be a good girl and don't find fault with me when I do the best I can. You little know my troubles and anxieties.

Horace and I made seventy-five cents apiece on our lecture.[1]

. . . I wish I could be with you up there among the grassy fields. I never hungered and thirsted after rest, and the country, as I do now. You may ask what I have done so wonderful to make me feel thus. Well, I don't know myself, except what you call 'no work' — thinking and teaching. I have nursed forty boys for over a year, and they have sucked a great deal of marrow and pith out of me. I feel

---

[1] He and a friend, Horace Fish, had engaged Bayard Taylor to lecture. On that occasion, he spoke to Taylor about some verses of Walt Whitman's, then appearing in the *Saturday Press*. Taylor replied, patronizingly, 'Oh, yes, there is *something* in him, but he is a man of colossal egotism.'

like a tree that has been dug up and exposed to the sun till it is nearly robbed of its juices. . . .

The hunt for work continuing is best told in his own words:

I suppose you have been daily expecting a letter from me full of good news, and I am sorry it could not be so. I have not yet got a place, and have neglected writing, hoping I would have something good to write.

I have had a place in view for a number of days as draftsman in a carriage manufactory, and worked faithfully for two days and nights on some drawings, but come to take them over yesterday they did not suit. If I had secured the place it would have paid me only ten dollars a week. . . .

I have another place in view as a writer, but I cannot hear from it in a week yet. I have raced and chased till I am pretty well fagged out; it is up-hill business. I should like to see you very much, but think you had better stay there till things look different with me. . . .

It is very bright and beautiful here this morning, and the trees in blossom make me inexpressibly sad. Write as soon as you get this. . . .

Five days later, still without a situation:

. . . I let no opportunity slip. . . . I have more hopes of getting a place to write than anything else. I sent an essay to the Saturday Press, and it came out as one of the leading articles. I took a copy of verses [1] to the Independent and they said they would publish them. As soon as I can get myself into notice in that way, I can get paid for all I write.

I answered an advertisement last Friday to write critical notices of new publications, which I hope to hear from by Saturday.

. . . I bought a hoop skirt for you the other day. I got a twenty shilling one for 5/6. I knew you wanted one. I have got eighty-five dollars left yet. . . .

Mr. Allen is going to read his poem in Newark on Friday night. . . .

E. M. Allen was a young man with whom Burroughs had formed an attachment during 1860, the beginning of an ardent friendship. The first published verses [2] by John Burroughs — 'To E.M.A.' ('Saturday Press,' 1869) — were addressed to Allen, after his visit to the Burroughs Homestead. They show the author's abiding love of comrades. Young Allen was a lover of poetry and a writer of good verse as well; he had fine literary taste, was companionable, had exceptional powers of

[1] 'Loss and Gain' — verses of a philosophical trend (*Our Friend John Burroughs*).
[2] See *Our Friend John Burroughs*.

mimicry, was a racy *raconteur*, could make clever caricatures, lecture well, sketch well, could, in fact, turn his hand to many things. At this period he was eking out a precarious living by giving occasional lectures. His letters [1] to John Burroughs during 1860 and 1863 supply some of the earliest data we have of the budding authorship of Burroughs.

In the summer, having failed to secure a business opening in the city, Burroughs returned to his father's farm for work and study. There in the south bedroom at the Old Home, at the age of twenty-three, he wrote the essay 'Expression,' which was published in the 'Atlantic Monthly,' November, 1860; an essay so Emersonian in tone that Lowell, then editor, looked through all of Emerson's published work before convinced that it was not a plagiarism. The 'Atlantic' articles were not signed in those days, and both 'Poole's Index' and 'Hill's Rhetoric' credited the essay to Emerson.

'Expression' has never been reprinted. Written some fifty years before its author was to come upon M. Bergson, it suggests him quite as much as it does Emerson. In it the philosophic Burroughs is epitomized. In truth, Burroughs began as a philosopher, and ended as a philosopher, though showing less of this trend in the middle years. In 'Expression' he approaches the universe solely from the philosophic point of view, setting forth the chart and compass which was to guide him through life. Much of biographic interest will be found in the accompanying excerpts from the essay:

... Nature exists to the mind not as an absolute realization, but as a condition, as something constantly becoming. ... It is suggestive and prospective; a body in motion, and not an object at rest. ...

The material universe seems a suspense, something arrested on the point of transition from nonentity to absolute being. ... Absolute space is not cognizable to the mind; we apprehend space only when limited and imprisoned in geometric figures. Absolute life we can have no conception of; the absolute must come down and incarnate itself in the conditioned, and cease to be absolute, before it comes within the plane of our knowledge. ...

And this is God's art of expression. We can behold nothing pure; all that we see is compounded and mixed. Nature stands related to us at a certain angle, and at a little remove either way — back toward its grosser side, or up towards its ideal tendency — would place it beyond our ken ... all things are made of one stuff, and on the prin-

[1] See *John Burroughs, Boy and Man.*

ciple that a difference in degree produces a difference in kind. . . .
From the zoöphyte up to man, more or less of spirit gives birth to the
intervening types. . . .

This law of degrees, pushed a little farther, amounts to detachment and separation, and gives birth to contrast and comparison. . . .
The chairs and pictures must come out from the wall before we can
see them. The tree must detach itself from the landscape . . . before
it becomes cognizable to us. . . .

So in higher matters. . . . The fullest experience is never defined,
and cannot be spoken. . . .

. . . Our thoughts lie in us like the granite rock in the earth, whole
and continuous, without break or rupture, and shaped by a law of
the spheres; but when they come to the surface in utterance, and
can be grasped and defined, they lose their entireness and become
partial and fragmentary. . . . We cannot speak entire and unmixed
truth, because utterance separates a part from the whole, and consequently in a measure distorts and exaggerates. . . . The fullest
truth . . . never shapes itself into words. What we speak is generally
only foam from the surface, with more or less sediment in it; while
the pure current flows untouched beneath. The deepest depths in a
man have no tongue. He is like the sea which finds expression only
in its shoals and rocks; the great heart of it has no voice, no utterance. . . .

. . . When one thought is spoken, all others become speakable. . . .
The difficulty in writing, is to utter the first thought, to break the
heavy silence . . . to disentangle one idea from the embarrassing
many. . . . We are burdened with unuttered and unutterable truth.
. . . But at last, when we are driven almost to despair, and in a semi-
passive state . . . the thought comes. . . . But if we drop the thread
of our idea without knotting it, or looping it to some fact . . . how
soon all becomes a blank! . . . Neither wife, nor friends nor fortune
nor appetite should call one from his work when he is possessed by
this spirit and can utter his thought. We are caught up into these
regions rarely enough, let us not come down till we are obliged. . . .

The spiritual canopies the material as the sky canopies the earth,
and is . . . expressed only by its aid. . . .

Ordinary minds inherit their language and form of expression; but
with the poet, or natural sayer, a new step is taken . . . he is distinguished from the second-hand man by the fullness and completeness
of his expression; his words are round and embrace the two hemi-
spheres, the actual and the ideal. He points out analogies under our
feet, and presents the near and the remote wedded in every act of his
mind. Nothing is old with him, but Nature is forever new like the
day. . . . The great writer says what we feel, but could not utter.
We have pearls that lie no deeper than his, but have not his art of
bringing them to the surface. We are mostly like an inland lake that
has no visible outlet; while he is the same lake gifted with a copious
channel.

The secret seems to lie in the temperament and in the transmuting and modifying medium. More or less of filtration does it all. Nature makes the poet, not by adding to, but by taking from; she takes all blur and opacity from him; condenses, intensifies; lifts his nerves nearer the surface, sharpens his senses, and brings his whole organization to an edge. . . .

Our expression is clogged by the rubbish in our minds, the foolish personal matters we load the memory with. . . .

What one has lived, that alone can he adequately say. . . . Every undulation of passion enriches and gives us a deeper soil. The most painful experiences are generally the most productive. Cutting teeth is by no means a pleasant operation, yet it increases our tools. . . .

Proverbs give us the best lessons in the art of expression. . . . *They give us pocket-editions of the most voluminous truths.*[1] . . . There is no waste material in a good proverb; it is clear meat, like an egg — a happy result of logic with the logic left out; and the writer who shall thus condense his wisdom, and as far as possible give the two poles of thought in every expression, will most thoroughly reach men's minds and hearts.

Secure in the wisdom and self-knowledge of which one gains a glimpse in the foregoing excerpts, the young writer could well afford to work and wait through all the coming vicissitudes between aspiration and fruition.

The following letter, written by Burroughs to Newark friends, curiously fell into my hands, some fifty years later, through association with Dr. Julia A. Fish, to whose parents it had been written. From it one learns something of his summer of 1860, in Roxbury:

DEAR FRIENDS, HORACE AND MARY,

. . . You know for the first three or four weeks in the country one naturally has a strong aversion to pens, paper, books — he only wants to live, to lounge and enjoy himself to the utmost extent of his sensuous nature. . . . Hunting and trouting I have revelled in; have planted corn and potatoes, and have been to a raising.

My friend Allen came up last Saturday. . . . Tomorrow we start for the region of trout and deer.[2] We intend to camp in the woods far beyond any settlement, for two weeks, and live on game. . . . Horace, I wish you could be with us; between telling stories, hunting, trouting, and sleeping, I think time would cease to be a burden. Suppose you leave the dingy old tannery and come up? I hope to catch a big trout for Barnum. I see he offers quite an inducement — $100. . . .

Mary, I picked some strawberries today, and in intention gave

---

[1] This is the quotation credited to Emerson in Hill's *Rhetoric*. Italics mine.
[2] The first camping-trip in the life of an inveterate camper. Of this experience he has written in 'Birch Browsings' (*Wake-Robin*).

half of them to you. Ursula has gone to the village to have a tooth drawn. She often speaks of you and would like to have you live near us.

They talk of making me school commissioner this fall, and I am not all averse to the idea, if they are fools enough to thrust the office upon me. It will pay me $600 a year for three years. . . .

Ursula says she would like to have you send that shirt-pattern.

Occasional essays were now gaining acceptance, but, as they brought little or no money, he was forced to resume teaching. The future was not rosy. Failing in what those nearest him counted success, he was being continually urged to quit writing, and 'go into business and be somebody.'

At Marlboro-on-the-Hudson, from the fall of 1860 till the spring of 1863, he taught school, with the usual work in midsummer on the home farm. Writing and reading were absorbing him more and more. Those were the days when the 'Atlantic Monthly' was his university. A subscriber from the first number, he continued to be one all his life. He was so eager to get it that when it was due he could not keep from running as he neared the post-office.

By autumn his wife was with him, keeping house, and in winter helping with the smaller pupils. In summer, they supplemented their earnings by picking raspberries at a cent a cup.

In his seventy-eighth year, when motoring through Marlboro, Mr. Burroughs said:

Here I taught school for two years. Lord! how green I was! I'm green enough yet. I roamed these hills, but had no interest then in the birds, except in game-birds — to shoot them. I even used to kill the little tip-ups — pretty little things that ran along the shore — for pot-pies. Think of it! But Mrs. B. made delicious pot-pies.

Here is where I lived when my first essay came out in the Atlantic. I was so set up by it that I wanted to send them another right away, so one Saturday I wanted to go in the little parlor by myself and write on another piece I had begun — 'Analogy' — but Mrs. B. thought it a desecration to use that precious parlor for 'scribbling.' When I insisted, she locked the door. That made me so angry I kicked the door till I broke the lock; then, of course, I was so upset I couldn't write. I took my gun and went into the woods all day. Poor 'Analogy' had a set-back that day that it was hard to recover from. After that, when I wanted to write, I used to go up in the attic and sit on the stairs, using the top step for my desk, and getting light from a little window. . . .

Shortly after the publication of 'Expression,' he began writing nature sketches for the 'Leader,' having concluded that it was a grave error to write like another, even Emerson. In order to get on ground of his own, he swung away from philosophical themes and wrote of things familiar to himself, developing at once a style of his own — fresh, individual, engaging. Under the general caption 'From the Back Country'[1] he wrote of butter-making, sugar-making, stone walls, and kindred topics.

His transition style is seen in the previously mentioned 'Analogy,' as first written, when he was dropping the Emersonian manner, and had not yet acquired a style of his own. The essay was refused by the 'Atlantic,' and five years passed before it accepted another by him. The return of 'Analogy' sent the hopeful author's stock much below par, but his friend Allen encouraged him thus:

> You may send them another not so good, and succeed. John G. Saxe said he sent a poem to Harper's and had it sent back, and sent them another the next week that would not compare with the first, and had it accepted. So at it again!

Taking Allen's advice, he rewrote parts of 'Analogy.' 'Knickerbocker's Magazine' printed it in December, 1862. Many years later he rewrote the entire essay, which was accepted (September, 1891) by Horace Scudder, then editor of the 'Atlantic.' More than a decade later, again rewriting it, he included it in 'Literary Values' (1902). It would be an interesting study of his mental growth and evolution as a writer to examine the three versions of 'Analogy,' written at such widely separated intervals; to learn to what things he held fast in the later versions, what let go. In the original paper, in the old 'Knickerbocker,' where Kinahan Cornwallis, the editor, published it as the initial essay, the young writer solemnly announces that he is dealing with 'the essential and eternal correlation of the material and spiritual world'; and that he who penetrates to the core of things must see the unity underlying diversity, after which announcement he proceeds to draw from all nature examples of telling analogies.

[1] Among the book-notices in the November *Atlantic*, 1860, — a number of such signal importance to J. B., — is notice of a book by Frederick Law Olmsted, called *A Journey in the Back-Country* — a title which probably suggested to Burroughs his caption for those first nature sketches.

Throughout, one finds the philosophic Burroughs, with the
Burroughs of the nature essays peeping through only occasionally. A few excerpts are culled from the essay:

Unity of cause and variety of effect, these are the center and circumference of all things. . . . Species stand to each other as ante-
cedent and consequent; one is the condition of the other. There
could be no man till first there was the zoöphyte. Darwin's hypothesis of the derivation of species is in keeping with the unity we everywhere discern.

(This is the only mention found in essay, letter, or journal
of his reading of Darwin till many years later, although his
acceptance of him goes without saying.)

The analogy drawn in the following excerpt reminds one
that the Civil War was in progress:

Nature is no disunionist, but forever aims at wholeness and continuity, linking the smallest with the greatest, the lowest with the
highest, the nearest with the remotest, and balancing the whole as
one body. Matter is the last issue of spirit. . . . The universe exists in
layers and strata, . . . and constantly refines as the grade ascends.
. . . Fluid is an advance on the solid; the aerial an advance on the
fluid; the imponderable an advance on the aerial; and so on up to
spirit, the law each time rising into higher regions.

The longings expressed in the next two excerpts were
assuredly brought to realization in his work of subsequent
years:

Oh! for Nature and sincerity, and vital, law-revealing analogy,
instead of hollow, heartless rhetoric. We would do well to imitate
the bees who, when they find themselves hiveless, or are offered a
decayed or unfit hive, go to the woods and seek one of Nature's
making. We would do well to read in the woods and fields; to muse
in the barn and barn-yard; to court familiarity with cows and sheep
and swine and hens and haymows; with backwoodsmen, with soldiers, with sailors, with mechanics, with farmers; with the thousand
forms of nature and life, that we may infuse something fresh and
real into our culture and speech. . . .

Continuing, he pleads for 'words that adhere to things,
that smell of the earth, and are warm with life.' In the closing
passage is glimpsed the high standard he set for every work
of art:

The end of all art is answered when we have obtained a pure and
natural result, and the work shall stand there as a legitimate off-

spring of the same Power that makes the rain to fall, and the grass to grow; and the end of all writing is answered when the piece shall affect us with a like sense of realness and beauty.

From Allen's letters to him one gathers much of what Burroughs was reading and doing at this period. He received twenty-eight dollars in payment for 'Expression'; Allen had taken Burroughs's 'Poetry' to the 'Saturday Press,' the editor liked it, but could not afford to pay for it; J. B. was reading 'The Count of Monte Cristo' and 'The French Revolution.' From Allen, too, one gets a glimpse of the literary Bohemians at Pfaff's (New York):

Walt Whitman was there looking rough, hairy, and 'gray-necked'; he had his hat on, looking reflective, listening to a nicely dressed young fellow who sat next him, which might have been Aldrich, for he is there sometimes. . . . I have become acquainted with 'Marion Harland,' Lucy Stone, and the Reverend Antoinette Brown Blackwell. . . .

Midsummer brought the usual interruption to literary efforts. His letters from the Old Home, in August, bear on the envelopes the Stars and Stripes in vivid colors. To Mrs. Burroughs:

I was glad to hear from you and that you are living in such fine style at Troy. For my part I am living at rather loose ends, as is usually my case when home — rough and hearty, and by no means up to your *punctillio* in dress.

. . . The expense of my journey was only about one dollar. From Kingston I got a ride to Olive, and the next morning your father took me to Shandaken Center. I am to work pretty hard, though the chances are I shall not earn over six or seven dollars, and be obliged to wait for that till winter. . . .

I have had one mess of tip-ups and several of trout. The other day Eden and I caught five that together measured five feet and a half. . . . I cannot think of getting clothes to come to Troy, so do not expect me. . . . Well, I must away to the hayfield. . . .

I wrote the trustees at Marlboro that I would be on hand to commence school by the 26th, though I am loath to return again to the drudgery of teaching, and the thousand and one vexations of housekeeping. . . .

Later, at Marlboro, when alone with two months of the vexatious housekeeping, after looking himself squarely in the face, he sent the contrite letter which follows, which evidently induced his wife to return and share his burdens:

DEAREST URSULA,

Your brief note was received yesterday. I am very glad you are coming back so soon. I am quite lonely and miss you very much more than I thought I should. I know what a blessed assurance it is to my wife to know that she is beloved by her erratic husband, and therefore I write that I love you more than I knew. Surrounded by objects that constantly suggest you, and your care and kindness to me, and still painfully remind me of your absence, I am more and more aware how deep you are in my affections. You know I am an excentric mortal, and have my ways, which I know are not altogether other folkses ways; and while reflecting on the subject tonight, it occurred to me that, uncommunicative as I often am, so much absorbed by my own thoughts, or in the reading of books, and depending so little for my society or companionship on those about me, that I must often be to you an intollerable bore. Your photograph lies before me as I write, and methinks reproaches me silently that I have been so neglectful of its original, and so little inclined to 'visit' when she coaxed so lovingly. 'Good for you,' it says, 'sitting there alone, looking so doleful! It would be serving you right if she would stay away six months, you selfish, heartless scribbler!' But 'the heart feels most when the lips move not,' you know; or, in other words, my love for you is always so deep and true, though it may not show itself outwardly; and I trust it will remain so through all the years to come.

This may sound foolish to you, and it certainly is unusual for me to write thus, but it may be all the more timely on that account. . . .

In the spring of 1861 the embryo essayist began writing to David A. Wasson, a Unitarian clergyman whose scholarly essays in the 'Atlantic' had so attracted him that he plucked up courage and wrote Wasson of his literary aspirations. The correspondence proved of incalculable value to John Burroughs at a time when sympathy and advice were greatly needed.[1]

A passage in Wasson's reply to Burroughs's first letter is singularly prophetic:

The essay that you sent me I read carefully twice. . . . It certainly shows in you, if my judgment may be trusted, unusual gifts of pure intellect — unusual, I mean, among scholars and literary men; and the literary execution is creditable, though by no means of the same grade with the mental power evinced. You must become a fine literary worker to be equal to the demands of such an intellect as yours. For the deeper the thought, the more difficult to give it a clear and attractive expression. You *can* write so as to command attention. I am sure you can. Will you? That is the only question.

[1] The Wasson letters are published in full in *Our Friend John Burroughs.*

Can you work and wait long enough? Have you the requisite patience and persistency? If you have, there is undoubtedly an honorable future before you.

But I will not conceal from you that I think you too young to have written 'numerous essays' of the class you attempt, or to publish a book consisting of such. No other kind of writing requires such mental maturity; stories may be written at any age, though good ones are seldom written early. Even poems and works of art have been produced by some Raphael or Milton at a comparatively early season of life. . . . But the purely reflective essay belongs emphatically to maturer life. Your twenty-four years have evidently been worth more to you than the longest life to most men; but my judgment is that you should give your genius more time yet, and should wait upon it with much labor. . . .

In the second letter his new friend admonished him:

You must be a little less careless about your spelling, simply because these slips will discredit your thought in the eyes of superficial critics. You understand, of course, that I speak above of the general public — not of the finer natures who will welcome you with warm hands.

I am obliged to you for informing me of your existence, *for I augur good for my country* from the discovery of every such intelligence as yours, and I pledge to you my warm interest and regard.

In connection with this prophecy in 1861 it is interesting to note that in 1876, in 'Scribner's Monthly,' 'The Old Cabinet' (R. W. Gilder) asserted: 'John Burroughs is one of the half-dozen or less American prose writers who *are adding anything vital by means of books to the thought and life of the country.*' And further, in 1905, Theodore Roosevelt, when dedicating one of his outdoor books to 'dear Oom John,' said, '*It is a good thing for our people that you have lived,* and surely no man can wish to have more said of him.' [1]

The winter, with its round of studying, teaching, and writing, was enlivened by letters from Allen, then in Washington, — lively pictures of the War, descriptions of interesting people, and other allurements of the Capital; letters which doubtless had much to do with the unsettled mind in which young Burroughs found himself for the greater part of the next two years.

Excerpts from letters to Mrs. Burroughs, written from Roxbury during the summer, carry along the story:

[1] Italics mine.

[June 16.] I was glad you wrote so soon. I thought it too bad that you should be near me so long, from Saturday till Monday, and I not see you. Why did you not come over in a dream, if no other way? . . .

Yesterday I put on my best 'bib and tucker,' and went down to the village to church. I even wore my silk gloves to cover my black hands, which, I suppose, if you had been here, and asked me to do, I should have refused. Such is human nature. The girls looked charmingly at me, and I looked charmingly back again. So, So.

I have only worked a day and a half since I came back, as there has not been much to do, but soon now corn will do to hoe, and I shall have to bend my back to it again. . . .

I am going to picking and kanning strawberries. I wish you would find out, if you go to Troy, what kaned strawberries will bring. . . . When I write for you to come back, you must start forthwith.

[June 28.] . . . I do not think I can come to Troy. It would cost me, at the least figure, six dollars, besides expenses while there, and my time. I should like much to come, but will have to wait. If there is any chance to get into something I would come of cours[e], but do not like to run the risk as matters look. I am working now, hoeing corn, picking berries, etc. Do not forget to inquire what berries sell for, put up in jars. Get some good receipts to make currant and berry wines.

Send me the Atlantic at once, and as many papers as you are a mind to.

My heart grows heavy every day but I shall not complain; stay as long as you are a mind to. Of course it is pleasanter there than here, but if you come back at all, or before haying, you ought to come soon after the Fourth, so as to pick and dry some berries. However, if you had rather stay in Troy till fall, and they want you, why I can stand it, if you can.

. . . Channy B. and I caught five trout today that weighed five pounds, one of them weighed one and a half pounds. I wish you was here to help eat them.

Bring or send me some stockings as I am about out. I had another letter from Wasson. He speaks very noble and cheering words to me. . . .

[July 10.]
DEAR URSULA,

I sit down in the P.O. to answer your letter which has just reached me. I expected you in with the mail tonight, as I have all the week, but must take up with a letter instead. You are very cool about the matter. Stay in Olive a week or two yet, eh? Well, act your own pleasure. Perhaps you had rather stay all summer! It would save expense up and back. I know not how the hearts of other people may be ossified, or turned to stone, but I know mine is flesh and blood, eminently so. The probabilities are that I shall enlist, and if you are not here before one week, you need not come, as by that time I shall (I hope) pass through Kingston as Lieutenant in the first Regm. of Delaware Blues. It is time every man took his musket, and I shall hold back no longer. If I should not return, of course you would not come to want — except it be to want another husband, which want can be easily supplied. I pity him, however, if you leave him as you do me.

. . . I will be at Dimmick's Corners when the stage comes in. If you come at all, come then, the 14th. You can certainly do all your visiting in Olive by that time. However, as I said, act your own pleasure. . . .

Doubtless when the 'stage' came, it brought the young wife; and doubtless by mid-September, when she was again in Olive, she was looking forward to the 'stage' bringing her husband there; for he writes her not to be impatient; that it will shell him out at her door one of these days, though then he was sorely afflicted with carbuncles; had had to stop work, and had made but five dollars, whereas, but for the carbuncles, he might have made ten. He must take care of his onions; he wants to go to Delhi to see the soldiers; he wants more to see her; and he sends fifty kisses condensed in one.

The onion seed he had planted had cost him a sum he could ill afford, and not one in a hundred had come up. The failure was a severe blow, and yielded him severer recriminations.

In October he began teaching in Olive at seventeen dollars a month, and reading medicine with Dr. Abram Hull. To his wife, then visiting in New York, he wrote of his plan of combining medicine with essay-writing, and proposed, since he could not find a house for rent, that she spend the winter at her father's, where he would pay her board:

I know my girl will stamp her pretty foot and say No, but let her think twice. . . . My utmost desire is to please you and promote our good. I beg of you to bear and forbear, and I know you will not be sorry. . . . I have got through one book [medical] and am making fair progress. . . .

Poor, disheartened, lonely, with scant means to support a wife, with the Civil War sounding its call, he was finding his affairs at their lowest ebb. However, one evening in November, as he sat in the doctor's dingy little office poring over Gray's Anatomy, something whispered that all would yet be well; that in good time his Own — that which his soul most craved and

deserved — would be his. Pushing aside his Gray, he began
scribbling. What he wrote was the now familiar 'Waiting.'[1]

Disappointing as that summer of 1862 had been, it brought
the embryo writer a friendship destined to become one of the
most helpful attachments of his life — the friendship with
Myron B. Benton, a rural philosopher and poet, and an advanced farmer; a man of ripe literary tastes. The previously
mentioned series of articles, 'From the Back Country,' had
attracted Mr. Benton. In early August he wrote their author.
It was the first letter John Burroughs ever received in appreciation of his writings.

. . . Longfellow somewhere compares the situation of an author
to 'one walking in the twilight' — he gives forth his thoughts to the
public, but seldom knows the impression they make on the reader.
. . . I thought as the expression of one obscure opinion, I would pen
you a word thanking you for the pleasure your writings have given
me. I have only seen them, to recognize them, in the Leader for the
past three or four months. . . . The essay some time since on 'Some
of the Ways of Power' was very fine indeed and full of deep and
excellent thought. Your sketches of country life and scenery I am
very much interested in, having always lived in the country myself,
being a farmer. I can well attest their accuracy. . . .

I perceive, too, that our tastes in reading are similar, as well as in
love of Nature. Hawthorne, with all his gloom, cynicism, and general conservatism on all the progressive ideas of the day, (after
passing his early radical-reformative fever, which culminated in the
Brook Farm bubble) I admire exceedingly. . . . But Thoreau — 'dear
departed Thoreau' — I read and re-read forever. . . . Only a few
weeks before his death I received a letter from Thoreau, in answer to
one I had written to him, though a stranger; and afterward his sister
sent me some verses, by his most intimate friend, William E. Chan-
ing,[2] which were sung at his funeral.

I have just received a copy of the Leader containing another of
your genial sketches, describing a walk in the woods.

A fortnight later Burroughs replied to his appreciative
reader:

Your friendly greeting found me in the hay-field. . . . I am sincerely obliged to you for your kindly expression of interest. I did
not suppose my scribblings in the Leader would attract attention in
any quarter, much less call forth expressions like your own. I merely

[1] Fifty-six years later, standing with him on the site of that little office, I heard
his voice, hesitant, yearning, reminiscent, recite the lines which had come to him
as an inspiration in those dark hours.

[2] William Ellery Channing, the younger.

wrote them for pastime — for a change of mental diet. . . . My style needed limbering up a little, needed more play and movement. So I took to writing about foxes and woodchucks. An essay of mine in the Atlantic for November, 1860, on 'Expression,' will reveal to you the faults I am striving to correct. You observe it travels a little stiff, like a ring-boned horse. 'The Ways of Power' has somewhat of the same fault. Writing about common and familiar objects, I find, is a good exercise. . . .

I first wrote for the Leader something over a year ago. In July, 1861, I contributed quite a long essay on 'Indirections,' which I like very well. After that a short one on 'Water and Rock'; also 'A Thought or Two.' I wish to write another sketch on 'Haymaking,' which will perhaps end my 'Back Country.' Fifty miles from the railroad, twelve miles from the stage-coach, and two miles from the Post Office — is not that Back Country? This is my native place.

. . . Two years past I have been stopping at Marlboro, Ulster County, keeping a school there, and expect shortly to start out again in search of a school or *Rebels*, or something else.

Tell me about yourself and what you have written — if a young man and single. I see your name in the Leader quite often. Your papers and essays are good. I should like to talk with you about Emerson and Thoreau, but could not do it on this sheet. . . .

Tomorrow I take down my scythe again to battle with the hordes of Timothy and Clover, then a week of walking and rambling!

Who is Agnes Franz that writes those essays and short pithy reviews for the Leader? They are capital, and I should like to know about their author.

A letter to Benton, dated September 12th, acquaints one with further circumstances and opinions:

Your letter found me still in the Back Country, in the harvest-field, oat-gathering. . . .

The war feeling runs high with me, but I have not enlisted and probably shall not. I have lost all confidence in our generals, and there is not one whom I would serve under without compulsion. McClellan I implicitly believed in once, but now consider a failure fully as much so as Pope, the Gasconade, is. Mac is a very proper general, a very mathematical gentleman, but, *me judice*, has not a spark of genius. And, mark this, so long as there is only engineering skill and mathematical precision on our side, and dash and bravery and rapidity of movement on the part of the Rebels, so long the battle will be against us. No great war can be successfully carried on purely on mathematical principles — (organizing Victory beforehand!) — any more than a great poem can be written by solely mastering 'Parker's Aids.' Forego spades and picks, and the idea of digging or engineering an active, vigilant enemy out of a place, and fall back upon pure bravery, and the ability to deal quick, hard

blows, and something may be done. Halleck engineered the enemy
out of Corinth, and we see now the fruits of it. Mac ditto out of
Yorktown, and see the harvest he gathered! Obliging an enemy to
retreat without fighting him is disastrous; it is winding the spring
up, and you know what effect that has — it narrows its compass, and
in the same measure intensifies its power.

I have not read the Tribune this summer, nor the Post. . . . I have
arrived at these views solely from studying our own movements,
and those of the rebels. Look at the contrast! I know it is very
naughty of them to 'cut up' as they have! They ought to have
come up in front of Washington, or of Pope's army, and gone to
digging. . . .

Your last two papers in the Leader on Thoreau and Clough are
among the best reviews I have seen in the columns of that paper. I
hail with great satisfaction the appearance of your articles among so
much that is prosy and heavy. I saw a bit of a poem of yours a week
or two ago in the Independent — 'From Under a Tree.' I only wish
I could meet more of the same sort. The Dial I never saw, though I
sent for it, with the money inclosed, but never got it. I guess it must
have been about the time it stopped. If you could send me the one
containing your 'Orchis,' I would return it again.

Did you know the Saturday Press? It died in 1860. It was an
excellent literary paper. Henry Clapp, the editor, is now connected
with the Leader. I wrote considerable for it — contributed a series
of papers called 'Fragments from the Table of an Intellectual Epicure,' under the *nom de plume* of 'All Souls.'

I have quite a number of essays that have never seen the light.
One on 'Analogy' I consider my best. I have so much matter on
hand that I have thought of publishing a book, calling it 'Studies in
Analogy.' But I shall wait a while yet. I have published only two
poems, one in the Saturday Press,[1] and one in The Independent.[2] I
am not a ready versifier and take to prose more naturally.

Who wrote the 'Forester'[3] in the Atlantic for April? Have you
noticed Wasson's essays in that magazine? Carefully read his
'Originality' in the July number. Notice the finish and lofty music
of the periods. With the exception of Emerson (whom he excels in
finish, if not in calm dignity), I know no writer so original, or so
profound. I have corresponded with him since spring. I prize his
letters much; he has spoken some noble words of hope and encouragement to me. . . .

You have the advantage of me in years as I am only twenty-five,
but I have the advantage of you on one point, I am a married man,
and I consider it an advantage for any man to be married. . . .
Try it.

. . . Do you ever come to Poughkeepsie? Perhaps we might meet
there. Suggest any place between here and New York that you may
have occasion to be at, and I could probably see you. . . .

[1] 'To E. M. A.' [2] 'Loss and Gain.'
[3] 'Alcott wrote it. In those days the articles were unsigned.' J. B.

The copious correspondence that continued for forty years — up to the death of Mr. Benton — is the chief source of exact knowledge of those years (aside from the Journals which began in 1876). It was an intimate interchange of thought and opinion that passed between the friends. The letters of Benton, the elder by a few years, show the more mature, conservative nature, the more scholarly type of mind. They doubtless had a distinct influence in moulding and ripening the mind and character of the younger, more impetuous man, with the more original nature. A passage in Benton's third letter to Burroughs reads:

Tell me all you know about Wasson. I always like to hear something personal about one whose writing interests me much. This may be impertinent curiosity, but it is certainly human nature.

I find that in a notice I wrote for our local paper on the Atlantic for November, 1860, that I made a little mistake, for 'Expression' was spoken of as 'another of Wasson's fine essays' — which you must pardon. By the way, you ought not to publish articles of that class, as 'The Ways of Power,' in the Leader. They should be in no lower place, certainly, than the Atlantic. 'Fall' is a gem, the best of the 'Back Country' series — 'tis a pity to terminate it now. 'Trouting' is one of the best also — myself being judge, who am no sportsman whatever, carrying more often a portfolio than hook or gun on my rambles. . . .

The friends soon arranged a meeting. The younger, reminding the elder what disenchanters are nearness and contact, said he expected to fall hugely in his estimation, as he was habitually stupid, his occasional bright spells seldom occurring with strangers: 'But if I should find that I have always known you,' he writes, 'though I have never happened to meet you before, why, we will get along first-rate together.' And they did. After a trip to New York, Burroughs wrote Benton of meeting Henry Clapp, 'Agnes Franz,' and 'Ada Clare' — clever Bohemians, contributors to the 'Leader.'

'Ada Clare' is really beautiful, not a characterless beauty, but a singular, unique beauty. . . .

Walt Whitman is at Pfaff's almost every night. He lives in Brooklyn, is unmarried, and 'manages,' Clapp says, to earn six or seven dollars a week writing for the papers. He wrote a number of articles for the Leader some time ago on the Hospitals. Do you remember them? . . .

My visit to Leedsville will always stand out in my memory as a rich autumnal day. . . .

In reply Benton said:

Your visit here will be retained in my own memory as well as
yours, very long and sweetly. My life has been somewhat destitute
of friends of a certain class. I mean those whose bias of mind is
such that they can call forth (of that kind which you can) sympathies in certain regions which had before been shut off by a kind
of impassable 'Northwest Passage' — a frigid strait for voyaging
undoubtedly, but there was a warm open sea around the Pole
within. . . .

Another significant friendship came to Burroughs that year
in James Brownlee Brown, whose essays in the 'Atlantic' had
challenged his attention. Brown was best known as the author of 'Thaleta,' a poem to be found in the older anthologies.
(Two of Brown's essays, 'Genius,' and 'The Ideal Tendency,'
Burroughs said were so fine and genuine that in advanced age
he could still read them with pleasure.) From Olive, in mid-
November, he wrote Benton:

I must fill up this letter by telling of a visit I paid to Brownlee
Brown.
. . . I found him in the field superintending the gathering of car-
rots. I had no idea of staying more than an hour or two, but as the
storm raged so furiously, and as he urged me so earnestly, I remained
till Monday, and a glorious time I had. . . .
He owns a splendid situation on the banks of the river, just out of
Newburgh, and lives as a scholar should — amid books and music,
Art and Nature. His wife sings and plays divinely. . . . He is thirty-
eight, a graduate of one of the eastern colleges, and a lawyer by
profession, though some eight years ago he gave up practice on
account of his eyes. He supports himself now by writing, gardening,
and teaching music and drawing. . . .
He frankly confesses his obligation to Emerson. He says, 'He is
the father of us all.' He thinks when a man gets through the crust
of things, and stands face to face with the ineffable mysteries of the
universe, he necessarily expresses himself somewhat after this style
— which I know is very near the truth. He has visited Emerson
twice. . . . He knows many literary men and artists. . . . He has
known Walt Whitman for a number of years and admires him
hugely. Only the other day he met him at Pfaff's. . . .
I told Brown of you. 'Why,' said he, 'there are three of us trav-
elling the same road, and living within a short distance of one
another, why should we not meet often and compare notes?' He
says he thinks it almost a sin for a brother heart to go by him without
calling, and chided me because I had not called before. So, Myron,
do you go and see him; he charged me to tell you to come, and Joel
[Benton] too. . . .

A little later Burroughs sent 'Waiting' to Brownlee Brown for criticism. The latter replied that the thought was good, but that it had been many times illustrated since Emerson had advanced it. Brown considered the poem hardly concrete enough to give satisfaction, and treated its author to a lengthy dissertation on poetry. David A. Wasson, too, gave but faint praise to 'Waiting.' He found the verses 'vigorous and flowing and good in sentiment,' but did not think they indicated that Burroughs had any special call to write verse, in fact thought his distinctly reflective cast of mind quite foreign to the lyrical. In short, he believed his 'own' would yield him more abundant fruitage in quite other fields — which again shows his prophetic insight.

Nevertheless, it is well that the unenthusiastic reception of 'Waiting' by his literary friends did not deter Burroughs from sending it forth. For, obscure as the poem remained for years, it has, perhaps, more than any other one thing from his pen, most endeared him to his readers.

First published in 'Knickerbocker's,' March, 1863, 'Waiting' was republished long after by Whittier in 'Songs of Three Centuries,' since which time it has had great vogue, many a reader treasuring it in his heart without knowing its author's name. It has been much quoted, misquoted, parodied, and set to music. Spurious stanzas have been added; and a stanza which the author himself discarded [1] many years ago, has been obstinately reinstated. For a few years in the early nineteen-hundreds, he himself substituted a new stanza [2] in place of the fifth, which he had never cared for, though subsequently returning to it as more in keeping with the whole. The authorship of the poem has been claimed by others. Some years ago, on the death of an obscure writer in the South, 'Waiting,' under a changed title, being found among his literary effects, in his handwriting, and signed by him, his literary executor, acquainting Mr. Burroughs with these facts, wrote:

'I understand you also claim to be the author of this poem. Can you show a date earlier than 1884?'

[1] Yon flowret, nodding in the wind
    Is ready plighted to the bee;
And, maiden, why that look unkind,
    For lo! thy lover seeketh thee?

[2] The law of love binds every heart,
    And knits it to its utmost kin;
Our lives cannot flow long apart
    From souls our secret souls would win.

Waiting

Serene, I fold my hands & wait,
  Nor care for wind nor tide nor sea;
I rave no more 'gainst time or fate
For lo! my own shall come to me.

I stay my haste, I make delays,
  For what avails this eager pace?
I stand amid the eternal ways,
And what is mine shall know my face.

Asleep, awake, by night or day,
  The friends I seek are seeking me;
No wind can drive my bark astray,
  Nor change the tide of destiny.

What matter if I stand alone?
  I wait with joy the coming years;
My heart shall reap where it hath sown,
And garner up its fruit of tears.

The waters know their own & draw
  The brook that springs in yonder heights;
So flows the good with equal law
Unto the soul of pure delights.

The stars come nightly to the sky
  The tidal wave comes to the sea.
Nor time, nor space, nor deep, nor high,
  Can keep my own away from me

                    John Burroughs

FACSIMILE OF AUTOGRAPH COPY OF 'WAITING'

'Yes,' replied its author, 'I can show one of 1864, and earlier.'

In December, an opening in the public school at Buttermilk Falls (now Highland Falls) decided the poorly paid teacher to give up the school at Olive for one in the river town. Judged by its results, it was a momentous move. Again the couple set up housekeeping.

I am quite pleasantly located [he writes Benton] right in the midst of the Highlands, and Nature looks at me with a very stern and rugged face. West Point is only two miles away, the river one quarter of a mile, and Cozzen's famous hotel in our very midst.

Did you read my 'Analogy' in old 'Knick'? The Evening Post calls it heavy, and I think justly. Poet Abbey says it is brilliant, but you know poets are apt to overstate.

Literary gossip and comments on the War pass between Buttermilk Falls and Leedsville. Benton thanks the Lord that they have the long-awaited [Emancipation] Proclamation at last, 'though it comes like Samson, shorn of its locks of strength.' Burroughs urges his friend to visit him, a letter in January running thus:

Oh, these long nights in our quiet household — what a god-send your company would be! I read and study incessantly, and find I am going over a good deal of surface at any rate.[1] By way of side dishes I have done 'Great Expectations,' and one volume of Prescott's 'Conquest of Peru.' I have been tempted to write a few times, but have merely cackled without laying a solitary egg.

. . . His [Wasson's] review on Buckle is very able and satisfactory to me. I think the deepest point he made was in stating the identity of Freedom and Necessity. It is pretty deep water there. Wasson sometimes has a smartness that I don't like, and a trick of underscoring that does not add to his force. Brownlee Brown spoke of seeing an essay of his some time ago, in a New England periodical which he characterized as grand. He says Wasson generally disappoints him on second reading. Have you remarked it? . . .

I took dinner with him [Brown] a couple of weeks ago, and he promised, as soon as the river should close up, to skate down and see me. I should like him better if there were a little more vigor and roughness about him. I suppose it is because I am such an uncouth bear myself. . . . He is a cousin of Henry Brown, the sculptor, who lives a few rods from him.

I am much pleased with my place here, and with my school also. The scenery is grand. It strikes me it would be a perfect paradise to a young unmarried man, as a certain element of the population

[1] After a few months more he abandoned the study of medicine.

which is much given to bonnets and blushes greatly predominates. Only a few hours ago I was whirling among a lot of the steel-shod beauties on the pond, and of course played the gallant in assisting them on and off with their skates. Think of that for a married man! . . .

The Leader I am clear disgusted with, and damn the thing every time I take it up. Clancy ought to be hung, and 'Ada Clare' condemned to forty years' silence. My heart bleeds for Abbey.[1] If I did not know him, I should say, 'Served him right — no need to make a book that contains no performance but only promise. Yet I trust it will do him good. She has greatly overstated the matter, and I suspect she knows it. So far he has received nothing but the cheapest kind of flattery, and even an over-dose of this caustic woman's wit will not hurt him. He must learn better than to daub on his colors so thick. He hunts too far for a subject, I suspect; looks at the sunset more than at the calm azure of the upper heavens with its immortal stars. Frissell showed me Joel's review in the Amenia Times. I think Joel does wrong to flatter him an atom. Nothing is valuable to a man but the truth. . . .

There is a splendid library at West Point which I feel like laying forcible hands on. I can go in and read for an hour or two, but cannot bring a book away with me. A good library at my disposal would be of inestimable value to me. . . .

The War troubles me much, in fact, keeps me in a kind of fever and ague all the time. I am going to pray for a long Rip Van Winkle sleep to fall upon me, if it keeps on at this rate. Please save a pile of daily papers for me, if you hear the spell is upon me. . . .

3. The Lure of the Flowers and the Birds

The early months of 1863 were trying ones in the Burroughs home. The wife was ill, her convalescence was followed by months of semi-invalidism — a harrowing time for both invalid and attendant. The latter chafed under his threefold occupation — nurse, housekeeper, and teacher — which so interfered with writing and meditation. But in May, a housemaid appearing, he wrote hopefully to Benton of the invalid's progress, and of his walks to the woods with Professor Eddy, a botanist. In the letter which follows, one sees John Burroughs in the first flush of wild-flower study. It is almost as though one were with him on those Sunday walks when he first learned to call the woodland flowers by name.

O, spring is marvellous! How my life goes out and up these joyous days! Today I worshipped in the mountains. The birds sang my

[1] About a review of Abbey's *May Dreams*.

psalms and the rocks preached my sermons. *When shall we know what these days and these rambles in the woods give us?* [Italics mine.] A book affects the quality of one's thought, but a May day in the woods, its tone and rhythm. I gathered my hands full of the Anemone today. . . . The Corydalis and Hepatica grow here in great abundance; also the Trailing Arbutus, I am told, but I have not found it yet. I have been looking for the Claytonia, but have not seen it yet, have you? Tell me the name of some very rare plant that you have found, and I will look for it here. . . .

And later:

I have taken an unusual interest in flowers this spring, chiefly, I suppose, because I live so near the woods. I have found some fine specimens, though I suppose they are common enough. The other day I gathered my hands full of the Lady's slipper, and never experienced so much delight over flowers as over them. I believe they belong to the family of orchids. I hear of a locality where the yellow one blooms, about seven miles from here, and I have a mind to go and see it. I have found the dwarf orchis, which seems to be very rare and delicate, and I wondered if it was the same species which suggested your poem.[1]

How does the Commonwealth get on? Some weeks ago I sent them some fragments called 'Kernels of Corn,' and suggested that if they would send me the paper I would send some more of the same sort. But evidently they do not consider such 'corn' an equivalent, for the paper has never come. The other day I sent them a poem of Brownlee Brown's, and threatened sending one of my own if they did not send the paper. This is the most ready currency I have, and if it does not bring the paper, I must go without it.

My friend in Washington[2] writes me charming letters of late; he has made the acquaintance of 'Florence Percy'[3] and is delighted with her, and, I suspect, in love, too. . . . I think her the very best of our female poets. He says also that between him and Walt Whitman has passed the bond of beer, and they are friends. Walt calls often in the store to see him, and they talk much. Walt says he has no sympathy with Abbey and that school of poetry, though he thinks Abbey shows promise. . . .

A little later from Allen comes this glimpse of Whitman:

Walt strolled in today as he frequently does. The whole front of our store is open and is shaded with an awning, and is a cool, pleasant place, coming in from the street. Sometimes when I am busy, I'll see Walt's picturesque form in one of the many camp-chairs, a fan in his hand; and then, after a while, he is gone. When I am not

---

[1] 'Orchis Vera,' by Myron B. Benton.   [2] E. M. Allen.
[3] The pen-name of Elizabeth Akers, author of 'Rock me to Sleep' and many other poems.

busy, I sit down and talk with him. He says he is going to give me a book of Thoreau's which the author sent him some years ago. . . . We projected an excursion for Sunday up the Branch to the same woods where Florence and I went. I wish you could be with us.

. . . We hold Fredericksburgh and the heights beyond. . . . For the last ten days Alexandria has been entrenched with rifle-pits, and the streets leading out barricaded. It seems there was an intimation of a raid by Stuart. If he had come, he'd have had a heavy time of it, for there were enough troops to bag him. I know Col. Kilpatrick, who has been raiding it so lately. He boarded where I did last summer . . . He is a small, blue-eyed man, and a graduate of West Point. . . .

Yours till death,

E. M. A.

Life for the budding writer was rich and full these days, with his ardor for the wild flowers, the comradeship with Allen, Benton, and Brown, the gossip about Whitman — Allen's letters making him so real — and now something richer still was about to come.

One day in June, at West Point,[1] Burroughs noticed a tall, striking-looking man going about with an alert, investigating air, much at variance with the perfunctory manner of the other official visitors. He seemed like a countryman away from home for the first time, and intent upon getting all there was out of it. A silk hat, much too large, was worn far back on the head; his sharp eyes were peering into everything, curious about everything. That night Benton burst into the Burroughs home announcing, 'Emerson is at West Point!' Instantly Burroughs knew who the alert, eager stranger was.

On the morrow Benton, Burroughs, and Donald G. Mitchell ('Ik Marvel') went over to West Point, met their hero, and walked and talked with him. He seemed to be glad to be with them, and as for them — they walked on air. Socrates, followed by the young Athenians, had no more ardent disciples. They asked him about Alcott, Thoreau, and Wasson. 'Wasson,' said Emerson, 'is one of the best heads among us, but he is the most indiscreet — if medicine is prescribed for him, he will double or triple the dose.' He charged them never to miss a chance to see Alcott and hear him talk, but admitted that when he put pen to paper his inspiration vanished. 'I get more pain than pleasure,' he confessed, 'from his writings.'

[1] Buttermilk Falls is near West Point.

Then, as though sorry to admit this, he glorified Alcott's eloquent, poetic vocabulary and orphic sayings.

That talk of Emerson to the young men was as water to a thirsty hart. They carried his bag to the boat-landing — a shiny black oilcloth bag; they hovered near as he bought his ticket, his talk scarcely interrupted by the transaction.

'We didn't cross the ferry with him,' Mr. Burroughs said regretfully; 'I suppose our sixpences were pretty short.' But, standing close to the boat, they listened, he still talking as it moved away. When he could no longer make himself heard, he smiled on them benignly — 'that angelic smile' — and with his long arm waved a sweeping farewell.

The day, to borrow a phrase from Emerson, was marked by the comrades with 'a vermillion pencil.' They had seen their hero 'plain'; the hour in which he had spoken to them was ever memorable. As they moved away from the pier, they were still enveloped in the aroma of his presence. The elation was slow to pass. Having seen the sun, Benton would fain see a satellite, so made a pilgrimage to Brownlee Brown, of which he writes in a long letter to his 'beloved John,' a part of which is given:

How near we came to not seeing him [Emerson] after all! Brown laughed heartily when I told him the gentleman's sentiments on Wasson's health. He said Emerson had little sympathy for sick folks — thinks sickness is a sin, and unnecessary if we obey the laws of health. . . .

Our farmers are busy with their tobacco. I have been ploughing my ground for it since I came home. Father told me that visiting interfered with work; I replied that it was just the contrary — work interferes with visiting. . . .

Burroughs writes Benton of finding a chewink's nest in one of his walks; of nearly breaking his neck clambering over rocks and finding some wild flax in bloom:

It has a wonderfully delicate blue bell-flower. Growing amid craggy rocks, it was inexpressibly beautiful. I never saw any before, and should not have known how to name it had I not consulted Mr. Eddy.

He writes of meeting 'Edmund Kirk' in New York (the author of 'Among the Pines'), whom he found a sociable, modest, and genuine fellow. He tells of buying a photograph of Emerson.

The Burroughs-Benton letters deepen in interest. Benton writes of his brother Charles being in great battles; of hearing Frederick Douglass; of fighting tobacco worms by day, and, in the summer evenings, reading Spenser's 'Faerie Queen'; and looking eagerly forward to a midsummer camping-trip with Burroughs.

Among the letters and mementoes dating back to that life at Buttermilk Falls is an empty envelope addressed to John Burroughs, by a New York editor. Presumably it had contained the rejected manuscript, appropriately called 'Loose Thoughts on Culture,' as that name is written on the envelope, which also has a memorandum from editor to author. One sees what pains they took in 1863 to temper the wind to the shorn writer.

The thoughts are good and original [wrote the editor], but the style is loose and rambling. It is consequently not accepted. The artist of the beautiful requires a mastery over form, as well as power over design and conception.

It is noteworthy that when the essay appeared in the 'Saturday Press,' the title was emended to 'A Thought on Culture'; and it is probable that, in rewriting it, the author eliminated some of the looseness and achieved some degree of mastery over its form.

The following note of July 29th, from Burroughs to Benton, is of special significance, in that it records the first glimmering of interest in bird-study, which was henceforth to be one of the absorbing pursuits of him whom a later poet-comrade (Richard Watson Gilder) named 'John o' Birds.'

I am not writing to answer your letter, but on a little matter of business. You know I am much interested in birds; at least of late I can think or talk of nothing else; and it sticks to me that the Atlantic[1] I let you have, containing Brown's 'Ideal Tendency,' contains also an article on birds. If it does, will you please mail it to me? I will send it to you again if you are not through with it.

What had aroused this interest in the birds?

On a Saturday in May or June of that momentous year, while browsing in the Library of the Military Academy at West Point, John Burroughs chanced upon Audubon's

---

[1] 'The Birds of the Pasture and Forest,' *Atlantic Monthly*, December, 1858. Unsigned, but written by Wilson Flagg.

'Birds.' Its spirited colored illustrations at once fired his imagination and kindled his enthusiasm. Thenceforth love of flowers and birds went hand in hand.

When in childhood he had noted with such wonder and delight that strange little warbler in the beechwoods, he had half promised himself that he would know the birds some day, but till now nothing had come of it. His observations had been aimless, his knowledge unsystematized. Now, with Audubon as guide, with the mounted birds at the Academy for reference, and with the throng of returning birds to quicken his ardor, he found a new world opened up in the midst of the old — a world so alluring as almost to blot out the perilous fortunes of the nation. 'Just think of it!' he said self-reproachfully, in later years, 'while the Battle of Gettysburg was being fought, I was in the woods studying the birds! And when we went to the Adirondacks in August, I was almost wild. The discovery of the Canada warbler, the black-throated green, the purple finch — what significance they had for me in the first flush of my bird studies!'

Shortly before that Adirondack excursion, the ardent Allen wrote Burroughs from hot and dusty Washington, with the din of war in his ears; wrote of his longings for the forest primeval; and of his own budding romance; and gave a glimpse of Whitman on his errands of mercy to the soldiers.

Walt just passed with his arms full of bottles and lemons, going to some hospital, he said, to give the boys a good time. He was sweating finely; his collar and shirt were thrown open, showing his great hairy throat and breast. I asked him about Brown and Thoreau some time ago. 'Fine fellows, fine fellows!' said he. That was all. He never gives a literary opinion of anyone, but always speaks of him in a personal sense. In fact, he is very reticent in book matters. He knew Thoreau and liked him much. . . .

I suppose you think we have been terribly excited here; not a bit of it, although 'Johnny Reb' has been raiding it within a few miles of us. As it is, all the citizens between the ages of eighteen and forty-five are called out for sixty days; we are all enrolled and ordered to muster on Monday at ten A.M. to be sworn into the U.S. service. I suppose we shall have to serve in the forts and rifle-pits. If the sixty days holds good, I am afraid I shall not see you this summer, which the Lord forbid!

Early in July from Allen comes another glimpse of those stirring times, and of Lincoln and Whitman:

At muster this morning we were informed that the stress was past and that the order had been revoked, whereat we grew jubilant. We thank General Meade and Co. for that. He has smitten them vigorously and they are having a refreshing season of it. I was up at the War Department today and saw 'Abe' twice as he passed me on the pavement. I touched my hat to him as I felt in duty bound to do, but he observed it not. He stoops some, and seems to have much on his mind, poor man! I send you a picture of Phil Kearny.

Walt and I quaffed beer today from great goblets that would become the halls of Valhalla. Walt is much interested in you, and I sketched your history some to him. He would like to know you. He is a good fellow, and although over fifty[1] belongs to the present generation. He was much interested in our trip to the Beaverkill, which I detailed to him.

In August, Allen came on from Washington, bent on going to the Adirondacks.

Go he must [writes Burroughs to Benton] and you must go with us. . . . What do you say? . . . Let not trifles detain you. We will have a glorious time. Write us by return mail and say you are with us. The expense will not be much, but the fun boundless. Joel [Benton] would be a valuable recruit also. . . .

The three friends, Allen, Benton, and Burroughs, with one 'Jaspar from Jersey,' made the trip into the north woods in mid-August. Jubilantly they set out, throwing cares to the winds, exulting in the prospect of two weeks of glorious freedom; but on reaching Troy the bird enthusiast began to be conscious-stricken about his young wife alone at home, and, evidently trying to keep his bubbling spirits within bounds, wrote urging her to make some visits till his return:

At least don't get lonesome and blubber. Be a good girl. Here's a kiss. I shall think of you often. I will spend as little money as possible.

Again the next day, just as they were to plunge into the woods:

We have had a very jolly trip so far. I find I shall need all my money. I regret much the expense, but cannot back out now. I would not have come had I known it would cost so much, but I will make the best of it, and make it up some other way. I should have taken the trip some time or other, and could never come better than now. Let my girl not scold or fret, and I will be good enough to her to make it up. . . .

[1] Whitman was but forty-four at that time.

He made it up when later he wrote 'With the Birds' and 'The Adirondacks' — essays begun shortly after this unwonted vacation.

In imagination one has camped and tramped with Burroughs on that expedition; spied with him the nest of the purple finch; seen the dainty warbler leading her young through the undergrowth; followed 'Bub Hewett' to the Stillwater of the Boreas; taken trout from its deep pools; paddled noiselessly among the lily-pads with the jack-light, and watched the startled deer fall a victim to the hunter's gun; has lounged by the camp-fire; slept on balsam boughs; and risen at dawn to see and feel and smell morning in the air. Further glimpses of it all are given in two tentative beginnings of the Adirondack essay (much different from the published account) found among his old manuscripts. The Mother Goose beginning acquaints one with the personnel of the party:

> Let us go to the woods, said Richard to Robin,
> Let us go to the woods, said Robin to Bobin,
> Let us go to the woods, said John all alone.

> What to do there? said Richard to Robin,
> What to do there? said Robin to Bobin,
> What to do there? said every one.

> To kill a fat wren, said Richard to Robin,
> To kill a fat wren, said Robin to Bobin,
> To kill a fat wren, said John all alone.

... Robin [E. M. A.] was mostly a city-bred youth of poetic temperament and mercantile pursuits, but full of spirit and vigor — taut and trim as a Yankee clipper, and with a breeze always in his sails — facile with pencil, he sketched or versified anything the occasion offered, ... weaving rhymes between bargains, and caricaturing an 'odd customer' while the latter was engaged in making out his bill. ... Latterly he had babbled much about green fields in his letters ... and an excursion to the Adirondacks had long been one of his day-dreams. ...

Richard [M. B. B.] was a poet and philosopher, a farmer, and a reviewer, cultivating the alluvium of his Webutuck Valley, but turning up the deepest sub-soil with his philosophical spade. Genial, quiet, good-natured, enamored of Thoreau and the wild, he received with enthusiasm every proposition that looked to an excursion to the woods.

Of 'John all alone' [J. B.] I can speak less positively. Indeed, I have never yet been able quite to make out the manner of being he is. This much, however, I can say: he was a poor, worn pedagogue

who looked to the green fields and the woods more wistfully than
any of his truant pupils; and the one of all others of the party who
was bent on obtaining the 'fat wren.'

Bobin, or 'Jaspar from Jersey,' was a youth of memorable fortitude and patience, pious, good-natured, and scarcely half through
his teens. . . .

In the second beginning is a view of the merry party riding
from Saratoga to the Fort in sunset and twilight, 'the large
few stars' (he is reading Whitman now) overhead:

Mystery and indefiniteness suited our already aroused imagina-
tions — the scenery dimly outlined, our songs keeping time to the
beating of the horses' hoofs on the resonant planks. . . .

Robin was not a youth to hide his light under a bushel, or [to]
button his coat too tightly across his whisky-flask, as our stage-
companions could testify. . . .

At Lake George, at a private house, we donned gray army shirts
and old clothes and walked off before breakfast. A farmer feeding his
pigs stared at us — he probably thought a squad of Confederate
soldiers had passed on their way to Canada.

In that fine passage where the author describes floating
for deer, a paragraph is omitted which it were a pity to lose.
It follows the sentence, 'We floated out into that spectral
shadow-land and moved slowly as before.' Continuing:

Was this the same earth and sky I had known so long? My own
identity seemed to slip away, and I moved a shadow among shadows.
Yonder planet hath its rings of fire, but here was the ring of Night
and the River of Lethe. The silence was impressive.

On that excursion Burroughs shot his first deer. His humiliating experiences as a lad in hunting (when he had a
superb fox, and, again, a host of wild pigeons, at his mercy,
but, fascinated, let them escape), were not repeated here.
Unhesitatingly he brought the deer, lured by the jack-light,
to the ground. In the published article he dismisses the occur-
rence as 'a very indifferent success after all,' but here one sees
his immediate reactions:

Instantly I saw it there, and the last quiver of life depart, the
sportsman in me was untrue to his allegiance, and I felt ashamed
that I had been so wrought upon by the prospect of slaying the poor
harmless creature. Besides, we had so played upon its credulity and
its innocent wonder, that it seemed a very unfair triumph. . . .

When bounding free through the forest, or snorting defiance a quarter of a mile away, it is something of a feat to send a bullet through its heart, but what sportsmanship is *this*?

It was the only deer he ever shot, or attempted to shoot. In middle life, having outgrown his earlier practice of study-ing the birds with a gun, he admitted, as though it were a weakness, 'I can't kill things any more.' As the years multi-plied, he grew still more averse to taking life — always ex-cepting woodchucks, and other 'varmints,' which continued to rouse in him the primitive instinct to kill.

Another unpublished passage throws light upon Benton and their comradeship:

In the twilight 'Richard' and I made our bed on a gentle slope, nearly overshadowed by a huge pine, where the moss was peculiarly thick and soft, and fell into one of our discursive, easy-going talks — the sport and play of the mind rather than the deliberate application of its powers. Rich and rare old 'Richard!' what depths there are in thee, and what heights! what quaintness, what subtlety, what clear-ness of vision, and what Norseman sturdiness and vigor! How we have tugged at the old problems, seeking again the unknown quan-tity whose symbol is not x, but the visible universe! Loafing and inviting our souls in forest and field, by lake and river and mountain, what converse we have had! what questionings, what glorious meta-physical wrestlings, what uplifting and liberation of spirit!

This night, in a kind of shadow-talk the hours went by. The slope was a little too rapid, and gravity, by inches and half inches and quarter inches, pulled us down toward the level, till finally we found our equilibrium around the camp-fire. 'Robin,' rolled up in his blanket, woke to find a gray log beside him which, he declared, was not there when he went to sleep. The gray log, being manipulated, disclosed 'Richard's' head at one end of it, and his boots at another, his butternut blanket, and his liberal length making the deception quite perfect.

The light from their camp-fire, extinguished so long ago, still shines in this passage:

... The sparks go up in their serpentine courses till the sparks seem stars, and the stars sparks. How true is Thoreau's remark that we do not know what our stoves and chimneys have concealed from us till we have built a fire in the woods at night! The sparks, the smoke, the deep shadows, the silent listening trees, and the great ocean of night kept at bay there by a little blaze! How cavernous the woods look, how spectral and pokerish! There in the deep flicker-ing shadows is the region of superstition and dread. Here one looks for the glaring eyes and the crouching forms of evil ... while getting wood and water he is inclined to whistle ... is unusually vigilant, and half expects to hear a stealthy tread behind him. [This calls up the Roxbury farm-boy with his fears of the dark.]

The ease with which Burroughs established intimacy and harmony with Nature is seen in subsequent passages in the essay. 'The mountain must come to me, not I to it. Beauty unsought is truest found.' And then, lured by a humming-bird, he strayed from the others, and, penetrating deep into the woods, reclined upon a moss-covered log, while a troop of chickadees, coming near, chattered and disputed; the little green flycatcher[1] came, too, to see what it was all about; then the blue-backed warbler, and the black and yellow; then a nuthatch — 'and in the goodly company,' he says, simply and truly, 'the woods satisfied me.'

In late September the embryo ornithologist writes Benton:

I am seriously contemplating going into the army. . . . I am getting dissatisfied and crave action. I do want to get nearer to this bugbear, War! I want to decide the matter this week, if possible. I have proposed to the Trustees to raise my wages, and if they refuse to do it, I shall stop the school at once and shoulder the musket. If I had some one like yourself to go with me, I should go at any rate.

Our campaign in the Adirondacks seems almost like a dream; it has idealized itself already, and my life will always be the sweeter and richer for it. How it enhances the value of living, does it not? to have something sweet to remember!

I am as absorbed in birds as ever, and 'fly-catchers' are my constant companions. I have succeeded in mounting them better than I had hoped, and now, as I write, a jay looks down at me from the top of my desk, 'as natural as life,' as they say. But few of the birds that I got in the mountains are fit for use, I find, owing to the imperfect state of plumage. The bird you spoke of is called the little green fly-catcher.

The month's Atlantic I find remarkably rich. Thoreau's article[2] is actually one of the best things I ever read. You see he discusses the point we talked about that Sunday on Lake Henderson. You remember my views were very nearly his. I stated, I believe, that I lived for my pleasure, or development, and had no other purpose before me.[3]

[1] A mistake in identification. Perhaps the yellow-bellied flycatcher.
[2] 'I think it was "Life without Principle."' J. B. This article appeared in the *Atlantic* for October, 1863.
[3] This rather bald admission of his hedonistic intentions must be taken *cum grano salis*. However, it expresses, in the main, an attitude he consistently held through life.

Wasson's article[1] I liked much. I would, however, that the style of it did not remind me of Carlyle himself. But doesn't he sock it to him? Whew! Did Trowbridge write the 'Pewee'? It is good. The fourth verse, I think, is very fine.

I liked your article on the Bishop in the Leader. In some parts of it you did yourself justice. I wish you would always sink your bucket down thus. . . .

Benton's protest comes forthwith:

. . . This matter of your going into the Army troubles me not a little. God forbid that I should throw a straw in the way of patriotism now. Our country needs sacrifices which should be offered willingly. But I do not see that the cause requires very much now in the mere matter of numbers, after the means which have been taken. One born with the genius to direct and control the great mass of raw material could do something for his country now; but I cannot see that the demand is such that *you* are called upon to enlist at this time. I beg of you, do not plunge into this thing out of rash uneasiness, and craving for excitement. Such feelings ought to be smothered before they lead you to bury all your opportunities of intellectual improvement, as you know you would. . . .

Being tired, I would not have answered tonight except to send my opinion on this subject; for I fear you are going to be very precipitate. Think of all you would forego to satisfy the 'craving' for the excitement of the 'big War.' One week would satisfy all that, and then — the long drudgery. If you think it is your duty to your country, I will not open my mouth, though it would be a sacrifice on my part to lose you. What you would sacrifice would be immense. I need not tell you that your after life will depend very much upon the way in which the next three or four years are spent — towards your 'development.'

Ten days later Burroughs replied that his plans had been 'knocked prematurely in the head' by the severe illness of his wife.

She has been very bad for nearly two weeks, and of course I could not leave her. . . . She undergoes the most excruciating pain. I can get no girl, and have to take the sole care of her myself and keep my school going. . . . If you happen to know a good girl in your neighborhood, I wish you would send her to me.

The draft has just come off here, and I believe I have not the honor to be a conscript. . . .

The housemaid did not materialize, but the wife soon con-

[1] 'A letter to Carlyle in answer to Carlyle's "Shooting Niagara," in which Wasson dealt Carlyle some good resounding blows. Carlyle had taken sides with the South.' J. B.

valesced. However, the undercurrent of unrest was waxing stronger and stronger. His meager salary was inadequate to meet the increased cost of living; domestic dissonances were occurring frequently. One night after reaching home, although he had, as usual, given out the lessons for the next day, he suddenly decided[1] to abandon teaching and get nearer to the seat of war.

Teaching had been but a means to an end, as had his brief study of medicine; while his business ventures had been foreign to all his tastes and aims. But the flowers and the birds continued absorbing, while the desire to write grew more insistent. And there was the War beckoning. So in the golden days of October, migrating South with the birds, he alighted in Washington in quest of work and adventure.

[1] A friend of his wrote me that awkwardness on his (J. B.'s) part, in overturning a 'spider' of hot grease on the floor, and the resulting recriminations, was the 'last straw' that prompted this sudden move.

CHAPTER IV
IN GOVERNMENT EMPLOY
1863–1872

The essential part of the life of a great writer, a great poet, is just this: to seize, grasp, and analyze the whole man at the moment when, by a concurrence more or less slow and easy, his genius, his education, his circumstances, accord in such a way that he has given birth to his first masterpiece. If you comprehend the poet at this critical moment, if you unravel the knot to which all within him will henceforth be bound, if you find, so to speak, the key to that mysterious ring, half iron, half diamond, which links his second existence — obscure, repressed, and solitary — the very memory of which he would oftentimes fain destroy, then it may be said of you that you possess and know your poet to the depths: you have entered with him the darksome regions of Dante and Virgil; you are worthy to accompany him side by side without fatigue, through his other marvels.

SAINTE-BEUVE

THE Nation's Capital was the scene of the growth and activities of John Burroughs for the greater part of the next decade. Emerging from the obscurity of rural surroundings, casting off the drudgery of teaching, freed from domestic cares, he found his new environment teeming with novelty and interest. The Washington of those closing years of the Civil War, then, as now, a city of magnificent distances, with its population of but sixty thousand, was like a country village with its dusty, unpaved streets, and its broad commons whereon the cattle grazed; where goats cropped the rose-bushes through the fences, and pigs dreamed dreams beneath them. Nature came up to the city's threshold. One could get to the primitive woods in ten minutes. Burroughs used to hunt snipe where now are solid blocks of buildings and rolling cars. Great apartments now loom in many of his former woodland haunts.

Reaching Washington in the fall of the year, when the Southern days, he said, had Northern blood in their veins, he drank deep of 'that vintage that intoxicates all lovers of the open air,' and basked in the soft brooding days and the enchanting nights. Never, he declared in 'Winter Sunshine,' had he seen anything but second-grade sunlight and moonlight until he reached Washington. There, dilating and expanding under the azure skies, he breathed deeper and stepped more proudly, as though inhaling the pure ether of mountain-tops.

Although he reacted with keen delight to his surroundings, a dismal period was yet to be passed before his 'Own' was to come to him. Genius, they say, lights its own fires; at this period John Burroughs not only had to light the fire, but to feed and fan it to keep it from going out.

He had written a part of the Adirondack essay before leaving Buttermilk Falls, and had begun another (on the birds), which, however, was destined to many interruptions.

As soon as he reached Washington, his friends E. M. Allen and Elizabeth Akers set about to help him find employment. To reduce expenses he slept on a cot in Allen's Army Supply store, and did a part of his own laundry.

The first work secured was in the Quartermaster General's Department, — burying negro soldiers, looking after supplies for the Cavalry, and keeping tally on loads of hay — occupations even more incongruous than that of Charles Lamb's 'thirty-three years of slavery' in London, seated on a stool in the East India House; of John Stuart Mill's clerkship there; and of Hawthorne's measuring coal on a British schooner in Boston.

I. Adjustments

During the six years of married life up to this point in his career, there had been many vicissitudes. Neither husband nor wife had found much satisfaction in their manner of living, with their reverses, his meager wages, her frequent illnesses, their long separations, and their many short and trying ventures at housekeeping; and, above all, with their diverse standards as to life's values, and irreconcilable points of view as to his ambition to become an author. His sudden decision to make a radical change having resulted in the journey to Washington, he soon made earnest attempts at a more satisfactory adjustment of their domestic problems, as letters of this period show. After a week of work in the Quartermaster General's Department, he wrote home:

DEAR WIFE:
I do not enclose any money because I have none to enclose. I will send you the first I get. I have already borrowed some, and will have to borrow more, I suppose. . . . Perhaps Amanda [North] can relieve you till I am replenished.

I am beginning to feel quite at home and can assure you appreciate my freedom. I am getting quite studious and think I shall do a big winter's work in the shape of study. Household cares and domestic duties, I think in time would about have spoiled me. There is nothing so deadening to intellectual pursuits. I feel as if I never wanted to go to housekeeping again till I can do so on quite a different plan.

I was sad and lonely for a few days, but am now getting over it. Books and work and my own thoughts must take the place of whatever I have lost. You don't know how good it seems to eat a meal of victuals without having to cook it, or be disturbed by the remembrance of the after-clap of dish-washing; or to sit down by a fire you did not kindle, or are not obliged to replenish. I enjoy other immunities which I need not mention, but which I deeply appreciate. It seems an age since I heard any one scold. Indeed, I seem to have taken a trip to the moon, and to be leading quite a new life.

I have seen 'Florence Percy,' and am not sure but she is the most beautiful woman I ever saw. I have seen Walt also, and think him glorious. I am glad you are getting better, and hope and trust that your temper may mend with your body. I believe it is good for us to be apart, don't you? I think our love increases as does the distance between us. When we are together I am sure to depart in some way from the course you seem to have marked out for me, and then you are sure to let loose the 'dogs of war' upon me, when all goes wrong. So let us brave it awhile, say till spring. Rent is so high here that it is useless to talk of housekeeping, and it would cost me $25 per month to board you here, to say nothing of fire, lights, washing, etc. I will have to board where my work is because I get it free. I do not feel warranted yet to calculate on staying long here. When I feel sure it is a permanent thing, then we will talk about your coming here. . . .

After you are through visiting, you had better hire your board some place where you can get it for $2.50 or $3.00 per week, and as fast as I get any money I will send you some. . . . Of our things at the Falls you had better sell all but a few. You know best about that. The preserves, etc., put up in jars, for I want some of them sent me. . . . I think you could get money of your father to straiten [sic] our affairs there till I can earn some. . . . I hope I can send you some money this week.

Allen sends love. So do I — to all. I cry daily in the depths of my heart, but mean to harden myself and be a Stoic. 'Tears, idle tears!' What do they avail?

Give my love to Amanda and tell her I hope again to see her in the flesh.

Your Good-for-nothing

John

A few days later, sending five dollars, — all he had to send, — he wrote of feeling ill; of having been transferred to another department, where he was assisting in giving out hospital supplies. Still later, November 13th:

Dear Ursula,

... I wrote you the other day and enclosed five dollars. I now enclose three, and have some change left. My daily expenses amount to five cents, which I pay for a pie every night on returning from work. I get only two meals per day so that I need the pie. . . . I have not much of anything to do yet and shall not feel safe and secure till I have. . . .

You speak of my happiness. You need not envy me. I hope yours may be no less. You would hardly know what to do with such happiness. I am afraid you would call it by another name. You cannot possibly crave sympathy and love and companionship more than I do, . . . but when I think of the past . . . I see no reason to be hopeful as to the future. . . .

On November 24, 1863:

I am writing to you much depressed and disheartened. I have lost my place and know not what I shall do next. I did not have much to do, and complained at Headquarters of the fact, when I pretty soon got my discharge. If I could have done nothing with as good a grace as some of the rest of the clerks, it might not have happened.[1]

Ah, well! it looks gloomy enough. I was paid $38 for the twenty-three days I was employed. . . . Allen thinks there is no danger but that I can find something. . . . I wish I had not left the Falls. . . . That cursed desire for more money is the destroyer of all peace.

I hope you will see all my creditors there and assure them that I will pay every farthing. . . . If you have any money to spare, pay the small debts first. . . . If I should get a place soon, I can send you some of the money I now have. Write by return mail. . . .

Subsequent letters tell of attempts to get a place; of seeing dissipated fellows in fat positions, and of supposing it will always be his fate to be in want of a situation. He was neither folding his hands nor waiting with any serenity at this period. He had almost a mind to go back to old Delaware County and hire out on a farm:

Nothing has gone with me in this world as I thought it would. My life is a failure. I am not as valuable as my old shoes. I wish for your sake you were at liberty to choose again. You might get some one who could provide you a home and care for you as you deserve. I have nothing but ideas, and do not see that I can ever bring them to bear. If you were well, you need not want, whatever might be-

---

[1] One day in a slack time he was reading a philosophical article in the *Westminster Review* (which, by the way, had a yellow cover), when the assistant quartermaster came in. The idle clerks immediately bustled about, but Burroughs kept on reading. In a few days he received his dismissal, the report which came later to his friend Allen being that 'about all Burroughs did was to sit around and read yellow-covered literature.'

come of me; but you are out of health, and I out of employment —
the Lord only knows what will become of us. . . .

If Charley writes for you to go to N.Y., and will defray your
expenses, go. A trip of the kind will do you good. . . .

In a few days, writing more cheerfully, he talks of buying a
clerkship provided he can borrow the money, if he can obtain
one no other way.

Let him who thinks the course of authorship, or of art in
any field, runs smooth, read this homely account of how he
'ate his bread with tears':

. . . I sleep on a little camp bedstead about two feet wide, and six
and a half long, here in the store. Army blankets form the bed under
me and the cover over me. Allen happened to have an old pillow his
mother gave him and one case for it. On that rests my head. When
the case is dirty, I turn it, and when both sides are soiled, I wash it
here in the sink and dry it before the fire. I also wash my socks and
handkerchiefs in the same way. The other day the laundry where
my clothes were burned up, and I thought I was shirtless and drawer-
less; but, luckey [sic] for me, my clothes were among the few that
were saved. I have plenty to eat, and better than I ever had before,
but my pants are pretty yellow, and my coat a little seedy. . . .

I go up to the Capitol often and walk through its marble halls and
down its long colonnades, and listen to the Senators and Repre-
sentatives; or saunter with glorious old Walt, and talk of the soul and
immortality; but I am not at peace, nor happy. I miss home and
quietness, and a wife's love and influence. . . .

The harrowing time continues. His letters of recommendation are delayed; the money he seeks to borrow is refused;
his Member of Congress is away; the weeks pass, and the new
year dawns, without the hoped-for situation:

Next week, if ever, I expect to be able to present my letters to
headquarters. . . . I think I shall go crazy waiting. You must not be
too sanguine; there are hundreds here figuring for places, backed by
strong influence, so that some of us must fail. If you expected I
would 'be in' by this time, you little know of what you are talking.
. . . I hope you had a happy Christmas and New Year. . . .

On January 8th he writes:

My prospects are beginning to brighten. . . . My M.C. returned
Monday. . . . Tuesday I got two letters of recommendation from
him, one to the Secretary of War, and one to the Comptroller of the
Currency. On Wednesday I went up to the War Department.
After waiting nearly three hours I was unable to get an audience, so

I rushed out desperately, saying I would not crawl on my belly to
them. With hardly any hope I took my other letter into the office
of Hugh McCulloch, Comptroller of the Currency. . . . I saw he was
a very kind-looking man, so felt encouraged at once. He entertained
my proposition favorably, and after considerable conversation told
me to come up next day. . . . Today at 9 I commenced, and worked
till 4, registering letters. Though I have not yet got my papers, the
clerks assure me I need feel no more uneasiness than if I had my
commission in my hand. I hope it is so. I do not expect to be able to
sleep for a week, I am so glad. My salary will be not less than $1200
a year. . . .

There are a number of ladies in our Office and a very beautiful one
sets[1] at my table, so that you may consider me in imminent danger!

The Comptroller has the entire currency of the U.S. under his
control, so that if I stay here, I will get an incite[1] into the entire
Banking System and money system of the Nation.[2] The piles of
'Green Backs' I have seen today would make a miser run mad. . . .

Write me how you are, and what you think of coming to Washington, in case I send for you. I shall be cruel and hard-hearted
enough to exact some promises before you come, and am willing you
should be equally cruel to me. If we cannot hit upon some plan of
agreement for the future, we had better love each other at a distance.
I say this in all kindness and love, seriously believing that our future
happiness requires some new understanding, and some new resolu-
tions. Write me how you feel. . . .

[Jan. 20.]

DEAR URSULA,

I have been expecting every day to hear from you. Why do you
not write and let me know how you are? . . . I am quite sure of the
position. I think I suit. I work hard enough, at any rate. . . .

Allen went North a week ago. I have attended several lectures
lately, among others, I heard John B. Gough. He is by no means a
great orator. I heard Miss Anna Dickinson also; she is not much.
You see I am as hard as ever to please. 'Florence Percy' accompanied me. She is a noble woman, and I prise her society much. A
man who has no female society here, of the right sort, is very apt to
go to the devil pretty fast. . . .

The Circumlocution Office experience being at last at an
end, the disheartened, bitter mood of certain letters yields to

[1] To call attention, in each instance, to carelessness in spelling and other early
errors would prove annoying to the reader who is here reminded that excerpts are
printed as in originals.

[2] It is interesting to remember that a brother of his great grandfather had (1740)
been conspicuously connected with the government's finances, having devised the
system of Federal money adopted under the secretaryship of Alexander Hamilton.
The new banking system, into which Stephen Burroughs's descendant was being
initiated, went into use (1863) under Secretary Chase.

optimism. However, the securing of work was but one of the difficulties disturbing him. A grave crisis existed in matters of far deeper concern. One hears the 'painful dissonances of the Actual.' It were not meet to lift the veil upon this trying period except to obtain a just understanding of developments then and in subsequent years.

In the correspondence is now disclosed the self-knowledge and self-development of John Burroughs at a crucial time in his career. His letters reveal the patience and long-suffering of an ardent, sensitive nature, subjected to discouragingly hampering conditions. They show him endeavoring to see clearly for himself and another, in order to bring about adjustments that will, if possible, secure a tolerant understanding between two persons who, widely opposed as were their points of view, were deeply attached to each other. They show also his struggle for freedom to live his own life.

In this connection, there is much to be said for the other, opposing, point of view — that of a proud, practical, energetic woman, in poor health, humiliated by reverses and the somewhat dependent position in which she found herself; unsustained by the aspirations which spurred on her husband; unsustained also by a belief in his ultimate success; in fact, unable to count as success that towards which he was striving. She had come of a thrifty, prosperous stock, their interests centered on material things. By nature and habit she had scant patience with the opposite qualities, as seen in her husband, and in the impecunious fortunes of his relatives. With an ingrained contempt for any one lacking the self-assertive prosperity of the Norths, she was at no pains to conceal her contempt.[1] Having only material standards, she could only test all efforts, all ambitions, all achievements by such standards. Poor crops, untoward circumstances, ill-luck — failure in any line — were set down to shiftlessness, or unpardonable weakness; while the 'everlasting scribbling' was brushed aside as a kind of self-indulgence — an excuse for shirking real duties.

A letter to his wife in late January, explaining in detail how he spent his time, continues:

[1] A *Mr.* Malaprop of Roxbury thus characterized Mrs. Burroughs: 'I never had much to say to John's wife when she was at Chauncey's — she was so *superlicious.*'

I am sorry that you took my allusions to the gentleman who hails from the Plutonic regions as swearing. . . . I meant really what I said: that men here are very apt to fall into dissolute, wicked ways, which, I believe, according to most christian beliefs, is literally going to the devil. . . . Because I often use words . . . that are commonly used in swearing, you think of necessity I must be swearing, too. It is a grave mistake, and this perpetual misunderstanding of me is the source of much of our trouble. . . .

I see plainly that there is but one way that we can live together again as we ought, and that is this: You must take me and love me and be satisfied with me just as I am, with all my faults and imperfections, or with all my coarseness and wickedness, if you choose to call it such. This is the only possible way under heaven whereby we can live in peace and love. If the good in me does not counterbalance the bad, in your estimation, then of course you cannot love me. I cannot sacrifice myself, or, what is the same, my tastes, my pursuits, my ideas, to anybody. I have much confidence in myself, in my rectitude, in my intellect, in my soundness of heart. . . . I see my way clearly. . . . If you can take me as I am, and, when you can't approve, say nothing, things would go smooth enough. Only let me alone and give me love. I expect to hoe my row alone, to cipher out my own problems. I do not complain. I do not ask help. I want only sympathy, but if you cannot give me that, you can let me alone. . . .

I often ask myself what there is in me that you love. I know there is so much that you do not love; I cannot see what there is left that you do love. Tell me what it is. I see plainly what I do, and what I do not, love in you: I do not love your pride, in the first place, nor your mathematical bump, nor your worldliness, nor your fear of other people's opinions, nor your self-approval, nor your uncharitableness, nor your scolding tendency, nor your disposition to lead and rule your husband. I do not *love*, though I *respect*, your religious belief. On the other hand, there is very much in you that I love: I love your warm, affectionate, confiding, sympathetic heart above all things; your bravery (though you sometimes have too much of it, and show "fight" when you ought not to); your thrift, your industry, your business tact, your domestic disposition, your wifely care and tenderness, your continence, etc.

I grant you the utmost freedom to chose and act for yourself; have and see what friends you please, go and come when you please, read, sleep, work, walk, ride, what and when and where you please. I shall love you the better for being thus free. I only ask the same for myself: To dress as I please, wear my hair and hat as I please, read and study and think and walk and hunt when I please, spend my Sundays as I please, go to church when I please (which you know will not be often), have and see what friends I please, in short, live and die as I please, by the grace of God. In this way we can live in peace and love; take the part of the apple that is good and sound and palatable to each, and say nothing about the other parts? Am I not right?

I am rejoiced that you are better. I know how much you have
suffered, and I know how much you have been tried. It seems very
long since I saw you. I have lived and suffered so much since I came
here that my past life seems removed a long way off.

I should be much happier to have you with me, if you can come in
the right frame of mind, and keep that old promise I heard you make
a long, long time ago, to take me 'for better or for worse.' You
remember also that you promised in the self-same moment to 'love
and obey' me; but I will ask only the former. . . .

The weather is very warm and beautiful here; the air soft and
smoky. . . . Last Sunday I went over to the Smithsonian grounds and
lay half the afternoon on the grass. . . . The nights are divine — too
beautiful to sleep away.

It is near twelve o'clock. . . . Think well of what I have written;
be equally candid with me. . . . I expect to be paid this week, when I
will send your father his money. I have bought no new clothes, but
have had my old ones cleaned. . . .

Write me by return mail and imitate me in length and candor.

This Declaration of Independence shows him already a
disciple of Whitman —

'Rest not till you publish your own personality.'

There had been 'ducking and deprecating long enough'; he
was nearing the point where he was to assume the mastership
of his own fate, the captaincy of his own soul. In a few days he
followed the foregoing letter with another long, friendly one,
inquiring whether his previous letter had seemed cruel or unjust, which he hoped was not the case. Again, on the last day
of January, he wrote:

You need expect no more long letters if you can repay with only a
stingy little sheet, part full. I am sure you have time enough to
write. Amanda wrote a good deal more than you did, and seems to
love me much more, and hers is only a sister's love. . . . If you have
nothing more to say on the subjects I wrote about, no confessions or
promises to make, then of course keep silent. I can alter and change
myself only as you alter and change toward me. I am not to blame
if you are no companion for me; you must *make* yourself such. I
know I am the cause of all the trouble — just as the North was the
cause of this War. If the North had not been the North, had not
loved freedom and been progressive and enterprising, there would
have been no war. But who commenced it, who fired the first shot?
Who bore and forebore, and was of long-suffering and tender patience? only now and then a fiery word or an angry look escaping?

I will not blame or recriminate. I know you have had a hard time
of it with me, and with your sickness and loneliness. I see plainly

what you have suffered, poor child! No friends, no society, no amusement, poor health, and, through so many past years, your sole companion a grum silent husband who talks little, and thinks less how he may seem to, or affect, others.

If you had had the love of Nature and of books that I have, I see you would have been much happier. Take from me my delight in reading and writing, and my love for the earth and the sky, and any part of my health, and I should be the most miserable of mortals. So I see that you have not had more than your share of happiness.

I wonder if you fully, or at all, appreciate my case. I sometimes get to thinking of it, and, in a sentimental mood, pity myself: Almost exiled from home, little love and no sympathy there,[1] and almost forgotten, yet with a deep affection for those left behind, for the old associations, and the old hills where I first saw the light; sent out into the world, friendless and alone, to make my way; a great hope and ambition in me, yet diffident, bashful, sensative, tongue-tied; grave and serious in thought, whatever I may be in word or deed; and always more or less occupied with the great questions of the universe, and with the ways and works of God, as shown in things around me; finding no encouragement or sympathy, and few friends; treated harshly and unjustly by those I love; *dis*couraged instead of *en*couraged; misunderstood and misinterpreted; poor, neglected, and, for ought I know (or care) despised, — all of which, I suppose, sounds very foolish, yet I sometimes pity myself.

And now, with a prospect of more worldly success, I seem poorer than ever. If fortune favors my purse but starves my heart, I have but little to be thankful for.

If you have ever thought of such things, you know there are two kinds of success: one is outward, apparent, worldly, seen and known of men — such as getting a fortune, fame, friends, position, wide and large connections, — the success of a general, statesman, politician. This is the only success the world knows or strives for; and I fear it is the kind of success you think most of, as it is for failing in this that you have blamed me most. And I see plainly it was the only kind of success I thought of, or was ambitious for. But I know I am wiser now. I see clearly that the only kind of success worth having is inward, virtual, unseen; the gaining of wisdom, the understanding of this universe; the seeing beauty and meaning in everything God has made — the success of Socrates who owned nothing; had no business or profession, and was at last poisoned by his countrymen. This is the only success — in one's soul — and not in his purse or title-deeds.

While I have not succeeded as I hoped, yet I have a success of which none but myself and my Creator know, a success of which I never hoped or dreamed, and which I now know is as immortal as myself. I am willing to be called wicked and irreligious; it matters

[1] His family sympathized with the South. 'I was a Union man from the first,' he said, 'but Father was a Copperhead. Hiram was on my side till he was drafted and had to pay bounty. We were all cowards — that's the truth of it.'

not; with the earth and the sky, and the summer of Infinite Peace in my soul, what need I care!

I am vexed that I have written so much, and have a mind to burn it up now. You do not deserve such a long letter.

I see from yours and Amanda's, that you have thought of going to Kingston to board. Well, if you do not want to come here, or think I require too much of you, and cannot come feeling as I want you to, I think you will do well to go to Kingston. Undoubtedly you could enjoy yourself there and live much cheaper than here. I will send you money as fast as I get it. If I stay here, I should expect to go home next summer, and could then stop and see you. Chose for yourself, and may you have health and peace and love, whatever happens to me.

Ever yours

JOHN

It is a relief to turn to the light-hearted, extravagant vein of the next letter, of the third of February, induced by the kind letter he had received from his wife:

MY DEAREST WIFE,

Your letter was awaiting me as I returned from the office. Surely, I said, as I have said of every one lately, this is a good fat one — two sheets at least. But on opening found the cause of its thickness, as usual, to be a foulded envelope. These envelopes have been the source of much speculation to me, and I generally look upon them pretty spitefully, for it seems as if they crowded out part of the letter. I think of taking one of them to a Government detective to see if he detects anything inimical in them. Whether you are laboring under the idea that there is no stationery in Washington; or whether you think envelopes come cheaper in York State; ... or whether you want your letters to come in immaculate white, and think there is nothing immaculate in Washington (which is pretty near the truth), I am at a loss to know. . . . You see those envelopes have wasted a whole side of a sheet. . . .

I expected this letter today as much as if I had seen you mail it. I see your faith was equally certain. I hope it went safe, and did not make you regret having written so kindly and cheerfully. I wonder if they recognized each other as they passed on the way. I reckon one of them must have looked pretty sour — the one Northward bound! Sunday was a gloomy day here — that may account for the tone of the letter. I received one from the Doctor today also. He thinks you have been wrongly treated, and that you can never become a mother, which makes me shudder. . . . If you go to Kingston, do try and take care of yourself, or I'll never forgive you. Your duty is to get well, and to use every possible precaution. . . .

If you fix up too much, I shall be ashamed to meet you. I have only had my Kingston suit cleaned, so that it looks like new; and my ribbed pants dyed. It crocks off on my hands a little. . . . I bought a new pair of boots and some undershirts, socks, etc. Allen presented me with a new hat on New Years. It is black and fine, has a broad brim, and suits me. Every distinguished man in town has since got a broad-brimmed hat, so that I should instantly get a narrow-brimmed one, if I did not know they would all be aping me again. Allen gets about three suits of clothes a week, and a hat and pair of boots a day. Pshaw! what is the use — I dress as well as the Comptroller does, and that is enough.

Taking my noon walk today I passed under the windows of Father Abraham's house, and walked as fast as I could, with head down, so as not to be recognized; but he saw me and came blustering out, bareheaded, got me by the button-hole, and insisted upon it that I should go in and lunch with him; and, do you believe it, I could hardly get away from him; and had to promise I would come next week, before he would let me go. When I walk again, I shall give the White House a wide birth!!!

I hear of a pretty woman here with a good mouth, fine teeth, and a sweet breath, who offers to kiss good-looking fellows for fifty cents, or three kisses for a dollar. I think of patronizing her, if you have no objections. It has been so long since I felt a woman's breath on my cheek, that I think I would give a month's wages for a warm, affectionate kiss. I shook your letter well, and turned the envelope inside out, but found no kisses, so you must have forgotten to enclose any.

When you get well, and I get well established, I will talk about getting you a place to count currency notes. If I get my appointment soon, I may not give my concent to your staying four or five weeks in Kingston. Why, bless you! you can sew here; there is no law against it. If I get time, I will have my photograph taken. . . . Saluting you with an imaginary kiss, I am as ever,

JOHN

[Feb. 18.] . . . I am rejoiced at the prospect of seeing you so soon. I hope your health may keep good, so that we may not be disappointed. . . .

I do not yet know about our boarding-place. I want to stay where I am, if I can get a room, as I am convinced we have the best board in Washington for the price. It is a dingy old house on the Avenue and may not suit you. . . . You must make up your mind that all boarding-houses are dirty. The work is done by darkies, and a slight sweeping is all the house ever gets. The tables are clean, and the victuals excellent, so it is best not to have too sharp eyes and peep around in holes and corners. . . . Have them [books and magazines] boxed and sent by express. Bring your preserves, if possible. Persuade your father to come with you. . . . I will be at the depot when the train comes in.

Spring finds the young couple reunited and boarding in Washington, the dissonances hushed in the harmony of reconciliation.

2. TREASURY CLERK AND SAUNTERER

In the Currency Bureau of the Treasury Department, for the greater part of the next ten years, John Burroughs sat at a high mahogany desk in front of an iron wall, behind which was the vault containing millions of bank-notes, of which he was the guardian. The office was on the second floor of the west side of the building, in what was the northwest corner before the North Wing was added.

('How I reacted against the door of that old safe!' Mr. Burroughs said in the nineteen-hundreds, when showing friends through his old office. 'But the rebound sent me back to the fields and woods of my boyhood.')

No captious quartermaster now objected to his reading or writing in his leisure. Accordingly, in slack times, and in that incongruous place, he wrote his first book on Whitman, and many of the essays which went into his first two nature books.[1]

His ardor in pursuing the birds was no whit less than when he had begun, the previous year. He spent Sundays and half-holidays in the woods. In self-condemnation, he once said, ' I was pursuing the birds in 1864, when our soldiers were dying in the Battle of the Wilderness.' In the same connection he spoke shamefacedly of his failure to attend Lincoln's second inauguration. An early note-book furnishes this:

Today [March 4, 1865], made my first excursion to the woods. Everett and I thought it more desirable to see Spring inaugurated than President Lincoln, significant and gratifying an event as the latter is. The afternoon was deliciously clear and warm — real vernal sunshine, though the wind roared like a lion over the woods.

When chiding himself concerning this defection, he said that about all he could remember of that excursion was finding some wild puppies in a hollow tree; but his note-book records hearing for the first time the soft, sweet note of the Canada sparrow, and finding bluets in bloom. The puppies, however, are what he best remembered. Thoreau was of like mind to Burroughs when he said he would rather see a snake cast its skin than to see a king crowned.

During the summer of 1864 Burroughs had the taste of soldiering for which, off and on, he had long been hankering.[2]

[1] *Wake-Robin* and *Winter Sunshine*.
[2] See 'Working for Uncle Sam' (*John Burroughs, Boy and Man*).

General Early was threatening the Capital. With his army stationed seven miles distant, apprehension grew apace. Burroughs was already a member of the Treasury Guards, and, having donned the blue, was being regularly drilled by Major Emory S. Turner. In a letter to Mrs. Burroughs, then on a visit in Troy, he gives a brief account of his bivouac with Grant's soldiers:

I have had a little taste of War, as I managed Monday and Tuesday nights to elude the pickets and get out to the front at Fort Stevens. I lay most all Tuesday night in the rifle-pits with the veterans of the Fifth Corps. I saw and heard the firing, and in the Hospitals saw all the horrors of War. Many bullets came very close to me.

How the soldiers did laugh to see me dodge! Allen was with me the first night and got enough of it. If the Rebels had not retreated, I should have tried my hand at fighting before this.

One can but smile at the confidence with which he spoke of what he would have done had the raid continued, for he frequently confessed what a sickening feeling he had when, from the rifle-pits, he watched a company of soldiers march toward the firing-line in the darkness. Recalling how appalled he always was by darkness as a child and youth, — the darkness of the door-way to his mother's bedroom, the black hole under the barn where the hobgoblins lurked, the fearsome borders of the woods at nightfall, — darkness always conspiring with his imagination to terrify him, one quite appreciates that, despite his hankering after the excitement of War, that near view, *at night*, filled him with consternation and dread. 'If they had ordered me to go that night,' he confessed, 'I should have collapsed — I couldn't have gone if they were to have shot me for the failure.' Yet by day he could laugh at his fears, even telling what he would have done had the need not passed.

It reminds one of his dog Lark, who, so long as he sat by his master in the buggy, would unburden his mind threateningly to every dog they met, but, if put upon the ground, would shrink back as if to say, 'Oh, I don't want to fight — I don't want to fight *at all!*' 'Lark had no more fight in him than I have,' he used to say; 'he was a pacifist through and through.'

In the sense of one who hates war, John Burroughs was a

pacifist. With his constitutional shrinking from all kinds of strife, he preferred the 'singing of birds to the singing of bullets'; and, admitting this, he courageously admitted, 'I fear at times I may have been a shirker,' though adding that he had shirked one duty that he might the more heartily give himself to another. His courage was of the kind that Lincoln showed when, in urging leniency toward a youth who had deserted, he confessed, 'I never felt sure but _I_ might drop my gun and run away, if I found myself in the line of battle.'

That Burroughs followed the Civil War with lively interest is seen in letters written and received by him during those years.[1] One which he wrote in the spring of 1864, to Dr. A. C. Hull, of Olive, New York, indicates his approval of the tactics then coming into play:[2]

FRIEND DOCTOR,

I have an item of news that will perhaps interest you: Burnside's army yesterday passed through Washington on its way to the front. It was over 40,000 strong, and was the grandest spectacle I ever witnessed. They occupied over three hours in passing. There were about 10,000 colored troops, which presented a very soldierly appearance.

It is difficult to conjecture what Grant's plans may be, but it is plain he means fight on the most gigantic scale. Burnside will probably go to Fredericksburg and move on Lee's flank, while 40 or 50 thousand move down the Shenandoah Valley and turn his left flank; Meade with 100,000 will press his immediate front.

I am very sanguine of Grant's success. I think this 'On to Richmond!' will not be checked.

I think there is no doubt but a large force is concentrated at Harpers Ferry to check Lee, should he attempt his old game of turning our flank. Thus, you see, Grant is keeping his whole army in supporting distance, and Lee cannot attack first one then the other, as he did McClellan, and Pope, and Fremont.

The comradeship between Whitman and Burroughs, which began shortly after the latter's arrival in Washington, is seen by the accompanying letter[3] to have been well advanced by the summer of 1864. This is probably the first letter written by Burroughs to Whitman. It is written from the Treasury Department, in early August:

[1] See _John Burroughs, Boy and Man._
[2] Lent by Mrs. M. E. Smith, daughter of Dr. Hull.
[3] This and other letters of J. B. to W. W. are reprinted from Traubel's _With Walt Whitman in Camden_, through the courtesy of Mrs. Traubel, and Messrs. Small, Maynard & Co.

DEAR WALT,

I am disconsolate at your long stay. What has become of you? On returning, the 7th of July, I found you had gone home sick. You have no business to be sick, so I expect you are well. I was so unlucky as to be sick all the time I was home — and most of the time since I came back. I am quite well now, however. . . . Benton and I looked for you at Leedsville, as I wrote you to come. If you have leisure now, you would enjoy hugely a visit up there.

I hope you are printing 'Drum Taps,' and that this universal drought does not reach your 'Grass.' But make haste and come back. The heat is delicious. I have a constant bath in my own perspiration.

I was out at the front during the siege of Washington and lay in the rifle-pits with the soldiers. I got quite a taste of war, and learned the song of those modern minstrels — the minnie [sic] bullets — by heart. A line from you would be prized.

A bereavement, the first he ever knew, came to Burroughs that summer, in the death of his brother Wilson. To his wife, visiting in the North, he wrote sadly:

I am constantly thinking of home and of him that is gone. His looks and ways are forever in my mind. I know where he is laid, and on the moonlight nights think of the shadows that fall across his last resting-place. It is appalling to think that I can never see him again, nor even look upon his grave till another summer has made it green.

In the spring of 1865, Mr. and Mrs. Burroughs began house-keeping in a quaint brick house on Capitol Hill, near where the Senate Offices now stand. Their frugal ways, and especially the wife's industry and thrift, enabled them each month to save fifty dollars of his earnings. They were soon out of debt and contemplating building.

In an April letter to Myron Benton, one gets a peep behind the high board fence into that city garden of which Burroughs writes so delightfully in his essay on the Rural Divinity — the garden so near the Capitol that he could look up from his weeding and cast a potato almost in the midst of the marble steps; the garden where he forgot the paved and blistered streets, and his high desk in the Treasury, and found an anti-dote for the blue devils and distempers fostered by life indoors.

Since April First [he writes Benton] I have been full of gardening, have taken a furnished house almost under the shadow of the Dome of the Capitol, and have been so absorbed with my acre that I get barely leisure to eat and sleep. I have not even time to read the Atlantic. The garden is a great help to me as an offset to the routine of office duties. I have nearly an acre of ground, and expect to raise lots of vegetables and fruit. I hope you will come down and take some hints in horticulture. . . .

Spring is earlier than last season by two weeks. I found Hepatica on the 12th of March. The woods are nearly full-fledged. I read nothing to speak of. . . . I share your surprise and delight at the amount of unpublished matter Thoreau left behind. I am vexed with Emerson that he did not publish his [Emerson's?] later poems. They are far the best, I think. One third of the old volume, I think, does not amount to much.

With all their simplicity of living, in that little house on Capitol Hill, life for the young author was rich in things of the spirit. Lincoln and Whitman were great stars in the firmament, the one remote though so near (until its light went out that fateful morning of the fifteenth of April); the other shining with a clear, steady light, and discerned by Burroughs, even then, as a star of the first magnitude. Emerson and Tyndall, and other great lights, shone there occasionally; and there were the treasures in the Library of Congress, and congenial and cultured friends. Perhaps, best of all, there was the intercourse with Nature, gained in frequent trips to the woods which, together with brief summer sojourns in the Catskills, were in time woven into the essays that went into his books.

Of Lincoln he saw but little, except often to see him from the window of the Treasury, stepping over huge piles of lumber, 'with his long, lank legs,' taking a short-cut to avoid the crowd, on his way to Seward. Once only he spoke with him — at a reception at the White House, in line with hundreds of others.

'When my turn came, I lingered a little,' he said; 'I can feel yet the pull of his great hand as he drew me along past him to make room for others.'

His deep appreciation of Lincoln showed itself in two diverse, but equally characteristic, ways. In the fall of 1864, when suffering from so-called malaria, he went home to recuperate, and to vote. He could hardly drag himself to the railway station, but as soon as he came in sight of his native hills he felt their strength pass into him, and, leaving the stageline, he struck off toward Roxbury, growing stronger at every step. He was overtaken by a farmer, who gave him a lift, and as they jogged along they discussed the War; but the farmer's disparaging comments about Lincoln so enraged his passenger that the latter jumped from the wagon and, shaking his fist at the astonished man, declared he would be d——d if he would ride further with such a d——d Copperhead. The 'd——d Copperhead' tried to coax him back into the wagon, but he, scorning to reply, trudged angrily on. The other instance was his tribute to Lincoln's Gettysburg speech, in the essay, 'Before Genius,' first printed in the 'Galaxy,' later incorporated in 'Birds and Poets.'[1] Many years later, reverting to that sublime utterance of Lincoln, he said:

When a thing has that inevitableness — that's the sign [of genius] — a studied thing — how different! Lincoln had been to school to the everlasting verities and was prepared. You knew when you looked at him — a man who didn't think of himself — that he was thinking of others, of the great duties thrust upon him. His terrible responsibilities brought out his heroism. He had not sought the Presidency — when some one had suggested the possibility of it, before his nomination, he had thrown up his hands and laughed, — 'A pretty President I'd make!' He came out of the dark days of Kentucky. His ancestral soil had been turned over deeply, — the pioneers before him — all had contributed to him. [Following this, when some one recalled Grierson's remark that Lincoln was the greatest human force since Robert Burns, Mr. Burroughs said, '*He* had penetration.']

John Burroughs always felt grateful that he had, in a small way, contributed something to the poem 'When Lilacs last in the Door-yard Bloomed' — that immortal threnody in which Whitman commemorated Lincoln and chanted a nation's sorrow; a poem characterized by Edward Dowden as 'one of the loftiest and most poignant dirges in all literature.' When, in outlining to Burroughs what he aimed to do in the poem, Whitman had asked for a bird to answer his purpose, Burroughs described to him the hermit thrush of boyhood memories — the bird whose song seemed to voice the deep, solemn joy that only the finest souls may know. At his description, Whitman exclaimed, 'That's my bird!' Thus it came about that the poet wove into the wreath for Lincoln's tomb those 'three beautiful facts of nature,' 'the early-blooming lilacs, which the poet may have plucked the day the dark shadow came; next the song of the hermit thrush, the most sweet and solemn of all our songsters, heard at twilight in the

---

[1] In commenting on this passage in 1917, he said: 'That isn't so well said as it might be — it is only partly said; but I think it was one of the earliest appreciations of the speech that got into print.'

dusky cedars; and, with these, the evening star, which, as many may remember, night after night, in the early part of that eventful spring, hung low in the west with unusual and tender brightness.' [1]

When arriving in Washington, in the fall of 1863, Burroughs wrote fitfully on the bird essay begun at Buttermilk Falls. He worked on it in the back part of Allen's store, while waiting for employment; but, when finding it too noisy there, sought quieter places to be had without price. He wrote a part of it on a little stand in the reception room of Willard's Hotel. The essay dragged during that discouraging period; but the following spring, on meeting the returning birds amid the new scenes; on hearing the mellow flute of the veery near the White House, as wild and sweet as in the Deacon woods at home; and on hearing the rich whistle of the fox sparrow on the Smithsonian grounds, the slow-growing essay received a new impetus. A letter which he wrote Benton in mid-March (1864), shows something of what went into the making of that first essay about the birds:

In these April days I am thinking of you — April days, as they seem to me, used to the Northern climate. Those silver poplars which you noticed as lining our streets are loaded with long drooping tresses, like those of the alder, only larger and softer. I enclose one. The effect is very beautiful. There is no more frost, and a thunder-shower the other evening seems to have inaugurated Spring thoroughly.

Many of my favorites, the fly-catchers, are here. Last Sunday, raw and cold as it was, I met the old acquaintances, and today quite a number more. Today has been singularly warm and beautiful. Allen and I made a dash off into the woods three or four miles distant, and among other rich spoils brought home our first Hepatica — two species, blue and white. I wished for you much. It has been a day of 'dear delights.' The fresh woodsy smell, the expectant air of things, the thousand nameless prophetic signs, the warm sun, the soft hazy atmosphere, the voices of birds, the flock of quail, and our thankful souls, made the Sunday worth having. For the first time in my life I saw and heard the fox sparrow sing — a round, firm note, reminding one of the oriole — and the gray Titmouse whistle. The purple finch sang also, the robin piped, the bluebird carolled, the snow-bird lisped, the great wren warbled, and the song sparrow sang. You see I am quite mad, and still on the subject of birds. If I could only infect you also! We saw butterflies, the phœbe bird, and the alder with its tassels also.

[1] From *Notes on Walt Whitman as Poet and Person;* also in *Whitman, a Study.*

What are you doing? What birds have come? (Robin told me he should start for your country next week.) Write instantly.

Walt is as glorious as ever, and, as usual, looks like a god. He expects to bring out his 'Drum Taps' soon. He discoursed with me an hour the other day on his plans and purposes. He anticipates a pecuniary success with the book. By and by he expects to make himself felt by lecturing. He is quite ambitious. Allen calls him an Old Goat! I tell him I wish I was an Old Goat.

I wish I could send you a Contraband, but I see none to send. I have a mind to come myself. I think we could get a variety of crops where most people reap nothing.

We have changed our quarters to Grant Place, near the Patent Office. . . . Mrs. Akers comes often to see us. On such occasions Allen is quite apt to drop in.[1] . . .

That first essay about the birds received a still greater impetus when its author went back to his native hills in the summer. The following autumn, with many misgivings, he sent it to the Atlantic, naming it, 'With the Birds.' It was printed as the leading paper in the spring of 1865.[2]

Unlike 'Expression,' this article had no Emersonian flavor (although F. B. Sanborn told Benton that Emerson was greatly interested in it). It could only have been written by John Burroughs. 'Genius,' says Mr. T. T. Munger, 'has no clear sign; nothing heralds it, and it has no true authentication until it does some work that stamps it as its own.'

Benton wrote Burroughs enthusiastically of the essay, which he thought in his best vein, and urged him to follow that vein whether he settled the abstruse questions of the soul or not. He wrote of having taken Sanborn to task for a 'mean cut' about it in the 'Commonwealth,' adding: 'You see where the shoe pinches — a Concord sage has been modestly called in question. . . . I think Sanborn an honest critic . . . but his appreciation has some harsh limits.' That the young essayist valued honest criticism, is seen in his reply:

I like Sanborn's criticism very much — I see that the great fault of the piece is what he calls affectation, or want of simplicity — that is, I see that an older and wiser head would not have been so ambitious, and would have written better. Mr. Sanborn will learn, how-

[1] E. M. Allen and Elizabeth Akers were married from the Burroughs house in October, 1865, soon moving to Richmond, after which time, with engrossing interests on both sides, the friends drifted apart: although letters exchanged during the last weeks of the life of Mr. Allen showed how abiding was the tie that bound them.

[2] Renamed 'The Return of the Birds,' and much altered and improved it formed the initial chapter in Wake-Robin (1871).

ever, that I do not hold Thoreau as infallible. . . . I have got two
eyes also, and shall see for myself. The piece has made a little stir
here and there. I have had letters of criticism, inquiry, congratula-
tion. A man from Canaan, Connecticut, is very enthusiastic, and is
studying the birds with great zeal. He writes well, and, I suspect, is
a dominie. . . . From Philadelphia a man writes and criticizes, and
convinces me that he knows nothing about the birds — more than
their Latin names.

Have you known the cuckoo to lay in another bird's nest? I
should like to know.

I make weekly and bi-weekly trips to the woods and contemplate
writing much more about the birds. . . . Allen and I and some others
talk of making a trip down the Potomac in a sail-boat, and making
raids upon Maryland from the river as a base. Come and go with us.

Poet Piatt calls on me occasionally. He is a clerk here like myself.
We walked in the woods the other Sunday. I like him very well,
though he is not quite up to my standard. Knowing you has made
me hard to please. He is very unpretending and modest. . . . There
is something in him; though his soul is not robust enough. His wife
[Sarah M. B.] writes also. . . . He has not much zeal for our own
favorites, and seems to be no hero-worshipper, which is not good in
a young man. I have met other literary people, but none that I
care for. . . .

I am reading Cape Cod betimes. Some chapters seem rather dull
to me, but some parts please me hugely. How so much juice can be
extracted from sand, is a mystery.

My chief work in these days is my garden. People stare at it over
the fence and wonder at my industry and skill. I think I have the
same interest in it a poet has in his poems, or an artist in his canvas.
It is a perpetual joy to me, notwithstanding the bugs and worms.
Ask Charley about my cherries. . . .

The correspondent from Connecticut to whom he refers,
and whom he thought a dominie, was the first woman reader
to write him about his essays. Of what a host was she the
forerunner![1] She asked why there should not be some attention given to the study of birds in our schools; why children
should not be taught to lift their eyes and open their ears
when rambling through the woods; she deplored the crass
ignorance concerning the birds — comments which, in these
days of nature-study, strike one as amusing; for, as some one
said at the time of Dickens's death, "He made charity fashionable," so may one say that John Burroughs made nature-
study fashionable. The author's reply to his unknown cor-

[1] To Mrs. S. W. Lyles, a niece of the correspondent, I am indebted for the loan of
the Burroughs letters.

respondent, and his subsequent letters, besides furnishing much first-hand ornithology, show what pains he took to aid the embryo bird-student — books on the subject and mounted specimens then being so scarce. He addressed his letter to S. W. Adams, Esq., Canaan, Connecticut, and so continued to do until she casually mentioned having no claim to the affix of 'Esq.' to her name and signed herself 'Sarah' W. Adams, — a revelation which did not tend to lessen the author's interest in the correspondence.

Letters passed back and forth painstakingly investigating whether it was the hermit or the wood thrush which she heard in her vicinity. He sent her quills from the tail and the wing of the hermit, told her (though then supposing he was writing to a dominie) that a gun was indispensable to the student of ornithology unless he spend years in the study. He gave careful differentiating descriptions of the three prevailing thrushes, saying the books were all muddled on the subject, and instanced errors of Wilson, Audubon, Thoreau, and Wilson Flagg in regard to these songsters. The greatest interest in the correspondence, however, is in two letters in which are found the germ of that matchless description of the song of the hermit with which Burroughs's reader is familiar.[1] Writing from his home in the Catskills in June, he says:

. . . I go to the woods daily to hear the hermit, and am more and more impressed with the beauty of his song. I often hear him over a quarter of a mile away. I imagine him saying, *O, holy, holy! O, purity, purity! O, clear away, clear away! O, clear up, clear up! silvery, silvery, so fine, so fine!* — sometimes in a high, sometimes in a low key.

And subsequently, on return to Washington:

In this dust and heat I sigh for the balm and coolness of the old Hemlocks. O, so fresh, so solemn, and so sweet! A few nights before I left home I went up to the top of a high mountain to see the moon come up and the night come down. As I neared the summit. . . the hermit thrush burst out in song close by me. What a new charm was imparted to the mountain at once, and a new significance to my walk! His song does not seem to me to express sorrow, or a memory strung by regrets, but perfect composure and serenity. It is the most spiritual sound I am acquainted with in nature, and has that sweet plaintiveness which is characteristic of the finest music.

One can imagine Miss Adams's surprised delight when she

[1] 'In the Hemlocks' (*Wake-Robin*).

came upon the more finished description later in the 'Atlantic,' and realized that its origin dated back to these letters to her. After learning that his correspondent is a young woman he tells her that of course she will not shoot the birds, but that much may be done by patience and a quick, sharp eyesight. To study the warblers, he says:

The best way is to sit down in the dense woods and watch the trees overhead. Attract their notice by some strange noise, or by hanging your handkerchief on a twig, and they will come within a few yards, as curious to make you out as you are them.

Referring to the difficulties that beset the student of ornithology, he wrote:

I felt quite helpless and discouraged at first. . . . You must forget that and master the first bird you meet. Get clearly in your mind the families and their characteristic traits. Get a sparrow and study it, and when you are master of the subject you know all the finches. So with the warblers, the flycatchers, the thrushes. The whole is known when you know half. One fact obtained, the rest comes easy. . . . I wish you had my gun-cane, or one like it. You would not hesitate to shoot it, and then it is so handy and portable. . . .

When Miss Adams inquires more about the gun-cane, he replies:

Its external appearance is precisely that of a cane. It is quite effectual at short range. . . . As to shooting the birds, I think a real lover of nature will indulge in no sentimentalism on the subject. Shoot them, of course, and no toying about it. . . .

I see no reason why you should not undertake taxidermy. . . . It requires, first, indomitable patience; second, delicate, skillful hands; third, love, imagination, and great familiarity with nature. . . . I have just set up a case of about fifty birds for my wife. It is the admired of all admirers. . . . It has little of the stiff artificial look of the work of a professional. . . . You see I think it good myself, and I am a severe judge of my own work. . . . A year ago I made a small case for my mother which soon became the wonder of the neighborhood.[1]

Although he had at first said so positively that one could make no real progress in knowing the birds unless with the bird in hand, he had confessed in a note-book of that period that he truly enjoyed the woods only when he did not outrage

[1] This case of birds, owned by a grandniece near Roxbury, is still in good preservation.

them by hunting down a bird. Still, in the beginning, the scientist in him could not be content without accurate knowledge. In truth, always he wanted the fact unadorned, after which he sought for the meaning in the fact, not that he might moralize about it, but that he might interpret it. It was not the 'sermons in stones' that interested him so much as the life under the stones. He grazed in all fields of science; selected what tasted good — the vital, nourishing truths — but had no appetite for the thistles of technical knowledge.

When 'In the Hemlocks' came out in the 'Atlantic,' Miss Adams's allegiance to 'With the Birds' (the first article of his which had so interested her) caused her still to write of that as the finer article. Dissenting from this opinion, its author wrote:

It ['In the Hemlocks'] has more directness and simplicity and is quite free from the affectation with which the other is almost fatally marred.[1] It shows much more maturity, and much closer observation, and contains one fact, at least, not hitherto known. I mean the air-song of the golden-crowned thrush, or wood wag-tail. . . .

I did not mean to say that a lady could not have a deep and permanent love of nature; I only meant to say that I had never known any such. Every lady professes the greatest love of Nature, but I find it does not go very deep. Do they go to the woods at all seasons and *alone?* — that is my test. Of course the same may be said of gentlemen. I think my friend Benton is the truest lover of Nature I have ever known.

To the same correspondent, many months later:

I hasten to answer and warn you against an act so rash as the procuring and attempting to read 'Leaves of Grass.' You do not know what is before you, or what an *awful* book it is — the very antithesis of the sweet and charming productions of the current poets. Read a literal description of Michael Angelo's 'Last Judgment,' and you will get a hint of the principle involved in the construction of 'Leaves of Grass.' Read 'Drum Taps,' but do not attempt the 'Leaves' yet awhile. Yet perhaps I am wrong in this, for, by some marvellous insight or higher spirituality, women often see clearly and instantly where men falter and stumble; and I have known those who made no pretension to literary ability or critical acumen — mothers of families, and, in one case, a lady who had long been an invalid — who yet saw at a glance, in reference to this book,

[1] It is interesting to see how he profited by criticism. He carefully revised 'With the Birds' before including it in *Wake-Robin* as 'The Return of the Birds.'

what it has taken me years to figure out. [Here follow comments on his own little book on Whitman, then about to be published, which he hoped would help prepare her for the 'Leaves' itself.]

3. WHITMAN, POET AND COMRADE

Walt Whitman and John Burroughs first met in Washington in the autumn of 1863, in the army supply store of Allen, Clapp & Co., introduced by E. M. Allen, Whitman being forty-four years of age, Burroughs twenty-six.

A brief account of the meeting occurs in an early note-book of Burroughs, dated December 14, 1865, accompanied by comments as to his first impression of 'Leaves of Grass,' which he had come upon two years before going to Washington:[1]

His [Whitman's] book, read with modern eyes, would seem to justify Emerson's characterization of him as 'half song thrush and half alligator;' and, by some means or other, I had got an impression that he was at least half rowdy. Imagine my surprise, therefore, when I beheld a well-dressed, large, benevolent-looking man, cleanly and neat, with a grizzly, shaggy appearance about the face and open throat.

Without rising he reached out to me a large, warm, soft hand, and regarded me with a look of infinite good nature and contentment. I was struck with the strange new beauty of him as he sat there in the gas light — the brightness of his eyes, the glow of his countenance, and the curious blending of youth and age in his expression. He was in that felicitous mood almost habitual to him, I have since found, during which his flesh and skin become, as it were, transparent, and allow his great summery, motherly soul to shine through. I was struck likewise with his rich, mellow voice — a voice that was at once an index to the man, implying not only deep human sympathies and affinities, but the finest blood and breeding, a gentle, strong, cultivated soul.

My interest was instant and profound. I said: Here is a new type of man, a new type of gentleman, a new type of philosopher — a veritable new ethics and gospel. I will observe his habits and movements, his manners and conversation, his life and doings, and see if expectation is justified. For two years, therefore, I have been studying this wonderful man, and have come, not only to love him as a friend, but to look to him as the greatest, sweetest soul I have yet met in this world.

Following this are copious impressions and comments on

---

[1] He had read some of Whitman's poems in the *Saturday Press*, perhaps as early as 1859.

Whitman's personality and writings, some of which went into Burroughs's first book, 'Notes on Walt Whitman as Poet and Person' (1867). The note-book gives this incident:

Sauntering with him one day by the Capitol, we met a soldier — dirty, travel-stained, and ragged, with a friendless, care-worn expression, whom Walt kindly accosted. I shall never forget how the soldier alter[ed] the tone in which he was about answering him, as he looked Walt in the face. . . . The sympathy and deep, yearning love that spoke in this man's voice and beamed in his face completely disarmed him; and in a blushing, bashful way he answered Walt's questions.

I stood a little apart and thought I had never seen anything so human and good. The soldier looked down at his boots, and began to be ashamed of his appearance, since here was some one who took an interest in him. He was a Western boy, and there was some curious history connected with his story and appearance. Walt, in his tender, curious way, asked him if he should not help him a little; not enough to hurt him, but enough to get him a bit of food, for he looked hungry. The soldier did not know how to meet this charge, and came near breaking down outright; and as Walt placed some small notes in his hand and turned away, he found his tongue to say, in that awkward, constrained way, that he hoped he would have good health and keep well. And I saw how deeply he responded to this act of kindness, and how poorly his words expressed what he felt.

That youth will not forget as long as he lives, the great kind man who accosted him under the walls of the Capitol, and spoke the first words of human sympathy and tenderness, perhaps, he had heard since his mother bid him farewell.

Walt said he had probably been guilty of some misdemeanor, perhaps was a deserter, or a returning rebel; but I saw this incident would do more to strengthen and encourage him, and help restore him to his lost manhood, if so it was, than all the sermons and homilies and tracts that have ever been preached or printed.

Very welcome is this fragment of description from the same note-book:

Notwithstanding the beauty and expressiveness of his [Whitman's] eyes, I occasionally see something in them as he bends them upon me, that almost makes me draw back. I cannot explain it — whether it is more, or less, than human. It is as if the earth looked at me — dumb, yearning, relentless, immodest, inhuman [unhuman?]. If the impersonal elements and forces were concentrated in an eye, that would be it. It is not piercing, but absorbing and devouring — the pupil expanded, the lid slightly drooping, and the eye set and fixed.

This information at first hand is so interesting one wonders

why he did not use it in his first book, or even in his later,
riper one,[1] instead of quoting descriptions by John James Piatt
and others. It may be that Whitman, who criticized and
pruned his earlier book, objected to being pictured so gentle
while declaring himself to be 'one of the roughs,' who cocked
his hat as he pleased, indoors and out. Burroughs does, however, give a brief but telling description of the poet on pages
85–86 in his 'Notes.'

Even more valuable, perhaps, than the foregoing account of
his first meeting with Whitman (written two years and more
after the meeting), are his brief, spontaneous impressions sent
to Myron Benton. On December 19, 1863, he wrote:

I have been much with Walt. Have even slept with him. I love
him very much. The more I see and talk with him, the greater he
becomes to me. He is as vast as the earth, and as loving and noble.
He is much handsomer than his picture represents him, goes well-
dressed, and there is nothing *outish* in his appearance, except, it
may be, his open throat. He walks very leisurely, rather saunters,
and looks straight forward, not down at his feet. He does not
talk readily, but his conversation is very rich and suggestive. He
regards Emerson as one of the great, eternal men, and thinks there
is not another living, nor has lived for the last two or three centuries.

I am convinced that Walt is as great as Emerson, though after a
different type. Walt has all types of men in him, there is not one
left out. I must write you all about him, but cannot now. If I get
settled here I want to give an account of him in the Commonwealth.
If you can get a New York Times of date October 4, 1863, you will
find a letter of his which is one of the finest pieces of writing I have
ever seen. It is just like Walt.[2]

Again, January 9, 1864, Burroughs writes Benton:

When I called on Walt[3] this morning I found him *en dishabille*,
reading 'Walden.' 'My impression of the book last night,' he said,
'was rather poor; I thought it puerile. But this morning after I
had sipped my coffee, I found it more satisfying. I opened near

[1] *Whitman, a Study*, 1896.
[2] 'I think it was his piece about the unfinished Capitol' (J. B.). This article,
and two others, of February 26 and August 16, 1863, contain graphic pictures of
Washington, and heart-rending scenes among the soldiers.
[3] J. B. said in later years: 'Walt lived on 4½ St., in a room with a bed and a table
and a broken down chair. He lived very frugally, mostly on bread and tea, ex-
pending everything he could get for the soldiers. Emerson and other Boston
friends sometimes sent him money for this purpose. He would stuff his pockets
with things and go and distribute them to the sick soldiers.' J. B. said that Walt
would sometimes come into Allen's store (1863) while writing *Drum Taps*, and jot
down things he had just seen — the tears still in his eyes.

the end and found it so good that I turned back and commenced again.'

He thinks his translations from Anacreon in the 'Week' far the best he ever saw; so good that he tore the leaves out that contained them, and put them among his choice tid-bits. He thinks Thoreau a very sweet, pure soul, but by no means a number-one man, as Emerson is. He was too timid, and too afraid of the world; did men and things injustice; was too exclusive; and not enough of a cosmopolitan.

The more I see of Walt, the more I like him. . . . He is far the wisest man I have ever met. There is nothing more to be said after he gives his views; it is as if Nature herself had spoken. And so kind, sympathetic, charitable, humane, tolerant a man I did not suppose was possible. He loves everything and everybody. I saw a soldier the other day stop on the street and kiss him. He kisses me as if I were a girl. He appreciates everybody, and no soul will get fuller justice in the next world than it gets at his hands here.

I related to him our Adirondack trip, the deer-shooting, etc., which so pleased him that he said seriously he should make a 'leaf of grass' about it. I related to him other country experiences which he relished hugely. In the spring he wants to go out to my home with me to make sugar and get a taste of that kind of life. If I can get off, I shall surely go. He also wants to go up to the Adirondacks and spend a season at the Upper Iron Works. He says a trip to Europe would be nothing compared to it.

He bathed today while I was there — such a handsome body, and such delicate, rosy flesh I never saw before. I told him he looked good enough to eat, which, he said, he should consider a poor recommendation if he were among the cannibals.

I have often told him of you, but without exciting any remark from him till the other day, without any provocation, he commenced to ask me about you: wanted to hear all about you, how you lived, and if you were 'a good fellow' (the highest praise he ever bestows upon a man). I told him what you had written. He said he did not want to hear about your poetry, but about you, what your type and temper and hair were, etc. So I fell to portraying you — a pleasant task — and Walt was much interested, and for all I know may immortalize you in a 'leaf of grass.' . . .

In an April letter 'Jack' wrote 'Myron':

Walt and I meet two or three times a week over a mug of ale, or a peck of oysters. Often his talk is so rich and suggestive that he sets every feeling and faculty in me on the alert. . . .

His note-book, on August 26, 1865, has this significant entry:

What a wonderful man is Walt! what a great, yearning love he has! what a hospitable soul, what soft, gentle ways! what a deep, sym-

pathetic voice![1] How he listens! The most cosmic and synthetical
mind I ever knew, he yet has a wonderful power of analysis — keen,
searching, discriminating, and subtle.

So commanding is one vital truth, he says, — so much else becomes knowable when one thing is thoroughly known — that he can
see how the theology of the day would fall before the standard of
him who has got even the insects. 'If these things are true, if these
facts are so, then these other things are not so.' I was trying to
express to him how, by some wonderful indirection, I was helped by
my knowledge of the birds, the animals, the cows, and common
objects. He could see, he said. The ancients had an axiom that he
who knew one truth, knew all truths. There are so many ways by
which Nature may be come at, so many sides to her, whether by
bird, or insect, or flower, or hunting, or science — when one thing is
really known, you can no longer be deceived. You possess a key, a
standard. You effect an entrance, and every thing else links on and
follows.

The comradeship with Whitman, and perhaps the very
conversation here hinted at, which made clear to Burroughs
the truth that 'a vast similitude interlocks all,' seems to mark
a significant epoch in the life of the young writer when, by a
concurrence more or less gradual, he arrived at the point of
becoming the writer we know; when his farm-boy experiences,
the rich sentient life he had enjoyed (and was always to enjoy),
his eager pursuit of knowledge in nature and books, his struggles as a teacher, his gropings, strivings, and yearnings — all
that had gone to make up his obscure existence were henceforth blended and linked with what was yet to be. *He had
found the key.*

Yet a little more of the same entry is apropos:

He [Whitman] thinks natural history, to be true to life, must be
inspired, as well as poetry. There ought to be intuitive perception of
truth, important conclusions ought to be jumped to — laws, facts,
results arrived at by a kind of insight or inspirational foreknowledge
that never could be obtained by mere observation or actual verification. In science — in astronomy — some of the most important dis-
coveries seem inspirations, or a kind of wingèd, ecstatic reasoning,
quite above and beyond the real facts.

It was always so with the great poet, with Shakespeare. He knew
all things without collecting the facts. Why not something like this
in natural history? So far as he had observed, he said, the au-

---

[1] A recent writer has spoken of Whitman's thin, high-pitched voice, but John
Burroughs always spoke of his deep, rich voice, sometimes characterizing it as a
tender baritone.

thorities on these subjects had been mere explorers, and had gone no farther than they could see; had caught no hint or clues by which large and important inferences could be drawn — and much more grand, glorious talk, entirely beyond my power to hint.

If the things Whitman talked of were beyond the power of the younger man to hint, one is at least not too bold in inferring that such talks had a broadening and deepening effect upon his attitude toward Nature; that to such intercourse no small part is due in having developed in Burroughs that happy combination of both the scientific and the poetic points of view.

That the poet and the scientist are not so far apart as they might at first seem, Burroughs himself points out in an unreclaimed essay written in the early eighteen-eighties. Does any one doubt that he had Whitman and himself in mind in this passage?

The true poet and the true scientist are close akin. They go forth into nature like friends. Behold them strolling through the summer fields and woods! The younger is much the more active and inquiring. He is ever and anon stepping aside to examine some object more minutely, plucking a flower, treasuring a shell, pursuing a bird, watching a butterfly; now he turns over a stone, peers into the marshes, chips off a fragment of rock, and everywhere seems intent on some special and particular knowledge of things about him. The elder man has more an air of leisurely contemplation and enjoyment — is less curious about special objects and features, and more desirous of putting himself *en rapport* with the spirit of the whole. But when his younger companion has any fresh and characteristic bit of information to impart to him, how attentively he listens, how sure and discriminating is his appreciation! The interests of the two in the universe are widely different, yet in no true sense are they hostile.

Whatever part Whitman played in influencing John Burroughs, certain it is that the latter's attitude came gradually to combine the scientist's, the poet's, and the philosopher's points of view; the poet in him lending wings to the scientist, and the scientist in him holding the poet in check, while the trail of the philosopher is over all. Vivid and poetic as was his apprehension of mere facts, his aim was to invest the facts of nature with living interest, without in the least lessening their value as facts. With Whitman he could say to the strict scientists:

'Gentlemen, to you the first honors always!
Your facts are useful, and yet they are not my dwelling,
I but enter by them to an area of my dwelling.'

In reverence for exact demonstration, blended with ability
to discern the spiritual meaning of things, Whitman and
Burroughs, so diverse in many ways, were one. This it was
that cemented their friendship. Together they could listen
while the learned astronomer lectured; could glean much from
his charts and figures; and, when wearied with it all, would together glide out into 'the mystical moist night air,' and gaze
'in perfect silence at the stars.'

Had Burroughs, gifted with the same powers of observation, lacked the poetic trend, he would probably have become
a famous naturalist; but the fortuitous combination made of
him the interpreter of nature instead. In Ruskin's statement
that the biggest thing in the world is to see something and
then tell it, is, in a nutshell, the secret of the unique excellence of Burroughs's work; especially since to his seeing
eye was added a precious thing, — 'the vision and faculty
divine.'

It seems impossible to exaggerate Whitman's influence
upon John Burroughs during that formative period between
his twenty-sixth and thirty-sixth years. What Coleridge's
friendship was to Wordsworth, what Carlyle's was to Emerson, and Emerson's to Thoreau, was Whitman's to Burroughs
— and more; for never a shadow of misunderstanding or
estrangement rested upon their comradeship, which lasted
from the autumn of 1863 till the death of Whitman in 1892.

Once, when commenting upon this period, Mr. Burroughs
said:

I loved him as I never loved any man. We were companionable
without talking. I owe more to him than to any other man in the
world. He brooded me; he gave me things to think of; he taught me
generosity, breadth, and an all-embracing charity. He was a tremendous force in my life. It was really Walt that drew me to
Washington — through Allen's letters.

He was the incarnation of Democracy, of the common, yet of the
uncommon. The indirect, orbicular style of the Leaves — he talked
in the same way — his talk always suggestive — 'Not to finish
specimens, but to shower them, as Nature does.'

Walt was very painstaking in his writing. He studied his lines;
would work long over one if it did not suit him — did not have the
right rhythm.

Early in 1866 William D. O'Connor wrote Burroughs, expressing gratitude for the latter's appreciation of his (then recent) pamphlet on Whitman ('The Good Gray Poet'). This letter marks the beginning of the friendship between Burroughs and the eloquent, doughty champion of the poet. It predicts that his pamphlet is 'but the preliminary skirmish of a war which will be fought under many flags for many years.' O'Connor wishes that the champions of Whitman had a magazine of their own; he speaks of the immortal times he has had with Walt; deeply regrets not having kept a diary of their days together during the War; and agrees with Burroughs that W. W. is 'an incarnation.'

Following this, Burroughs used to drop in at the O'Connors' of a Sunday evening, where Whitman and the host would hold a sort of symposium, with Burroughs, Charles W. Eldridge, and others as listeners. Never, Burroughs said, had he heard talks to equal that between the two — O'Connor with his Irish wit, ardor, eloquence, and learning, and Whitman, with his own wide, assimilated reading, and vision. When warmed up, Whitman met O'Connor as a foeman worthy of his steel.

There were other companionships during those years, among which were those with J. T. Trowbridge, Dr. Frank Baker, and Mr. Aaron Johns. There were Sunday-evening receptions in the home of Professor Spencer F. Baird, of the Smithsonian, where Burroughs met many well-known men and women.

For a time when Burroughs was living on Capitol Hill, O'Connor had a room in the attic, where, stimulated by coffee and tobacco, he wrote his story, 'The Carpenter.' Protesting against this suicidal way of working, Burroughs would often throw plums into the open window to divert O'Connor from his task.

In the Burroughs-Benton correspondence one finds a record of the growth of the first book published by John Burroughs — the small volume on Whitman already mentioned. In a letter by Burroughs dated January 17th may be traced other interests and activities as well:

Since I recovered my health I have enjoyed life intensely. To live has been a luxury to me. I have done considerable writing, and *much has been begun in me*. I have found where the game lurks, and *will take it at my leisure*. [Italics mine.]

I have just finished correcting proof of an article called 'Snow Walkers,' that will appear in the March Atlantic. They have one of mine called 'In the Hemlocks,' which they will publish in May or June. I have another on hand on Walt Whitman which, I suppose, would throw them into 'catnip fits,' if I were to send it to them. I seriously contemplate putting it into a book.

How do you like 'The Good Gray Poet'? I know O'Connor; he is a good fellow. If you are writing book-notices now, I wish you would notice it. Have you read 'Drum Taps'? There are no other poems in the language that go into me like some of those. I have some immortal times with Walt. . . .

I wish you could see my case of birds. Walt says it is a poem.

I am doing well in a pecuniary way, and save $100 a month easily. I want to make enough in the next two years to purchase my freedom. My wife is quite well, and the cow also.[1]

As to 'In the Hemlocks,' he had written Benton the previous autumn of the delicious time he had had in the summer among the old Delaware County hills, picking up material for another paper on the birds, at which he was 'pecking away.' Almost apologetically he said that he saw he must have his say out about the birds, perhaps even make a little book about them. He himself regarded this essay as about the best he had then written. In it he has given some of his best characterizations of the birds, has caught and preserved the freshness of the dim old forest where he roamed as a boy. Reading it, one walks with him under the ancient hemlocks, and stands awed and silenced by the inscrutable processes of life transpiring there.

Although he did not always exert the forbearance enjoined by Emerson, and name the birds without a gun, he did enter into their lives with sympathy, and translate the meaning of their songs. One feels this, standing with him on the mountain-top in the moonlight, and listening to the hermit chanting its evening hymn. And when with him one stoops to note the solitary *Dalibarda repens*, the tinted pyrola, and the pink-veined wood-sorrel, one gladly leaves them on their stems. Of his own lack of forbearance during his early study of the birds, he says in a note-book (May 26, 1865) that his excursions to the woods are often vitiated by going forth in quest of a certain species:

The full fruition of enjoyment and delight comes when I go out

[1] Chloe, the 'rural divinity.'

without any purpose except to get near the earth and sky and accept the whole, ready to entertain bird and beast and tree alike — full of faith and self-forgetfulness, and pledged to no special end. . . .

As I saunter through the woods and by the brook, the kindly and hospitable influences of the air and earth come nearer to me; nothing escapes my eye or ear or nose. . . . A more intimate and harmonious relation is established between me and Nature. I do not outrage the woods, I do not hunt down a bird. . . .

It was in this spirit that he walked with Nature the greater part of his life. In those early note-books his spring rambles are recorded often with as much charm as is found in his books of that period. Reading them, one experiences the glow that attended every fresh discovery.

Benton writes Burroughs anent the nature essays then coming from his pen:

I see more and more that you have found your proper field. . . . Your essays show constant improvement. 'Snow Walkers' is altogether a fine treatment of quite an original classification. 'In the Hemlocks' is brim-full of wit and acute observation. [He adds that he finds his suggested title for a book of such sketches ('Experiences with Nature') a bit commonplace.]

In a letter dated March 20, 1866, Burroughs sets forth the plan of his Whitman book as it was shaping itself in his mind:

Walt is well and hearty and often asks after Benton. The more I study him, the more I am impressed. He is the best answer to the riddles and problems, I am convinced, I shall ever see.

Some time ago a letter from the Atlantic, in answer to one of mine, in which they stated they were quite ready to *see* an article on W. W., though their editors were not prepared to champion him in so unqualified a manner as Mr. Emerson had, led me to prepare an article on 'Drum Taps.'[1] Hearing that Howells was going there on the editorial staff, I hurried it off, but not in time — 'Willie, dear' was there ahead of me, and of course it was not accepted. It was short, and not strong — not a defense of Walt, but biographical and descriptive, with an underrunning hint of what might and sometime would be said. But if I could write to please Howells and 'Babie Bell' Aldrich, I should be ashamed to let my left hand know what my right hand doeth.

The article is only one of a series which I am preparing on Walt, and which I am going to put into a little book — the drift or con-

[1] 'Walt Whitman and his Drum Taps,' John Burroughs, *The Galaxy*, December, 1866. 'It was the first essay in the U.S. about W. W. that made any attempt at appreciation. I wrote it while Walt was in N.Y. He never saw it till it was in print.' J. B.

clusion to be that Walt Whitman is a return to Nature — that
'Leaves of Grass' is an utterance from Nature, and opposite to
modern literature, which is an utterance from Art; that W. W. gives
the analogies of the earth, and that he is the only modern or democratic man who has yet spoken, and our only hope from utter literary
inanition. The chapters are to be 1. Biographical, 2. Drum Taps,
3. Beauty, 4. The Earth, 5. Modern Literature, 6. Leaves of Grass
— with one central idea running through all and culminating in the
last chapter, in which chapter I open up the whole length. . . . [The
remainder of the letter is missing. One can only conjecture that
when Benton reviewed the book, he may have abstracted this part
(evidently the author's summing-up of the 'Notes'), to save himself
the bother of transcribing the passage.]

Since the 'Notes on Walt Whitman as Poet and Person'
is long since out of print, and not readily accessible to many,
it may be interesting to give here the data for comparing the
form the table of contents finally took with the tentative
plan as outlined by its author in the foregoing letter:

Part First has the general title, 'Leaves of Grass,' with the
section-titles, 'First Acquaintance with Poem and Poet,' 'The
Early Issues or Editions,' 'Review of the Completed Poem,'
'Standard of the Natural Universal,' 'Beauty,' 'Personality,'
'Further Presentation and Points.' Part Second has the section-titles, 'Personal Sketch,' and 'Drum Taps.' The second
edition (1871), the one I have by me, which, however, varies
but slightly from the first, contains one hundred and eight
pages, followed by about sixteen pages of 'Supplementary
Notes' and two pages consisting chiefly of extracts from the
newspapers.

The accompanying excerpt from his note-book further re-
flects Burroughs's ruminations about the bard at this time:

W. W.'s intention to let 'L of G' speak directly from the facts of
the human body and soul, without reference to established customs.
. . . It is only from the standpoint of usage that our poet offends. Is
any part of the body more indecent than another? Is life more
indecent than death? He violates no principle of nature, or of the
body, or of the soul, but, on the contrary, gives them unrestricted
utterance. For myself, I was shocked as much as anyone by such
overwhelming freedom of speech and metaphor, but from the first I
had faith in the spirit of the book, and, without being able to justify
it all, believed that there was ground for justification, when it
should be reached.

[J. B. to M. B. B. June 6, 1866]

I am glad you take such a lively interest in your barn. I can see that it may and will have an esthetic value to you, as my garden does to me. I think, and think strongly, that that which literary men need the least of is books; and that what they need the most of is the *un*literary element. On this point there is a chance to preach a sermon to every living writer, save W. W., and I mean sometime to preach it.

I mean to preach it by a kind of indirection in my book on Walt. Said book will be quite different from what you think. I don't seek to defend 'Leaves of Grass,' as O'Connor did, for instance, but to state the principle from which the poet starts, and which justifies him in saying such terrible things. I want to show that literature has become so artificial and petty and dainty and gaudy that a tremendous plunge was needed in the other direction; and that Walt Whitman is the great reaction against the puny, feeble way into which we have fallen.

The book is substantially done, but I am going to let it lay — to empty myself of it — and see how it reads next fall, when I hope to publish it.

I saw a long letter the other day from [Moncure D.] Conway to O'Connor, in which he spoke of Walt in the highest terms, and said if asked to describe New York he should say it is the place where Walt Whitman lives. He has written an article on Walt which is shortly to appear in the Fortnightly Review.

Your little notice of 'Drum Taps' was very well done — by far the best that has been written. Walt was much pleased with it, I think.

I should subscribe to the Radical if it would throw half of its theology overboard. I think the New Theology as bad as the Old. Theology, as such, anyway, is death to me. I have no hopes of Wasson since he has gone to hair-splitting.

I think I have had my say about the birds, for the present, at least. *Sometime I may make a book of these, and other articles*, but am in no hurry. [Italics mine.]

He was in no hurry chiefly because of the great Whitman planet that had swum into his ken, and, as he said, because he had found where the game lurked, and could take it at leisure.

In his 'Notes on Walt Whitman,' Burroughs starts out naïvely by telling how it began with himself, as a preliminary to tracing the effect which 'Leaves of Grass' had had upon him; tells of his life as a farm-boy who 'loved few books much, but . . . Nature with a love passing all the books of the world.' He then relates that in his first dip into the strange book he recognized in it a quality akin to a fine sunrise, or to a dim old hemlock forest. He took the book with him, he

said, on his tramps across the hills; and, after five years of
reading it, during the last three of which he had known the
man, he wrote the 'Notes.' It was not only his first book, but
was the first book ever written about Whitman.

Of this, many years later, he said:

> I plume myself that I did not have to wait for somebody to say to
> me, 'This [the 'Leaves'] is great.' I knew it was as soon as I read it.
> I picked out what I could understand, and let the rest go till I grew
> to understand it.

In his 'Notes' he credits Whitman's book with having
rendered him a moral service beyond statement, coming as
it did to him, a young man full of inquiry, of emotion, of
doubt. It strengthened his faith and curiously contributed
to his sense of self. One glimpses that Catskill mountain
farm-boy in this passage:

> I never knew how beautiful a redbird [scarlet tanager] was till I
> saw one darting through the recesses of a shaggy old hemlock wood.
> In like manner the birds of the naturalist can never interest us like
> the thrush the farm-boy heard singing in the cedars at twilight as he
> drove the cows to pasture, or like that swallow that flew gleefully in
> the air above him as he picked the stones from the early May
> meadows.

The following excerpt from the same source reveals the
high artistic standard he thus early set for him who aims to
report Nature — a standard to which his own work has
closely approximated:

> Every object as it stands in the sequence of cause and effect, has a
> history which involves its surroundings; and the depth of the interest
> which it awakens in us is in proportion to which its integrity in this
> respect is preserved.

Here, and in much of his writing in the note-books, as well
as in the 'Notes,' we see the philosophic Burroughs of those
early essays, between 1860 and 1862, — the essays published
in the 'Saturday Press,' and the New York 'Leader,' and 'Expression.' Quite a different Burroughs than the genial interpreter of nature of his subsequent books, yet the one we
first met, when examining his earlier writings.

At the time of writing his 'Notes,' Burroughs was fairly
obsessed by Whitman. He was firmly convinced that in Walt

Whitman America was superbly illustrated; in him Democracy was embodied; while in his poetry both were grandly uttered. Book and man became fused in his mind, nevermore to be separated. Out of this conviction he wrote the little book, which, whatever its limitations, is pervaded by insight and sincerity; and, in the main, by a calmness and surety of judgment beyond that looked for in an untrained writer of nine and twenty. However, one recalls that he matured early; and that David A. Wasson, after reading his early essays, said that Burroughs's twenty-four years had been worth more to him than the longest life to most men.

The story of his days, and the progress of his book, are carried along in the letters which follow. To Benton, on August 26th:

... Office work light, political aspect threatening. A. J. and 'My Policy,' and my clerkship also, may go to the dogs — I will not support him.

I am still pecking away at my book, but hope to have it to suit me by October. Walt is in New York bringing out 'Leaves of Grass.' I am going to see what can be done with the Galaxy, though I have little hope of getting an article in it favorable to Walt. It is getting to be quite a bright magazine, by the way — some articles there by Eugene Benson[1] wake one up a little.

The Round Table is at last on the right track, if it has the courage to stick to it, and the ability to hit hard. I refer more particularly to the last number. . . .

J. S. Clark of Ticknor and Fields called here at the office to see me while I was home. I can only conjecture his business. Willie Howells will not soon have the fun of pronouncing on one of my articles.

I had a letter from Miss Juliette H. Beach[2] the other day in which she took occasion to say that my name was familiar to her as the 'signature of some of the most delightful essays' she had ever read. I am surprised that so many people not interested in the birds should be interested in my articles. I have begun a piece on 'Sheep Pastures.' Any suggestions?

What are you doing? I wish you would come down this fall. Why not? I see O'Connor much. He is a tip-top fellow, but awfully learned and sharp, and smooth-tongued. . . .

Again on October 27th:

My book is not yet finished. I have rewritten it a good many

[1] 'An artist who had some vogue at that time.' J. B.
[2] The friend to whom Whitman wrote 'Out of the rolling ocean.' She wrote many beautiful letters to Walt which J. B. tried in vain to get her consent to publish. She died many years ago.

times, and it has grown amazingly on my hands. I think there are
some things in it that will make you open your eyes.[1] I believe I
have revived and illustrated a principle that is entirely obsolete in
this age, and that if carried out would revolutionize modern literature. The principle may be come at by asking yourself what Nature
means in Literature — what is the analogy of the open air in a
poem?

I wrote quite a long article on Walt and his 'Drum Taps' for the
Galaxy. I think it will be out soon. *In it all the points are hinted at,
and some openly stated, that I shall make in the book.* [Italics mine.]
The last clause contains the main point. . . . The history of their declining it, and then reversing their decision, is a curious one, and I
will tell it to you some time. They also have an article of mine
called 'A Night Hunt in the Adirondacks,' which Walt says is by far
my best piece, which is my own opinion. I do not think the Galaxy
amounts to much, however, or ever will.

I sometimes get heartily sick of what we call our literature, and
feel like going back home among the mountains and forgetting it all,
and driving oxen and prying rocks. I am not certain but after I have
freed my mind upon the subject, I shall do so; or, better yet, go to
the Far West. This 'piddling and pottering' here in a government
office is still more contemptible than modern poetry.

What has happened to you that you are so melancholy? Love,
bile, business, or what? Speak out.

I saw a letter from Wendell Phillips in which he said O'Connor's
pamphlet was the most vigorous and brilliant production he knew of
in all controversial literature. Also a letter from Matthew Arnold in
which he acknowledges Walt's power and originality but thinks —
to give his meaning in short — that Americans will have to fall into
the European movement, and that we had better not attempt anything on our own hook. Cool, ain't it?

In mid-February, he wrote Benton:

I meant to have had my book out by this time, but if I get it
published next month, I will do well. I am getting up the plates
here, and shall try for a publisher in New York, and in the West.
The plates will be done in about ten days. I enclose you a slip of a
proof that you may see how it will look.

The book has taken many shapes since I began to write it, and has
finally assumed the form of Notes arranged under five or six different
headings. I am very well pleased with it. I think the main idea of
the book sticks out so prominently that no reader can escape getting
it into him. I call it 'Notes on Walt Whitman as Person and Poet.'
Of course I expect great things from it, but I expect to wait. [In the
title finally chosen 'poet' preceded 'person.']

[1] Years later, J. B. said of this early comment, 'How a young man always thinks
he has found a mare's nest! and it usually turns out to be nothing but a field
pumpkin!'

On February 25th he further discusses Whitman, and his forthcoming book about him:

I think your notion about Walt's culture from books quite a natural one, and one that most readers of 'Leaves of Grass' will share. I myself felt in the same way till I had deliberately set myself to studying the book, and now every year the feeling becomes stronger with me, that there is no book in the language projected from a higher water mark of culture than 'Leaves of Grass,' or one that implies a greater maturity of the moral and intellectual faculties and perceptions. There is something or other in the productions of an unlettered man which betrays him and weakens him at every step. He uses his tools awkwardly — cuts his own fingers. I think the attitude of the author of 'Leaves of Grass,' in every page, is that of a man who knows all that can be said upon the subject, and who knows precisely what he is doing. You say it would damage your notion of Walt as a poet to know that he was a 'book-worm.' Of course it would; for a worm is a worm, whether he bore in books, or in rotten wood; but would it not increase your respect for him to know that he had looked over the whole field of literature, and, without having extensively read, had yet thoroughly absorbed the *spirit* of the great bards; and so knew precisely the nature and relative importance of his own undertaking? Such is the fact, at any rate.

I doubt if he has ever read Catullus, but I [have] heard him speak of Lucretius as one of the 'great mountains,' and Homer, and the Greek dramatists, he is much more familiar with than with more modern poets.

He has the faculty of measuring and predicting a man from a small fragment of him, as the great naturalist will build an animal from a tooth or a claw, or from his track in the sand.

He says at the outset of his book that he 'conned old times,' 'sat studying at the feet of the great masters' — and pays due obeisance to all great men — 'priests, poets, philosophers, languages, shapes' — of other times. Read 'Savantism,' and 'Beginners.' But of course, and very properly, his emphasis is not upon these things, like the scholar's, or the man of mere intellect, but upon personal qualities, democracy, life, love.

Walt Whitman is much greater, both as a poet and as a man, than you have ever begun to conceive. After years of study, I feel that I am only just beginning to realize his magnitude. . . .

I expect you will rebel against the main conclusions of my book; if you do, don't hesitate to 'pitch in.' I don't fear any attacks upon my principles. I only fear silence and indifference. Said book yesterday took rail for N.Y. to seek its fortunes. I expect it will have a hard time, and I presume I shall have to go on there myself. If I do, I shall go home to make sugar in the woods. . . .

[*J. B. to M. B. B. June* 1, 1867]

I would give all my interest in the Russian possessions to be with you this perfect June day. It is one of the finest days of the season, and the country must be a brimming cup of delight.

Next week I hope to send you my little book. I will send you also a copy of proofs, in case you should want to 'cut it up.' I print the book here, and the American News Company of N.Y. are to publish it.

I hear from Conway that an English doctor is writing an article on W. W. for the Edinburgh Review. But I think they are all on the wrong track over there.

I sent you the other day a copy of the Times containing O'Connor's review of Ball's claim to be considered the author of Mrs. Aker's poem, 'Rock me to sleep, Mother.' I think it is one of the best reviews of the kind I ever saw. I have never seen anything in any of the British Quarterlies which in its way equalled it. I am convinced there is no other American writer who could have riddled Ball in that style. Raymond was so well pleased with it that he sent O'Connor a draft for $50.00. I am curious to see what kind of a reply Ball's friends can make.

I talk of building a house this fall. Send me a plan for an eight-room cottage, built on strictly economical principles. . . .

[*J. B. to M. B. B. June* 19, 1867]

Your letter came this morning. I really hope the 'Notes' have got life and enthusiasm in them. I was afraid they were too quiet and tame. I wanted to make a book with warm blood in its veins, and as unruly and revolutionary as possible. I hardly expected you to make a notice of it. Do not by any means do so for the mere sake of noticing it, or because I sent the proofs. I had laid out a copy for Joel which I will mail today. The first hundred were put up in the style I sent you; the remaining four hundred I shall have put up in this latter style, which suits me[1] better. Make my regards to Joel, and tell him if he feels like reviewing the book, not to spare me. I am by no means sanguine about the immediate success of the book. I am fortified against any indifference on the part of the public and literary men generally.

After a generous distribution of complimentary copies of the 'Notes,' and a goodly supply furnished to Whitman, stacks of unsold copies were grudgingly given room in Mrs. Burroughs's tidy parlor, the annoyance, especially when they had to be dusted, doubtless accounting for the slighting remarks

[1] As some copies of the first edition of this rare little volume are bound in green, and others in brown, this is probably the explanation of the reference to the two styles of binding.

she sometimes made as to both writer and subject. Mr. Julian Burroughs, in his boyhood recollections of his father, records the scornful emphasis which Mrs. Burroughs would, even many years later, throw upon that word 'person' — 'poet and *person*.' Unquestionably the hue and cry raised about the poet, in those early Washington days, had its effect in discrediting both Whitman and his champion in the eyes of one so conventional as Mrs. Burroughs — an effect, however, that was invariably neutralized when that obnoxious 'person' appeared; for she ministered to that person in many kindly ways, succumbing, in spite of herself, to his lovable personality.

In a reminiscent letter to me, in 1914, Mr. Charles E. Benton writes:

It was probably in 1868, when Joel and I were in Washington, that Burroughs showed me, piled up in his parlor, what must have been nearly the whole edition of his then recently issued book, 'Walt Whitman as Poet and Person.' The Public had not grasped for it! But he remarked indifferently that if it was wanted, it would eventually be called for. He had said his say, and seemed indifferent as to whether the public would listen.

[*M. B. B. to J. B. August 2*, 1867]

The Times you kindly sent me some time ago was received bearing Mr. O'Connor's gallant championship of your little book. He gives you a high seat, and enviable praise. I have seen but very few of the current periodicals lately, and so know nothing of the manner in which the 'Notes' are being treated, except the notices of the Tribune and the Commonwealth. I saw an extract the other day in the Times from the London Chronicle which places Walt on a pedestal high as those of Homer and Shakespeare.

. . . I am sadly in earnest in this thing, John, and have told you a secret. I recollect you have a way of leaving your letters in all manner of coat-tail pockets and indiscriminate dove-holes and drawers; now please ignite this and pass the contents to no second person whatsoever. . . .

[*J. B. to M. B. B. August 5*, 1867]

Your letter gave me much pleasure. I had a hearty laugh over the little secret which I esteem was my right and privilege. You have my sympathy. You are just where I have been wanting to see you for years. You are testing the cup which is such a strange mixture of pleasure and pain; yea, I may say of bliss and despair. But it will do you good, and I have no doubt you are master of the situation. It will do you immense good, and the new relation which it foreshadows, and to which, I trust, it will lead, is the one thing needed to complete your life. Tell me all about it — all about her, and how it came about. Your secret shall be kept with religious fidelity.

My book has not excited much comment yet, though its reception has been much more favorable than I had expected. The Citizen, Leader, and Evening Post have had eminently friendly notices of it. Mr. [William] Rossetti in his article on Walt in the London Chronicle speaks in commendatory terms of it; so did the article in the London Review some time ago. Conway, in a letter which I received a few days ago, says it is the best critical work ever produced in this country, which, of course, I take with a grain of allowance. The Chronicle article is magnificent, and has had a profound effect. The Round Table completely goes back on its statement of a year ago. Church of the Galaxy is trying to get a poem out of Walt for the October number of his magazine, and I guess will succeed. Subject, the Harvest which the returned soldiers have sown and gathered. Conway says other articles will appear in the English periodicals. The editor of the Pall Mall Gazette says 'Leaves of Grass' is the most wonderful work he has ever read of any country or age. The victory is ours beyond all doubt.

Little and Brown of Boston have been writing to me about editing a new edition of Nuttall's Ornithology, or writing a new work on the subject. I do not know what it will amount to; not much, I expect, as Nuttall does not need much editing, and as I am decidedly averse to undertaking any new work on Ornithology at present.

I had a very frank letter from Miss [Sarah] Adams the other day about my book. She accepts W. W. as 'person,' but not as 'poet.' I will send a copy of the 'Notes' to Morse of the Radical in a few days.

Excerpts from Conway's letter containing further mention of the Whitman cause, read:

If you were pleased with the London Review article (and we can hardly hope to have John Bull at his best see Walt as we see him), how much more will you be delighted with Rossetti's article which I am about sending you! I fancy I see the glow of O'Connor's eyes when he reads it. More will come. Rossetti tells me he was misquoted by Swinburne in thinking that there was anything in 'Leaves of Grass' that couldn't be published in England. Our Cause, as you well call it, gains continually. The editor of the Pall Mall Gazette told me he had been reading it and thought it one of the most wonderful productions of any age. . . . I have met a good deal of Philistinism here in this matter, but a great deal of insight, too. We can afford to wait, for Walt is as sure to be recognized as the sun.

Give my love to the old youth, and tell him I hope to see him over here yet before I return; and remember me to O'Connor.

I am writing weekly now to the Tribune, and you will now and then see some sly mention of what we are interested in.

Benton reviewed the 'Notes' in the November Radical. Burroughs wrote him of the review:

It is better than I deserve. It will keep the ball moving. There is little or no sale of the book — not fifty copies have yet been disposed of; which is proof, I think, that the book has something in it.

I hear from Conway occasionally. He says my book irritates and interests Matthew Arnold, who has written Conway a letter about it. . . .

The space here occupied by this 'little big book about Whitman,' as one of Burroughs's correspondents characterized it, is justifiable 'for reasons.' It has long been out of print, and is practically inaccessible; comparatively little of it has been reprinted, although much of 'Beauty' was incorporated in 'Before Beauty,' in 'Birds and Poets,' in 1877; and much of the section on 'Drum Taps' (which as its author indicated in a previously-quoted letter to Benton, forms the spinal column of the book) was reprinted in 'Whitman: A Study,' in 1896. Moreover, since the passing of Mr. Burroughs, rumors have come to me, as previously they came to him, that Whitman, not Burroughs, wrote the most of 'Notes on Walt Whitman.'

To one actually crediting this rumor it is only necessary for refutation to adduce the early note-books of Burroughs, wherein may be traced in his own handwriting, the inception and growth of the book. In this connection alone, Burroughs's letters to Benton, herein quoted, are important; there is also important evidence in letters to Dowden, Trowbridge, and Higginson.

Mr. Burroughs always frankly said that Whitman helped him conspicuously with the book; frequently talked it over with him; trimmed and cut, and wrote the part named 'Standards of the Natural Universal.' Whitman supplied the title, and some of the chapter-titles, and arranged and wrote a large part of the 'Supplementary Notes' (second edition).

I recall once when Mr. Burroughs was helping me with one of my articles, adding a little, and pruning a good deal, he said, 'I am doing for you just what Walt used to do for me — cut out and amend my early efforts.'

Fortunately there are conclusive written statements from him on the subject, called forth by inquiries from a stranger. On October 10, 1920, a correspondent who signed himself Egmont H. Arens and said he was 'a student and collector of Walt Whitman,' was moved to inquiry because of persistent rumors to the effect that the 'Notes on Walt Whitman' were largely written by Whitman himself; and he thought it only fair to give Mr. Burroughs a chance to 'quiet the title.'

Why this correspondent should have written Mr. Burroughs under an assumed name, is something of a mystery — quite as much as the 'literary mystery' he claims to solve in a recent magazine article dealing with the little book and settling, to his own satisfaction, that the book is chiefly the work of Whitman. As author of the article he signed another name, Frederick P. Hier, Jr., presumably his real name, since it is the one he is known by in his (legal) profession. In the article he says that the letters from Mr. Burroughs (which he quotes), were replies to *his* letters, and *were addressed to him*, whereas, they were addressed as already indicated. (I have his inquiries, and the original drafts of Mr. Burroughs's replies.)

This chapter, written long before the publication of the article in question, answers automatically its erroneous implications. It would seem that Mr. Burroughs's candid replies to his pseudonymous correspondent should have forestalled such an ambiguous article as that of Mr. Hier's, with its unpleasant and unjust insinuations, especially after Mr. Burroughs could no longer answer them.

It seems only fair to add that reticence in the earlier years, on the part of Mr. Burroughs, as to Whitman's emendations and contributions to the book, were hardly on his own account; but the rather to spare the poet the criticism sure to follow if it were known that he had taken this means (one of many such instances, as has since been learned) to expound himself. And it seems only fair to Whitman to point out that he did this, not as 'outrageous self-puffery' (of which he has been accused) but from an earnest desire to contribute to the better understanding of his message.

The frank reply of Mr. Burroughs to his unknown correspondent (I quote from the pencilled rough draft by Mr. Burroughs, from which I made the typed copy that went from Roxbury, New York, October 15, 1920, to the so-called Egmont H. Arens of New York City) should have been sufficient to dissolve any sense of 'mystery' lingering in the inquirer's mind as to false claims on the part of John Burroughs concerning the first book he ever wrote:

I have received yours of the 10th, relative to my little book 'Notes on Walt Whitman as Poet and Person.' *There is a modicum of truth in what you have been told.* [Italics mine.] Whitman's mark is on several of my books and magazine articles which were written during the Washington days. He was a great critic, and I was in the habit of submitting my Mss. to him for his strictures.

The first thing I wrote about him was in the Galaxy, in the late sixties, and was called, 'Walt Whitman and his Drum Taps.' This was written while Whitman was absent in New York, and he never saw it till it was in print.

My next piece was called 'The Flight of the Eagle' (in 'Birds and Poets'). This he named, and there are a few sentences scattered through it from his pencil. Page 197 was written by him. He told me the incident, and I asked him to write it out, which he did, and I put it in.

I have not a copy of my 'Notes on W. W.' here, and I have not looked into it for years, but I know it abounds in the marks of Whitman's hand. I had a more ambitious title — I forget what — and he renamed it and pruned it, and reshaped many of the paragraphs. The most suggestive and profound passage in it is from his hand, nearly a whole page, but I cannot refer you to the page.

Whitman named my first volume ('Wake-Robin')[1] for me. I took a number of titles to him, and he held me to that one. He named William O'Connor's eloquent defense of him — 'The Good Gray Poet.'[2] It is certain that my 'Notes' would not have been what they are without his help. *If I remember rightly* [italics mine] the Supplementary Notes to the last edition were entirely written by him.[3] My volume, 'Whitman, a Study,' would have been of much greater value could he have pruned it. It is too heady and literary.

---

[1] In the recent 'mysterious' article referred to, which labors to prove that Whitman wrote the book, one of the 'evidences' adduced by its author is that J. B. here speaks of *Wake-Robin* (published in 1871) as 'my first volume.' His *Notes* had been out of circulation for almost half a century, so that he had long come to think, and loosely to speak, of his first nature book, *Wake-Robin*, as his first book. But the legal mind grasps at this straw, and convicts the author out of his own mouth! And yet, since he builds his case on such 'evidence,' how can he ignore the fact that throughout this same letter J. B. speaks of the little book on Whitman (published in 1867) as 'my' book?

[2] This title is reminiscent of Tennyson's line in his 'Ode on the Death of Wellington' — 'Oh, good gray head that all men know.' Anent his statement: J. B. had evidently forgotten the fact that an early letter to him, from Charles W. Eldridge (an intimate of W. W.'s and W. D. O'C.'s), distinctly states that O'C. himself named his pamphlet. Furthermore, Horace Traubel quotes Whitman himself as saying, 'The "good gray," William's other name for me, has stuck.'

[3] These 'Supplementary Notes,' a sort of Appendix, cover less than sixteen pages, of smaller type than the text, and are largely made up of data as to the various editions of *Leaves of Grass*, and the various groupings of the poems; with quotations from certain poems, and a setting forth of the author's aims regarding them. They contain a short account of the poet's ancestry; copious excerpts from Emerson's letter to Whitman, indorsing the first edition of *Leaves of Grass*; and from Anne Gilchrist's paper, 'A Woman's Estimate of Walt Whitman' — *addenda* which were clearly not *written* by Whitman; but which Whitman was naturally better prepared to compile than was Burroughs.

When I get back to West Park, I will look over the 'Notes,' and if I can throw any new light on the subject, I will write again.

On November 6, 1920, in response to a second letter signed Egmont H. Arens, (but which Mr. F. P. Hier avers was written by himself), Mr. Burroughs replied:

I have been looking over my little book, 'Notes on Walt Whitman as Poet and Person,' and am a great deal at sea about it. I find it hard to separate the parts I wrote from those he wrote.[1] The fine passage I referred to, by him, begins on page 37, Chapter XXI, and includes the whole chapter [595 words]. In other places I see *where he touched up my work, leaving the thought my own.* [Italics mine.] The chapters on Beauty, and on 'Drum Taps,' are all my own. The Biographical Notes he enlarged and improved in the proof from notes which he had given me verbally. I have no doubt that half the book is his.[2] He was a great critic, and he did me great service by pruning and simplifying. The title, too, is his. I had a much more ambitious title.

And yet, after these straightforward letters from Mr. Burroughs (which, by the way, the legal gentleman, who can hardly plead ignorance of the law, prints without the permission of Mr. Burroughs's literary executor), the writer of the article, F. P. Hier, Jr., with the *alias*, E. H. Arens, asserts that it may be fairly (!) said that the book is virtually Whitman's!

In my own copy of the 'Notes' (second edition) are many little turns of expression which I marked years ago as sounding like Whitman, and concerning which Mr. Burroughs concurred, instancing others as 'probably Walt's' — quite a different matter, however, from Mr. Hier's assertion that the book which John Burroughs said he wrote was mostly written by Whitman!

It was Whitman as person, even more than as poet, that influenced Burroughs in those Washington days; and it is as person that one welcomes the familiar glimpses one gets of

[1] It had been fifty-three years since he wrote the book, and he was then long past eighty-three, and in failing health.

[2] This statement should be taken in connection with the fact that of the 108 pages in the book (excluding the 'Supplementary Notes,' *compiled from many sources, and arranged by Whitman*), space which would at least fill twenty-two pages is taken up with quotations from *Leaves of Grass*.

him as a frequenter of the Burroughs household, of a Sunday
morning, drawn by the delicious coffee and pancakes that
Mrs. Burroughs made, with maple syrup from the old sap-
bush in the Catskills; but also drawn by the thought of a stroll
that he and 'Jack' would take after breakfast, and their *séance*
on the marble steps of the Capitol. Invariably he came late.
Invariably the punctual housewife would 'get in a pucker' at
the delay. And is it not enough to try a woman's soul when
her coffee and the piping-hot griddle have to wait, while the
guest comes not?

'Car after car would go jingling by,' said Mr. Burroughs,
'and still no Walt! At last one would stop, and Walt would
roll off it and saunter up to the door — cheery, vigorous,
serene — and all evidence of ill-humor would vanish before
his compelling charm.'

Whenever they strolled past the White House, Whitman
would always stop and bring from its hiding-place in one of
the fence-posts a smooth round stone which he tossed from
hand to hand as they walked, on return tucking it away in
its niche till they came that way again. 'What would I not
give for that stone now!' Mr. Burroughs would say, sighing
regretfully that he had kept no record of their talks.

He told of the oyster orgies he and Whitman had, seated on
high stools at the counter in Harvey's, the genial darkies who
opened the oysters marvelling at the quantities they consumed. Doubtless their talk, translated, would, in spirit,
have tallied with Pistol's when Falstaff refused him a penny;
only that they would have substituted the 'mightier weapon'
for the 'sword':

> 'Why, then, the world's mine oyster,
> Which I with [pen] will open.'

Women who disapproved of Whitman as poet found their
disapproval vanishing in his presence. Elizabeth Akers, being
a writer of correct, rhythmical verse, looked askance at Whitman's revolutionary, 'uncouth' lines, and studiously avoided
meeting him.

'One day she came tripping down the stairs to meet me,'
said Mr. Burroughs, 'and there was Walt!' She couldn't
help liking him — no one could — and surrendered to his
personality, but she wasn't big enough to accept his poetry.

JOHN BURROUGHS
In the Early Seventies

MRS. JOHN BURROUGHS
In the Washington Period

I laugh whenever I think of her look of dismay when she saw
Walt. He appeared not to notice it, but laughed about it
afterwards.'

Although she scolded about the poet, Mrs. Burroughs made
shirts for him. She was the only one who would make them
loose and comfortable. Later, after his stroke of paralysis,
she used to carry him delicacies, and do for him other little
services. Mrs. O'Connor used to darn his socks, and, especially during and just after the Civil War, look after him with
affectionate solicitude — when he was spending himself on
the sick soldiers with such lavish self-forgetfulness; spending
himself with a like compassion to that expressed in 'Drum
Taps' — those poems in which, as William O'Connor said,
is voiced 'the madonna tenderness — the mother's unutter-
erable love and woe.' After all, poet *and* person were
appreciated in the Burroughs and O'Connor households.

Unforgettable were those scenes in the Washington hospitals when John Burroughs, so unused to the sight of suffering,
would occasionally accompany Whitman on his errands of
mercy; for Whitman's services continued long after the War.
On Thanksgiving, and other holidays, he would wheedle
Mrs. Burroughs into making pies and cookies, which he and
'Jack' would distribute to the soldiers. Sometimes the dis-
tressing sights would almost floor the younger man; but with
Whitman pity as an emotion had long given place to practical
sympathy. As his friend watched him move from cot to cot,
dispensing fruit, tobacco, writing-paper, clover-blooms, some
little thing for each, and, with each gift, dispensing cheer and
tenderness, he, too, would try to help, but made poor work of it.

During that Washington decade, but few letters passed
between the comrades, since they were seeing each other
almost daily; those few when one or the other was absent from
the city. Whitman's letters are lacking in literary quality —
homely, commonplace letters, with a strong human heart-
beat in each. His remembrances to friends never seem perfunctory; his affection breathes in the very mention of their
names. It is as though the one so remembered had received
a blessing.

Although a little out of sequence, chronologically, excerpts
from a letter of July, 1866, written by Whitman in Washington, to Burroughs in the Catskills, are given here:

I went up to your house this morning and took a look at the garden — Everything growing first rate, — potatoes, tomatoes, corn, cabbages, and all — I guess upon the whole the garden never looked better at this time of year. We have had opportune rains — I inquired about the cow, and received a favorable report. . . .

John, about coming, I am not able to say anything decisive in this letter. . . . Up in your Bureau all seems to go on as usual — . . .

I am feeling hearty and in good spirits — go around more than usual — go to such doings as base-ball matches and the music Performances in the Public grounds — Marine Band, etc. . . .

I hope your parents are well — I wish you to give them my love — tho' I don't know them, I hope to one of these days — remember me to the wife, also.

I am writing this by my window in the office, — the breeze is blowing moderate, and the view down the river and off along Virginia hills opposite is most delightful — the pardon clerks are middling busy — I have plenty of leisure, as usual — I spent yesterday afternoon at the Hospital, and took tea in the evening at O'Connor's.

Piatt is trying to get transferred to New York, to the Custom House — Well, good by for present, you dear friend, and God bless you and wife, and bring you both safe back

WALT

To the inquiry as to what caused the estrangement between Whitman and O'Connor which one sometimes sees mentioned in books about Whitman, Mr. Burroughs said that Eldridge, who was probably more intimate with the poet during his life in Washington than any one else save the O'Connors, told him that the estrangement originated in a heated argument over the Fifteenth Amendment; that W. W. thought the negroes unfit to vote, which enraged O'Connor. In time a complete reconciliation was effected.

Reverting to those long-gone days, as he reread the old letters from Walt, Mr. Burroughs said, 'Oh, those Washington days! how these bring them all back! I see the monument when I shut my eyes, the Potomac gleaming, and the Virginia hills through the shimmering light.'

One of Whitman's letters asks Burroughs, if convenient, to send him a draft for one hundred dollars. In explanation, Mr. Burroughs said that this was probably a loan to himself; that sometimes Walt borrowed from him, and sometimes he from Walt; and that *Walt was always punctilious in returning every cent he borrowed.* He was the more emphatic about this because certain biographers have said that Whitman's debts sat lightly upon him. He characterized such libelous charges in no gentle terms, whether made by inconsequential persons, or by those who, because their statements carry weight, should have taken the more pains to learn the facts.

The story of Whitman's removal from his clerkship in the Department of the Interior, in 1865, has been told many times in print, but nowhere with the scornful fire that burns in O'Connor's memorable pamphlet. This it was which gave rise to the ardent championship of Whitman in which O'Connor led off, and Burroughs followed, though in a saner, calmer way, as befitted his type. The first blow struck by Burroughs was the already-mentioned essay, 'Walt Whitman and his Drum Taps,' published in the December Galaxy, 1866. This, as has been seen, was the germ of the 'Notes,' in 1867, with a second edition in 1871. Then came a lull till 1876, when an editorial in the Tribune set him going again, the result being a paper for the Tribune, April 13, 1876, followed by 'The Flight of the Eagle' ('Birds and Poets'). Afterward, in countless ways, throughout the years, he dealt many a direct and indirect blow in the bard's behalf.

His boyhood capacity for enthusiasm, his marked reactions to the influence of Emerson, his ardent pursuit of the birds and flowers, are all of a piece with the ardor with which he espoused the cause of Whitman. Outside of Nature herself, nothing throughout his life had anything like the effect upon his plastic nature that was wrought by Whitman and his work. In later years he admitted that, for a time, in his partisanship for Whitman, he had decried many an author of whose worth he was well aware. In the earlier period he spoke superiorly of the 'Tennysonian wine,' which had gone to the heads of the younger poets, all unaware that he himself was 'half seas over' with Whitmanian wine.

If a writer damned his hero with faint praise, or damned him without praise, the sarcasm of Burroughs was forthcoming, his sentence severe. In truth, he also merited the term which Mr. Bliss Perry gave to the Camden group of loyal Whitmanites — 'hot little prophets.' In Burroughs's later years, however, he avowed:

It is a mistake a young man makes — if he sets up an idol, he thinks he must tear down all others. As he gets older and broader, he learns to see the good in all.

This, however, in face of the fact that, with the years, he was increasingly impressed with the greatness of Whitman.

Important events and plans are touched upon in two letters from Burroughs to Benton in the spring of 1868:

[Feb. 29.] . . . I built a brick house in the north edge of the city. By turning my face to the north I am in the country, turning it to the south I am in the city. I have about a mile to walk to the office, though the street cars go within half a block of our house.

If I had gone out of town I should have used the plan you sent me, but it was not so available where I am. I have ten rooms, a large cellar, coal- and wood-house, and plenty of verandas.

O'Connor and his family occupy half the house with us. I have enough ground for a small fruit and vegetable garden. I am the owner of three hens, one of which has nine chickens, ten days old. Can you beat that? I have more delights with them than most people have with their children.

What are you up to? I have been writing away nearly all winter, but have got nothing into shape. It has been mainly experimental. I heed your suggestions about the book. My plan is to make two — one about the birds, and one of farm sketches. But I cannot afford to undertake them yet. I have sent an Adirondack sketch to Putnams, which he says he will use in the summer.

The house (still standing — Number 1332, V Street), which Whitman named 'the house that Jack built,' is a substantial brick dwelling, — a house in which its mistress took great pride. Its owner, when inviting friends of the East Orange days to come and see their tidy new home, wrote, 'Ursula does her own work, and even the cat wipes her feet on the mat before she ventures inside.'

To Benton, in March, Burroughs writes of his plans and achievements:

Your letter was so full and rich and entertaining that it deserves a longer and better answer than it will get at my hands. . . . I heartily respond to your expressions of regard. I have often said to my wife that I have no friend or acquaintance whom I would like so much to have near me as Benton. Between Allen and me, and between O'Connor and me, there is always an impassable gulf. With you I have no such feeling. When I build my nest up along the Hudson, we will have some jolly old times. . . .

My Adirondack piece only described the deer-shooting, and is called 'A Night Hunt in the Adirondacks.'[1] Why do you not try your hand at the 'Deserted Village' and Indian Pass?

[1] Putnam's Magazine, 12:149. Later incorporated in 'The Adirondacks': *Wake-Robin.*

I have spent nearly the whole winter writing upon the subject of Art — literary art — with a view to settle in my own mind the question as it relates to 'Leaves of Grass.' The more I have explored the matter, the stronger has become my conviction that this poem fulfills all the conditions of great art. One of my foundation stones is this: that a work of art differs from a didactic or philosophical treatise in this, that it is not a thought, but an act, as Creation is; it is the deed transferred to a higher plane, and implies a like totality of the human being. The grand artist is not merely the knower or sayer, he is the doer.

No modern production certainly compares with 'Leaves of Grass' in this respect. No other poet *so moves one*. Again, I have settled to my own satisfaction that the antithesis of Art is Science. Both aim at truth, but with this difference: Science aims at truth in detail, Art at truth of *ensemble*. The results of Science relatively to its aim, must be parts and pieces, but Art must give the whole in every act; not quantitatively, of course, but qualitatively. Hence, I have no difficulty, after lifting the subject out of the petty, superficial grounds of finish and lineal regularity, in proving 'Leaves of Grass' to be in the highest sense a poem and a work of art.[1]

Give me the benefit of your opinion. What do you think constitutes a work of art?

I have been reading, or rereading Carlyle also. The only two living writers with whom I do not get disgusted are Carlyle and Emerson. With all those Boston wits — with Lowell, Higginson, Wasson, Howells, — I am thoroughly sick. I cannot read a line Wasson writes nowadays. In my piece ['Before Genius'] I speak of Carlyle as having a fuller measure of the great religious artist-mind than any of his contemporary poets or others. He has more of that which makes a man of action, and has injected into his pages more of the stuff of which strong manly characters are made.

I must tell you that your notice of my book [the 'Notes'] in the Radical was the means of at least selling one copy of that illustrious work. A man by the name of Greene, in Rochester, Wisconsin,[2] wrote me that on seeing Myron Benton's notice, etc. etc. . . .

Yesterday by a warm bank in the woods I found Houstonia in bloom. . . .

Two letters to Trowbridge[3] give further light on Burroughs's championship of Whitman, as well as his own views of the poetic art. One in early March says:

The result of my scribblings and cogitations upon Art, of which I

---

[1] I haven't outgrown this opinion,' said J. B., years later. 'I got hints of it from Lessing and Goethe.'

[2] Perhaps Calvin H. Greene, of Rochester, *Michigan*, who corresponded with Thoreau, 1856–59.

[3] These, and other letters for selection, were kindly lent by Mrs. J. T. Trowbridge.

told you when you were here, is a brief essay which I think of offering
to some magazine. To help it with editors, at least not to hinder it,
I have not discussed the question of 'Leaves of Grass' as a work of
art, but have only touched upon it incidentally.

It has occurred to me to ask you if it would be in your way to put
the piece in the hands of Mr. Fields, in case I should send it to you?
I know very well what would be its fate if I send it in the regular
course, and it falls into the hands of his subs, but with Fields himself,
I think, the piece would stand a good chance. I think the Galaxy or
Putnam would publish it, but the Atlantic is much to be preferred.

Again, March 11:

I am quite of your opinion about the probable fate of the essay if I
sent it to the Atlantic. On looking it over again, after I had written
you, I saw it was not the thing they would like.

The most I say directly about Walt is this: that he is an artist in
this, at least, that he has not preached Democracy as a doctrine, but
has predicated his poems upon it as a living, dominating fact, which
I claim to be the method of all first-class artists. Also that in making
himself the staple of his poems, he is strictly artistic, since it is himself only in his universal human attributes, and not in his local or
accidental traits at all. I claim that any obtrusion of himself in the
character of *poet*, or *artist*, or as a person with a point to make, or
theory to divulge, would be the height of the inartistic. My notion
is that the artist, ideally, is the universal man, or that Art aims at
the universal, the All, and that its antithesis is science. . . .

I shall give the piece one or two more revisions, and, if it keeps
well, send it to the Galaxy, or to Lippincott's.

Rossetti's edition of Walt's poems is out. It looks first rate, and,
save two or three very absurd and stultifying statements in the
introductory essay, is all that we had expected. . . .

When calling Benton's attention to an article on Personalism by Whitman, he thus commented:

There is meat in it, and bone, too. I do not object to the style.
I think we all write too smoothly and flippantly. The need of literature always is for something deep-cut and characteristic. Alcott
writes Walt that he and Emerson are enthusiastic. He says he
(Walt) is on the road to empire.

My little squib in the Galaxy ['Before Genius'] stirred them up
considerable. (I regret the name — 'The Manhood Test,' it should
have been called.)

Higginson was exercised to the point of writing me a letter. I am
letting him have it right and left; though, of course, good-naturedly.
There are many things in heaven and earth not dreamt of in his
philosophy. The article is only a chip from what I hope is a real log,
though one can hardly tell, at the time, at least. As I told you

before, it is something about Art. Church praises the article, but
thinks it is too soon to publish it.

Benton replied that he hoped the essay, 'Before Genius,'
was not as obscure as its title. In this article, the author's
contention is that manliness must go before genius, as, in
a previous essay ('Before Beauty') he had contended that
power must precede beauty. The essays, taken together, set
forth his gospel of Art, which he began preaching in his 'Notes'
on Whitman, and by which, in the main, he continued to live.
When, however, he incorporated 'Before Beauty' (much
of which, it will be remembered, had formed a part of his
'Notes') in 'Birds and Poets,' he studiously avoided mention
of Whitman, though Whitman looms large in the background.

In a series of letters which passed between Burroughs and
Higginson at this time, the latter comments appreciatively
on the freshness and vigor of 'Before Genius,' and the generally impregnable position taken by its author; but thinks
him wrong in assuming incompatibility between native force
and high polish, any more than between manliness and refined manners. His chief objection to Whitman, he says, is
that 'he has not been strong enough to combine cosmopolitan culture with indigenous strength.'

'Your only two great American writers,' adds Higginson,
'are Emerson and Whitman; mine are Emerson and Hawthorne: I am glad to have even fifty per cent agreement with
one who writes so heartily.' To a second letter, in which
Higginson emphasizes the need of good-natured, hearty
coöperation from all classes, in order to make either a nation
or a literature, Burroughs replies:

I can hardly see how two reasonable persons can differ materially
on so important a subject as culture, when they come to understand
each other.
Of course we must have culture. We can be nothing without it,
either as a nation, or as individuals. We do not want crab apples in
literature, or politics, or religion, or manners, but the fullest fruit
Nature can bring forth.
I should differ with you perhaps as to the relative value or importance of artificial culture (culture from books, art, society, ex-
clusively) in the production of a national literature, and the broader
culture of life and real things. The question with me now is not what
will conduce to the production of scholars, or a class of witty, elegant,
accomplished *littérateurs*, for such obscure the true ends of literature,

as the priests pervert religion; but what comports with grand, primary bards upon whom a nation can build. I think of Homer's teachers, and of Shakespeare's, and of all monumental, everlasting men, and I see how little what is now called culture had to do with what they were, or what they achieved.

Whether or not we have culture enough in America, it is plain that there is as yet no full fruition of culture here, no triumph of the man-quality in our literature over the conventional, and, what is worse, there is not likely to be.

The matter often shapes itself in some such formula as this: the first step in culture is marked by a love for, and an acquiescence in, the artificial; the second step shows a revolt against the artificial, as in Byron; the third and last step, which not one poet in a century takes, shows no revolt against society, or civilization, or art, but an absorption of them, and a rising above them.

I do not see that any of our popular poets have ever taken the second step, the step which disturbs and unsettles, and presages new things. To me, Longfellow, sweet and gentle spirit that he is, is no more tonic than confectionery is. Lowell's whip has got a good snapper on it, and he knows how to make it crack like a pistol, but is that enough? I think Emerson has taken the highest step in morals and religion; but the only modern who has taken it in Art, according to my judgment, is Walt Whitman. From the standpoint of culture I regard 'Leaves of Grass' as a supreme work. It shows a maturity of the man beyond any other modern poem — the man done with toys, done with ornaments, done with criticism, and solemnly confronting the terrible beauty and majesty of things.

You must allow me the frankness to say that I think you do not understand it. You look into it for what the poet had no design of putting there — at least of making the main thing — namely, gems, specimens, 'fine things,' highly wrought, intellectual porcelain ware. It must be understood at the outset that this poem does not enter into competition with other modern works with reference to these things. It differs from them just as the landscape differs from a flower-garden. It is absolutely new, both in the theory of art upon which it is based, and in the ends which the poet had in view. This theory of art I have attempted to suggest in my book.[1] It is briefly this: that Nature affords the only adequate standard for a first-class modern artist. That to elaborate is of no avail, but to hint, to stimulate, to vitalize, set going, is everything.

Nature is perpetual transition. Everything passes and presses on; there is no pause, no completion, no exhaustive elaboration. To produce and multiply endlessly, and commit herself to no end or scheme, is the law of Nature. Something like this is in 'Leaves of Grass.' A hint, a word, a significant look, and on the author goes, follow who can.

I am as little in love with crudeness and awkward or bungling workmanship as you are, or with acrid, unripe fruit; and any such

[1] *Notes on Walt Whitman as Poet and Person.*

thing in W. W. would be to me his instant condemnation. Against any such charge I set the fact that his most hearty recognition, both in this country and in Europe, has been from men of the most liberal and ample culture. To partially cultivated people, he is meaningless and repulsive.

You are wrong in saying I think the West superior to the East as respects literature and general culture. It would be silly to affirm such a thing. I think the West *prospectively* superior to the East. I think a type of character is forming there which will eclipse anything that has yet appeared in the Atlantic states, though that character may yet be a long way off from literature. Neither did I wish to be understood as referring to 'Katrina' as a work of true culture. It perhaps represents the average culture of the schools and churches, and its author has doubtless been cultivated fully up to his capacity for culture.

I appreciate the need of good nature and hearty coöperation among literary men,[1] as much as any one, but we must be aware what price we are paying for them. I think Lessing's example as a critic a good one for young men to emulate; and that soft words may not always be the best. The class of poets who aspire to foster and lead public taste in this country is intensely obnoxious to me, because I see such are the sworn enemies of any large, generous growth. The great standards, and the principle of universal Nature, need to be revived and enforced at all hazards.

Let me call your attention to Whitman's article on *Personalism* in the May Galaxy, which I think contains the deepest, largest word ever spoken on the subject of culture.

Illustrative of the pervasive influence of Whitman upon Burroughs, are the facts that not only was his first book about Whitman, but that the last essay ('The Poet of the Cosmos') in his last book published during his lifetime ('Accepting the Universe'), was also about him. He was never done with Whitman, any more than with the birds.

4. The Literary Craftsman

Absorbing as was the comradeship with Whitman, and much as it stimulated to mental activity, the daily work of the Currency Bureau exacted of the Treasury Clerk its toll of hours. Still, as already seen, there were times when, seated at his high mahogany desk, his imagination playing truant, he roamed far afield, first living over again his days in the

---

[1] Burroughs and Higginson met pleasantly some months later, and again and again, years later; and while Burroughs succumbed to the personal charm of Higginson, the latter was always something of a thorn in the flesh to him, because of his jibes and slighting remarks about Whitman throughout the years.

open, then re-creating them with his pen. On holidays, Nature beckoned from the nearby wilds, and in the summer vacations in his native State his experiences yielded, among other essays, the well-known 'Birch Browsings' ('Wake-Robin'), 'Speckled Trout,' and 'A Bed of Boughs' ('Locusts and Wild Honey'). Thus, with shreds and patches of time, slowly but steadily, he acquired the confidence and skill of the literary craftsman.

A glimpse of the trip to the elusive Thomas's Lake, familiar to his reader, is given in a letter to Mrs. Burroughs, in the summer of 1868:

When your letter was being written, your 'country correspondent' was wandering about, half famished, torn and dirty, and with the points of the compass sadly mixed up in his head, in the Beaverkill mountains. On Saturday afternoon, about five o'clock, we (Hi Corbin, Hi Burroughs, and I) left our team at the head of Millbrook, and, knapsacks on our backs, plunged into the woods, bound for a trout lake far in the mountains. On Monday afternoon, about the same time of day, we emerged from the woods not three rods from the place where we went in, expecting or fearing we were coming out ten miles away.

In the mean time we had done some fearful marching, had been lost two or three times, but had found the lake and tasted its trout. Tuesday night we got home. I am in hopes I can make a piece of it — 'Among the Birches' ['Birch Browsings']. At any rate, it was fruitful to me in much besides trout. . . .

The next summer he gives the following account of his camping experiences:

We have eaten trout by the hundred. I am meditating an article on 'Speckled Trout.' I was headachey the first day, but since have been as hearty as a bear. So has [Aaron] Johns. He is a capital fellow in the woods or out of them. Yesterday we marched about fifteen miles in half a day, over mountains and through woods. . . . You would have fainted away if you could have seen us, we were so 'nasty.' John's gaiters just hung to his feet when we got here, and I was in tatters and rags, but both of us good for any number of miles more. I wish you could have had some of the trout we caught. At Balsam Lake, during a thunder shower that drenched Johns and me to the skin, I caught from a dugout 75 as beautiful trout in about two hours as ever swam. It was such fun! Sometimes I would haul in two at a time, as I had two flies on my line. . . .

I long to see you again and to be with you. You must keep your spirits up and not get lonely; and take it easy at all hazards. Write to me at once how you are getting along. . . .

A dearly loved nephew, Chauncey B. Deyo, affectionately called, 'Channy B.,' who had many a camp and tramp with John Burroughs in the Catskills, was in Washington during a part of Burroughs's sojourn there. The companionship of Channy was one of the most precious things in his uncle's life. 'Channy B.' is found on many pages of his books. He it was in the hemlocks who helped gather much of the material for that essay; together they followed the streams for trout, and they shared many a wild-honey quest. It was Channy who caught a swarm of bees in his hat; and who, on seeing frog-spawn in the creek (see 'Spring at the Capital'), said it looked good enough to eat; it was Channy who skated with him on Rock Creek, and with him tramped about the city. He was 'the bright and curious boy' mentioned in 'Birds' Nests,' who found a certain chickadee's nest in a wild-cherry on the summit of Old Clump, when even John o' Birds would have given it up; and who helped find the nests of the black-throated blue, and the mourning ground-warbler, which John Burroughs was the first to describe.[1]

A letter to Benton, dated January 27th, hints at the current activities and opinions of Burroughs:

The Atlantic gave me $250 for three articles. . . . The Galaxy has an article of mine which I look for in the next number, called 'A Hint from Lessing.' I have another bird article partly finished which I shall send to Lippincott. Do you know what they pay? 'Putt' is too slow. I am now meditating an article on the Cow. I dare say you have many observations and incidents that would be valuable to me if I could get them out of you. I have the germ of another article, on the Bumble-bee, and have in my drawer, awaiting revision, an article on Victor Hugo.

I spent an evening not long since with Higginson. He lectured here. . . . He is bright and witty in conversation, and no doubt a good fellow. I feel the same want in the man that I do in the author — a want of unction, heartiness, common and broad grounds of character. The god of his idolatry is a well-turned sentence. Higginson will make a graceful, but not a deep and lasting mark. Last evening we were at a little party where Grace Greenwood was one of the lions. She is bright and amusing, like all literary persons — but myself. . . .

I am glad you have undertaken a story. I really think you can do something big in this direction if you only throw yourself into it. Your touch certainly recalls Hawthorne's, but you have not Haw-

[1] Baird, Brewer, and Ridgway's *History of North American Birds.*

thorne's industry, nor his ready command of all his resources. You
need to work like Jehu, and to let yourself out. The great trouble of
men of your temperament, and of my temperament, is that we are
too reserved, too cautious. We do not get up heat and motion
enough. Such men as O'Connor and Victor Hugo err in the other
direction. They beat the air wildly. Their writing is a conflagration.
I constantly feel that I need more swing. We want nothing sensa-
tional, but a work cannot be too striking and deep-cut. I think you
will not fail for want of dramatic talent. You need to look to the
features of your work, to give it point and variety. . . .

I have been led to investigate Victor Hugo from hearing O'Connor
blow so much about him. I could not bear him at all at one time, but
think much better of him after reading him. He is great in some
directions and monstrous in others. I can never accept him as a
creator, but there are lyrical touches in his works which are wonderful. My article is severe upon him as an artist or a novelist, but I
find much in him to admire. When I begin an article I cannot rest
day or night till I have finished it. I am happy only when I am working at it. I do most of my writing in the office. My work is such that
I have two or three hours each day to myself. Intrenched behind my
high desk, I can defy any uproar and confusion. When the weather
is cold, and the air full of oxygen, I can write nights.

I have not read the 'Spanish Gypsy.' I read 'Adam Bede' not
long since, and liked it, though I should not expect a great work of
any kind from the author, much less a great poem. Browning I do
not read. He is not much to me and never can be. I see his marvellous skill, his wit, his 'many-colored intellectual lights,' to use a
phrase of the London Spectator, but I do not see[1] a great personality, or a lovable man, and I doubt if he has the final touch which
makes a man a creator.

All I know of Eugene Benson is that he is a New York artist. I
read his essays with pleasure, but am often vexed at his want of
discrimination. His praise of Henry James makes me distrust his
judgment in other matters: in writing of one of the World editors he
compares him to all the great French wits, past and present. He is
in the wilderness in regard to all matters in art or life or politics, and
will always remain there. But he is a great advance on the old,
prosy, respectable essayist.

Why not come down and help me inaugurate Grant? . . .

That year Burroughs reviewed in the Nation the 'Life of
Audubon,' by Mrs. Audubon, revealing in the review his own
enthusiasm for the pioneer ornithologist whose work had so
signally influenced his own career.

[1] One is reminded here of Turner's rejoinder when a lady told him she did not
see the colors he saw in nature — 'But don't you wish you *could*, madam?' Mr.
Burroughs never read enough of George Eliot to form a fair estimate; and never
overcame these early limitations in his appreciation of Browning.

During 1870 he wrote chiefly for the Galaxy and Appleton. 'Spring and the Poets' and 'More About Nature and the Poets' are essays of this period.

The wife's health again declining, and his attempts at combining clerical, literary, and domestic work proving too exacting, they sub-let their house, she going North to relatives, he boarding in the city.

Toward the close of the year he wrote Benton of his forthcoming book of nature sketches:

What do you suppose I have christened the book? I know you will not like the title at first, for none of my friends have, but all are delighted with it after a while. I have tried in vain to hit on a specific title that was not hackneyed, and so sought for some word or phrase or name that should be thoroughly in the atmosphere of the book. Hence I call it 'Wake-Robin,' the common name, you know, for the nodding trillium.

The first piece is called 'The Return of the Birds,' and I casually introduce the name of the flower whose name I have appropriated, on the first page, as suggestive of the universal awakening of Nature. Tell me what you think. When does the trillium bloom with you?

If Hurd and Houghton do not take the book, I will try some one else.[1]

Did you see O'Connor's onslaught in Appleton's? It was the latter part of October. He walked into my 'Mad Dog' [an article characterizing Hugo's as a 'mad-dog nature'] in his usual style, and belabored the poor beast well. I sent my reply off the next week, but Appleton refused to allow the controversy to go on. They thought my reply excellent, but, I suspect, as the publishers of Victor Hugo, did not like to have his works attacked. So I doubled the dose and sent it to the Galaxy; but as it generally takes three months to hear from the Galaxy, I probably shall not know the fate of the article till Spring; or the fate of another called 'Bull in our Book-shop again,' which I sent shortly after. The latter piece was written *apropos* of the article in the Westminster Review on American literature. . . .

In an essay written in 1870, 'More About Nature and the Poets' ('Appleton's Journal'), after taking Victor Hugo, Byron, and others to task for not having dealt honestly with Nature, Burroughs ends with a passage characteristic of his writing at the time — either an allusion, or a direct mention of Whitman:

[1] Hurd and Houghton took the book, and that firm, long since Houghton Mifflin Company, has been his publishers ever since.

Where is the poet who strikes his roots down deep and draws up for us the rude vigor and freshness of the earth itself? a poet in whom Nature wells up full and lusty, overriding and keeping under all mere prettiness and excrescences, and making his words rank and savory, and an insult to our dainty euphemisms, and to the sentimental gallantries with Nature?

If we except Walt Whitman, a bard certainly aboriginal and virile enough, and one thoroughly Greek in his attitude toward man, who else is there?

In April, Mr. and Mrs. Burroughs again installed themselves in their house on V Street. From Roxbury, in midsummer, writing his wife of his adventures on the Beaverkill, he adds:

I found our folks glad to see me and sorry you did not come along. ... Sentence of death has been pronounced against the old rooster, and tomorrow his head will come to the block. I wish you were here to pick a bone with me. Take good care of yourself and don't worry or fret. They like your picture much, and have many questions to ask about you. I tell them you are a trump — a right bower. ...

About that time he and a friend contemplated engaging in trout-culture, a copious cold spring near Washington seeming well adapted for the purpose. Counting his fish before they were hatched, his dreams were similar, if soberer, to those anent the patent harness-buckle of the earlier days. Fortunately, difficulties in getting control of the land caused them to relinquish the plan.

The following entry is from his note-book, December 21st:

Walt said a friend of his, Mr. Marvin, met Emerson in Boston the other day and when Walt was mentioned Mr. Emerson said, 'Yes, Walt[1] sends me his books. But tell Walt I am not satisfied, not satisfied. I expect — him — to make — the songs of the — nation — but he seems to be contented to — make the inventories.' Walt laughed and said it tickled him much. It was capital. But it did not disturb him at all. 'I know what I am about better than Emerson does. Yet I love to hear what the gods have to say.' And, continuing, he said: 'I see how I might have wandered into other and easier paths than I did — paths that would have paid better, and gained me popularity — and I wonder how my feet were guided as they were. Indeed, I am more than satisfied with myself for having the courage to do what I have.'

Among the influences of the early seventies in Washington, besides those already named, were Tyndall's great illustrated

[1] Isn't it probable that Emerson said 'Whitman,' rather than 'Walt'?

lectures on Light (which furnished Burroughs a felicitous comparison in his essay on Emerson in 'Birds and Poets'), Youmans's lecture 'The Chemistry of a Sunbeam,' and Agassiz's on the Amazon. 'He held the Amazon, as it were, in the hollow of his hand,' he said years later in speaking of Agassiz. Justin McCarthy and Judge John P. Hale were also among those he remembered hearing in those years.

When 'Wake-Robin' was published, its author, writing Benton about it, said he thought now he was about done writing about the birds![1]

The book gained a gratifying reception from the reviewers. Helen Hunt reviewed it in 'Scribner's,' and Howells in the 'Atlantic.' Among the many time-stained book-notices, it is characterized as 'the best summer book yet seen,' as 'a perfect pastoral, with the voices of birds ringing through it, its chapters all held together by a thread of song.' Some reviewers likened the new author to Thoreau, others to Higginson. One, delighting in the birds 'about which he gossips so pleasantly,' pertinently said that, like White's 'Selborne,' 'Wake-Robin' had a character of its own. Some thought it chiefly interesting in recalling one's childish memories. Another hoped it would prevent boys from throwing stones at birds! Still another pronounced it 'a book about the birds by one who knows and loves them — not a dry catalogue, but an exhibition of live birds on the wing, and in the nest; birds in love, and birds in song; birds at work, and birds at play.' Helen Hunt said that all lovers of the woods would surely find it; and recommended it for the spiritually halt and maimed and blind, 'as one would crutches for cripples, or glasses for short-sighted eyes.' 'Begin the book and you will finish it,' said another reviewer, 'and finish it, and you will again begin it.' Howells said of it, in part:

The dusk and cool and quiet of the forest seem to wrap the reader. ... It is a sort of summer vacation to turn its pages. It is written with a grace which continually subordinates itself to the material, but which we hope will not escape the recognition of the reader. ... Perhaps it would be difficult not to be natural and simple in writing of such things as our author treats ... but Mr. Burroughs adds a

[1] He was still writing about them in the beginning of 1921 when the illness came upon him which forced him forever to lay aside his pen,
'My heart shoots into the heart of the bird,
And it will for sheer love till the last long sigh.'

strain of genuine poetry which makes his papers unusually delightful, while he has more humor than generally falls to the ornithological tribe. His nerves have a poetic sensitiveness, his eye a
poetical quickness; and many of his descriptive passages impart all
the thrill of his subtle observation. It is in every way an uncommon
book that he has given us; fresh, wholesome, sweet, and full of a
gentle and thoughtful spirit; a beautiful book within, and (thanks to
the growing taste of our publishers) an exceedingly pretty book
without.

After such appreciation, it seems as though John Burroughs
must have begun to feel that his 'Own' had come to him; and,
since honor in his own country was not withheld, he was
perhaps the less surprised to receive generous criticism
abroad. Moncure D. Conway wrote enthusiastically from
London; and from Dublin, Edward Dowden[1] sent gracious
acknowledgment of the book in which he found 'a sense of
life and growth and secret nourishment . . . so genuine, even
at second hand, as to make it restorative to the mind's eye
. . . like a growth of nature . . . sunlit, fresh, nutritious. . . .
Virtue proceeds out of anything so real, so faithful, and
affectionate.'

The high-water mark of gratification must, however, have
been reached by the author when (though not until the wake-
robins had bloomed and faded for three more seasons) he
received the following from one so competent to judge as was
Dr. Elliott Coues, who wrote as follows on February 5, 1874:

My normal state has been for some years that of a 'wader'
through books about birds, till I have come to regard ornithological
literature as just so much shop-work. . . . Your book has been to me
a green spot in the wilderness, where I have lingered with rare
pleasure, enjoying the birds as nowhere else excepting in the woods
and fields — where you carry me straightway.

. . . I . . . can bear witness to the minute fidelity and vividness of
your portraiture. How many things you saw — how many more you
felt. . . . You bring it all back to me — things which I felt at the
time, but which passed like last night's dream, I find here fixed and
crystallized clear.

I have learned from you, too; the golden-crowned thrush never
sang to me as he has to you; when the grass-finch spoke to me, I did

[1] To Mrs. Edward Dowden I am indebted for the gift of the letters from J. B.
to E. D.; and for her permission to quote from her husband's letters. She and Miss
Hilda Dowden, and J. M. Dent & Co., also gave permission to quote from the
letters of both E. D. and J. B., already published in *Edward Dowden and his Correspondents.*

not understand. . . . I never read thrush-music entirely aright before, nor had the least idea where the Canadian warbler built its nest.

Years ago, when I bent almost breathless over Audubon, he told me of strange, wonderful things that fairly made my heart leap. . . . Now you come to tell me things no longer strange or wonderful, indeed, but, like a friend, pointing out new beauties I missed before, and recalling vividly those which I knew, but which, like jewels long possessed, were not appreciated, were even neglected. . . .

Nearly all the reviewers felt it necessary to explain that 'Wake-Robin,' though named from an early spring flower, was about the birds. Indeed, the title, at first glance, does seem a little remote from the birds, while the word 'robin' has, in this connection, ever proved misleading. Only a few years ago Mr. Burroughs came into the house one morning, his eyes twinkling merrily, as he told of meeting a strange workman up the road, in carpenter's apron, who had stopped him to tell of his neighbor in Esopus who knew him well: 'She has one of your books — about a robin — Wake up, Robin, or something like that — and says *she knew that robin* — it had a nest near her house, when she lived in this neighborhood.'

5. OVERSEAS

In the closing months of 1871 the Treasury clerk and two other employees were sent to England by the Government to convey fifteen millions in United States bonds, and to superintend the destruction of the old ones.

Four inimitable essays in 'Winter Sunshine' grew out of that October abroad. In them one sees the untraveled writer who, 'like a wolf clamorous to be fed,' devours each novel sight and sound. The landsman's first experience with the savage sea; his sympathy with the little wood-bird that, having lost its reckoning, came aboard ship as they were losing sight of land; the keenness of delight on going ashore — all is detailed with charm and originality. He approached England in a way all his own, and in his own way he gives the lay of the land, and the look of its people. One is somewhat prepared for his enthusiasm for the mother country, but hardly for the account of his London experiences, notably the emotion he felt on entering St. Paul's cathedral. Even more welcome than the published description is a letter he wrote Whitman, on that first day, from Inns of Court Hotel:

Dear Walt,

I am writing to you on the spur of the moment in hopes it will bring me to my senses, for I am quite stunned at the first glance of London. I have just come from St. Paul's and feel very strange. I don't know what is the matter with me but I seem in a dream. St. Paul's was too much for me and my brain actually reels. I have never seen architecture before. It made me drunk. I have seen a building with a living soul. I can't tell you about it now. I saw for the first time what power and imagination could be put in form and design — I felt for a moment what great genius was in this field. But I had to retreat after sitting down a half-hour and trying to absorb it. I feel as if I should go nowhere else while in London. I must master it or it will kill me. I actually grew faint. I was not prepared for it and I thought my companions, the Treasury clerks, would drive me mad, they rushed around so. I had to leave them and sit down. Hereafter I must go alone everywhere. My brain is too sensitive. I am not strong enough to confront these things all at once.

I would give anything if you was [sic] here. I see now that you belong here — these things are akin to your spirit. You would see your own in St. Paul's; but it took my breath away. It was more than I could bear, and I will have to gird up my loins and try it many times. Outside it has the beauty and grandeur of rocks and crags and ledges. It is nature and art fused into one. Of course Time has done much for it, it is so stained and weatherworn. It is like a Rembrandt picture, so strong and deep is the light and shade.

It is more to see the Old World than I had dreamed, much more. I thought Art was of little account, but now I get a glimpse of the real article, I am overwhelmed.

I had designed to go on the Continent, but I shall not stir out of London until I have vanquished some part of it at least. If I lose my wits here, why go further? But I shall make a brave fight. I only wish I had help. These fellows are like monkeys.

I have seen no one yet, but shall try to see Conway tomorrow. I write this, dear Walt, to help recover myself. I know it contains nothing you might expect to hear from me in London, but I have got into Niagara without knowing it, and you must bear with me. I will give facts and details next time.

Go and see Ursula.

With much love

John Burroughs

Other aspects than are recorded in the essays are found in his letters home:

I am now in London and can hear the great city roar around me. Our safes have been delivered and all is well. Judge R—— says we are at liberty to do and go where we please. . . . He said we would be allowed 6 dollars a day in gold for expenses from the time we landed till we sailed on our return, and he thought we could go around a good deal on that. I shall go to Paris, and perhaps to Switzerland. I think I can live on 3 dollars a day and travel on 3.[1] . . .

Today we have come through the heart of England, and such a country I never saw — one vast garden. The train from Liverpool to London rushes at a fearful rate of speed — from 50 to 60, and occasionally 70, miles an hour. I shall probably write some letters to the Sunday Chronicle.[2] . . . I wish you were here very much. You would enjoy the whole thing hugely. We will come sometime. I think of you and dream of you often. I do hope you keep well and are not too lonely. . . .

[J. B. to U. B. October 10]

. . . We have just heard of the appalling fire in Chicago. How terrible it is! I do hope Mr. and Mrs. Johns are not sufferers by it. I have been in London now one week and a day. . . . I am out sight-seeing every day in museums, parks, cathedrals, picture halls, and galleries, and am more and more astonished at the magnitude of London and the vastness of its collections of all kinds. I look and look till my head swims. . . . I am beginning to long for the country, . . . and tomorrow or next day shall go out to Oxford and Stratford, and toward the end of the week leave for Paris, again to be stunned with sights and sounds.

I have seen Conway and dined at his house, and in the evening, to my unbounded delight, he took me down to see Carlyle. The great man was in a very pleasant, genial mood and delighted us for over two hours with his rich and eloquent talk. It was a memorable night for me. Yesterday I dined at the Rossetti's, and spent the evening there. The family consists of two brothers and two sisters, and the mother; the brothers and one of the sisters being noted poets and artists.

I see lots of things here I should like to buy, but I shall make no purchases till I get back from the Continent. . . .

I hope you are well and enjoying yourself. I would give a pound sterling for a kiss, though a saucy little girl at a concert the other night offered to kiss me for half a crown, but I was afraid she would bite me. I won't trust them, would you?

With much love, your devoted   John

A letter written from Paris to H. R. Hulburd, Comptroller of the Currency, October 19th, reads in part as follows:

I believe when I wrote you before I had just entered upon my sight-seeing, and was in a queer kind of commotion. Since then I have cooled down a good deal. Indeed I am nearly sated with sight-seeing, and shall be thoroughly glad when it is all over with. It seems

[1] J. B. said that he made the clerks angry because he held the purse-strings so tight, refusing to let them charge up personal expenses to Uncle Sam.

[2] Search through *Sunday Chronicles* of this period reveals no letters from J. B.

to me I have seen enough museums and pictures and collections of one kind and another to stand me all the rest of my mortal life, be it ever so long. . . . I don't think anything could tempt me now to go on and *do* the rest of the continent. . . . Tennyson says, 'Better forty years of Europe than a cycle of Cathay,' but a little of Cathay would be very acceptable to me just at this time.

After my feast of London joints I came to Paris for my dessert, but my appetite was nearly gone and I have been very dainty in Paris, the most dainty of cities. It really seems to me that Paris is quite monotonous. After you have seen one square, or one Boulevard, you have seen it all. It is certainly very elegant and beautiful, and everything is in excellent taste. The ruins are in admirable taste and the best-behaved I ever saw. One has to look twice to see that they are ruins; the tide of battle and blood that so recently ebbed and flowed through the streets seems to have deported itself most seemly and has left hardly a trace.

The theatres and music halls are the finest I ever saw, and the manners of the waiters in the hotels please one like a work of art; but I have seen the most ugly women since I entered France I ever saw, . . . and the *demi-monde*, as it appears on the streets of Paris, will not compare with what one sees in London.

I came alone to Paris. . . . I regret now that I did not brush up my French before I started, as I have had to pay the most fancy prices for all the English I have got in Paris. Indeed, I have learned to avoid the shops and cafés where English is spoken. . . .

One of the best days I have had was at New Haven, an old town on the south coast of England. It was a beautiful October day and I spent most of it wandering over the South Down hills amid the singing of sky-larks. To hear the famous English larks was one of the things I had fondly hoped for, but hardly expected so late in the season, but this day I heard scores of them. I was disappointed in some respects. The song is not so sweet and melodious as I had expected. In this particular it falls far short of many of our own familiar songsters; but the wonder is its length and continuity, and its strength. There the bird is spread out against the sky two or three hundred feet above the earth, pouring out his song in a perfect ecstacy for eight or ten minutes. It is quite wonderful. The song is of the sparrow kind, and its best notes seem as if copied from the songs of our sparrows. Now if I could only hear the nightingale I should be more than satisfied, but this cannot be.

Another streak of good luck was seeing Carlyle in London and spending an evening at his house. He was in a delightful mood, and it was a rare treat to me to meet the glorious old Scotchman face to face, and hear his voice. There is no British author I so venerate. He was very gentle and grandfatherly, and delighted me with reminiscences about the birds, and about Scott and Scotland. . . .

When he and Conway reached the house in Cheyne Row, in the gloaming, Carlyle was out walking, but soon came in, wearing a long gray coat and slouch hat, his cheeks glowing faintly through the tan. His face had a weather-beaten look. He was then six and seventy years of age. They were there more than two hours, a detaining sign from Carlyle, as they started to leave sooner, causing them to extend their visit.

His [Carlyle's] hair was iron-gray [said Mr. Burroughs]. His eyes were full of unshed tears, and whenever he lapsed into silence, there was a look of unutterable yearning in them. He rested his elbow on the table, and leaned his head upon his hand — this way — his fingers thrust through his hair. He let Conway lead the talk, while he regarded us intently. Yet he talked a good deal, especially of his recent visit to Scotland. The yearning look in his face, and that 'dying fall' in his voice, went to my heart. When he found I was interested in birds, he talked of their birds — the mavis, the linnet, the skylark, the nightingale, and the house-sparrow. He called the sparrow 'a comical little wretch,' imitated its pert ways, cocking his head on one side as he did it. He said it was so bold it would dispute the passage with you. When I told him we had introduced it into America, how he laughed! 'Introduced it, have you? Well, you will rue the day ye did it!' And again that strange, soliloquizing laugh! — I can't describe it — he often laughed during his talk — the laugh seemed to take the sting out of what he said.

Carlyle was the biggest event of that trip, but other personalities yielded him much, and the mellow old-world atmosphere, most of all. He heard James Martineau, Spurgeon, and Conway. Of Spurgeon, many years later, he wrote in his Journal:

Why did a man like Spurgeon, a man of real power, produce no literature? His expression, says the London Academy, was as direct as a blow; and yet very little that he left or said has any literary value. His quality was a personal quality that you felt in his speech, but do not feel in his writing. He could not give himself through his pen. He was a coarse-grained man, and literature demands something fine.

In a letter to Benton on his return:

I saw quite a good deal of Conway while in London, and we used to take some long walks. He is tall and homely, with a sharp, penetrating look, though not a profound look. He holds you in high regard, and had many inquiries to make about you, declaring his intention to visit you when he comes to America.

Of the Conway book I have read only a few chapters. I have no doubt your objections are well taken. I think the book is extremely clever and valuable, but I cannot help but feel that Conway is a little deficient in the heart of him. I fear he is not finally to be relied upon, or is liable to make some great blunder or mistake. I saw quite a good deal of him and his family, and was very kindly treated.

He is a good suggestive talker, and a good walker. He is tall and gaunt, with a homely, fluid, mobile face; the nose a little too fat, and the mouth large and coarse.

I heard him lecture one Sunday night at one of his small chapels, on Sadi, the old Persian poet. It was a good talk. His voice is rather harsh. He has a congregation before which he preaches in the morning, in Conway Chapel. . . .

To Mrs. Burroughs:

I have spent the afternoon wandering over the South Downs (where the famous South Down sheep come from) amid the singing of sky-larks. I enjoyed it hugely and shall write about it. I found a little village sitting on the green grass among the hills, with a very old church — perhaps five or six hundred years old.

I leave for Paris tonight. To go from London to Paris and return costs thirty-six shillings, or about nine dollars. Most of the clerks here have made quite an extended continental tour, but I do not wish to run along so fast. What I see, I wish to see well, though I may go to Antwerp and Brussels and Cologne.

I had a good suit of clothes made in London, and an extra pair of pants, for about twenty dollars. I also got me a fine overcoat for about $15½. I ordered me a sole-leather trunk, extra large, but find I cannot get forty yards of carpet in it and put in my other things. I intend to bring you a silk dress, and perhaps a cloak, or a sealskin jacket. These last take my eye. I see all the best-dressed ladies have them on. I can get a fine one for five guineas, or $26 in gold, and a cloak for 3 guineas. But I will see how my money holds out.

. . . This little withered flower I plucked today on the South Down hills (a scarlet poppy).

On October 28th:

Your letter came this morning. I looked for it two weeks ago. . . . I was very glad to get it, I assure you, but sorry you have been sick, and that you and William's [O'Connor's] family did not get along well. But let it pass.

I bo't one dozen pairs of gloves in Paris and some other things. . . . I shall bring some pictures, though not paintings, but some splendid photographs of celebrated paintings. Good paintings are far beyond my purse, but the photos suit me admirably. . . .

I hope to see you by the 24th of November. At any rate, may the sea not seperate [sic] us always, or, as the old song says,

'May the heavens above me guide me and bring me safe home back again
   To the girl I left behind me.'

                              Your faithful

                                        JOHN

And on November 2d:

I have only received one letter from you yet. . . . I think every day I will not write again, and then in a day or two I find I am at it again.

The Judge has fixed the 16th as the day upon which we may sail. . . . We seldom get to work before 11½ o'clock, and work till five or six, counting, arranging, and cancelling bonds. . . .

Yesterday I made some purchases for you, a silk dress, 18 yds, and a seal-skin jacket. The dress is what they call 'grow-grained silk' [sic], it cost 7/6 per yard, or about two dollars in gold of our money. A N.Y. merchant who came over with us . . . told me it was very cheap, and could not be bought in N.Y. for 5 dollars per yard. The Jacket cost 10 guineas, or 55 dollars in gold — more than I intended to pay, but after I had seen it, I could not buy anything less. They are all the style here and in Paris. In N.Y. it would be worth $125. You see you will have to be a very good girl to pay for all these things, but I guess you have already paid for them. I shall buy a carpet in a few days. The best will cost about $1.25 in gold. . . .

I hope this will be my last letter. . . .

Among old mementoes is found an unfinished letter, written from Stratford on Avon, in November, to an unnamed friend, which contains some passages like certain ones in 'From London to New York.' The subjoined excerpt pictures the traveler at ease in his inn:

I reached Oxford yesterday and came on to Stratford today, and am at this moment seated in the coffee-room of the Red Horse Inn, beside a blazing fire.

There is nothing like home-brewed ale, and one of the cosy coffee-rooms with a bright fire in the grate, to make one contented. Then I have only to touch the bell and in there comes such a pretty house-maid, as fresh and whole as a clover blossom! and I find myself touching the bell pretty often. I ask for some cold meat and bread, and she spreads the cloth and sets before me a whole haunch of mutton, a loaf of bread, and a pint of ale, and, bringing up a chair says, 'It's ready.'

The Red Horse is indeed a comfortable steed, and I would the 'home-brewed' might be my drink for life. I appear to be the only guest, and the quiet and privacy are complete, which are all the more acceptable to me after the rush and roar of London.

The only person I have seen about the Red Horse — except that I got one glimpse of the Boots — is the rosy damsel above referred to. She received me, took charge of my luggage, designated my room, informed me about the trains, and, indeed, has me quite under her wing (not so much under her wing, though, as I would like to be). She has just now popped in to poke up the 'coals,' and to say it is a cold night. I wonder what Will Shakespeare would have said to her?

I see in this sweet homely life the occasion for the exercise of that marvelous mother wit of which he was so full. Here it was where it was fostered and fed, and this delicious domestic ale has played its part.

Stratford is a quiet quaint old town, situated in a level stretch of rich farming country. I seem to see none but common working people here, and no very marked signs of either riches or poverty. Many of the houses evidently date back to Shakespeare's time, and their heavy oak frames with the spaces filled in with brick, still look firm. The church that contains the Poet's tomb is a little out of town, and is a much finer structure than I expected to see, its tall graceful stone spires being visible from all points. The central portion and tower date back to the 12th century, and the other parts to the 15th. The old oak doors of the Poet's time, and before, seem as sound as ever. The architecture is worn and defaced by time — the queer heads and images that project from the walls being barely suggestive of the original design. The Avon — a stream 12 or 15 yards wide, and full to its grassy brim, like all English streams — flows or rather slides noiselessly by.

I expected to see a name and date on Shakespeare's tomb, but there is only the inscription which is so often quoted. . . .

As the sun was about half an hour high I set out for Shatterick [Shottery] to see the house of Anne Hathaway — followed a path that followed hedgerows, skirted turnip fields and cabbage patches and meadows, and crossed pastures to a quaint gathering of low thatched houses. I took a good look at Anne's house, and could easily see the divine William leaning against the door-jamb, or gazing out of the two-by-three window-panes.

Returning I stepped into the Shakespeare Inn, a small, homely, home-made tavern, and the goodwife brought me some home-brewed, which I drank, sitting by a rude table on a rude bench in a little low room with a stone floor and an immense chimney. The fire burned cheerily, and the crane and hooks called up visions of my earliest infancy. Apparently the house, and the atmosphere of it, and the ways of the inmates, were what they were three hundred years ago.

Dublin was memorable to the traveler chiefly from the encounter with the scholarly and winsome Edward Dowden, of whom he wrote Benton:

He is a grave, serious young man of English descent, but of Irish birth and brogue, and I liked him immensely, and his wife — a cultivated, enthusiastic Irish woman.

Walt has many fervent readers in Dublin, and I should have met more of them but for an indisposition caused by a rough passage over the Channel. . . .

An amusing experience in London came near being a serious

one. Almost duped by a scheming German and a wily Englishman, the confiding American was saved in the nick of
time through his unfailing instinct for the genuine. The
episode is described at length in 'John Burroughs, Boy and
Man.' Burroughs himself wrote of it in 'Scribner's Monthly'
(May, 1887) under the title 'A London Adventure.'

In 'From London to New York' Burroughs records that
when abreast of New England, and many miles out at sea, he
distinctly smelt land — 'a subtle, delicious odor of farms and
homesteads, warm and human, that floated on the wild sea
air' — one out of many proofs of the preternatural keenness
of his sense of smell. His nose was not, like Wordsworth's,
'an idle promontory projecting into the desert air,' but one
of the five free channels through which he received messages
from Nature.

Excerpts from a January letter to Benton detail subsequent experiences in Washington:

... I had hardly got settled back into the old routine, when along
comes Emerson and unsettles me for a week, my planet showing
great perturbation in its orbit whenever such a body comes in my
neighborhood. He was advertized to lecture in Baltimore, and away
I go, dragging Walt with me, to hear him; and as Fate would have
it, he enters the vestibule of the hall just as we do, and we have a
little talk.

Walt introduced me. He received me quite warmly, unusually so,
Walt said; and to my consternation proceeded to put me at once on
trial for a remark I made about an observation of Thoreau's, in
'With the Birds.' I defended myself as well as I could, and explained
that I had left it out of the book ['Wake-Robin'] because I had not
been to the Maine Woods. He was good-natured about it. Said he
had 'Wake-Robin' on his table, and had looked into it with a good
deal of interest. Thought the title a capital one — expected to see
an older man in me, etc.

The lecture was on the 'Sources of Inspiration.' His delivery was
not so marked as I expected, yet it was good, his voice having the
ring of purest metal.

From Baltimore he came here and stopped with Senator Sumner.
When he went away I waylaid him at the depot. I stood off at one
side and saw him purchase his ticket. It was amusing to see what
hard work he made of it, fussing and fumbling, at a loss to know what
to do with his gloves, his umbrella, his parcels — very anxious and
earnest, apparently charging himself: 'Now, Old Forgetfulness,
don't leave your ticket or your money, or miss your train, as you
have so often done before.'

He was alone, and had ten or fifteen minutes to spare, so I got him aboard the train, and sat down beside him. He has not changed much since we saw him, except perhaps his nose is a little more hooked, and his hair a little thinner.

I drew him out on Walt, and found out what was the matter. He thought Walt's friends ought to quarrel a little more with him, and insist on his being a little more tame and orderly, more mindful of the requirements of beauty, of art, of culture, all of which was very pitiful to me, and I wanted to tell him so; but the train started just then and I got off. However, I wrote him a letter telling what I thought, and sent him my book. I do not expect to hear from it, but I was determined to give him a shot.[1]

Viewed in the light of the wants or needs of the American people today, and of the great questions and issues about us, nothing can be more irrelevant or pitiful than those lectures he is now delivering. It is like a wriggling of thumbs. I am utterly tired of these scholarly things. Night before last he lectured here on 'Homes,' and I heard him again. It was a good talk, but hardly seemed worth his while to speak, or us to hear. He came and went the same night, and I did not seek him this time.[2]

My nephew [Channy] has been with me since I got home, and we have had lots of fun. Every Sunday we go for a long tramp. He is deeply absorbed in Emerson's books, and they are doing him good. Here is where Emerson is invaluable. At a certain age he is an angel of light to one.

I am sorry to hear you think of overhauling your house ['Trout-beck']. I had rather have the old nest than any house you can build. . . .

The London Athenæum reviews my 'Wake-Robin' rather sharply, and amusingly to me. It makes the mistake of reviewing it under the head of Science instead of Literature, and says my egotism needs taking down; that I tell too much about myself, and not enough about the birds; that I am a master of rounded sentences and fault-less periods with nothing in them; that it is a pity when I got lost in the woods, that I had not staid lost, etc. On the other hand, Pro-fessor Dowden, of Trinity College, writes me very enthusiastically about it, and tells me things from others, as Robert Buchanan,[3] that are very gratifying. . . .

---

[1] An attempt to recover this letter was futile, Mrs. Edward Emerson writing that since the letter was written in 1872 (the year the Emerson house was burned), it was probably burned also.

[2] Whitman said the lectures were like the second brewing of tea. Years later, commenting on his own criticism of them, Mr. Burroughs explained:

It was during the reconstruction period. The lectures were full of idealism, but they seemed unsuited to our needs. In a book such an essay is like a star, but on the lecture platform it was rather ineffectual. But they were all right, in a way. Emerson couldn't unhitch his wagon from a star to drag our little burdens to market.

[3] 'Robert Buchanan,' J. B. explained, 'was a Scottish poet and critic who pitched into the fleshly school — Rossetti and others — and also wrote about Whitman, but treated him in a jaunty sort of way — did not appreciate his greatness.'

An appreciative letter from Dowden to Burroughs concerning the latter's 'Notes' on Whitman, called forth the response which follows, which, apart from the value of its critical comments, gives a glimpse into the innermost nature of Burroughs. In this letter he speaks of his companionship with Nature:

Your letter sent a warm glow through me, under the influence of which I took out my little book and read parts of it over for the first time in a long while. In the light of your approval it seemed better than it had ever seemed before. Mr. Whitman himself likes the book, and thinks it will stand, so does Mr. O'Connor; and *I am indebted largely to both of them for aid in getting the matter into shape.* [Italics mine.] But the book has had no audience in this country. I sent it to most of the critics and literary men, but they said not a word. The N.Y. Tribune gave me a good notice, but the other journals steered clear of it. Less than a hundred copies have been sold.

I have myself never been satisfied with the passage on Wordsworth, and it never would have been allowed to stand, had not Whitman and O'Connor both commended it highly, neither of whom, I have since made up my mind, do Wordsworth justice.

I read Wordsworth a good deal, and find my own in his pages, and shall soon attempt an essay upon him. The right word about him I have not yet seen spoken, nor has it come to me to speak it. I think he is the first and the highest of the modern solitary poets, and that he speaks, or sings, warmly and genuinely, even grandly, out of that solitude which lurks by mountain lakes, and broods over lonely moors. He is to me the greatest of the interpreters of this phase of nature, but I do not recognize the creative touch in him. Wordsworth expresses to me that delicious companionship which I have with the silent forms and shows of rural nature, and which I am half ashamed I do not have with men, and with towns and cities. I think it is something of the 'homesickness' that Schiller speaks of; while Whitman expresses to me the life and power of the globe itself, and lets me into the secret of creation. His poems rival the elemental laws and the great dynamic forces. They are *deeds* and not *thoughts*, and have the same intimate direct personal relation to himself that a man's proper act has to himself.

I am not satisfied with my allusion to Tennyson, either, though it is doubtless true in that connection. But I think Tennyson a noble poet — that he has the real 'fluid and attaching character,' and will live. He does not belong to the morning of the world, like Whitman, but rather to its sunset; but this phase has its place also.

Whitman has been absent in New York over a month, bringing out another edition of his books. Do you know of John Addington Symonds? He writes Whitman some very appreciative letters, and has sent him quite a long poem in print, inspired, he says, by Whitman's 'Calamus.' It is lofty and symphonous, and reminds of Shelley. . . .

I am not going to allow you to disparage your article in the Westminster. At that distance from Whitman it is a marvel to me how you could grasp him so completely. I am sure I could never have written my book, had I not known Whitman intimately and long. There is no distinction between the man and the poet, and to know one is to know the other. The article is very lofty and effective, and the first half of it is positively a new contribution to the science of criticism. It makes a new and for us immensely important classification. . . .

I think his treatment of the sexual part of man perfectly consistent with his scheme, and no more bold and unconventional or inartistic than his treatment of any other part. Poetry must be as pure as science, and the subject, if handled at all, must be handled without reservation or insinuation, and solely with reference to offspring. If people are shocked — and they *are* shocked — I was shocked — it is because we are not used to cold water upon this subject, but expect something much more sweet and spicy. . . .

The year of 1872 was comparatively uneventful for Burroughs. Besides the work in the Currency Bureau, he wrote on his European trip, tramped the woods, and fled to his native hills when vacation came.

In November, he wrote Benton of having just finished a paper on 'The Birds of the Poets,' adding:

Of course I voted for Grant. I was never a believer in Greeley. To me he was neither fish, flesh, nor fowl. We know well enough what would undoubtedly have happened, had he been in Lincoln's place, and that settled him for me, as I guess it did for the people. . . .

By this time, weary of Washington, — 'tired of eating Government dirt,' — Burroughs was casting about for something whereby he could 'earn his victuals and have plenty of time to scribble.'

On the last day of the year, resigning his position in the Treasury Department, Burroughs left Washington almost as abruptly as he had quit school-teaching some nine years before. By this time it will have been gathered that, however deliberate he was in thought, he was often impulsive, even precipitate, in action. Under trying conditions he could be patient and long-suffering; could submit to irksome tasks, and to a surprising amount of routine and drudgery; but suddenly something within him would take the bit in its teeth, when, with unreasoning impetuosity, he would kick over the traces, leap over, or break through, the bars, and escape to pastures new.

In leaving Washington, however, he was by no means freed from the coat-tails of Uncle Sam; for, being appointed receiver of a broken bank in the city of Middletown, New York, he immediately went there and engaged in the unaccustomed work.

One of the last pieces of writing he did in Washington was 'The Exhilarations of the Road' ('Winter Sunshine') — an essay which takes the reader forth on a gleesome saunter, the foot striking fire at every step; the air tasting like a new and finer mixture; the walkers accumulating force and gladness as they go. On such jaunts about Washington, he had, among others, as companions, W. L. Shoemaker, E. J. Loomis, one Parnell, and Mr. Henry Litchfield West. Shoemaker and Loomis came to him, attracted by his writings. Loomis had once boarded with the mother of Thoreau; had eaten at the table with her gifted son, walked with him in the Concord woods and along the Musketaquid, and bathed with him in Walden Pond. One likes to think of the talks the happy saunterers had in the environs of Washington, with reminiscences of Concord by the way.

Once, within the last few years, when, along a country road, we encountered some young pedestrians with their camping equipment swung across their shoulders, Mr. Burroughs said: 'Whenever I see young men walking through the country like that, I sometimes flatter myself that maybe my books have had a share in sending them forth.' To read the before-mentioned essay, in which he preaches so alluringly the gospel of walking, is to agree that it undoubtedly had such a share.

What a walker he himself was! and how he loved the old paths where he walked! — about Roxbury, Washington, Middletown, and his Hudson River home, and in countless other haunts in woods and fields, — alone, or with friends! There was something peculiarly characteristic in the way he walked — the way he put down and lifted his feet; a direct, firm implantation of the feet upon the ground; no fumbling, but an involuntary precision and surefootedness, as though spirit and body were in perfect unison, the spirit informing the feet — a quiet tread in the woods, a directness and eager-

ness upon the hills — something in the press of his foot to
the earth that seemed peculiarly his; a something difficult to
describe, but which those who have followed him up a hill,
or along a woodland path, must have noticed. I used to
search in my mind for words to describe it when following his
footsteps, but could not find them. Nor can I now; but the
paths he frequented with his friends, the trees under which
they tarried, the springs at which they have quenched their
thirst, the mountain-tops from which they have looked off
— a something intangible will ever linger in those places, and
in them, together, in silence, the friends will walk forever.

CHAPTER V

BACK TO THE SOIL

1873–1876

Smile, O voluptuous cool-breath'd earth!
Earth of the slumbering and liquid trees!
Earth of departed sunset — earth of the mountains misty-topt!
Earth of the vitreous pour of the full moon just tinged with blue!
Earth of shine and dark mottling the tide of the river!
Earth of the limpid gray of clouds brighter and clearer for my sake!
Far-swooping elbow'd earth — rich apple-blossomed earth!
Smile, for your lover comes.

WHITMAN

WHEN, at the age of thirty-six, Burroughs resigned his position in the Treasury Department, and went back to his native State, he began truly to come into his own. Nature, during the preceding ten years in the city, had called him unceasingly; now he was to heed her call; he would 'hear the bravuras of birds,' and 'the bustle of growing wheat,' and give himself freely to that which satisfies 'more than the metaphysics of books.' Before leaving Washington, his yeoman ancestry becoming rampant, he had written Benton that he felt like a fowl with no gravel in its gizzard — was hungry for the earth — could almost eat it like a horse if he could get at it.

He was now by way of becoming the essayist whose page savors of the soil and of the hardiness and plenitude of rural things. In Washington he had published two books; the other twenty-five were to follow gradually.

Although in resigning his clerkship he had taken the first step toward realizing his dream of a home in the country, he was to remain for several succeeding years in the service of the government. Beginning his work as receiver of an insolvent bank in Middletown, New York, on January 1, 1873, he was occupied with the disentangling of the bank's affairs and long-drawn-out litigations for four or five years. He also acted as special National Bank Examiner for districts along the Hudson, in other sections of the Empire State, and in certain sections of Virginia — work consuming four or five months of each year, which, with his receivership, yielded him between fourteen and fifteen hundred dollars. The bank-examining lasted till 1885, or a little later, when he was ousted by the

Cleveland Administration and his twenty-one years in Government employ terminated.

Once, to the remark that it was difficult to associate him with banks, he rejoined, 'Well, I did it for a good many years, but "I know a bank where the wild thyme grows," and I like to examine that kind a great deal better.' When a correspondent who had found delight in his bird articles learned of his new occupation, he begged him not to let broken banks interfere too much with the birds. The danger was that the birds would interfere with the banks. Certain it is, he had an eye on the birds when driving about the country, and much that went into the essays of that period was gathered while going from bank to bank.

To his wife, still in Washington, he wrote of the mixed-up affairs of the insolvent bank being dumped upon him all at once:

A receiver, to thoroughly know his business, ought to be a practical lawyer, a practical banker, and ought to have been a receiver of at least four banks. So you see how much I have to learn.

'I was not a good examiner,' he acknowledged, 'was not up to their ways; had not the training, and made hard work of it. I was painstaking, but was easily deceived. I made a good many angry because I reported things I found unsatisfactory.'

Yet, distasteful and incongruous as was the work, he pursued it with a fidelity that won ready recognition; and in time offered aid most acceptable to men engaged in banking business as a life-work, a case in point being an article called 'Broken Banks and Lax Directors.'[1]

From the accompanying letter to Whitman, written from Middletown, January 12th, one gets a glimpse of the new work upon which Burroughs had entered:

I have thought of you very often since I have been up here, but have hardly had the time to write and tell you so. I left W[ashington] in great haste, and since I have been here have been in the midst of a very maelstrom of business, all new, all strange, and very mixed. But I am now fairly master of the situation; and though I do not expect my troubles are over, yet I am better prepared to meet them. I have got a good accountant, a competent attorney, a balance in the bank, and ought to be happy; but it cost me a pang to leave W. I was so warm and snug and my nest was so well-feathered;

[1] *Century Magazine*, March, 1882.

but I have really cut loose and do not expect to return again except briefly. I can make more money here, be much freer, be nearer home, and have a new field for duties. My greatest loss will be in you, my dear Walt; but then I shall look forward to having you up here a good long time at a stretch, which will be better than the crumbs I used to get of you in W.

I expect it will take me a year or more to close up this bank; then I shall make me another nest, among the rocks of the Hudson, and try life, my own master.

I hope you are well and will write to me, and will go up and see my wife. . . .

I have collected and turned over to the Government thirteen thousand dollars since I have been here, and have about a hundred thousand dollars more to collect. By and by I shall have plenty of time to myself.

The letters which passed back and forth between Middletown and Washington during the first part of 1873 show how dependent was the bank-examiner upon the comforts of a home and wifely care; show the wife's solicitude for him, and his anxious thought of her, lest she be lonely or 'blue.' He praises her for being brave, but chides her for letting the maid go, fearing she will work too hard. She asks about his 'peaces,' and he tells of their acceptance, sending on checks for the same. The baby-talk (in which, on occasion, she indulged even in her eighty-first year), and the pet names she gives him, are amusingly queer — Lunkey Punkey, Jolly Dolly, Domp, and Dompey — while his for her are Baby, Blue-Jay, Periwinkle, Chicken, and Pickaninny.

She writes of Walt's bringing her magazines with her husband's essays in them, one of which elicited the comment, 'It pleased me very much, some of it was real funny.' She tells of a powerful sermon she heard, wishing he could have heard it also, and adds, 'Be a good child and do what's right, and the Lord will reward you in due time.' She writes of seeing Janauschek; of regular visits to her physician; of the persons who come to look at their advertised house; of the curls and the 'switch' she has had made; and gives explicit details as to her wardrobe, with statements of the costs. He comments amiably; is pleased that she is pleased about her 'switch' and her dress-making; but begs her not to render him an account of such expenditures, as he knows she is economical; she must rent or sell the house as seems best to her; and he hopes they can find a cosy little place in Middletown, and begin housekeeping in the spring:

I see the Lord takes good care that, because of my grumbling about your sweeping and over-neatness, I shall get a good dose of the opposite thing when I am away. The woman, I guess, never sweeps, never scours her knives and forks, and only about half washes her dishes.

You are so fond of sausage, I wish you could breakfast with me: we have sausage five mornings out of six! Then her pancakes! How she can pervert innocent flour so, I do not understand. They are either heavy or sour, and are always black as if baked in the ashes.

He tells her of a merchant, one of her old flames, who he is expecting will soon call for his dividends:

I shall take him in to the Directors' room, and with an air of great mystery, ask him if he ever knew 'black-eyed Susan.' If he pleads guilty, I shall make him own up to all the little pleasant pastimes you and he used to engage in. Then — oh, then — I shall take him out to take a drink!

Replying, she urges him, on the coming of her friend, to try to be as dignified as possible. (Dignity always was one of her strong points, and it was ever a sore trial that her husband was so lacking in it, or in what she considered dignity. His simple, natural manner was never quite to her liking. It would have pleased her better had he shown more pride in himself, taken more pains in dress, impressed people more with his importance. His meekness, or humility, was something she could neither understand nor abide.) She hopes he will get a more satisfactory boarding-place; tells how lonely she is; sends him the 'Sunday Chronicle,' a wash-cloth, and her photograph, and tells of Whitman's illness. A significant paragraph in his reply runs thus:

It made me feel quite proud that Professor Tyndall at a farewell dinner given in New York the other day referred in his speech to an article in the Galaxy which had touched a sympathetic chord in his bosom, which article was written by your good-for-nothing 'Domp.' Go and see Walt and write how he is. . . .

Almost a half-century later Mr. Burroughs said that Tyndall, in speaking to a friend of that article ('From London to New York'), had declared it made him so homesick he wanted to take the first steamer for England. Praise as mere praise had little weight with John Burroughs; it was the source that counted, and this from Tyndall had gratified him exceedingly.

In a later letter to his wife he writes:

I see the Nation gave my Galaxy article a big puff last week, but I hate the Nation for all that. [Because it was unfriendly to Whitman.] I am so glad Walt is better. . . . Nurse him up well, if he comes up. Keep up your courage, and send me lots of love, and I will send much back again.

At another time he writes characteristically: 'I am glad to hear about Walt, and that you are kind to him. Love me, love Walt.'

RIVERBY

Early in 1873, prospecting for his home in the country, first on Long Island, then along the Hudson, Burroughs finally decided upon a nine-acre farm on the west shore of the river, some eighty miles north of New York.[1]

Though he was eagerly looking for a place to build, he could not regard the sale of their house in Washington without a reminiscent sigh, — the Celt in him always loving a thing most when it had become a part of the past: 'So we are now homeless, and you can drop a tear over the memory of our little home. Adieu, cosy nest, ours no more!'

On first stepping off the boat at the landing near the farm which he finally purchased, something seemed to say to him, 'This is to be your home.' While still undecided he wrote his wife:

I could make a very pretty place of it in a few years. I have made a plan of our house, and have made the house itself in pasteboard. It has taken me three days to build it. It looks very nice. It is half wood and half stone. If we could reduce ourselves to the size of mice, we could go to keeping house in it right off. I may have it photographed. It is a modification of one of the plans we looked at in Benton's book. It has a glorious old hall, 12 × 16, and the rooms are all large. . . . Tell me all about things, *and feed my trout*.

And later:

If we were not alone I should not hesitate about the Deyo place [later named Riverby], but the great bane of my life has been loneliness. We two are not enough in a house. I pine for a companion of my own sex; so, no doubt, do you. What shall we do? Can we make it up by dogs and cats, and a pig and a horse, a cow, hens, etc.?

[1] Esopus, two miles distant, was the nearest post-office until after the building of the West Shore Railway, when one was established at West Park.

You know the place and the house one has in mind he can never find. I want a spring, but when I see a spring, I would not live there. Sometimes I think I will look no further, . . . then I begin to doubt, and have misgivings, and feel unhappy, and groan. . . .

One of the things which helped him decide on 'the Deyo place,' was that it was 'so handy to home,' meaning Roxbury.[1] Another favoring condition was a neighboring stone-heap. Those vast piles of warm gray weathered stone which give, *en masse*, the mottled, lively character of the bole of a beech tree, decided him to close the bargain.

Waxing enthusiastic over his few acres, dreaming and planning, in August he began to build, going back and forth between his work in Middletown, and the growing structure. Benton had tried to dissuade him from building in late summer, but he would not heed the counsel.

At first he called his place 'Rock Ribs.' 'Gritty, isn't it? but I don't mind if it does grate a little on the teeth,' he said to Benton, while trying out that name. Still he did mind, and in time settled upon the felicitous name of 'Riverby' (the short sound of the *y*) for his place by the river. He added to his acreage in later years, so that the estate came in time to comprise twenty acres. The land slopes east by south from the State highway to the river's brim — ideal for fruit-growing.

He must have decided upon this avocation with much the same thought that actuated Sir Walter Scott when, in giving up law for literature, he sought a clerkship in the Supreme Court — literature might be his staff, but not his crutch. As Scott made a fair barrister, but a better novelist, so with John Burroughs in his various avocations — a conscientious teacher, a painstaking Treasury clerk and bank-examiner, and a successful fruit-farmer, he made a far better essayist. Still, popular as his writings have been, the income from his books, even supplemented by magazine-writing, was comparatively small. However, he did not write for the money in it. In his vineyard he had a dependable crutch; but it was his staff that he loved, and upon which his spirit leaned.

The enthusiasm with which he worked is reflected in 'Roof-Tree' ('Signs and Seasons'):

---

[1] In all the succeeding years of dwelling in his river home — seven and forty — he continued to speak of Roxbury as home.

THE STONE HOUSE AT RIVERBY

JOHN BURROUGHS'S PASTEBOARD MODEL OF HIS
HOUSE AT RIVERBY

It seems to me that I built into my house every one of those superb autumn days which I spent in the woods getting out stone. I did not quarry the limestone ledge into blocks any more than I quarried the delicious weather into memories to adorn my walls. Every load that was sent home carried my heart and happiness with it. The jewels I had uncovered in the *débris*, or torn from the ledge in the morning, I saw in the jambs, or mounted high on the corners at night. Every day was filled with great events. . . .

He watched the masons sharply lest they smooth the stone-work too much, or leave the mortar too conspicuous. ·He eagerly climbed the hills and helped fell the trees and haul them to the planing-mill; and even went back to his Catskill haunts for butternut, cherry, curly maple, and ash, one bleak winter's day climbing the home mountains for an old butternut about which a hunter had told him, and which, a year later, he saw in base and panel in his home.

The Burroughs–Benton letters of this period are rich in the history of how the house grew. Benton wrote at the outset:

Your model strikes me as exceedingly picturesque, though probably the photograph does not show the full beauty of your ideal. The long strip of court-plaster passes my comprehension, unless it be to make the gutter of the roof water-tight. And how you expect to force the lady sorrel to grow as high as the peak of the gable in this climate, I cannot imagine.

How and by what process did you manage to get the photograph? Is it from a drawing, or from a miniature model of pasteboard? But it represents a bold and picturesque piece of architecture and I like it well. Be sure to make its ornaments in the general shape and solid outlines, and not much by frail appendages. . . . [Much valuable advice follows.]

Burroughs reports progress:

I carried the stone-work up to the eaves, and on the whole am pleased with the work and proud of the design. The wall has a bold and rocky look which is much heightened by the projections on all the ends or gables. I had the luck to get some long strong stone in the woods, which enabled me to jut the wall out where it left the chamber-floor joist, one foot. Around the top of the bay-window also, I made a projection of stone. The stone-work, including the digging, etc., cost between fourteen and fifteen hundred dollars. The lintels to the windows and doors, and the sills, are all stone obtained in the woods near by.

I hope to get the roof on this week. The gables with the timber-finish are all in, and the house will soon be inclosed. I have ceiled the gables with white pine, and used yellow pine for the outside timber-work. I have painted it with a transparent paint made of tar, turpentine, and oil, and like it much. It shows the grain of the wood, and, I think, when completed, will have a good effect.

He was right in this. One who sees the stone-work to-day can reëcho his words concerning it:

'When the rising or the setting sun shines athwart it, and brings out the shadows, how powerful and picturesque it looks!'

The original pleasing effect of the stained wood in combination with the stone, has, however, been considerably modified for many years by the cold gray paint which, contrary to his plan, has covered the timber-work. In building he aimed to have the house express shelter, comfort, hospitality; he planned the interior 'to eat in, sleep in, be born in, and die in' — to accord with homely, everyday usages, and with its surroundings.

The pains he took to give an individual touch to his house is glimpsed in a passage from one of his letters to Benton:

I wish you would help me invent a new style of trimming out a room. I want to hit on a different finish for my parlor than is commonly used, and I enclose a little sketch of about my idea. The vine running around the openings is designed to be cut out of ¼ inch black walnut — all the rest of the wood butternut. I have got tired of mouldings, and think this a simpler finish. I want to show plenty of wood, and some such plan as this will do it. How does it strike you? Will it look too spotty and calico-y? Any flowing form will do, but I want no blocks or kaleidoscope figures. . . .

Benton's foresightedness is shown in his reply, which, in this particular, fortunately, his friend heeded:

You asked about the wood-work. . . . The finish for the door-casings would, I think, be quite pretty, if it does not seem too fanciful. Molly says the leaf-work would catch dust fearfully, and the black walnut would make every part of it show. Probably it would stick, too, as it would be difficult to get the sawed edges of the leaf-work perfectly smooth. I imagine Mrs. Burroughs with a step-ladder, dusting them night and day. At least, that is the way my wife would do. I think on this account, and also for the effect, I should have the leaf-work, or vine, of chestnut, the same as the casing. It would not be as conspicuous, and yet would show as much as you wish. . . .

The impetuous builder brooked no delay. If the workmen were slack or dilatory, he took their places himself. He was as

good as six men, the old Scottish mason said, in getting out
stone; and when the mason himself, after a 'wee drap' too
much, absented himself, just as the chimney was nearing completion, the 'boss' climbed on the roof and nearly finished the
job, his work receiving from the sobered Scot an approving
'Weel, sir-r-r, ye are a hondy mon!'

In time, the house-builder came to regret that he had not
heeded more of Benton's suggestions, for, on moving in,
many things were found unsatisfactory. With dining-room
and kitchen in the basement; library, parlor, bedroom, and
bath on the floor above; and other sleeping-rooms still above;
it proved a house in which it was hard to do the work, and
doubly so for Mrs. Burroughs, to whom immaculate housekeeping was an inexorable law, and who was, moreover, subject to prolonged periods of semi-invalidism.

'We never seemed to think we were going to grow old,'
said Mr. Burroughs in commenting on the mistakes made in
building. The library, where he had hoped to do his writing,
could not be on the river side, that being appropriated by the
large unused parlor, the pride of the housekeeper's heart; and
the cramped little fireplace, an offense to him from the start,
was never used, except when he and his dog were housekeeping, and did not mind the litter its use occasioned.

By the time he wrote 'Roof-Tree,' he wrote from the
vantage-ground of dear experience. To his regret he found
that the interior of his house expressed neither his own, nor
his wife's, taste; he had not been bold enough in supplying
windows, and those supplied, being heavily curtained, made
the inadequacy still more apparent. In 'Roof-Tree' he pleads
for dark furniture and hangings, with a dash of color here and
there, and floods of light. He got the dark, even somber, and
neutral tones in walls and furnishings, without the saving
grace of flashes of color and floods of light; while the marble
mantelpiece (and other concessions to a taste formed in that
period in Washington), with 'its senseless vases,' gave to the
dignified, irreproachable parlor the 'finishing touch of coldness
and stiffness,' which, though yielding to, he abhorred; not,
however, without his little fling in the essay, — 'Marble
makes good tombstones, but is an abomination in a house,
either in furniture or in mantels.'

Fortunately, however, the scales did not fall from his eyes

all at once, and the joy in building was not tempered in those busy days of 1873 and 1874. Fondly he lingered about the house, walking pensively from one imaginary room to another, sat in reverie on the naked joists, climbed the skeleton stairs, and looked out of the vacant windows; and though the house grew surprisingly fast, it seemed long a-finishing, the heart moving in, he said, long before the workmen moved out.

Essay-writing was almost at a standstill during 1873 and 1874. Before leaving Washington, as he wrote Benton, his mind had begun to sprout in several different places; but the new occupation had acted like a sudden frost; though by spring he began to feel the buds swelling again. 'The Birds of the Poets,' which first appeared in 'Scribner's,' and later as the initial chapter, with the amended title, in 'Birds and Poets,' was the result of that second sprouting. A passage from one of Whitman's letters shows the poet's way of reviewing:

John, I think 'The Birds of the Poets' your best article in many respects — it has a jaunty air, *in a perfectly natural way* — flits, and hops, and soars and sings around, in a birdish way itself.

Early in the year, while awaiting court proceedings, Burroughs wrote his wife of being forced to sit and chew his cud, the cud just then being Trowbridge, Trowbridge having chosen Burroughs to be his headsman because of his 'spirit of honest criticism.' This biographical sketch was published in 'Scribner's' in November, 1874. It has humor, and some good criticism, but impresses one as being one of the (happily) few things he wrote in which the subject chose him, rather than he the subject.

In a May letter to Whitman, one sees that neither banks, nor birds, nor building could take the place of his absent comrade:

I rec'd a magazine (The Galaxy) from you yesterday which I have been peeping into today, but the day has been so beautiful, and the charm of the open air so great, that I could not long keep my eyes on the printed page.

The season is at last fairly in for it, and the fruit trees are all getting in bloom. My bees are working like beavers, and there is a stream of golden thighs passing into the hive all the time. I can do almost anything with them and they won't sting me. Yesterday I turned a hive up and pruned it, that is, cut out a lot of old dirty comb; the little fellows were badly frightened and came pouring out in great consternation, but did not offer to sting me. I am going to transfer a swarm in a day or two to a new style of hive. I spend all my time at work about the place and like it much. I run over to M[iddletown] to look after bank matters for a day or two, then back here. The house is being plastered and will be finished during the summer. The wrens and robins and phoebe birds have already taken possession of various nooks of it, and if they are allowed to go on with their building I must stop mine. During that snowstorm the last of April the hermit thrush took refuge in it. We are surrounded with birds here and they are a great comfort and delight to me.[1] Your room is ready for you and your breakfast-plate warmed. When will you come? The change would do you good, and your presence would certainly do us good.

How comes on the rustic porch? [writes Benton in September] Cedar, peeled, would make one very durable. I am told that if the bark is left on, there is a worm gets into it and makes it unsightly. With plenty of knots left rather prominent, peeled sticks would be sufficiently rustic. [He followed this suggestion.]

In late December, writing Benton of being nicely settled in their new house, Burroughs added:

We are quite cosy, and I really have felt for the last few days as if I should get back my literary cud, lost nearly two years ago. . . .

My wood-work stands the ordeal of the furnace very well. It is over two months now and only a little of it has opened at the joints. The worst is some pine doors that were not kiln-dried. My ash and butternut doors are as tight as a drum yet. . . .

My rustic porch takes the eyes of the bluebirds. There are two or three here that act as if they would stay all winter. Mrs. Burroughs, however, threatens to clean them out, as she does not like the souvenirs they leave on the door-stone.

I like to hear you talk of going to Catskill; then you will not dare to go by here and not stop. . . . Too little company, too few calls, is going to be our chief source of discontent here. Come and see us as soon as the river closes. . . .

Benton responds:

It's a pity about your losing your cud. I shall set you on a three-legged stool in the midst of forty ruminating cows, and watch to see the infection take hold. No artificial, made-up cud would amount to anything. There are thousands of such literary quids undergoing mastication the country over to the great demoralization of the community. Let the machines grind away on their juiceless cuds, but never do you put one into your mouth. Rather yield no milk for a twel'-month. . . .

[1] They were then living in an old cottage on their place by the river.

That is about what happened, for the bank affairs kept him going from place to place, making writing impossible. Once, when enduring a tedious season in New York, during court proceedings, he complained to his wife, in Roxbury: 'I had ten times rather be on the mountains with Eden and his hounds than here.' He wished she could take his place, since cities and traveling were to her taste; and signed himself disconsolately, 'Your rail-bound Domp.'

Channy B. Deyo, a youth winsome and affectionate, held, as has been seen, a peculiar place in the heart of John Burroughs. When as a boy he had lived at the Burroughs homestead, his uncle had seen in him a second self, — his love of Nature, his aspiration for learning, so like his own. From Washington he had written the lad stimulating letters, advising him what books to read, and encouraging him to get away to school; and Channy's letters to him had been as welcome as the first song sparrow in March, telling, as they did, the homely news of the farm — the price of butter, the scarcity of eggs, the news of the sap-bush, the advent of the first robin, the recrudescence of Hiram's Western fever, the lad's quest of the gray-cheeked thrush (which later he sent to the Smithsonian); telling of the calf he was raising, in hopes that it would carry him to Washington, though it would 'have to have a pretty stiff back to do it'; and when Channy did get to Washington, the congeniality had deepened between him and 'Uncle John,' while the attraction the lad felt for Whitman had proved another strong bond of union.

Later, in the spring of 1874, while Channy was studying medicine at Long Island College Hospital, he wrote his uncle of visiting Whitman in Camden:

How good it seemed to be with him! Then, if ever, I was happy. Every word seemed to go to the spot. To look at him inspired my soul. I do not see how anyone could help but love him. It seems to me that he is the perfection of the fruit of the earth. I remember that once, while looking at him when he was still, I wondered how he had lived the calm and easy life he had — how it happened that he had not been a great general, or a king, or shaken the nation or the world in some way; and then I thought of his writing, and how that had been his work — that instead of commanding armies and conquering worlds, as Napoleon or Cæsar, he had written poems; and I believe as sure as the earth rolls, they will yet help America more, far more, than Washington helped it, or Napoleon France, or Cæsar Rome.

It seemed hard to see the great man afflicted, bowed down, and I could not suppress my tears, and cannot suppress them now when I think of it. His death would be a heavy, heavy blow to me, Uncle John; I can't think of it without crying, as I do now.

Some weeks later, his uncle received from Channy a long, eloquent letter, full of the dreams and seething emotions of adolescence; a letter showing humor, altruism, and insight, yet showing unmistakably an abnormal state of exaltation — a graphic self-portrayal of a state all too well known to the psychiatrist. The lad recognized his own fits of exaltation and depression; prophesied (then ridiculed himself for turning seer) the approach of a new movement of uplift; saw visions of old orders to pass away, and new ones to come; and felt that he might bear a part in it all if only — pathetic insight — it did not 'drive him crazy.' His 'frightful headaches,' and insomnia, and apprehension, complete the picture.

Preserved by his uncle, this and other exalted letters, are found in Channy's hand. Some of these sound like a mute, inglorious Whitman. One such, written at a railway station, records the impressions he received from the passing throng — girls, old men bowed with care, carpenters, and other sturdy workmen; the young mystic reads their souls as they pass; something is exchanged between him and them in their quick glances:

I catch the eye of a girl. Her look produces its impression upon me, and my look produces its impression upon her. Nothing . . . can produce the impression that the eye produces. By no other means do we come so near each other's souls. . . . I catch the eyes of men and boys. It is good. I love them, but there isn't that affinity, that love, that sympathy. Such cannot be. It is contrary to nature. . . . How good it is to see such men [workmen]. . . . Oh, that we could feel our indebtedness to them! that we could feel the deepest reverence for the large brawny arms, the coarse, tough hands, the tanned, sweaty faces! . . .

The following letter which Burroughs wrote to his wife in May, from the Long Island College Hospital, reveals how the uncle's heart was wrung when, summoned to Channy's bedside, he found the condition he describes:

Channy B. is fearfully crazy and has to be tied in his bed. I am overwhelmed with grief. I hear his ravings as I write. It is all religion. He knows me, but I can have no influence upon him. He had the operation performed, but it was only slight, and could not have caused this. . . . I shall stay till there is a change. It seems like a horrid dream to me, and my heart is broken. . . . Get somebody to stay with you. . . . Keep up your courage, my dear wife. I think often of you in my distress. This is a fearful blow to me. It may be worse even than death. . . .

The sad sequel is traced in a June letter to Myron Benton:

The early summer days have brought no pleasure to me, but the deepest sorrow. A nephew of mine, a young man of twenty-three years of age, whom I loved with all my heart, died the twenty-seventh of May. Orville may remember him, as he was in the party that went with us over on the Neversink a-fishing. He died in Brooklyn (where he was taking a course of medical lectures) of some cerebral disease — perhaps the result of overstudy.

I was by his side the most of the ten days of his illness, and suffered more than I ever expect to suffer again. He was both son and brother and dear comrade to me, and of all my kindred I could least afford to lose him. Life looks dreary indeed to me since he has gone out. He was a young man of great worth and promise, and one of the most conscientious persons I ever knew. . . . Ah! how the heart bleeds and bleeds, and finds no balm anywhere! I am busy here with my farm, and try to make the multitude of little cares divert my mind. . . .

The pipings of the orioles which he heard that month of May became so associated with his sorrow that he could never dissociate the sound. 'Oh, that oriole!' he said to me one day in May, forty-one years later, — 'when Channy B. died, I used to hear it calling all the day, — every day. I thought it would kill me!' With what poignancy he speaks of this, his first great sorrow, in his 'Bird Medley' ('Birds and Poets'):

During any unusual tension of the feelings, how the note or song of a single bird will sink into the memory, and become inseparably associated with your grief or joy. Shall I ever again be able to hear the song of the oriole without being pierced through and through? Can it ever be other than a dirge for me? Day after day, and week after week, this bird whistled and warbled in a mulberry-tree by the door, while sorrow, like a pall, darkened my day.

Throughout the years, in Journal and in conversation, he seldom failed to mention Channy B. when the sad anniversary recurred.

News of Whitman, and of himself, goes to Edward Dowden, May 4th:

... I have had you in mind during these years though I have heard nothing directly from you. I have rather thought you would come over to this country and see us by this time — you and Rossetti. . . . You ought to come, both of you, while Whitman is living. . . . He may live yet many years, but I fear his sun is getting low in the horizon, and you, of all men, should see him and know him in life.

For the past year a dark dread has beset my mind whenever I have thought of him. He is so unspeakably dear to me that the earth would not seem habitable if he were gone. And yet he does not seem to be getting worse. I saw him for a few hours about the middle of April, and thought him fully as bright and hopeful as when I saw him in December. He told me with a reassuring laugh that he had heard that his physician had said he was not as ill as he (W) thought he was. It was at night, and near eleven o'clock; he walked out with me several squares as I left, and his voice and manner were like the old times in Washington. He looks as well as ever, only a little more bleached in his hair and beard. His brother, with whom he lives, thinks he is slowly gaining strength. I have great hopes of having him up here with me part of the summer, and great expectation of benefit to him by the change of air and scenes. . . .

I am established here in a rather lonely place on the Hudson River, in a house of my own (of stone, and of my own building), with a small fruit-farm attached.

I come of a race of farmers and have always had a hungering for the soil, and am now bound to take my fill of it and let the empty artificial world go its own way, which is not mine. I only lack some one near to talk books with, but then I have the birds, and one can't have everything.

I congratulate you both on the advent of the son, and pray the fates to pass the favor round this way.

One of the joys, and one of the griefs, of that first year at Riverby came to John Burroughs in the form of a common little cur named Rab, a mixture of black-and-tan and mastiff, with an uncommon amount of intelligence and devotion. The two were boon companions, but the companionship was brief. While Rab was ill, Curtis Burroughs wrote his brother:

John, I hope Rab has got well. You must not think so much of a dog. It was the shock of lightning that hurt him. Must rub him and get his blood in circulation.

When too weak to lift his head, Rab recognized the voice of his master. The accompanying letter from Burroughs to Benton, August 31st, recalls the incident of Scott's cancelling a dinner engagement the day that his dog Camp died, 'on account of the death of a dear old friend':

Your card came last night. I am glad you propose a postponement of our visit as we could not have come today as promised. Rab is still alive, though we expect every hour will be his last. It is almost like losing a child. Indeed, half the people do not mourn so much over the death of their children as we do over Rab. He is a homely cur, but you can hardly imagine how much he has been to us. He has been the life and light of the place for a year. Some nights I have heard the clock strike every hour in listening to hear him kick his last. I tried not to listen, but could not help it. . . .

He buried Rab beside the rock that led to the spring, and for his monument thrust into the ground, at the head of the grave, the staff he had so often carried to the woods in their rambles.

His next dog friend, Rover, was a well-bred, spirited black-and-tan, whom he rechristened Rosemary Rose, apparently for no other reason than because his eyes were like a girl's, and his tongue like a rose-leaf. Rose was his companion on many a tramp for two or three succeeding years, often accompanied him on his drives to the various banks, and camped with him and Aaron Johns on the Rondout.

The life at Riverby was in turn cheered and saddened by six different dog chums, most of which met a tragic end, the four dearest being Rab, Rose, Lark, and Laddie. The wounds caused by their deaths never healed. To the last of life, when speaking of them or pointing out their graves, he showed by his tender, wistful tone how deeply he had loved them.[1] At this period, aside from Myron Benton, Burroughs had few associates, and his dog friends were perhaps the more deeply cherished.

In one of Benton's letters occurs a hint of the good cookery with which Riverby's mistress was justly credited:

Tell Mrs. Burroughs that the fame of those corn-cakes has gone through the length and breadth of this part of the country. I cannot begin to tell how many times, I have heard that recipe repeated. We tried it on the very fag-end of our green-corn, and were more successful than would be expected. Next summer there will be a corn-cake revival in this region that would make Moody and Sankey put back from London. . . .

To this Burroughs replied:

. . . When I read that part about the corn-cakes, Wife purred so I could hear her clear across the room.

[1] See 'Dog Friends and a Boy Chum' (*John Burroughs, Boy and Man*).

I have been at home pretty closely since you were here, excepting a long and tedious trip to Titusville, Pa. I have been writing some — have finished three pieces and sent away two to Scribner's. The Atlantic editor liked the piece on the Apple, but could not use it in time to be out of the way of the book, which comes out this month.

What can you tell me about the Cow? I am finishing up a piece on that poetical creature, and have no doubt you have material I could use. What cunning tricks have you known her up to? What do you know about her hiding her calf? and what is your theory about her devouring the after-birth? Is it not a vestige of her wild habits? Does your herd always have a boss cow? ...

In his well-known essay, 'Our Rural Divinity,' Burroughs made use of parts of Benton's reply, and of his poem 'Rumination.'

The apprenticeship as a writer which had begun in 1854 and continued through the groping years, moving rapidly forward during the Washington period, had now reached an advanced stage of craftsmanship, yet had resulted in but two books. Still, whatever his avocations, he had held steadfastly to the purpose of becoming an author; and, slowly as the books continued to come, in the long row of them which he left at the last the honest craftsmanship which insensibly merged into artistry may be traced. From 'Wake-Robin' to 'The Last Harvest,' his skill and proficiency in the use of tools steadily increased; yet almost never is one conscious of the painstaking work that went to their making — there stands the temple, but 'neither hammer, nor axe, nor any tool,' was heard in the building of it.

The publication of his third book, 'Winter Sunshine,' seems to have been the most significant event for Burroughs in 1875. The book had been begun in Washington. Most gratifying to the author must have been this gracious note:

When an author sends out a book like 'Winter Sunshine' to charm and instruct the whole country, somebody ought to thank him heartily for a service done to America. I dare say many a reader has already expressed deep obligation to you for writing this most welcome volume, but I wish to be among the first to say what enjoyment you have given personally to

Cordially yours
JAMES T. FIELDS

Professor Dowden wrote him that parts of the book were 'like an immediate off-growth of nature, and as full of juice as a bonny-cheeked Newton pippin, or a red astrachan.' He had found the song of the apple, parts of which are lyrical, so persuasive that he had felt a sudden craving for American apples, and had suffered from a bad conscience those mornings he had not diverged from his regular route to College, to seek a shop where there was a ruddy store of them. Several other correspondents wrote that the apple piece set them to eating apples, while 'Exhilarations of the Road' sent them out over the hills.

An outstanding event early in the Centennial year was a visit from his father, thus recorded in his Journal:

In the 74th year of his age, and after I have been a housekeeper for nearly twenty years, Father comes and sits at my table and smokes his pipe on my porch, and sleeps in my chamber. I can hardly realize it. He is like a boy, remarkably well and hearty; has an enormous appetite, and it does me good to see him eat. . . .

The son's frequent visits to the Old Home at Roxbury began when he settled down on the Hudson, and were kept up every year, and many times a year, throughout his life; but the rare visits from his parents and sisters were indeed red-letter days.

His literary activities may be traced in excerpts from a mid-January letter to Benton:

Both the Cow and the Spring pieces were returned by the Atlantic, and I guess with reason. I have already begun to slaughter the Cow, and mean at least to get something out of the hide and tallow. The piece on Springs, I think, is worth printing, and I shall take it to Scribner's or the Galaxy. Mr. Hurd[1] has asked me several times to write for the Atlantic, so I sent them these pieces, but they are hard to please.

The next Galaxy will have a piece of mine on Emerson, which I find I do not feel just right about. It needed another revision.

Calvert Vaux wrote me about the House article in a very pleasant strain.[2] I expected the old architects like him would shake their heads over the article. You must get Alfred Barrow's 'Foot Notes.' It is very good, for all it is so much like Thoreau in manner.

As to the 'Cow,' Burroughs wrote Benton that he had de-

[1] Mr. M. M. Hurd, of the firm of Hurd & Houghton, publishers of the Atlantic.
[2] Calvert Vaux, author of a book on Domestic Architecture had commended 'Roof-Tree.' In truth, some of the ideas expressed in this essay are so much in advance of their day that one credits J. B. with a little pioneer work in house-building. In 1912 an architect in Portland, Oregon, wrote J. B. that the principles set forth in 'Roof-Tree' had long been of signal help to him in designing houses which he hoped had proved to be real homes.

cided to 'stall-feed the critter' instead of slaughtering her out
of hand for nothing but her hide and tallow — a decision of
which his friend approved, adding: 'That Cow, with its stall-
feeding and currying and cajoling, will be a wonderful specimen of livestock breeding.' Then, rejoicing that he and she
would go down to posterity hand in hand, or, rather, hoof in
hand, Benton admonished him not to dare, in his revisings,
to expunge 'Rumination' from the essay.

As to Burroughs's delineation of Emerson at this period,
keen and trenchant as it is, it was without doubt much modified by reason of his disappointment at Emerson's failure to
follow up his original endorsement of Whitman; and especially at Emerson's omission of Whitman from his 'Parnassus.'
Still, despite Burroughs's reservations, where, in any other
writer, can be found such a just and telling estimate of Emerson as may, all in all, be found in the writings of Burroughs?[1]
Whatever fluctuations his enthusiasm for Emerson suffered
throughout the years, the hero of his youth and early manhood remained his hero to the end. Although in advanced age
he pointed out the flies in the Emersonian amber, he reread his
essays, and repeated favorite passages from his poems with
unabated admiration, while his final testimony, in 'The Last
Harvest,' shows unswerving allegiance:

I find that something one gets from Emerson in early life does not
leave one when he grows old. It is a habit of mind, a test of values,
a strengthening of one's faith in the essential soundness and goodness of creation. He helps to make you feel at home in nature, and
in your land and generation.

With the appearance of Burroughs's first essay on Emerson,
there followed a lengthy discussion about their hero between
him and Benton, the latter considering Emerson's poetry by
far the finest flower yet sprung from American soil. Benton
admitted Emerson's lack of the lyrical quality, in the ordinary
sense, but declared that his words spring from his thoughts as
inevitably as the oak-leaf develops from the acorn; which
opinion led Burroughs to reply:

It belongs to you to write a defense of Emerson's poetry, especially

[1] See ' Emerson' (*Birds and Poets*), 'Arnold's View of Emerson and Carlyle'
(*Indoor Studies*), and 'Emerson and his Journals ' and 'Flies in Amber' (*The Last
Harvest*).

its form, which to me, too, seems complete, but which dainty critics like Howells, pick at.

I sat down after I came home from Washington, and in about a week wrote another piece on Emerson called 'A Final Word,' which I took to the Galaxy, and which they said they would print in the April number. I like it better than the other. I wrote it easier and freer, and I think it is less Emersonian in style. I shall be curious to know how it strikes you. I growl considerable, but hope I give him his full meed of praise. The other piece, which I wrote last winter, did not relieve me, but I feel delivered of the subject at last.[1]

I have felt pretty ugly toward Emerson because he ignored Walt Whitman in his 'Parnassus.' I think Walt can afford to be overlooked, but I don't think Emerson can afford to overlook him, much less Bryant and Whittier, as they have done. [In anthologies prepared by them.] It is the weakest thing I ever knew Emerson to do, and has been a great help to me in criticizing him. Yet I hardly feel that I have been criticizing him in either article, but rather sounding him, and trying to determine exactly what he is. He is not a man to be criticized, but rather to be defined and appreciated.

Yes, I read 'Peter's' article in the Contemporary, which Henry Abbey sent me. He is a hopeless old granny. A noble article on W. W. appeared about the same time in the Gentleman's Magazine, by Arthur Cline, that pleased me immensely. Of course 'Littell's Fossil Age,' as O'Connor calls it, would not reprint that. . . .

I have just finished a paper called 'Touches of Nature' [in 'Birds and Poets'] a kind of patchwork, or coat of many colors. I write quite easily this winter, often an article a week, and often, I fear, only a weak article.

I want to write a piece on the natural history of the boy.[2] Can't you furnish me some material — characteristic traits or anecdotes of boys, of yourself, for instance? . . .

Continuing, during 1876, to study the birds, and the poets as well, he wrote the essays later incorporated in the volume, 'Birds and Poets.'

In May, 1876, John Burroughs began regularly to keep a journal. This had been preceded by occasional note-books, already referred to, the earliest dated 1854. His Journal, kept till within a few weeks of his death, is the source of much henceforth to be found in these pages.

[1] It is probable that when he reëdited the original Emerson essay for *Birds and Poets*, he incorporated in that 'A Final Word on Emerson.' In connection with his statement of being at last delivered of Emerson, it is noteworthy that his last (posthumous) volume, *The Last Harvest*, contains some one hundred pages devoted to Emerson. Never was he delivered of Emerson, or of Whitman, or of the birds, any more than he was of Nature.

[2] Sections XVI and XVII in 'Touches of Nature' in *Birds and Poets*, are as near as he came to carrying out this intention. Some of his own boyhood experiences are recorded there.

News about the warblers opens the record, and doings of the familiar birds, observations of outdoor life, and unfailing concern about the weather, form a large part of the daily records. His reflections on what he is reading, tentative beginnings of essays, now familiar to his reader, a mingling of subjective and objective interests, brief but pregnant characterizations of friends, places, events, are also faithfully chronicled. In late May he is meditating essays on Association, April,[1] Strawberries,[2] My Possessions, The Swallow, Saint-Pierre, Notes of a Walker,[3] Roads, Rain and Dew, Dirt. That he carried his meditations to fulfillment concerning several of these, his reader knows. The essay on Dirt had a long germination — not until 1908 did it appear, and then as 'The Divine Soil,'[4] in the 'Atlantic,' later in 'Leaf and Tendril.' The essay on Roads at last had its turning, also in the 'Atlantic,' in 1909, in that masterly setting forth of the principles of evolution, in 'The Long Road' ('Time and Change') — an essay in which science and literature are so felicitously combined that the reader is informed as much as he is charmed.

The birds and the flowers, the Journal shows, punctuate his days. Adown the years he records with an abiding interest the return of the birds, the blossoming of the flowers, with as creative a touch as Spring herself achieves.

It is a quiet life in which the reading of Cowley's essays, beside Black Creek Falls, is a noteworthy event (he prefers 'Obscurity' and 'Solitude'); the swarming of his bees, another; while the resurrected steamer, Sunnyside, moving by, 'like a funeral procession,' after having lain in her watery grave for months, makes a ripple in his mind, as well as in the river.

Here he preserves a day in June:

Yesterday and today are the shining days. How the river dances and sparkles, how the new leaves of all the trees shine under the sun! The air has a soft lustre; there is a haze; it is not blue, but a kind of shining, diffused nimbus — no clouds, but the sky is a bluish-white, very soft and delicate.

[1] 'April': *Scribner's*, April, 1877 (*Birds and Poets*).
[2] 'Strawberries': *Scribner's*, August, 1877 (*Locusts and Wild Honey*).
[3] 'Notes of a Walker': *Scribner's*, 20: 97.
[4] The title, suggested by a friend, is reminiscent of Whitman's lines,
'Underneath, the divine soil,
Overhead, the sun.'

Excerpts from letters which he wrote to Edward Dowden in April, furnish entertaining literary gossip as well as trenchant criticism:

I presume you have seen what a stir Buchanan's letter to the *London News*, in behalf of Whitman, has created. I do not see the British journals, but it set the geese to cackling here beautifully.

The papers all encouraged themselves with the remark that Robert Buchanan was quite unknown in this country, but the ado they have made over his letter is astonishing.

If you see him, or correspond with him, tell him that there is one man in America, at least, who is grateful to him for what he has done. I wish he would shy another missile into our barnyard the first opportunity that offers. Our fowls are getting too complacent.

The papers have nearly all made his letter an excuse to attack Whitman, and it is pitiful and humiliating to see the littleness and cur-dog spite and bluster exhibited. . . . The New York Tribune, of which we had some hope, has an editorial every day or two full of abuse of Whitman. . . .[1]

What makes it doubly annoying is that his friends can make no reply — the papers and journals are all closed to them. If we only had an organ, you would see the fur fly, and something under the fur. It makes me blood-thirsty to have to stand by and see and hear such things. A scalping-knife would feel better in my hand than a pen.

You can hardly understand, from your distance, what a miserable puling set of editors and poets we have in this country. Such an utter absence of anything manly, broad, robust, is disheartening. They say that the reason Whitman is more popular in England than here is that the Englishman has grown *blasé*, sated with order and conformity, and craves the wild and lawless. But the real reason is that we are a race of pigmies, and in comparison, your authors and reviewers are a race of giants.

All our rising literary men in this country are of the superfine sort — very knowing, very quick, bright, deft, smart, but without any port, or stomach, or bowels, or carnality, or sexuality, or proper manliness.

I heartily wish some British reviewer would take them up fairly, dispassionately, and show how they all run to mere refinement, mere finger-tips, and that in trying so hard, as the Tribune says they are, to get away from the conditions represented by Whitman, they are getting away from the only sources of power and fresh inspiration. I should like to furnish the names and facts for such an article.

I see by a paragraph in the Tribune that you have been reviewing Lowell's 'Study Windows.' I hope you smashed some of them in. I can't endure the man. The harshness and rawness, as well as the brightness, of the New England climate has come to a head in him.

[1] 'I think Bayard Taylor wrote them.' J. B. (See editorials, March 28 and 30, and April 12, 1876.)

He seems to me one of those minds that never get ripe, but are crude and puckery to the last. He has great verbal brightness and 'smartness,' and that is all. There are incessant fire-fly flashes of wit over a dull prosy ground. He is an 'embroiderer.' It is a kind of torture to me to read him. Such an absence of tone, of mellowness, of harmony, of poetic quality from a man of his ability, is remarkable. . . .[1]

Have you seen his [Whitman's] 'Two Rivulets?' The prose parts are very noble, and the Hospital Sketches priceless, but I do not care much for the new poems. They have not the leaven of poetry, as have his old pieces.

And later:

I saw the article in the *Gentleman's Magazine* on Whitman, while visiting him last January. He was much pleased with it, as he might well be. It was a noble tribute.

In his remarks upon the significance of the Calamus, or friendship pieces, the author turned new and deep ground, and set me to thinking. In fact, he broke new soil all through the piece. Arthur Cline, then, is only a *nom de plume?* The article was not reprinted here, as, of course, stupid Peter Baynes's was. What a leather-head Baynes is!

I think if Whitman's friends in England feel like doing anything for him in the shape of pecuniary aid, it would be rightly received by him. I should recommend taking the difficulty by the horns boldly, and a point-blank gift of money, and no beating around the bush. As soon as I can bring it about, I shall make no apologies at all for sending him my check. He is not in want, so far as food, shelter, raiment, goes, but I suspect he has little or no money. A few years ago, some wretch picked his pocket of $400, which made a sad hole in his savings.

We expected he would have a position in one of the Departments at Washington again before this, as it was promised last winter, but nothing seems to come of it yet. Yes, the Government ought to pension him, but the only way it can be done is by a nominal place in one of the executive departments. There is no law under which he could be pensioned, and you know we do things according to law in this country!

A brief picture of midsummer at Riverby is found in the Journal:

The heated term apparently over, the air clear and pure, and looking toward August. All day the indigo bird sings in the trees about, and all day the scarlet tanager sings also, and between them the wood or bush-sparrow sings. The tolling of the crickets, or nocturnal insects, has just begun, to go on increasing till fall. Wife gone to Elmira to the Cure.

[1] 'That is pretty severe — an exaggerated truth,' said J. B. in 1914.

To his wife at the Water-Cure he writes requesting a full report of what the doctors think of her case, and tells how he and Rosemary Rose are faring in her absence:

He [Rose] has talked a good deal since of the wonders he saw at Poughkeepsie that day. He made the acquaintance of lots of dogs. I had to keep an eye on him. . . . He sits at the table and helps himself, and I take what's left. . . . I like housekeeping first rate. It takes me one hour to get breakfast, eat it, do up the work, and ten minutes to do the dinner. In one and one half minutes after dinner is done, the dishes are washed and put away. I am at leisure 25 hours out of the 24. . . . Keep a stiff upper lip, and don't worry about me. . . .

Later, when sending her trunk, he writes that he and Rose want to go along with it, but can't scrape up enough money; that Rose does not like boarding with him, as he has his meals too irregularly, and sometimes none at all. Still, from the account of the chickens they consumed, it is gathered that, on that score, he and Rose were not to be pitied. They are planning a big walk; they are going to make up a box of 'grub' and send her; she is not to let the people at the Water-Cure humbug her; and he hopes the check he incloses will answer her purpose.

A pathetic situation is revealed in the low-spirited reply: Lonely and homesick, the invalid's hypersensitiveness and self-pity stand out clearly; her husband's careless comment about the check had caused crying-spells and sleepless nights. He, however, continues to write cheerily. He tells of picking and canning huckleberries; of a visit from her brother and his family; of what he gave them to eat before taking them for a row on the river; tells of his hired man clearing out the strawberries, and of *his* trying to write a piece about them; and then, sending on his photograph, he rallies his wife thus:

How do you like the looks of the young man? Look at him sharp, and see if you don't think you have been pretty hard on him sometimes. He is not a bad fellow, but his skin is pretty thin, worn so in some places, and his wife ought to be pretty careful of him — he may amount to something, one of these days. . . .

Rosemary Rose is well, but talks about the Water-Cure every day. A few days ago he fought the battle of Lundy's Bridge, and great was the carnage — one drop of 'claret' on his antagonist after half an hour's fighting! But he routed the enemy, and pursued it vigorously. Since then he has been a great hero! . . .

Concerning the photograph sent, his wife protests:

It gives one the impression that the animal predominates, which is not so; besides, it looks coarse and uncouth. I am sorry to have a picture misrepresent[ing] you as that does, put in the magazines to go all over the country. I would not let them use it. I feel certain it would impress most people unfavorably, and when we can just as well impress them the opposite I think it is your duty to do so. Because, my Dear, you are a much better man than that makes you out to be.[1]

Later, when he writes her of camping-trips on Coney Island, and on the Rondout, she begs him not to get 'all tanned up,' as some young ladies at the Cure who admire him much are reckoning on seeing him when he visits her, and she wants him to look 'as sweet as a peach.' The chances are it was a sun-tanned 'peach' that subsequently made its appearance at the Cure, after his tramps with 'Aaron' in the wilds.

Aaron helps me wash the dishes [he writes]. We have corn-cakes and melon for breakfast, and chicken or steak for dinner. House-work does not make slaves of us. We are masters of the situation, and of most of our time every day. You may see a piece of mine in the September Galaxy. Your day lillies are in full bloom.

The 'jolly, idyllic times' which he and 'Aaron' had on the Rondout are recorded in the Journal, and then this brief entry:

August 28. Aaron left me at noon today, and left me sad. The air is loaded with smoke, the day is obscure and dreamy. Our trip seems like a beautiful dream that ended too soon. A melancholy haze envelops my mind.

The camping is followed by lonely days at Riverby — hot, dry September — the canning of peaches and pears, and other domestic tasks, mingled with bank-examining, and the writing of 'A Bed of Boughs,' ('Locusts and Wild Honey').

'Rose and I do the minimum amount of work,' he writes the invalid, 'and have the maximum of good times.' As the weeks pass, and he urges a trip to the seashore, rather than a longer sojourn at the Water Cure, his wife replies, citing conscientiously the advantages of a longer stay: To leave then would be to lose the time and money spent; the physicians think she should stay two or three months more; the treatment is being

[1] This is probably the illustration used later in Joel Benton's discriminating and interpretive article on J. B. in *Scribner's Monthly*, January, 1877.

directed to her sterility, and she believes that their desire for a
child may yet be realized. Details follow, after which she
urges attention to things at home; he must have his clothes
pressed before he visits her, must not let things run down; and
she hopes he will get track of a girl, — a consummation which
he wished far more devoutly than did she, for it was ever difficult for her to surrender the reins of housekeeping into the
hands of a maid. 'It fairly makes her sick,' her husband was
wont to say,'to see any one else handling her pots and pans.'
Yet a return to housekeeping, aided or unaided, was, because
of her strenuousness, usually followed by physical and emotional upsets.

To one like Ursula Burroughs those lines in Proverbs must
have been applied: 'She riseth also while it is yet night, and
giveth meat to her household. . . . She looketh well to the
ways of her household, and eateth not the bread of idleness.'

Although progress toward recovery was slow, with the advancing autumn the invalid's thought turned to her home and
the fall housecleaning. Affectionate letters pass back and
forth. She asks her husband to gather ferns and press autumn
leaves that she may make bouquets on return; she urges repairs on the furnace and out-buildings — a veritable Martha
cumbered with cares, much of which, it must be said, was
necessary, since attention to such matters sat rather lightly
upon her husband. He liked exceedingly the results of a well-
ordered house, but was ever impatient of the requisite fore-
thought and care. In short, he and she represented opposite
poles here. Still, under her tutelage, he became one of the
handiest of men about a house, and one of the most resourceful
in fending for himself.

Soon the Journal chronicles a visit to his wife; a sojourn in
Philadelphia, and his impressions of the Centennial Exhibition. Of the journey to Elmira:

Rode all afternoon down the Susquehanna. New scenery to me
and very beautiful — the green water, the long still reaches alternat-
ing with broad, pebbly shallow places; the bluff-like hills, now on
one side, now on the other, and the long winding curves of the river.
. . . When we passed the Wyalusing I thought of Father and Mother;
for, many years ago, while on their way to uncle Henry's in a wagon,
they had to ford this stream, and came near being drowned. There
were no bridges on the Susquehanna till we reached the Tunkhan-
nock — a stream like a fair Indian maiden. . . .

Of the Centennial he wrote Benton that he could stand only a day and a half of it; that he would be afraid to take a woman there lest she die on his hands; the affair, he said, was well worth seeing in the lump, and a few things in detail, but he was never more fatigued in his life.

In Philadelphia he met Anne Gilchrist, who had recently come over from England to be near Whitman, and to educate her children in this country, with whose democratic principles she was in close sympathy. While staying at the same hotel with the Gilchrists, he writes Mrs. Burroughs his impressions of them:

Walt came over every evening from Camden and took supper with us, and we had much talk. He likes Mrs. Gilchrist and her family, and they like him. They are going to housekeeping, and expect to spend several years in this country. It will be a god-send to Walt, and he anticipates much pleasure in visiting them.

Mrs. Gilchrist is a rosy woman without a gray hair in her head. I liked her much. The daughters are fresh and comely, like soft, light-skinned peaches. I went house-hunting with them. You will see an article of mine in October Scribner's. . . .

He sends the home news in a later letter:

Rose and I have been hunting today and got a partridge, a pigeon [1] and a gray squirrel. I never saw a dog hunt so. Tonight he is tired out and groans, and wants me to hold him.

I have a coal fire in the grate, and the game is now cooking over it. That little kettle just sets on the grate, and all the steam goes up chimney. I often broil my steak here. I wish you had the partridge. He was a fat fellow. He would do you good; but Rose and I will think of you when we eat him.

I have picked you a fine lot of chestnuts. Rose is keeping them for you, and today we got some more brilliant maple leaves.

At last comes the welcome word. The wife is soon to return. Eagerly the husband hurries to a neighboring city to meet her. Accompanying her is a comely young woman as ally in the anticipated warfare against the accumulated dirt and disorder of four months' absence. The renewed health and energy quickly find their old channels; sanitarium habits are forgotten; the 'demon of Housekeeping,' rampant, eggs her on. It turns the neglected house topsy-turvy. The master and his dog flee to the woods.

---

[1] The last wild pigeon he ever saw, he often mourned to think he shot it. He little dreamed the species was soon to become extinct.

Irritation at the general upheaval, and at the inability of the leopard to change its spots, finds expression in acute, analytic comments in the Journal, November 8th:

Wife returned from the Water-Cure on the Second, after an absence since the 20th of July. She is in better health, but still unchanged — still bent on making the kitchen rule the house. The chief end of man is to clean up his own dirt — health, happiness, comfort, must give way before the broom and scrub-brush. . . . As a housekeeper, Wife has many excellent qualities — prudence, thrift, good cooking; but she is never master of the situation; is always mastered by it. . . . The extreme literary woman who cares nothing for the kitchen, and the extreme housekeeper who cares for nothing else — which is the worse?

With order again prevailing, however, and a strong maid in the kitchen, much of the customary friction was obviated, and the current of their lives ran fairly smooth during the autumn and winter.

A December letter to Benton, and a Journal entry, picture the winter days at Riverby:

It is from no want of sympathy for you that I have not written before. I have daily put from me the thought of the great sorrow that has fallen upon you, and if I had any words that could have dulled the edge of your grief, I should not have withheld them, rest assured. The wonder is, considering the way things go in this world, that one's mother — his best and truest friend — is spared to him at all; but both you and I have had more than the average luck of mortals in this respect, though this fact, I am aware, cannot lessen the loss when the terrible blow comes. . . .

We have been hauling and moving a large number of hemlock trees, five and six feet high, from a hedge along the road. I have moved quite a large oak and maple also, and contemplate trying my luck with a few red cedars.

I have finished four sketches recently which I shall take down to Scribners tomorrow — 'The Pine Tree,' 'Strawberries,' 'An April Leaf,' and 'Bird Types.' I have sworn off on bird pieces several times, but I don't stick. My wife is always pointing out the bird's nest in my hair, but she doesn't see deep enough — it is in my brain; but I trust the last brood has flown now. This last piece is mainly a comparison of our birds with the English. My 'Strawberries' needed more literary cream than I had for them, and my 'Pine Tree' will not make more than two good saw logs — that is, two pages in the magazine. The 'April Leaf,' I hope, is tender, but any browsing magazine reader like you will find it a small mouthful.

What are you up to? Can't you and your wife come over and see us this winter? Mrs. B. seems well again, and, I hope, has a good girl.

[Journal] Dec. 3. A day of wonderful brightness and purity. The Fishkill mountains are nearly hidden by the haze, and the river valley is beginning to be obscured by soft white vapor — a day for one to take his skates and go to the ponds and still reaches in the streams and woods, and let himself loose on the transparent ice. Such a day I went once with dear Channy, to Rock Creek. With what glee we flew up and down the winding stream!

With the closing year, the Journalist makes this query:

Without a center-board your sail-boat slides upon the water. It does not take deep hold of it. You cannot beat up to the wind. What is the center-board of a man's character — will, integrity, depth of purpose, or what?

CHAPTER VI
WORKS AND DAYS
1877–1878

His daily teachers had been woods and rills,
The silence that is in the starry sky,
The sleep that is among the lonely hills.
WORDSWORTH

MR. BURROUGHS used to say that he had often thought of writing an essay and calling it, after Hesiod, 'Works and Days.' Those quiet early years at Riverby, in which he was steadfastly pursuing his work, yet attentively regarding the face of each new day, and pensively watching it fade into oblivion, fall naturally under this comprehensive title. His work was henceforth to profit incalculably through this fruition of hopes held for twenty years — a home in the country, with interests that rooted him to the soil, yet gave leisure for writing. The work of those years lives, and, when one reads the record of his days, one feels that the days themselves live also. He reverenced each day. Closely he scanned each one — a concrete piece of time rescued from the ocean of eternity. None was like another; none an object of indifference. Each was new every morning, fresh every evening. As with Emerson, the spectacle of the day was, in truth, a new speech of God to him. Sketches of his days, culled from the Journal, picture his work as well.

During 1877 there were many little ripples in the mental and emotional life at Riverby. The bank-examining went on, also the fruit-growing, and magazine-writing. There were brief jaunts from home, occasional visits from relatives and friends, deep joys and heavy sorrows; and there was the publication of his fourth book, 'Birds and Poets.'

While the title of this book was under consideration, there came the following suggestion from Whitman:

I think 'Birds and Poets' not only much the best name for the book, but a first rate good name — appropriate, original, and fresh, without being at all affected or strained. The piece you put fourth should be first, should lead the book, giving it its title, and having the name of the piece changed to 'Birds and Poets' [instead of 'The Birds of the Poets'] which, I think, would be an improvement. The

whole collection would be sufficiently homogeneous (and it were a
fault to be too much so) — you just want a hint for the name of the
book — Only it must be in the spirit of the book, and not too much
so either — 'Nature and Genius' is too Emersony altogether.

Some of his difficulties as an author are mentioned in this
entry:

I find it quite impossible to make my pump hold water from one
day to the next. I write away today and am very full of my theme,
and the stream of ideas flows freely; but if I am broken off for a few
hours, or lose a night's sleep, I am nearly dry again, and must pump
and pump next day a long time to bring the column up again; and
often have to prime a little by reading a page or two of some virile
author.

To Richard Watson Gilder,[1] in late January, he sends this
heart-warming bit of appreciation:

I think you go up head in this number of the Old Cabinet. If you
go on writing in this way you will have to be looked after. Most of
your things have a permanent value as literature, and you will soon
have to begin to sort them out and put them in a volume. Your
point always has a good ample basis — it is never the result of an
accidental or momentary angle of vision, like that which makes a
jewel of a dew-drop; it is a jewel from any point of view.
I like especially the hint from Shakespeare, and the remarks on
the typical quality of great art. You also say just the right thing
about Boyesen, and about the other superfine story writers.
You have very marked one precious quality that is so rare among
our younger writers — an honest, sincere, inquiring attitude of mind.
You are not thinking to show off your parts, but are ready to be
nothing for the sake of what you have to say. . . .

After a ten years' lull in writing about Whitman, Burroughs
had been set going again by some editorials (mentioned in the
foregoing chapter) in the New York 'Tribune.' The last one[2]
had provoked his rejoinder of April 13, 1876 ('Walt Whitman's Poetry'), which the poet marveled that the 'Tribune'
printed, characterizing it as 'an artillery and bayonet charge
combined.' Warming to the task, Burroughs later wrote 'The
Flight of the Eagle,' which he hurried off to Philadelphia for
Whitman's criticism and approval, as the Journal entry,
February 17th, shows:

[1] The letters to Gilder are kindly lent by Miss Rosamond Gilder.
[2] 'American *versus* English Criticism,' April 12, 1876.

Returned yesterday from Philadelphia where I spent the night of the 15th with Walt at Mrs. Gilchrist's. Never saw Walt look so handsome — so new and fresh. His new, light gray clothes, his white beard and hair, and his rosy, god-like, yet infantile face, all combined to make a rare picture.

After ten o'clock we went up to his room and sat and talked till near one o'clock. I wanted him to say how he liked my piece on him, but he did not say. We talked about it, what had best go in, and what were best left out, but he was provokingly silent about [its] merits.

Speaking of his poems, he said it was a very audacious and risky thing he had done, and the wonder was, not that they made their way so slowly, but that they had got any foot-hold at all. When the conditions were all considered, and the want of anything like matured and robust æsthetic perception in this country remembered, it was a great success to have effected a lodgment at all.

It is a feast to me to look at Walt's face — it is incomparably the grandest face I ever saw — such sweetness and harmony, and such strength — strength like the Roman arches and pieces. If that is not the face of a poet, then it is the face of a god. None of his pictures do it half justice.[1]

The original manuscript of 'The Flight of the Eagle' shows emendations in Whitman's handwriting, doubtless those referred to in the foregoing entry. One sees the poet's hand supplying, deleting, and altering words, phrases, and sentences. Besides the passage (pages 197–98, 'Birds and Poets') to which Burroughs refers in a letter to E. H. A., quoted in Chapter IV, as having been written by Whitman, as well as those seen in the accompanying illustration (a facsimile of parts of the manuscript), the most noteworthy passages contributed in whole, or in part, by Whitman, are here transcribed:

In fact, the main clue to Walt Whitman's life and personality, and the expression of them in his poems, is to be found in about the largest emotional element that has appeared anywhere. This, if not controlled by a potent rational balance, would either have tossed him helplessly forever, or wrecked him as disastrously as ever storm and gale drove ship to ruin. These volcanic emotional fires appear everywhere in his books; and it is really these, aroused to intense activity and unnatural strain during the four years of the War, and his persistent labors in the hospitals, that have resulted in his illness and paralysis since.

[1] In Brooklyn, at the Whitman Centenary Celebration, he said of a painting by Walters: 'It gives Walt's benevolent look, but not his powerful, elemental look. It makes him out rather soft — like a sort of Benjamin Franklin.'

welcome any evidence to the contrary, or any evidence that deeper & counteracting agencies are at work, as unspeakably precious, I do not know where this evidence is furnished in such ample measure as in the pages of Walt Whitman. †

The point is fully settled in him that ~~however they may have been held~~ in abeyance, or restricted to other channels, there is still sap & fecundity & depth of virgin soil in the race sufficient to produce a man of the largest type, & the most audacious & unconquerable egoism, & on a plane the last to be reached by these qualities; — a man of antique stature, of Greek fibre & grip, with science & the modern added without abating one jot or tittle his native force ✱ adhesiveness, Americanism & democracy;

✱ The great lesson of Nature I take it is that a dire serenity must be preserved at all hazards; and that, it seems to me, is also the great lesson of this writing

PAGE OF MANUSCRIPT OF 'THE FLIGHT OF THE EAGLE' WITH
EMENDATIONS BY WALT WHITMAN

The French *Revue des Deux Mondes* pronounces his war poems the most vivid, the most humanly passionate, and the most modern, of all the verse of the nineteenth century.

In the next sentence the italicized words only are emendations by Whitman:

Is there not a decay — *a deliberate, strange abnegation and dread* — of sane sexuality, or maternity and paternity among us, and in our *literary ideals and social* types of men and women?

The great lesson of Nature, I take it, is that a sane sensuality must be preserved at all hazards, and this, it seems to me, is also the great lesson of his writings.

I know that Walt Whitman has written many passages with reference far more to their position, interpretation, and scanning ages hence, than for current reading.

Concerning the 'Memoranda During the War' — the account of Whitman's nursing of the soldiers — these subjoined additions are in Whitman's hand:

...and puts in practical form that unprecedented and fervid comradeship which is his leading element, even more than his elaborate works. It is printed almost *verbatim*, just as the notes were jotted down at the time and on the spot.

The last paragraph in the essay is entirely in Whitman's handwriting.

Of Whitman's first visit to Riverby, March 21, the Journalist says:

A great event! Walt came home with me from New York Friday night, the 16th, and stayed till 4 this afternoon. Harry Stafford came with Walt. They cut up like two boys and annoyed me sometimes. Great tribulation in the kitchen in the morning. Can't get them up to breakfast in time.

Walt takes Harry with him as a kind of foil or refuge from the intellectual bores. Walt is mending, and said he walked better the morning he left than he had for five years.

May 10. New book came today. Like the dress much, and am well pleased with all the pieces but the last — the one I set my heart on. It generally happens that the father's pride turns out the worst of all. . . . [He refers to 'Birds and Poets,' the last piece of which is 'The Flight of the Eagle.']

Whitman's verdict, which followed a week later, reads:

I read it all over with appreciative and, I think, critical eyes. My impression of liking it, as a curiously homogeneous work (just enough radiation to make it piquant) and in connection *liking the name*, all deepened and clinched.

I especially much like — and more like — the chapter about me. There has certainly been nothing yet said that so makes the points (and eloquently makes them) I most want brought out and put on record.

Anne Gilchrist wrote enthusiastically about the book. She felt sure the heartiness of conviction breathing through the essay on Whitman would waken some out of their lethargy with a start. She found the essay on the Rural Divinity 're-dolent of all homey, enjoyable, sweet-tasted country things.' Myron Benton considered the Eagle essay by far the ablest defense of Whitman's poetry yet made on either side of the Alantic:

It is alive with eloquence and noble fire, as well as good hard sense [he wrote]. Enthusiastic as it is, there is a sanity about your criticism which not all his admirers possess. It awakens anew my old enthusiasm for some of those deep-fathoming lines that we first read together when we took 'Leaves of Grass' with us and lay down under the shade of Mulberry Rock that summer day so long ago. . . .

In re-reading your critique on Emerson [in 'Birds and Poets'], I am impressed that it is about the most searching estimate of the man that has ever come under my eyes; and at Emerson so many more able hands for the past forty years have been tugging, of course, than have tried Walt Whitman's case. I know this is saying a good deal, but really, so far as I know, there has been no such analysis as yours. The very marrow in his bones seems to quiver like jelly. I love him so much that I cannot help wincing a little myself at some of your thrusts. . . .

To Benton's letter Burroughs warmly replied:

I was greatly tickled at your hearty commendation of my essays. I sip your words slowly like some rare and costly wine that I would not miss any flavor of. Your praise is not cheap, and it does a fellow good when it does come. You say a most superb thing about W. W. — better than I have said — and I much regret that I did not have it to put in the piece. I refer to the statue and statuette comparison. I shall revolve that under my tongue as a sweet morsel. . . .

I have had several warm letters from strangers about the essay. One from Lathrop full of enthusiasm for Whitman — quite a startling letter to come from Cambridge. . . . But I expect some of the old foxes will be after me by and by, like Taylor, or the Nation man. But I don't care — let them have their say, I have had mine, tho' not about *them*.

. . . I have had no sign as to what he [Emerson] or his friends think of it.¹ I met Dudley Warner at Mr. Gilder's . . . he said much the same as you do. . . . I had thought to go to Boston this month, but the desire has about dried up, like my strawberries. . . .

I have just had a three days' visit from a young Englishman [Edward Carpenter] from Cambridge, who came to this country to see Whitman. I liked him much. . . . He is now in Boston and has letters to Emerson and others.

No rain here since April to wet the ground; things all drying up . . . but I had one berry — 'Agriculturist' — today that measured 4½ inches in circumference. Potato bugs came early; indeed, sat on the hills waiting for the potatoes to come up. . . .

Mrs. B. is not very well this spring, and is now furnishing her parlor; it is serious business. Do you know anything against this raw-silk furniture? I like the homely look of it much.

P.S. O—— does not know a wood-thrush from a long-tailed thrush, or thrasher, nor a cow blackbird from a crow blackbird. I should like to put a hot griddle under him for his patronizing familiarity.

Burroughs describes Edward Carpenter in the Journal as 'a modest, hearty, thoughtful young Englishman.' Mr. Carpenter wrote from Boston in early June:

I have not met with a spark of appreciation (intelligent or otherwise) of Walt Whitman here yet. I had a long talk with O. W. Holmes about him. He 'whinnied' (I find they all do) at the mention of his name and then launched forth as follows: It was very curious how he [Whitman] was admired in England. Lord Napier had said he was the one thing that interested him in the States, and then Lord Houghton came plump out about him at a dinner party, and was attacked so fiercely by Willie Everett that conversation was silenced. And he knew that Rossetti, and others in England, thought much of him. But — but — but — he could only say that in America no one read him. Well, their best critic, Lowell, for instance — he and Lowell and Longfellow were talking about Whitman together one day, and Lowell said, 'Why, there's *nothing* in him' — Longfellow seemed to think, 'Poor fellow, something might have been made of him, if he had been trained,' and 'for myself I knew what I thought about him — Oh, there's *something* in him, no doubt' — that thrown in by way of a sop to me — 'but — but — but' . . . and then off he went with the usual rant about W.'s sexuality, etc.

I said that his nakedness was no more than the nakedness of a Greek statue; and that his flavour, which Holmes found so strong, would perhaps flavour the dishes of America for a great many centuries — but it was obvious that I might as well have argued with the wind.

So much for Holmes. Of course he isn't important; but I think, he

¹ [The paper on Emerson.]

is just the kind of man who, having little or no real mind of his own, represents the literary world around him very well.

With Emerson I spent a whole day (and night), and a most enjoyable one. He was so good and gentle (by no means of the race of 'savage old men') that I could not feel angry with him for the part he took. He did not abuse Whitman, or rant against him in any way. He spoke of him more in sorrow than in anger. Said of course that he 'thought he had some merit at one time — there was a good deal of promise in his first edition' — 'but he was a wayward, fanciful man.' (It appears that Whitman took Emerson to see his Bohemian[?] society in New York — and Emerson thought it very noisy and rowdy; and couldn't understand his friendliness with firemen. In fact, Whitman baffled and puzzled him.) The truth is, as it appears to me now, that Emerson is a purely 'literary' man. I never understood that before. And I believe no 'literary' man can accept Whitman.

I saw Lowell, too, but did not say a word on the subject to *him*.

I was fortunate enough to find Lathrop at home last night. I like him much. He is a sensitive, emotional sort of fellow, perhaps almost morbidly so — as unlike the hard literary type as possible. He is very anxious to see you and Walt Whitman.

Matters quite other than literary were soon claiming the attention of Burroughs. Mid-June found him in Roxbury attending to the sale of the farm belonging to his brother Curtis (on the east end of the Homestead property — the house which years later became known as 'Woodchuck Lodge').

[Journal] Mother has worried and grieved herself nearly sick over the failure of Curtis. 'To look up at his back fields,' she says, 'and think they are to be his no more!' Looking through the kitchen door that evening I saw her busy washing a huge pile of milk-pans, standing there where she has stood and washed pans for over fifty years. Her face looked quite haggard and discouraged. It revealed all the care and toil and trouble she has gone through. As she came in it brightened up, and she looked more like herself. Mary Jane [his sister] came back with me — the first time she ever visited me.

In early July, Mrs. Burroughs went away for further medical treatment, and Mr. Aaron Johns and Burroughs went to the Canadian wilds. Out of this jaunt grew 'The Halcyon in Canada.'[1] They went by way of Boston, and our author made his first acquaintance with that city. In the excitement of getting away he forgot his fishing-rod. In the essay just mentioned, he speaks of pausing and angling in Boston, where they caught 'an editor, a philosopher, and a poet

[1] *Scribner's Monthly*, February, 1878, and *Locusts and Wild Honey*.

[Guernsey, Bronson Alcott, and George Parsons Lathrop], and might have caught more, if we had had a mind to, for these waters are full of 'em, and big ones, too.'

Frank B. Sanborn took them to see Alcott, and Alcott almost immediately began, as one would make a casual remark about the weather, to say, 'When are we to have the idyllic age?' Much to his and Aaron's disappointment, however, Sanborn snuffed him out abruptly, preventing them from hearing one of those transcendental monologues of which Emerson, years before, had told him and Benton at West Point. He had said that they must hear Alcott talk; that he talked divinely; and here was Alcott willing to talk to them, and Sanborn would have none of it! 'So we missed the orphic sayings, and the transcendental flow which was "like a train of fifteen railway cars and only one passenger."'

A heavy sorrow visited the traveler the day after his return:

[Journal] August 5. My beloved dog, Rosemary Rose, died this morning from poison — strychnine. . . . I do not need to write it in my diary to remember it — it is burnt into my heart. Oh! a bitter day. None may know what that dog was to me. He and Rab were my children, and my only comrades. I am quite desolate. Wife is away . . . and the house is struck with death. We dug his grave this afternoon — Aaron and I — but tonight he lies in his bed at the foot of the stairs for the last time.

His life was identified with mine as that of no human being ever has been, or perhaps can be. He seemed more than usually affectionate and demonstrative in the morning when I got up. Did he have a presentiment of his coming fate? He came to my bedside and whined and licked my feet all the time I was dressing, and came near tripping me up as we came down stairs.

August 6. Aaron and I returned from our Canadian trip the 4th, having been gone since July 16th, a long hard trip of 2300 miles and not very agreeable or satisfying, except the week spent in the woods, on Jacques Cartier river, 65 miles north of Quebec.

August 8. Aaron left me this morning. I am sad and depressed to the very marrow of my bones. The thought of my poor dog keeps me from sleeping.

August 15. Got a new dog in Poughkeepsie, with which I am trying to bridge over the chasm — have named him Lark.

To Whitman he writes of his recent jaunt:

. . . I called on Guernsey of the Boston Herald and found him a thoroughly good fellow. . . . We poked about Cambridge some, and then went over to Concord. . . . I like Sanborn all except his lofty coldness and reserve. It seems to be the style out there to affect ignorance of everything you are interested in. He showed me the home and some of the haunts of Thoreau, and then his grave, and that of Hawthorne. He took me to see Alcott, whom I liked. Alcott praised my Emerson piece, but Sanborn appeared not to know anything about my writings. . . . [Alcott] spoke in a friendly way about you. We passed by Emerson's house, and I admired his woodpile, but did not feel like calling on him of my own motion. . . .

I got the Literary Table with Blood's sanguinary review of my book. It is very petty criticism, and I think I can stand it better than Blood can. He evidently wanted to pitch into my Eagle, but was afraid of the claws. . . .

Burroughs seldom wrote a perfunctory letter. In acknowledging a book of poems, he wrote thus to Trowbridge:

Your beautiful and opulent 'Book of Gold' came this evening and captivated my wife at once. As becomes a critic I am slower to give it my allegiance. I tried to read 'Tom's Come Home' aloud, but broke down before I was half done; then Wife tried to finish it and she broke down. You do find the tender and human side of one very quick. Your poems have always been great favorites of my wife, and she said tonight with bedewed eyes, 'How much I should like to have Mr. Trowbridge come and see us!' I told her she was altogether too sincere and honest for a critic. I would scalp any poet that dared show himself on this side the river! He would find out that 'Tom' had come home.

Your book is certainly characteristic and savors of you in every line, and it is a good savor.

I did not look for you last summer, or for any one else. I was sick and disgusted, and was going a-fishing. I passed by Mr. Emerson's house and looked my defiance towards it. . . . I mean to come again when my liver is not a stone, then look out!

[Journal, Nov. 6] Finished the Canada piece[1] begun three weeks ago. New girl came this afternoon, and I resign the dishcloth to her willingly — the 12th girl since we moved here, three and one half years ago, and yet we have been whole seasons without any — besides the precarious help picked up here. . . .

Nov. 14. New girl gone. Another takes up the task.

Nov. 18. At Walden N.Y. on the 15th to examine the bank — walked down in the evening and discovered the Walkill, and stood on the bridge half an hour listening to the roar of the water below me. It set me to spouting poetry, when no one was in sight. The roar of the water always seems to set one going. The Walkill is a very noble, picturesque stream at this point. — Solitude is only more

[1] 'The Halcyon in Canada' (*Scribner's*, February, 1878) and *Locusts and Wild Honey*.

and closer company than one can have elsewhere — the company of one's self. One's best companions are those that affect him like his own waking thoughts and sympathies — himself seen at a little remove. The lover of solitude understands well Thoreau's dry remark that in his hut there on Walden Pond 'he had a good deal of company, especially the mornings when nobody called.' Solitude is a severe test of a man, but it is no doubt necessary to insure deep and fast colors of the spirit. Those who are most alone are most like themselves. Travel and society polish one, but a rolling stone gathers no moss, and a little moss is a good thing on a man. It gives him a local flavor and coloring that one likes. Solitude makes one a shining mark for the arrows that men dread, — misfortune, the loss of friends by death — he must meet them alone, unprotected.

The lover of solitude sows himself wherever he walks — the woods and fields and hills and lanes where he strolls come to reflect himself. There is a deposit of him all over the landscape where he has lived. He likes to go the same route each time because he meets himself at every turn. He says to the silent trees, or gray rocks, or still pool, or to the waterfall: 'We have met before. My spirit has worn you as a garment, and you are near to me.'

He is such a lover of the earth that a new landscape looks alien to him. After a time, maybe a long time, it becomes colored, or more properly, enriched more or less by his spirit. The mountains where one was born remind him of his father and mother, and he has a filial yearning for them. When Father and Mother are gone, I know I shall have a sad pleasure in the look of the hills where they lived and died.[1]

It often happens that I have many unoccupied hours or days upon my hands in strange towns and cities. I walk out into the country and over the hills and along the roads with long, sad thoughts. Why sad? I don't know. I gaze longingly into the houses and upon the farms and homely country scenes and occupations. What do I want? what does my heart crave? I don't know; but I know I leave myself all along the road; and I know I send out messengers that never return. As the bird feathers her nest with down plucked from her own breast, so one's spirit must shed itself upon its environment before it can brood and be at all content.

Nov. 27. Today is the 25th anniversary of the death of my little sister, Evaline, the youngest of the family. A quarter of a century has passed and Mother and Father are still living. She would have been a woman now, doubtless with children of her own. I have thought of her much today, and called up that sad, far-gone time. I helped Wilson skin a fox in the morning; he had caught it in a trap in a hole in the rocks; and now he, too, has been in his grave thirteen years!

[1] See his poem 'The Return' (in *Bird and Bough*), in which he has condensed in three stanzas his chronic nostalgia, and wistful yearning for his lost youth.

Dec. 5. My health is perfect these crisp December days, exquisite, keen as a razor; and out of this fine, delicious feeling I am writing my essay on the rain. I write from 10 till 2 or 3 o'clock then, after dinner, which I help get, I walk four miles in great glee, my dog and I. Then read Boswell's Johnson in the evening, or the paper.

I try to keep my appetite for my work eager and fresh.

[There is a note added one year later which says, 'Rain piece not so good as I had hoped.']

Dec. 8. A change has come over the spirit of my dreams. I am on the crest of the wave no longer, but in the hollow. Can't write a word, and have not for three days. It is ebb tide with me. I am not sick, but empty. My literary appetite is gone. Oh! my Rain! when will you pour down again? Hiram came Thursday night. Today, Sunday, we had a long tramp in the woods, and up toward Black Pond.

Dec. 18. In writing I observe that it is a great point to get a nest-egg. When you have made a beginning, got one good sentence, or fact, or observation, you add to it with comparative ease. 'It's the first step that costs,' as the French say. I want to write an essay on Solitude, but I have my nest egg yet to get.

The year 1878 was comparatively uneventful, with a few outstanding features, of which the birth of his son in April was the chief. The year also brought new and valued friends and correspondents, the most signal being the poet Emma Lazarus and E. S. Gilbert, a young farmer and naturalist in embryo. The bank-examining and fruit-growing continued, the essay-writing increased. Early in the year he wrote 'Sharp Eyes' ('Locusts and Wild Honey'), and began an essay, 'Phases of Farm Life,' which he undertook reluctantly at the suggestion of Gilder, and about which he wrote Myron Benton for suggestions. In his reply Benton gives a welcome picture of his friend:

You are fairly in for the winter campaign — teeth all sharp for that long big hole of the meatiest kind of nuts that you have been stowing away there all the past season — sharp, nimble little squirrel that you are! I know just how you will enjoy yourself sorting over those stores, nibbling now a rough but'nut, and now a chestnut, or a hickory. You are a wise, cunning rodent, and generous to share all those delectable things with the world. . . .

In the Journal in late January occurs an entry which (when the incident it records was more fully described to Whitman) gave rise to the poem 'The Dalliance of the

Eagles.' Whitman himself never saw the 'rushing amorous contact high in space,' which he has pictured so graphically. It is one of several instances where Burroughs, by supplying descriptions of things in nature, contributed to the making of the 'Leaves':

[Journal.] A clear sharp day. Saw three eagles today. Two were sailing round and round over the river by the dock. They approached each other and appeared to clasp claws, then swung round and round several times, like two school girls a-hold of hands.

The printed page of Burroughs seldom shows the smoky atmosphere to which he confesses in the entry given here:

Smoke seems to be the equivalent of flame: when the fire bursts out, the smoke is gone. I think that, intellectually speaking, I have many smoky days when a little more draught, a little excitement, a lucky hit or thought, or maybe a determined effort, would cause the flame to come forth. Something like this always occurs with me when I write: I begin by 'smoking' and feeling discouraged, but, by and by, if I put the screws on, the clear leaping thoughts and the glow come. But for the past three or four days I cannot get beyond the smoke. The combustible matter in me is very soggy for some reason; mainly, I think, because spring is here. . . .

In late March he and 'Smith'[1] are planting peach trees and 'telling yarns' amid the bird music:

[Journal.] . . . The medley of notes now and then shot through with the smooth, strong, piercing shaft of the meadow lark. It is bliss to be alive and be out of doors. That indescribable spring air is over all, that quality of newness and firstness — the sunlight is white, the naked branches shine, the deepening tinge of green is about the yard and in the moist places in the fields.

His forty-first birthday was spent in Washington on banking affairs. Things crowded fast that eventful April which held for him so much of joy and pain. He had to be in Elmira for a week on bank-litigation matters; his son was born on the fifteenth; and on the same day he was attacked by neuralgia in arm and shoulder — 'the severest pain of my life last night.'

Despite his suffering, which lasted some weeks, one finds him writing critically, in an April letter to Gilder, of poems the latter had sent him for his opinion:

I have dipped into Fawcett's poems a little and think it poor stuff; there is such an utter absence of passion, spontaneity, feeling.

[1] A nephew by marriage, his helper on the fruit-farm.

It is all carving and polishing. I can find no fault with his birds; he keeps on the safe side and attempts to delineate nothing characteristic of them; but he should know that the bat is not a 'blunderer,' any more than the toad is a 'stumbler.' He should know also that when 'dew meets dust' the result is mud ('In Hemlocks'). There are some capital descriptive lines in the poems, and that is all. There is no music or harmony or passion. I will dip into it again when I am better. I am in great distress at present. . . .

Those [the natural history] poems, however, I consider the best in the book, despite their occasional lapses from the strict truth. 'The Bat,' 'The Toad,' 'The Oriole,' 'Wrens,' are full of strong characterization. . . . He says that the dragon-flies emit 'rosy flashes' from their wings. The tint is rather steel-blue, never rosy, according to my observation. But that is a capital line,

'Dank with foul mire and rank with woody rot.'

. . . I cannot catch him taking liberties with the birds. I wish I could. . . . This from 'The Ice-berg' is good,

'When the red aurora, at the world's wild ending,
Opens in heaven with its awful fan of light.' . . .

Burroughs's record of a Sunday walk in May shows that the new dog had won its way to his heart:

Lark and I went on a long walk through the woods — found the nests of a robin, a kingbird, a bush sparrow, a hawk, and a gray squirrel, and started a rabbit from her form. Besides, Lark had a tussle with a mink, and the mink got away. I first saw the mink coming up the creek along on the rocks and stones. I sat down and waited for him to come up, but within a few rods of me he saw or smelled me, and ran under some large stones. Then I poked him with my cane and he came boldly out in Lark's face. Lark caught him, but dropped him in a hurry, both dog and mink crying out; and then he escaped as quickly as if he had dropped into the earth. Where he went to, I have no idea. He made a strong, not disagreeable smell, and gave us an adventure. The sweet-scented orchis in bloom.

May 29. Heard a rare thrush in the woods — the gray-cheeked thrush, I think. Its song reminded me of the veery's more than any other, but it was low and slight, as if the bird were only humming the air. The first part was more broken than the veery's — more like the syllabling of the wood- or hermit, but low and fine, and not very effective. Saw a pewee attacking a gray squirrel in a tree.

June 14. Attended the funeral of Bryant today with Walt and Gilder. Walt and Bryant used to be old friends, and had many long walks and talks together before Walt wrote poetry — after that, Bryant was cold and distant.

In June, Whitman visited Riverby. His 'Specimen Days and Collect' pictures the roomy, honeysuckle-and-rose-embowered cottage of John Burroughs; the hospitality; the raspberries; the perfect bed; the ample view of the Hudson; the early, Venus-heralded dawn; the noiseless splash of sunrise; and the delicious coffee, with cream, strawberries, and many substantials, for breakfast.

With the hot days of July, the little family went to the Old Home, where all three throve in the cooler air of the Catskills. The baby had not yet been named; but while camping with 'Aaron' on the Neversink, in August, Burroughs wrote his wife hoping 'the little man' was not giving her too much trouble, and suggested that they call him 'Julian,' in which suggestion she concurred.

On return to Riverby in the autumn, a willing maid was found, and life went more smoothly than ever before, despite the increased care a baby brought to the silent house. The beckonings of Dame Nature were less heeded; housekeeping was perforce less strenuously pursued; and in the sharing of parental joys and anxieties, husband and wife found more in common than heretofore.

His mother visits Riverby. He fills pages of the Journal with her tales of olden times. Deep in his heart he treasured the sight of her as she sat and tended his child.

In November, Benton warns Burroughs not to let paternal cares wean him from old friends. Commenting on the venerableness of their correspondence, he says: 'What a different world was that to our eyes, in the days of those first letters! . . . There was a freshness, a glory to everything that seems to have vanished.' Burroughs replies in the same vein, only more so — these men, only a little past forty, viewing everything in the light of the setting sun!

Yes [writes Burroughs], it is a sad fact that life and the world lose their freshness and glory as we grow older. The future becomes the past, and we turn more and more from what is, or is to be, to what has been. I think one begins to lose time after he is thirty-five; that is, his hopes and his spirits do not keep pace with the fast flitting years. It is this pack at our back, this burden of memory, that grows more and more as the days pass.

I look upon this baby of mine and think how late he has come into the world — how much he has missed; what a faded and dilapidated inheritance he has come into possession of. The spring and the summer are gone. Ah! me, what a delusion it is! The eye thinks the sun is fading, when it is our vision that is growing dim. No doubt the youth will find the glory we miss; and in his turn pity us that lived at such an unseasonable time.

The youngster, by the way, is doing well. His sense and his intelligence are very keen, and I think I see a future poet in him. He and I have great times already. I am writing a little again, getting my things in shape for another book in the spring, but not breaking much new ground. . . . I am reading the old authors, Tacitus and Cicero. Tacitus is very noble and good. . . .

When 'Phases of Farm Life' ('Signs and Seasons'), comes out in 'Scribner's,' Benton, writing that it bears the impress of having been written to order, adds:

I cannot bear to have you fall into this sort of hack-work, notwithstanding you have the example of the greater part of other eminent writers. Such examples, in fact, ought to be warning enough in themselves. I beg of you, I beseech you, resist all such temptations as you would the Adversary himself. Fortunately you are not in the predicament of many a poor fellow who must hack away to keep the wolf from his door.

At this period a correspondence started between Burroughs and E. S. Gilbert, a young farmer in Canaseraga, New York, which, mutually helpful, extended over many years, and which, as a whole, forms a valuable contribution to the wild life of the Hudson and Canaseraga Valleys. It furnishes a good example of the friendly aid Burroughs gave to countless young men who brought to him their natural history observations and problems. In Gilbert's letters one traces, under the tutelage of Burroughs, a natural observer's evolution into a trained observer. Burroughs, with his appetite for facts (which, however, he never offers to his reader as mere facts), welcomed young Gilbert's letters, which chronicle facts about the flowers, the rocks, the birds, and all the wild creatures with a fidelity strikingly like to 'White of Selborne's loving view.'

They compared notes, raised queries, and checked each other up in hasty observations. Burroughs sent Gilbert reading-matter and encouraged him to write for the magazines; he quoted from his letters in 'Sharp Eyes' ('Locusts and Wild Honey') and placed some early essays for him. One traces the self-distrustful young farmer, abashed at the elder's words of commendation, but grateful, working with a will; in time

editing a column of 'Notes and Queries' in a scientific magazine; writing valuable papers on 'The Formation of Sand-
banks,' and the 'Surface Geology of Canaseraga County'; and
seriously contemplating a popular work on botany.[1]

As to the botany which Gilbert contemplated writing,
Burroughs advised:

I am glad you are going to try your hand at a popular botany,
I cherished such a purpose myself at one time, but my ambition
gradually faded out.

Among other things, you must have an Appendix in which the
flowers are arranged *according to color*. Also arranged *according to
their blooming*, March, April, May, etc., so that one can identify any
flower they find, without having to analyze it. [Italics mine.]

The key in the botanies is no key at all to most people, but a
combination-lock. Make the subject clear and easy and your book
will be a success.[2]

[1] I am indebted to the son of E. S. Gilbert, a namesake of John Burroughs, for
the loan of the latter's letters to his father.

[2] Gilbert never wrote his botany, but Mrs. William Starr Dana (later Parsons),
in *How to Know the Wild Flowers*, and *According to Season*, followed a similar suggestion made by Burroughs in his essay 'Among the Wild Flowers.' (St. Nicholas,
1891; *Riverby*, 1894) quoting in her first-named book, the passage which gave her
the hint for her helpful books about the wild flowers.

CHAPTER VII

BITTER–SWEET

1879–1881

Whether the Cup with sweet or bitter run,
The Wine of Life keeps oozing drop by drop,
The Leaves of Life keep falling one by one.

OMAR KHAYYÁM

IN the ensuing three years our author drank deep of Time's bitter-sweet vintage. Birds and flowers held rivalry with banks; essay-writing and fruit-growing continued; another book was published; the baby was an increasing delight; new friends came; satisfying comrades lingered; but amid experiences fraught with joy came two bereavements that darkened his life.

In the Journal, January 10th, writing from the Old Home, he says:

Mother as active as usual. Father . . . is quite childish at times — cries on the slightest provocation; the least thing that touches his feelings brings the tears and chokes his voice. I could see myself in him perpetually.

As he sat reading and trying to sing from his hymn-book Sunday night, I thought I saw more dignity and strength in the lower part of his face than I had ever before seen in it. . . .

The accompanying letter to Gilder shows his ready appreciation of a brother author:

Your 'Poet and his Master' is still lying upon my table, and I take a sip of it now and then (since the first and second reading) to see what the after-flavor of it really is. Its atmosphere is more familiar to me, more akin to our thoughts and ways in this country than that of the New Day. . . . The literary quality of the book is very pure and ripe, and in some of the poems there is a pathos that shakes the heart, and Landor, you remember, says that unless the heart is shaken the gods thunder and stride in vain. That Sonnet on the Sonnet is a gem of the first water. Those last two lines are like a 'header' the boys take from some high bridge or precipice. When you get more leisure and health you will put a lifting force in your poems that will test our foundations.

Eaton's [Wyatt] Emerson is the best thing yet. There is not quite enough power in the mouth, yet the picture is a better success than I had dared to hope. I do not like his leaving the bust in blank that way, and I find the picture is more acceptable to my eye when this part is covered up.

I expect to send you proof of the Pastoral Bees in a few days....

Letters to Benton carry along the story:

February 9.... I am writing a little, and moping and yearning a good deal.

The proof of my new volume is coming along,[1] and that occupies me a little, but on the whole my celestial heifer seems to have gone farrow, and I shall get but little out of her.

The baby is a refuge from my barren and unhappy moods. He grows finely, and he and I have quite an understanding already. I take him out riding on the hand-sled, and he crows and exults like any other boy. You must come and see him and his fond parents before the spring has laid its detaining hand upon you.

I expect to go to Washington the latter half of this month, but would postpone it to see you here.

I like Hardy, too, and shall read any of his books I can lay my hands on. I have only read 'Far from the Madding Crowd.' He is too consciously an artist to be as great as Hawthorne, I think.

Mrs. Gilchrist told me she visited Emerson last fall in Concord. He is very serene and cheerful — remembers earlier things and events, but is fast losing his hold upon later. He saw Walt Whitman's photograph in her album, and on being told who it was, asked her if he was one of her English friends.

'What was the name of my best friend?' he will inquire of his wife. 'Henry Thoreau,' she will answer. 'Oh, yes, Henry Thoreau.'

Dean Stanley stopped some time with him, and Emerson drove him about in the antiquated wagon, holding the lines himself.

I like Sanborn's article on him. He [Emerson] does not forget that Shakespeare was the greatest writer that ever lived. He and Carlyle have ceased corresponding on account of their ages and infirmities....

April 20. While sitting on the border of the woods, was attracted by a soft, uncertain, purring sound in the dry leaves, which I soon traced to a spider. I saw and heard several; never heard a sound from a spider before.

The little piping frogs were in the fields and woods; long and long I watched and waited to see and catch one, but gave it up; but on my way home, in the cedar lane, I saw one hop, then another, and still another. I captured them all. It never rains but it pours. In the marsh I caught another. They were of different colors, but seemed to belong to the same species. Were they going from or to the marshes?

Heard a blue jay secreted in some pines and cedars indulging in a rehearsal that quite astonished me. It was a medley of notes worthy

[1] *Locusts and Wild Honey.*

of the mocking-bird, but delivered in a suppressed key — trills, quavers, warbles — very sweet and musical; occasionally there was a note like that of the red squirrel.

26. These days I am happy. The days are perfection — sweet, bright, uncloying April days — and then Walt Whitman is here. He sits in the open bay-window, reading, writing, musing, and looking down upon Smith and me grafting the trees or ploughing among the currants, or upon me alone wheeling baby Julian about the grounds. His white beard and ruddy face make a picture there I delight to see. Occasionally he comes out and strolls about, or sits on the wall on the brink of the hill, and looks out upon the scene. Presently I join him and we have much talk.

30. A most delicious April day — the flower of the whole month. Walt and I drove over in the Russell woods and visited the falls. Walt was much impressed with the scene and made some notes.

Turning to 'Specimen Days,' one reads the notes which Whitman made that day, while seated upon a fallen hemlock. Mr. Burroughs never failed to point out the place where Whitman sat as he wrote:

I jot this memorandum in a wild scene of woods and hills where we have come to visit a waterfall. I never saw finer or more copious hemlocks, many of them large, some old and hoary. Such a sentiment to them, secretive, shaggy, what I call weather-beaten, and let-alone — a rich underlay of ferns, yew sprouts, and mosses, beginning to be spotted with the early summer wild flowers. Enveloping all, the monotone and liquid gurgle from the hoarse, impetuous, copious fall — the greenish-tawny, darkly transparent waters plunging with velocity down the rocks, with patches of milk-white foam — a stream of hurrying amber. . . .
As we drove, lingering along the road, we heard, just after sundown, the song of the wood thrush. We stopp'd without a word, and listen'd long. The delicious notes — a sweet, artless, voluntary, simple anthem, as from the flute-stops of some organ, wafted through the twilight — echoing well to us from the perpendicular high rock, where, in some thick young trees' recesses at the base, sat the bird — fill'd our senses, our souls.

On May 3d the Journal reads:

Walt left today. The weather has been nearly perfect, and his visit has been a great treat to me — April days with Homer and Socrates for company.

The May records are quite as engaging as those of April. One lives them over with him as he leisurely drives through the sunlit country to examine the various banks; spies his old love, the white-crowned sparrow; hears the bobolink music in the meadows; looks through the yellow-green mist of foliage, and breathes the perfume of the sugar-maple blooms.

After a few days' trouting on the Rondout, he declares himself almost surfeited with rocks and waterfalls, yet says the scenery at the head of the Rondout, he is convinced, is unequaled by anything in the State. Again his father visits him, and again the son records his ways and many of his sayings.

An early June letter to Benton shows the preliminaries to the summer voyage of which Burroughs writes in 'Pepacton':

I have just finished a boat for a trip down the Delaware [the east branch of which is called the Pepacton] and I want you to come and go with me. I suppose the absurdity of the proposition fairly takes your breath away, but I mean it. My farm is not my master yet, and I hope you dare to snub yours. I say to my berries and my garden, and all the rest, 'Get behind me, Satan.' Do you do the same. I want to start soon after the fifteenth and go down [to] the Delaware Water Gap. We could make the trip from where I should put the boat in in Delaware county to Hancock ... in about five days. ... It will take us through a wild, picturesque country, and we will just live on Locusts and Wild Honey. Write me by return mail and say you will go. ...

Whether Benton's farm would not be snubbed, or whether the diet promised was not alluring enough, one knows not. He did not go, but asks about the voyage in an August letter, adding:

It will doubtless be a grist of golden wheat for the upper and nether stones of magazine and book, but let me have a loaf from the toll, which latter, you know, is always taken before the regular flouring is begun.

Burroughs replied:

I had no adventures, and no hair-breadth escapes; and but little to write about, but you know a writer gets only the seed-corn of his article from without; he grows the main crop himself, as he writes; at least I do.

In writing to each other these farmer-friends frequently used the homely rural language, taking their figures from familiar phases of farm-life. A correspondent, recently commenting on this trait in Burroughs, said: 'His wholesome philosophy, and homely vocabulary always makes me think of

graham bread, and apple-sauce, — clean, fine country life —
so refreshing after the "jazz" of our present day.'

To Joel Benton, the poet, Burroughs writes from Roxbury:

Your letter found me up here with wife and baby among the delectable mountains of old Delaware, where we propose to spend
August and a part of September. A man may live out all his days
here; the air and water are such as I expect to have in Paradise. . . .

I wrote a short article for the Christian Union which brought
me an invitation from Lyman Abbott, and a family by the name of
Valentine (with two pretty daughters), to camp with them on 'Tip-
top,' somewhere near the Highlands, but I could not be tempted
from my retreat here.

I am now writing a piece about the natural history of the poets —
picking flaws in the wood-lore of Emerson, Whittier, Bryant, Longfellow, Trowbridge, and others. I am in want of more victims. Have
you the poems of Mary Clemmer? If you have, or those of Howells,
Aldrich, Celia Thaxter, or any other younger, well-known poet, and
will send them to me, I will return them, and I will use them as
gently as I can. [The volumes, or the poets?]

Send me the Independent if you have it, with Mary Clemmer's
sharp stick. [She had objected to his frequent use of the word
'virility.'] I can think of nothing in my last volume that should have
offended her. Higginson, I see, sticks pins into me in the last North
American, but I stuck pins into him first.

My Ohio girl [Mary Sprague, author of 'The Earnest Trifler']
whose story I showed you last fall, has done well. At my suggestion
she re-wrote her story and sent it to Howells. He was greatly taken
with it, and Houghton, Osgood and Co. will publish it this fall.
Howells would have put it into the Atlantic, if he had not had so
many serials on hand. . . .

From the Old Home in late August he writes to Whitman:

I wish you here daily, it is so cool and salubrious. I imagined you
off to some watering-places. . . . I shall not rest till I have you up
here. . . .

I have written an article on Nature and the Poets, showing where
our poets trip in their wood-lore and natural history, and where they
hit the mark. I catch them all napping. Emerson, Bryant, Whittier,
Longfellow. I shall have something to say about you, with extracts;
but I cannot catch you in any mistake as I wish I could, for that is
my game. I wish I could also find a slip in Shakespeare or Tennyson;
but I cannot according to my knowledge, except where Shakespeare
follows the unscientific thought of his times, as in his treatment of
the honey-bee. . . . I will send you proof of the article before it goes
into the magazine.

There are two articles in the August Appleton's Journal that are
worth glancing over — Arnold on Wordsworth, and Earl D. on

moose-hunting. What simple good hearty fellows those English earls must be; not a false or conventional note in this one.

The baby is doing well and completely fills my heart. Wife is about as usual.

I find I cannot read Whittier and Longfellow and Lowell with any satisfaction. Your poems spoil me for any but the greatest. Coming from them to you is like coming from a hothouse to the shore or the mountain. I know this is so, and is no pre-determined partiality of mine.

A quarter of a century later, while strolling through the Deacon woods on the Old Home farm, Mr. Burroughs said: 'It was in these woods that I did my reading when I rather ungraciously attacked the poets.[1] I wanted to teach them a lesson — to make them more careful how they took liberties with Nature; but it was rather small business — going through the poets with a fine-tooth comb for the purpose.' He spoke of having taken Lowell to task for making the dandelions bloom with the buttercups and clover, and said that while, of course, dandelions bloom nearly every month in the year, his contention had been that, since Lowell was describing the full tide of summer there were riches enough then, without robbing May of her dandelions. He said that when, some years later, he had met Lowell, and referred a bit apologetically to his early criticism of him, Lowell had waved away his remark good-naturedly and said, 'Inasmuch as I was looking at a dandelion when I wrote it, I didn't mind.' Higginson, however, did mind. In the 'Contributors' Club' of the 'Atlantic' (March, 1880), he sharply commented upon Burroughs's criticism of Bryant and Lowell, and still later returned to the charge in a letter to Burroughs.

In a subsequent essay, after Burroughs had learned how capricious certain wild flowers are as to perfume, recalling his criticism of Bryant's 'Yellow Violet,' he conceded that there might occasionally be found one with the gift of fragrance, though with much searching he himself had never found one. He went further and said that it is the general truth we expect from the poet, and that, in his early criticism, intent upon detecting the alloy of error, he had perhaps unwisely sought to smelt the gold of the poet in the pot of the naturalist; and that while he had found the general truth on his side, the poets criticized may have had an accidental fact on theirs. 'Dogmatism

[1] 'Nature and the Poets,' *Scribner's Monthly*, December, 1879; also *Pepacton.*

about nature, or about anything else,' he added, 'very often turns out to be an ungrateful cur that bites the hand that reared it. I speak from experience.' Nevertheless, his tendency to be dogmatic led him again and again to get his hand bitten.

In this connection he instanced the pains which Tennyson took to be exact in all natural-history allusions. Anne Gilchrist once told him of walking through the fields with Tennyson, who, on spying a spring bubbling through the sand, got down on hands and knees, and peered a long time into the water, to see exactly how it behaved.

To Benton, who referred to some one having drawn comparisons between Thoreau and Burroughs, he sent the following discriminating comments:

That Thoreau business, I think, will play out pretty soon. There is really little or no resemblance between us, not near so much as between Thoreau and Cowley.

This is the way we must be set apart, each on his own pedestal: Thoreau's aim is mainly ethical, as much so as Emerson's is. The aim of White of Selborne was mainly scientific. My own aim, so far as I have any, is entirely artistic. I care little for the merely scientific aspects of these things, and nothing for the ethical. I will not preach one word. I will have a pure result, or nothing. I paint the bird, or the trout, or the scene, for its own sake, truthfully anyhow, and picturesquely if I can. Now when you criticize my books, put these points strong.

Burroughs suffered a great shock when, in early September, his mother had an apoplectic seizure. Much cast down, he lingered on at the Old Home till she rallied, and again returned there after a few weeks at his river home. In his Journal he writes:

Found Mother much improved. When I came in the room she said, 'Oh, John,' and wept for some moments. I was deeply moved. In a broken and disconnected way she told me how she heard the train, then thought of me, then all was still; then, in about half an hour, the door suddenly opened, and in I came. Poor Mother! her mind is in fragments, like a shattered vase, and she can fit only a few pieces together. . . .

Taking comfort, however, in signs of improvement, he returns to Riverby and seeks diversion in wild-honey quests on Mount Hymettus; later in what might be called a bit of a climb on Parnassus; for, with the closing year, he, who was then mingling so little with fellow-authors, attended a birth-

day breakfast in Boston for Oliver Wendell Holmes given by
the publishers of the 'Atlantic Monthly.'

The Journal barely mentions the affair, but in letters to
Benton and Whitman, and in conversation in later years, he
has left vivid accounts of that brilliant occasion. He merely
says in the Journal:

A good time at the Holmes festivities. Saw and spoke with
Emerson. He is the most divine-looking man I ever saw — does not
look like a saint, but like a god.

To Benton:

Yes, I had a pretty good time at the Holmes breakfast — saw
Emerson, and all the lesser Eastern lights, and was kindly and flatter-
ingly received by many persons. Miss [Mary] Sprague is a sweet,
charming young woman, and I felt flattered when told I was the
first person she inquired after when she reached Boston. She is good,
gentle, unassuming; not a dashing, brilliant talker, but full of quiet
fun and brightness. You would never have predicted such a book
from her. Her sister, whom I have known for many years, seems
more like a woman of genius, though one can see she has not the
intellectual grip of the author of the now famous 'Earnest Trifler.' I
saw Miss Sprague again several times in New York, and went about
with her, to a reception at Dr. Holland's among other places. She
has now gone back to Ohio and hopes to resume her pen. I marvel,
as she does herself, at the success of her book. It is less entertaining
to me than a book of Howells, or Henry James, and yet it far outsells
the works of either. If it was poorer, I could understand its success
better. . . .

Early in the following year, from St. Louis, Whitman wrote
Burroughs, acknowledging a gift from an unknown friend —
a check for two hundred dollars which James T. Fields had
asked Burroughs to convey to Whitman without disclosing his
name. With this letter came a picture of the great bridge
across the Mississippi at East St. Louis, where the poet said he
loafed many hours, adding: 'I don't believe there can be a
grander thing of the kind on earth.' Referring to Burroughs's
account of the Holmes breakfast, Whitman said: 'Your letter
made me see Emerson, no doubt just as he is — the good,
pure soul. John, I sympathize with you in the arm, and the
treatment, too.'

This was the time I had neuritis in my left arm [J. B. explained].
It came on after getting wet through and chilled, while fishing,
culminating in a fierce attack. The pains used to come in waves

down my arm — my thumb and index finger were numb. They used a cautery on it, and gave me hypodermics. Digitalis and hot sea-baths finally helped me. The arm was weak for years, but the power gradually came back.

At this time, learning of the whereabouts of his old teacher, James Oliver, Burroughs wrote recalling himself to him as one of his West Settlement school-boys; for the personality of James Oliver had been a light along his path since his teens. Excerpts from Mr. Oliver's reply are given here:

I think Mrs. Oliver has already mentioned to you we were very much interested in your writings long before we surmised that we had any interest in you personally.

Last fall I took a trip through Roxbury . . . and there and then was fully satisfied that the John Burroughs of literary fame was the West Settlement boy of a quarter of a century ago. But even then we could not decide certainly that you were a pupil of mine. I remember the family well, and the children in a general way, and your sister, now Mrs. H. Corbin, very distinctly; but I could not recall one by the name of 'John.' Your letter, however, solves all doubt, and I am indeed pleased to know that the hills of Delaware may claim you, and that they have at least one child not insensible to their charms.

The grand old Roxbury hills are enough to stir the blood and loosen the tongue. I well remember one summer evening, when I was spending the night at your father's house, climbing the hill to the north, and from the inspiration drawn from air, earth, and starry sky, composing, and afterwards reducing to writing, some fervid verses, the sole poetical(?) product of my life.[1]

This letter was one of the treasured possessions of John Burroughs. His old teacher, who retained vivid recollections of one Kennedy (afterwards of 'Kennedy's Medical Discovery' fame), and of other promising pupils, had seen no promise in the bashful lad; had even slighted him when telling Jay Gould and Andrew Corbin (in the same class) to get themselves a grammar; and, beyond showing a mild surprise when John had produced *his* grammar, had in no way been impressed by the lad. But now, at last, he had commended him; and his old teacher's 'Well done!' was more precious to the grown man than many a greater honor from a greater source!

Excerpts from the Journal carry along the story:

[1] 'I remember the occasion,' J. B. wrote on the margin of the letter; 'he brought back the skull of a fox.'

Jan. 30. How true it is that every person has his or her permanent water-level, like a mountain lake! We can hold only just so much happiness. A streak of great good fortune raises one for a short time, but we surely settle back again to the old water-line. So ill-luck, sorrow, the loss of friends and kindred, lower one for a season, but we recover and come back to the old measure, be it little or big. How much I love little Julian, and what a god-send he is to me, and yet is not my water-level permanently raised.

Feb. 3. Myron Benton came today, and this afternoon and evening we have sat in a 'tumultuous privacy of storm,' and talked the old, old talks.

Feb. 9. A clear, bright, rather cold winter day, and a sad one to me, for this morning Smith and Emma left me, to come back no more. For five years have they been here, and much have they helped to fill up the chasm of time. Going up there in the evening and sitting in their little kitchen, was like going home. It was a touch of the old times. Smith has been much company for me. He has written himself — his honest, silent, continent, manly self — all over my little farm. His work here will abide long after we are both in the dust. Little Channy, too — [their baby, named after Emma's brother, Channy B. Deyo] my heart clings to him. But they are gone, and another chapter in my life is closed!

Weeks of sleepless nights and anxious days are recorded in March, when baby Julian had scarlet fever. Writing of this to Benton, the father adds:

Your visit is about the only bright spot in my winter. . . . I have not written much, and now the season is past. I have already shed my antlers, and they will not sprout again for many weeks. They are 'in the velvet' all summer, and do not become hard and serviceable till the frosts of the fall. I am full of sap in the spring, and all my thoughts are watery and opaque. . . .

[Journal] May 7. Saw and heard an English skylark in full song up and up towards the clouds back of the hill over Hibbard's meadow. Must write it up. The bird was trying to mate with the field or vesper sparrow.[1]

A year later, from Cornwall, England, Mr. Charles R. Rowe, having read of the English skylark on the Hudson, in one of the above-mentioned essays, sent the author some larks to liberate along the river. The result of the experiment is found in a letter to Benton, in 1881:

[1] See 'Notes by the Way,' *Pepacton*, and 'Lovers of Nature,' *Riverby*.

Only seven out of the twenty-four [sent] reached me, and two of those died on my hands. The rest I let out in a field back of the hill, and two of them, at least, are still there, and, I think, will breed. When you come over I think you can hear the original of Shelley's sky-lark.

[Journal] May 17. Returned today from Auchmoody's lake [he and Mr. Ernest Ingersoll]. Had an idyllic time. The woods dry, clean, and delicious. What talks and yarns, and mutual confessions. . . . The time sped all too quickly. It seems like a beautiful dream. . . . In the moonlight we floated up and down the glassy lake and mused and talked; then captured the little green piping frogs by the light of a match.

From there they went to the Old Home, and the records are full of the May loveliness — 'acres of meadow-land down by the river covered with bluets — they tinged the ground like a bluish hoar frost'; handfuls of Canada violets, with a delicious odor, suggesting apple-blossoms; wild-ginger in bloom, and the painted trillium. They climbed Old Clump. The meadows are gay with buttercups; the bobolinks are in all their glory — their songs ring through his dreams; but his spirit was enveloped in a cloud. Already his heart was crying for his mother, as he tried to brace himself for the loss he knew must come soon.

'A Taste of Maine Birch' ('Signs and Seasons') records a trip Burroughs took that summer. The loon he describes, which had laughed so many hunters to scorn, laughed its last when he aimed his breech-loading rifle at him. Stuffed by its captor, it stood for many years in the dignified hall at Riverby, a mute reminder of that camp in the Maine wilds. Of that jaunt, among other topics, he wrote Benton:

Mr. Johns and I, and two others, went to Maine the latter part of August. We went up the Valley of the Kennebec to Moxie Lake . . . saw five bears, one moose, and three deer, and caught lots and lots of big trout. I am sorry you do not get off to the woods. Come over here and we will encamp on a beautiful lake near by, in the primitive woods. Gilder was up in September and we encamped three days over there, and enjoyed it hugely — poetry and pickerel every day with keen relish.

It is fearfully dry here, but the woods are golden, and I am out every day looking for wild honey of various kinds.

. . . I must resume my pen soon, or starve. . . .

I don't know why I should have delayed so long to thank you for your splendid article [about J. B.] in the Literary World. It is much more and better than I expected or deserved. . . . Be assured I appreciate it. . . .

Your poem in the Commonwealth took my eye, and the flavor of it lingers long upon my palate. Your poems all have as distinct a character and quality of their own as have Emerson's, or Whitman's. . . . It is a pity you have not my leisure, — without my laziness; you would be heard from well up on Parnassus.

To E. C. Stedman,[1] on October 9th, he wrote of Stedman's forthcoming essay on Whitman:

I have been looking for your article on Whitman with a good deal of interest. You told me when you were here that it would make all of Whitman's friends mad, and I have felt justified in getting mad a little in advance. In fact my wrath has been slowly fermenting and rising for the past month, and had you not sent me this letter I do not know what might have happened on the appearance of your article.

. . . But really I do not expect to be mad, but rather to be glad. It is not fair and honest criticism that W. W.'s friends resent, but insult, like that which Whipple and Holland and many others have dealt in. I know you will be respectful and appreciative, whatever flaws you may find in his work.

The tone and style in which you have treated Taylor and Poe are eminently judicial, and such as any poet could wish to receive at the hands of another — the treatment is affectionate though impartial. No doubt you have approached dear old Walt in the same spirit, and I am half disposed to resent the insinuation that you expect his friends to be mad. I am sure that neither O'Connor nor myself would ever have taken up the cudgels in behalf of Whitman in the way we have, had not his treatment at the hands of the literary men of this country been simply outrageous. Your article I trust and hope marks the beginning of a different state of affairs — that of honest and respectful criticism, and I for one expect to cry Bravo!

I myself have never felt like criticising Whitman any more than I have Nature itself; his very defects, if they are such, are vital, and such as belong only to the first order of minds. Much of his poetry is what may be called negative poetry, just as so much of the beauty of Nature is negative. . . . In his most arid stretches and catalogues I feel the same poetic throb, the same tremendous spirit that knows well enough what it is doing. . . .

I must give Holland credit for more liberality than I thought he possessed in allowing you your own way in the matter, portrait and all. You must have made a spirited fight.

On seeing Stedman's critique, he wrote Joel Benton:

[1] This and other letters from J. B. to E. C. S. are lent by Mrs. Laura Stedman Gould.

Stedman's article on Walt Whitman will do its subject good —
help sell his books, I think. Some parts of it are very fine, but it does
not settle the case. It will not do to compare the sexual passion and
procreation to the mud and slime that Nature covers up. Nature
covers up mud when she can, but she does not cover up procreation.
This part of the article is weak.

Although more proof is unnecessary, the subjoined letter, to
Gilder, dated November 28th, shows how ready Burroughs
always was to take up the cudgels in Whitman's behalf:

Walt Whitman has written to me about the piratical course
Worthington has been pursuing with regard to *Leaves of Grass*. I
have written to Walt recommending that he be sued at Camden at
once. The first step to be taken is to have an injunction served upon
him forbidding him to print [and] sell the book. Do you know any
lawyer whom you would be willing to ask to serve Walt in the matter
without a fee? If you do not, and Walt does not employ one in
Camden, then I will do it here. I think I can raise a fund to put the
scoundrel through. If you see Stedman speak to him about it.
Is there any way you can find out to what extent Worthington has
printed and sold the book? Go in to Legget Brothers book-store and
you will see the book there; ask them about it, where they get it, and
what the sales have been. I hate to trouble you, but I can't come
down just now, and I hate to see Walt Whitman, or anyone else,
robbed.

With the waning year Burroughs suffered the heaviest bereavement of his life. In his sorrow he turns to his Journal:

December 20. Mother died today at 10.25. It is Father's 78th
birthday. I came home Saturday night. Mother kissed me and
seemed quite bright. She looked better on Sunday, and Father said
he felt quite encouraged about her; but in the afternoon she was
taken with vomiting and grew worse. I was up with her nearly all
night. Paroxysms set in at eleven o'clock, and continued more or
less all night. The last words I heard her speak, or that she ever
spoke, were to Margaret [Eden's wife]: 'Go to bed, do go to bed!' she
said, as if wearied with our efforts to relieve her. I went to bed at
2 am, but they called me at 4. While dressing I felt that the end was
near. The paroxysms (of an epileptic character) [probably apoplectic
convulsions] grew more and more severe. I could not stay in the
room. [In view of his extreme sensitiveness to witnessing suffering,
it is a marvel that he could have forced himself to endure that
nightly vigil.]
About 9 o'clock I went over to the stack where the boys had
foddered the cattle. It was a relief to get out and look at cold, im-
passive Nature, and at the tranquil feeding cattle. I know Mother

would not have deserted my dying bed in that way, but I could not stand it.

As we returned, Eden and I were standing out in the road on the big hill, by the pennyroyal rock, when they called us to hurry up. How my heart sank! When I entered the room, Mother was bolstered up with chairs and pillows, and was evidently within a few minutes of her end. The Doctor sat by her side, and the family stood round, silent or weeping. Mother was getting purple, the heart was beginning to fail; the eyes rolled from side to side; her breathing grew shorter and shorter, and then ceased, and her eyes closed; her lips quivered, and our dear Mother was dead.

It was a cold, still winter's day. Father's grief is touching at times, but the clouds come and go quickly with him, as with a child. Homer and Jane came in the evening.

This picture of his mother's death-bed is characteristic. No detail of the physical dissolution escaped that seeing eye; every harrowing glimpse was burnt into his consciousness. As if in expiation for having left her side in that last hour, he forced himself to live it over again with his Journal. Morever, it was like him to make the most of his sorrows, as well as his joys — to extract from grief the last bitter drop. His brooding, imaginative nature met all sorrows and joys in this way.

On the home farm, in a hillside pasture (the one now known as Memorial Field), is a tumbled heap of stones — the foundations of an old house, the ruins of which were there in his boyhood. There, on that winter's day, he sat alone with his grief, while his mother's life was ebbing away; there faced the oncoming wave of sorrow that almost engulfed him. Speaking of this, years later, he said:

It was an hour of agony — my soul's Gethsemane. When I arose to join Curt and Eden, I could hardly walk — the emotional strain did something to me — there was a difference after that in the left side of my face, and in my whole left side — I was an older man, physically, from that hour.

Turning again to the Journal:

Dec. 22. Today Mother was buried. A bright, cold day, the air full of glistening frost particles, and a curious fog clinging to the mountain-tops. Mother looked as if wrapped in a profound calm. Her features wore a more severe and noble expression than they ever had in life.

After they carried the coffin down and placed it in the sleigh, Father stood by the window and looked out after it, and I heard his agonized words, 'I shall see her no more — my dear wife — I shall see her no more!'

Few men have ever loved a woman more. He clung to her more than she to him. Mother's heart and life were devoted to her children; she could not do enough for them; but she was often curt and unkind to Father. Not so with him; his children were secondary — she was first always. 'There was never a better mother,' he said, 'and never a better wife.'

Elder Hewitt preached one of his curious, incoherent sermons on the Elect — such a sermon as poor Mother has listened to a thousand times and thought she enjoyed. In the course of it, he stated that he thought we should not know and love our friends and kindred, as such, in the other world. He thought it contrary to Scripture. The reason was that some of them might be in hell, in everlasting torment, and we could not be happy, even in heaven, if we knew this was so. Of course we could not. It was a poor foolish sermon, in one sense, and yet it was sincere and heartfelt.

25. It is Christmas, and I have but one thought, 'Mother is dead.' Her toil-worn hands and aching heart are at last at rest. After life's fitful fever she sleeps well.

30. Every hour in the day I see Mother's image and hear her voice. In the night I awake and my heart cries, 'Mother, Mother!' The saddest of all is that I can eat and sleep, and read and laugh, and go about my affairs cheerfully, with Mother in her grave.

To Benton on Christmas Eve:

Your letter came tonight just as the snow-flakes began to come down. It promises indeed to be an old fashioned Christmas, and an old fashioned winter, too. I am beginning to have great faith in the 'probabilities' of the muskrats. This is the third winter they have hit the mark — three bull's eyes in succession. Their houses were scarcely finished when winter was upon them. I think it would have taken about three nights more to have completed the particular house I had my eye on.

This can be but a gloomy Christmas to me. I returned on Thursday from my mother's funeral. . . . You have drunk this cup and you know how bitter it is. My nature quickly rallies from such a shock, but the world looks very dark and cold to me now, and then this snow — how it drifts across my heart!

We have been planning for some weeks to go to Florida to spend the winter. . . . So be persuaded to come over early in January and go with us, you and Mrs. Benton. We will never be younger, and it will be a new world to us. We can go down there and spend a couple of months for about $100 a person. . . . I know there are a thousand and one obstacles in your way, but put them all behind you, as I do, and be a free man once in your life. . . .

CURTIS BURROUGHS

JOHN AND EDEN BURROUGHS

A tone of sadness in letters and Journal prevails throughout the following year; but his writings were bringing new friends and correspondents, and the old ones grew ever more dear. The usual avocations were pursued, but the real life was that lived with Nature, with books, with friends.

The first entry for the new year records the unprecedented cold all over the country, and the ice-harvesting in full blast on the river, but soon recurs to the sorrow hovering near:

Everywhere I turn the image of Mother — her voice, form, features, ways, are all before me. She appears always a little withdrawn, a little in shadow, as in life. Mother was not a bright, chirp, smiling woman, though as happy, perhaps, as most persons; but her happiness was always shaded — never in a strong light. The sadness which motherhood and the care of a large family, and a large yearning heart, beget, was upon her. I see myself in her perpetually. A longing which nothing can satisfy I share with her; whatever is most valuable in my books comes from her — the background of feeling, of pity, of love, comes from her.

Jan. 10. Julian is my comfort, my life. How my soul clings to him! He is a remarkably bright, handsome, engaging child. He just now begins to use the word 'wish.' Among other things he says, 'I wish you get me seven league boots.' . . . He cannot understand the death of Grandma. He insists, with great emphasis, however, that Grandpa is not buried in the ground. 'Grandpa live,' he says, 'and coming to see Dudy this day.'

15. It seems incredible that Mother should be dead. How many times during recent years, when I was home, or she was here, have I charged myself to observe her well, and note all her ways, and all she said, and show her every kindness, for before I saw her again she might be snatched away.

I have tried to remember her last words to me, and her last look when we parted, for my heart was full of blind fear that that might really be the last.

Well, she has lived her life, 72 years. How little she knew and saw of what there was in the world to see and know; and how much she felt and underwent! Her life was one ceaseless round of toil from childhood. After she married there was the housework and the dairy, and a baby nearly every year. [Here he rehearses in detail the thousand and one tasks that filled her days; tells of her berry-gathering; how she loved it; how the day before her fatal stroke came, September 5, 1879, she had come in fatigued from picking a pail of blackberries — the last berries she ever picked.] The morning of her attack, she went to the stove to fill the tea-kettle, when her extended hand was arrested. The blow fell. Her head dropped, and she staggered, and Father and Margaret caught her.

Her work was done. Great Nature said, 'Enough. No more toil for thee. Thy rest is at hand.'

In February, responding to Gilder, who had sent him a poem ('The Voice of the Pine') reminiscent of their encampment on Auchmoody Lake, he said:

I suppose you think I will say I like your poem out of mere complacency and compliment; but I shall not. I shall say honestly and frankly what I think, which is that it is a great success — one of the best things you have yet done, or that I have seen for many a day. You have cut out the heart of the matter with great ease and skill, and given it a lofty poetical cast, or rather, developed its latent capacity to assume a noble form. The last lines express my own definite view and feelings, and I shall hug that pine tree the next time I go to those woods for putting them into such portable pine-cone shape.

I do not seem to like that word 'mannered' — mannered secrets — but perhaps it fits the case in your own mind. [Mr. Gilder omitted the word 'mannered' in publishing the poem.]

Mrs. B. is going to N.Y. to the Women's Hospital this week, and 'Nay-Nay' and I will keep house alone. Come up and we will make the chimney roar with obstreperous talk — philosophical back-logs, and poetical kindling-wood, piled to the throat.

This refreshingly outspoken letter (somewhat condensed here), goes in mid-March from Burroughs to Whitman:

I send you a little remembrance — enough to pay your expenses up here when you get ready to come, which I hope will be before long. I have rec'd reminders from you from time to time in shape of papers which I have been glad to get. The sketch of Carlyle in the London paper was the best I have seen. Your own words upon his death were very noble and touching. It was a proper thing for you to do, and it became you well. The more one reads and knows of Carlyle, the more one loves and reverences him. He was worth all other Britons put together to me. What have we to do with his opinions? He was a towering and godlike man and that was enough. He is to be judged as a poet and prophet, and not as a molder of opinion. He was better and greater than any opinion he could have. His style too I would not have different. To me it was not the 'Mary-had-a-little-lamb' style of most of his critics, any more than your own prose style is; but grand and manly and full of thunder and lightning.

The robins are just here, and the ice on the river is moving this afternoon, bag and baggage. Ursula is still in N.Y., but hopes to be home soon. Julian and I have all sorts of ups and downs.

I am correcting the proof of 'Pepacton' and writing an article for Scrib. on Thoreau. I first wrote them a notice of his Journal just published, which they were pleased to say was too good for a book-notice and that I must make a body article out of it. Scrib. has displayed some remarkable journalistic enterprise lately. They have got from Emerson his article on Carlyle for their May number. This is *sub rosa.* . . .

I hope your clouds lift as spring comes. . . . If you see young [William Sloane] Kennedy tell him I will write him bye and bye. I guess he is a good fellow, but he needs hetcheling to get the tow out of the flax.

One learns from the letters to Benton that 'Notes by the Way' ('Pepacton') was bringing the author more letters from strangers than anything he had yet written. An Episcopalian clergyman in Philadelphia wrote that it furnished him material for his Sunday-school class. He writes of finishing an essay on Gilbert White.

At the Old Home, February 9th, he records in the Journal:

'Fifty-five years today,' said Father, 'I and your Mother were married,' and his tears flowed afresh. 'Fifty-five years ago last Sunday night,' he went on, 'I stayed with her the last time before we were married. I rode your Uncle Martin's old sorrel mare over to her father's.' Poor Father talks of Mother nearly all the time, and kisses her likeness many times a day. He cannot utter a sentence about her without breaking down before it is finished. He tried many times to recall where she had been one time, a few years ago, when he had met her at the depot and was so glad to see her. 'I suppose I was on a half cry,' he said, — 'I wanted to kiss her, but I knew she would be mad. Seeing how overjoyed I was, she said, "Chauncey, don't be foolish."'

Julian became alarmingly ill in February. Helpful as were the neighbors, since the child would suffer no one but his father to hold him, he tended him, day and night. Later the father's letters give graphic pictures of mingling housework with amusing the child; of stuffing an owl, and tinkering at his essays. The child soon has a relapse, the father a return of neuritis; the wife, still in the hospital, is gaining but slowly, — decidedly, 'life is not all beer and skittles'; but with the coming of sap-weather the skies brighten, indoors and out, as the Journal of March 8th shows:

Another crystalline sap-day of melted frost, or liquid ice and snow, wind N.E. The veins of the maples fairly thrill. Under the maple by the spring there is a shower of sap from the branches, where probably the squirrels have bitten them. Julian and I make a fire in the leaves by the old maple at the spring.

And on the 14th, an ever welcome event:

4 pm. The ice on the river has just started. Presto! what a change! the dead is alive again! resurrected! Where was that white, rigid, death-like expanse but an hour ago is now the tender, dimpling, sparkling water.

All the forenoon I have noted the signs: the river stirred a little, put forth a little streak of water here and there, made breathing holes, as it were. At 3 o'clock the ice was rent here and there, and shoved one piece upon another slightly. There was something alive and restless underneath them. Then by and by the whole body of ice began to move down stream very gently, almost imperceptibly at first, then with a steady, deliberate pace, till the whole expanse of the river in front of the house lay dancing in the light again. The resurrection of the river, but the dead — oh, the dead![1]

More joyous notes follow as April days come before April herself appears:

March 17. April-like weather. One sparrow yesterday, dozens of them this morning, and all singing. Snowbirds chattering, nuthatches calling, and woodpeckers drumming. It is not at the door of any grub he raps, but at the door of Spring. Am writing my Thoreau article, and doing fairly well.

To the invalid in the hospital, concerned about the house, he writes:

The house doesn't suffer, but if it should, it were better than that we suffered. There will be houses and things after we are food for worms. Julian is well. His last want is that I shall get him a little well, 'wiv' a bucket and rope, and a wheel to go round,' . . . I am living poor and thinking high nowadays. Julian eats like a tiger when he is away from home. I fear he does not like my cooking, but he is well and rugged, and more of a steam-engine than ever.

Ever reluctant to return to the grind of housekeeping, he proposes several courses for consideration when she returns: to spend a little time in Washington; to board in Poughkeepsie; in summer to board at Roxbury; and, in the autumn, a sojourn by the sea. Meanwhile he is making butter, and finishing an article on Thoreau:

About one hundred dollars worth of manuscript. It is a good article. If I had had some one to take care of Julian and do the work, I could have written much more. . . . Write me how you are. Shall I send you any magazines? . . .

[1] This passage, much elaborated, occurs in 'A River View' in *Signs and Seasons.*

[Journal] April 3. Sunday. My 44th birthday. My first motherless birthday. She who gave me birth sleeps her last sleep. A clear bright day and rather sharp dry wind in the north. . . . Julian and I still alone and peace reigns in the house. . . .

As the weeks drag by, and his wife's coming is indefinitely postponed, — the procrastinating physicians talking of keeping her there still longer, — his letters show him 'much put out.' He can't find any needles to sew on his buttons; his chicks are out of the shell, but it is so cold they wish themselves back; Julian takes so much of his time he can hardly say his prayers; and if he can't find 'Black Mary,' or some one to help them out, they will go out to the Old Home, or to New Haven to visit, or — or *something*.

He always was a persuasive writer: in three days, though far from well, the wife came home.

[Journal] April 10. A gloomy house, a gloomy outlook. In the afternoon walked back of the hill. The finest fox sparrow song I ever heard. How it went to my sad heart! Of all sparrow songs that is the finest. . . . It almost made me weep, it echoed in my heart, and the thought of it clung to me long and long. So plaintive, so bright, so prophetic — of what? sadness or joy?

Presently, however, he writes Benton cheerfully:

As you surmise, Mrs. B. is much better than when she first came from that horrid hospital, where they think and dream and talk of nothing but tumors. . . . She is now busy cleaning house (or hoeing out the thickest of the dirt, as she says), and works with her old vim. If we succeed in getting a decent girl, we may stay here a part of the summer. . . .

Julian, too, is quite well again, and grows finely. We have long walks and talks together. He knows the sparrow, the blue jay, and the robin. The crow he persists in calling a black robin, which shows that his ornithological eye needs training yet. He said that one day a robin called him to come up in the clouds to sit down. He speaks of 'smooth' as an extraneous or independent something; of this or that he says, 'It has "smoove" on it.' . . . He asks ten thousand questions a day. He is a bright boy, and we love him more and more.

Stoddard's criticism [of 'Pepacton,' published that month] did not hurt *me* much, and it did my wife a great deal of good. I think it is the only piece about me, or my books, that she ever took any interest in, or thoroughly appreciated. She thinks I have had too much 'soft soap.' If you see or write to Stoddard, thank him for me; tell him my better half was highly edified and delighted, and that the other half is none the worse.

I reluctantly admit that I am 'very good,' and often exclaim with Thoreau, 'What demon possesses me that I behave so well?' But about being young, except in wisdom, and in appreciation of Stoddard's poetry, — alas! alas! It does not trouble me at all to be compared to a cow in clover, especially when he puts me among such celestial cattle as Emerson and Thoreau; and I shall not drop my sweet cud for the barking of any cur that may leap the fence. Poor Stoddard! more clover and less beer would make him better-natured, and a better poet, too.

I do not see many notices of the book. 'H. H.' had a good one in the last Critic, too good; and somebody sent me a good one from the Sunday Times. I feel little interest in the work, and don't care whether they blame or praise. I always do as well as I can — do not water my milk one drop — and there my duty ends; and my interest too, sometimes. I have kept a copy for you, but you must come after it.

I am sorry to hear of [Walter] Pomeroy's illness. I trust your air and hospitality will do him good. We must get him off in the woods in the course of the summer.

The Nation has sent me, to notice, Miss Preston's translations of Virgil's Georgics. I found that she and other translators make Virgil say absurd things; so I have been digging out the original, and find that Virgil was not always so wide of the truth in his natural history as they made him out to be. I wish I had hold of Pomeroy to help me through with some of the tough passages. . . .

I enclose a specimen letter, such as I frequently receive from invalids, and that arm me completely against such critics as Stoddard.

The letter of which he speaks was from Amelia Beardslee, in Manchester, Iowa, and proved to be the beginning of a valued correspondence. Twelve years an invalid, and unable to step outside her room, she said that he had enabled her to forget that; she had gone with him through the fields and woods. 'You have the rare power of enabling others to see with your eyes,' she added, 'and I feel grateful to you for the moments in which the blessed sense of strength has come back to me.'

'Notes from the Prairie' ('Riverby') is largely made up of excerpts from Mrs. Beardslee's letters, in which she recorded remembered observations of her childhood. On the first appearance of the essay, as a magazine article, the author wrote tendering her a share in the proceeds; he said the bigger and better part was hers; but, declining this, she said: 'When Christmas morning comes, give your birds and squirrels an extra measure of food in my name — only this and nothing more.' By now he had changed the opinion expressed in the sixties to his first woman correspondent — as to the scarcity of nature-lovers among women; he even averred in 'Notes from the Prairie' that women are about the best lovers of nature, after all.

One woman friend, of this period, Mrs. Sarah Booth, a bird-student, protesting against his gifts being suffocated in kitchen smoke and steam, said:

There are hosts of biddies with no brains, but plenty of hands, and they must do the work which needs only hands. . . . I would turn New York City as inside out as the turned hemisphere of a peeled orange to supply myself with hands, that I might have the freedom of my brain, if I were endowed like yourself. . . .

The biddies, however, were hard to find, and, when found, harder still to keep. Hence his literary activities, then and always, were inextricably mingled with activities in the kitchen. In later years guests at his rustic cabin in the woods marveled at his handiness in fending for himself, little realizing what a long apprenticeship he had served.

Only rarely does he mention public events in the Journal, and then briefly.

July 4. A sad Fourth. Much depressed by the shooting of Garfield. Whether he lives or dies, the event will be productive of incalculable injury. Great crimes are sure to repeat themselves. Other presidents will be shot in the future, either by madmen or by assassins. We shall probably have an epidemic of shooting at once. When a thing has been done once, it is much easier to do it a second time. The pent-up madness and villainy will now set toward this new vent — shooting distinguished men.

August 10. Wife and Julian and Gilder and family join me and Lark today. We remain in camp till the 19th, when I carry Julian, who is sick, out in a pouring rain. Much alarmed about the dear boy, but in a few days he is better.

The experiment was not entirely satisfactory. It is a mistake to take one's family to the woods. They stand between you and the wild nature you are after, and between you and your male companions. Gilder and I could not, or did not, get at each other. We had no intimacy, no comradeship, no talks. Leave the women at home next time. The camp is for men alone.[1]

[1] He modified these views, in later years, and had many delightful times in the Adirondacks, and elsewhere, when he found women to be good camp-mates. It was only one of his dangerous generalizations. What he meant was that one's camp-mates, men or women, need to be chosen from those who are true lovers of the woods and of camp-life.

Sept. 20. The President's death oppresses me like a personal bereavement. . . .

Sept. 21. We go down to Ocean Grove and spend a week by the sea. The beach attracts me much. Its purity, its odor, its elemental wildness, its rustling liquid drapery, the great white, lace-like spreads which it is forever throwing and forever withdrawing from the smooth face of the sands. I never tire of it. Day after day I walk for miles on the beach, bare-foot, skirting the thin edges of the waves, alone, soliloquizing with the soliloquizing sea.

28. Back home tonight and much distressed by the illness of my dog, Lark, from the bite of a large Newfoundland dog.

30. My dear dog, Lark, died today. I sat by him the last two hours of his life. So he, too, is already of the past! Oh, greedy, remorseless Past! not even is one's dog safe from your all-devouring maw! This was (ah! that fatal 'was'!) my third dog, and the most tender and affectionate of them all. Dog of the gentle heart! more a child than a dog! How much have I buried in the grave with thee! How can I again resume my walks through the old lanes and by-paths and wood-roads where we have strolled together for four years past, summer and winter, without thy gentle comradeship? All the landscape for miles and miles we have read over and over together, as two boys read a story-book. No forest-way or nook or retreat but knew us many times. The 'Idyl of the Honey-Bee' was thine as well as mine. The 'Notes of a Walker' were thy notes as well. It seems as if I could almost give my right hand to have thee back. A vital part of me is gone, something that knitted me to the fields and woods, and that made life more sweet.

Lark was always childlike, not puppyish, but like a proud and pampered child. He could not stand even the look of anger from me. Let me approach him any time or place and look sternly at him, and he would throw himself upon his back and put up his little red feet supplicatingly. There was no blame he would not take upon himself, and humbly beg forgiveness for. He had no prowess, no courage, could hardly kill a squirrel unaided.

How pathetic now seem his wanderings with his faint yet yearning human and sagacious heart, when I lost him in Kingston, on my return from Roxbury, and he made his way back, ten miles to Father North's in Olive, where I spent Sunday, and where we had left Wife and Julian! What trepidation, what bewilderment had he not suffered! The hostile dogs, the hooting boys, the threatening cattle, and the long, dusty, tedious way! If I knew where he passed the night, or where he rested by day, I think I would go there just to gaze on the spot. The dry leaves upon which he made his bed, and where he renewed his resolution not to be discouraged, or to give up the search for me, would be precious to my eyes.

One's pleasure with a dog is unmixed. There are no set-backs.

They make no demands upon you as does a child; no care, no interruption, no intrusion. If you are busy, or want to sleep, or read, or be with your friend, they are as if they were not. When you want them, there they are at your elbow, and ready for any enterprise. And the measure of your love they always return, heaped up.

Ah, well! I cannot help but mourn — my daily companion and comrade is gone. The door that opens and shuts but once, to dogs as well as men, has closed behind him, and I shall see him no more, no more. I buried him at the north end of the rock where my other dogs lie. In the afternoon I dug his grave, and in the twilight buried him, Julian looking on, the only mourner.

Years later, in various essays (in 'Ways of Nature,' 'Leaf and Tendril,' and 'Field and Study') he wrote many passages about dogs in which the gentle Lark is traceable. He is mentioned by name in the essay 'Human Traits in the Animals.' Along with Scott, Dr. John Brown, Count de Foix, John Muir, Lowell, and Maeterlinck, to name a few, of John Burroughs also, it may be said, 'He mightily loved dogs above all other animals.'

Cursory readers who have not followed him closely in the above-named essay, in 'Animal and Plant Intelligence,' in 'What do Animals Know?' and in 'The Reasonable but Unreasoning Animals,' have felt aggrieved at his seeming to run counter to what they have observed in dogs and other household pets. A careful reading would correct such impressions. His endeavor is always to help his reader to love the animals as animals, not as men:

Such sweet companionship as one may have with a dog, simply because he is a dog, and does not invade your own exclusive sphere! He is, in a way, like your youth come back to you and taking form — all instinct and joy and adventure. You can ignore him and he is not offended; you can reprove him and he still loves you; you can hail him and he bounds with joy; you can camp and tramp and ride with him, and his interest and curiosity and adventurous spirit give to the days and the nights the true holiday atmosphere. With him you are alone and not alone; you have both companionship and solitude.

Who would have him more human and less canine? He divines your thought through your love, and feels your will in the glance of your eye. He is not a rational being, yet he is a very susceptible one, and touches us at so many points that we come to look upon him with a fraternal regard.

Sound psychology, this, and sound human-heartedness, at which only a hopeless sentimentalist, who dares not follow facts to their conclusion, could take offense. Always in study-ing John Burroughs one is convinced of his reverence for 'things as they are.' What *is*, is best, and worthy of all ac-ceptation; he will not bedeck it with false attributes, but will love it for what it is, whether it be his dog or the Cosmos.

To Benton he writes of his loss:

Your letter came tonight and I tore it open with hands cold from the picking of about my last peaches.

Eventful months have sped by since last I heard from you. . . . We are all here, except poor Lark. . . . He has joined my other dogs beneath the grass beside the old rock, and also, I have no doubt, in the happy hunting-grounds beyond. . . . I have mourned and still mourn him deeply. He was my muse and the inspiration of all my walks. The 'Notes of a Walker' were mainly his. He would sniff out the fact, and I, as his secretary, would chronicle it. I doubt if I shall ever give my heart to another dog to be widowed in this way — it is too painful.

Now I am trying to take up my pen again, but my ink will not flow yet. I am coming your way soon, perhaps next week, and the banks of your placid stream are among the banks I hope to inspect. Wife and Julian would like to come, but the ride is too far. . . .

If you can come over, don't wait for me. . . . These are good days to crack our literary nuts. How gregarious and jovial the birds are in the fall — let us go and do and be likewise. . . .

The rustic Study at Riverby, on the bench of land some rods below the dwelling-house, was begun in the autumn of 1881. It must have occupied much of the author's time and thought, yet is but briefly mentioned in the Journal. Did he guess, at the time, how much the little refuge was to mean to him in the years to come?

As the year wanes, a year in which the bitter had mingled with the sweet to the very end, he writes in his Journal:

Nov. 25. A bright clear day. Snow on the ground. All alone in the house since last Saturday, Wife and Julian in Troy. How many days and nights of solitary confinement have I spent in this house! The sad, sad thoughts and remembrances, how they find one out and prey upon him in solitude!

Dec. 15. Finished my article on the bank question for the Century last night; ink hardly dry on last page when I was ordered to P——, to look after a defalcation in the P—— National Bank.

Of the essay, 'Broken Banks and Lax Directors,' he said: 'I didn't know I had such an article in me till Gilder told me I had. It made quite a hit. Experts in banking circles wrote me about it. One man said he took it as his chart and compass.' At the time it was published (March, 1882), directors of many of the national banks wrote urging him to write a manual for bank directors. The paper attests to the thoroughness of his work as bank-examiner. There was nothing slipshod in his searching methods. An expertness not looked for in one with so much ideality is here revealed. One sees quite another Burroughs than the one of the books. In truth, in one sentence only can we detect the writer of the nature essays:

Bees carry off honey from the hive and leave the comb all intact; and cashiers have been known to exhibit as clean and straight a set of books as need be, when their accounts were little more than empty combs.

Evidently, if he had not let the banks interfere with the birds, he had also not let the birds interfere with the banks. One finds, despite his avowal to the contrary, that he *could* spy on something besides a chipmunk; for, airing the devious ways of dishonest cashiers, he gave explicit instructions to unwary stockholders and directors, lest 'the golden apple of bank-shares and expected dividends turn to ashes' on their lips. All these seemingly foreign activities in one we associate with such different interests and aims, all the reams on reams of paper he covered with wearying columns of figures (and had preserved for old association's sake), make one marvel that the untrammeled man one knew, who came and went freely in nature, could so steadily have held himself, and for so many years, to work so alien to his tastes and temperament.

CHAPTER VIII

IN PASTURES NEW

1882

The scenery of the Clyde is unequaled by any other approach to Europe. . . . The landscape closes around us. We can almost hear the cattle ripping off the lush grass in the fields. One feels as if he could eat grass himself. It is pastoral paradise.

From *Fresh Fields*

EARLY in the ensuing year — a year that was to yield so much of varied interest — Burroughs settled in new quarters, his cosy, one-room bark study, a few rods from his dwelling. Its huge fireplace,[1] its book-lined walls, and its wide windows looking out upon vineyard and river, and its detachment from domestic affairs, afforded the place and atmosphere needed for work. He himself fashioned the book-shelves, table, and settle from native oak.

Much joy went into the making of this snug little refuge where, in succeeding years, besides many magazine articles, he was to write 'Fresh Fields,' 'Signs and Seasons,' 'Indoor Studies,' and 'Riverby.' He records in the Journal, January 5th:

The first day in my new Study. Moved in yesterday. My books in their new places last night. I contemplated them with a strange, sad feeling, my faithful, silent companions.

'Signs and Seasons' was the first essay he wrote there; the Carlyle essay, next.

In January, urging Benton to come over and visit them, he says:

We are well, have a good girl, a full larder, a bursting coal-bin, and hospitable hearts. . . . We have had little or no company this winter and have had to crack the social hickory, and eat the juicy Nelli's, and toothsome Spies, alone. . . . Come over, and like two mice, we will nibble away on such cheese-rinds as my poor board, literary and other, affords.

I have builded me a new house, and there is a big chair in it for you. I am alone with my books and my thoughts now, down on the brink of the hill, beyond the orbit of household matters, and hardly

---

[1] Its brick chimney which did not draw well, was supplanted by a wood-stove, and later by a picturesque cobble-stone chimney.

ever perturbed by them. I have the solitude of Bruin in his den, and
I suck my paws pretty industriously.

I am writing a little and reading a little — reading mainly African
travels.

If you have got copies of the old Radical, see if you can find the
one with a poem by John Weiss called 'Dark,' or something like that
(it was a very dark poem, at any rate), and send it to me, or bring it
with you. I want to contrast it with Emerson's 'Brahma' in a little
essay for the Critic.

Benton came, as the Journal shows:

Feb. 13. Myron left for home today. . . . Much talk down in my
little house, trying our teeth as usual upon the old uncrackable nuts.
The logico-metaphysical lines in Myron's mind much stronger and
deeper than in my own. The inward eye of his mind is very clear.

Feb. 27. . . . A suggestion of spring this morning, clear and soft
and hazy. The bluebird (here all winter) has the amorous warble of
spring. The purple finches sitting in all the apple trees, indulged in a
fine, half-suppressed chorus; it was very pleasing. My little wood-
pecker has not begun to drum yet. A hard snow covers the ground.
Ice men began to put in poor six-inch ice on Saturday in front of me.
A sun-dog yesterday afternoon; and a soft rosy glow diffused over
the clouds at sunrise this morning, reaching nearly to the zenith.
Do these signs indicate fair weather? First chipmunk today, back on
Manning's ridge.

March 1. . . . Finished my 'Signs and Seasons' today,[1] begun two
weeks ago. Writing is like fishing: you do not know that there are
fish in that hole till you have caught them. I did not know there was
an article in me on this subject till I fished it out. I tried many
times before I had a bite, and I did much better some days than
others. Stormy days (either snow or rain, though snow is best) were
my best days.

The stimulus of Benton's comradeship is further acknowledged in this letter:

I have been pretty busy since you left. Your visit put about two
inches of fat on my ribs, and I have been working it off. It was most
timely and satisfactory. I needed a pause, a breathing spell, and to
have my thoughts crossed with some vigorous species. You know
Darwin has shown (I have got nearly all his works since you were
here) that cross-fertilization is best in the vegetable kingdom, and I
know it is in the intellectual. One must have pollen from other

---

[1] This essay was published in the *Century Magazine* in 1883. Its title was
changed to 'A Sharp Lookout' on becoming the initial chapter in the volume
Signs and Seasons.

minds if he would keep up a race of vigorous seedlings of his own. The next two weeks after you were here I wrote quite a long article, and one of my best, I think, on Observation of Nature — nothing that we discussed, yet I doubt if it would have been written if you had not come. I have also written another short essay.

I send you the Critic with my little Emerson essay, which you may return sometime.

I will send you advance sheets of my Thoreau article soon.[1]

I like your poem on the Mowers much. It is one of your best, and is no doubt destined to a permanent place amid our rural poetry. If you dug into your mind as persistently as I do in mine, you might write many such, and many prose sketches of permanent value. The muse is not going to seize one's hand and make him write; he has got to wait upon her, and court her assiduously. I bore her unmercifully sometimes. . . .

Well, spring has come, the tender, yearning, wistful spring, and the heroic winter is gone. I confess I am sorry. One can nestle so close to himself, and to his friend, in winter, but spring drives one forth. I experience all the pain and sadness of the annual migration of my Aryan ancestors in the spring. . . .

[Journal] April 3. My 45th birthday. Clear, crisp, and delightful. All day in the old sap-bush at home, boiling sap, Father, Julian, and Hiram there much of the time. How delighted I am again amid the old scenes and at the old occupations!

Now, on my 45th birthday, my hair is about half gray, beard ditto, mustache unchanged, except on close inspection, when three or four gray hairs appear. Health good, and much of a boy yet at heart, but the boy is growing more and more sad with longer and more frequent retrospections.

Indeed, the Past begins to grow at my back like a great pack, and it seems as if it would overwhelm me quite before I get to be really an old man. As time passes, the world becomes more and more a Gethsemane [Golgotha?] — a place of graves, even if one does not actually lose by death his friends and kindred. The days do not merely pass, we bury them; they are of us, like us, and in them we bury our own images, a real part of our selves. With what longing and regret we look back athwart this cemetery of the years where our days, many of them so beautiful and happy and bright, lie hushed and still. They cannot rise, they cannot come back to us; they were the offspring of our loins. Many of them we have entirely forgotten the look and aspect of; we cannot recall what they were like, and this makes us sad. Occasionally a word, a forgotten tune, or a perfume, brings back for a moment the buried Past, and a mournful thrill goes through the soul.

It was of such passages that he spoke when, on giving me his Journals, he said, 'I seem to have put all my gloom in them,

---

[1] First published in the *Century Magazine;* later in *Indoor Studies*.

and all my sunshine in my books.' One does find in the Journals much too much of the pensive mood; hears too often the 'sad whisper of autumn leaves.' Nevertheless, retrospections are often relieved by sunnier reflections. For example, on the same day that he made the pathetic birthday record, he sent a note to Myron Benton which shows him looking forward:

We have made up our minds to go to England in May and spend part of the summer there. We have also made up our minds that you and Mrs. B. are just the couple to go with us. I have been in N.Y. to see about passage. Write that you will go with us. . . . We are younger this year than we will ever be again.

Meanwhile his pen was not idle, as an amusing Journal entry attests:

April 26. Am writing on Carlyle, and hitting the mark now and then. Just at this moment my wife calls me to drop my Carlyle and come and shake the carpet — a Carlylean task that makes me wrathful. I will whip the seams open!

Mrs. Burroughs had a dinner-bell of no uncertain sound, with which she used to summon him from his Study to the house. 'Many an essay has that hateful bell ruined for me,' he said in later years. 'Sometimes I would pretend not to hear it — no use — if I didn't respond, Mrs. B. herself would soon appear — I might better have gone at the first clang. For when I would get angry, my Muse would desert me, and it sometimes took days to woo her back.' The exasperating part was that the bell exacted tasks of a kind which his hired man could have done far better than he.

The departing April days brought sad tidings:

[Journal] April 28. Emerson died last night at 8.30 o'clock. At that hour I was sitting with Benton in his house, talking of him [Emerson] and his probable death.[1]

With Emerson dead, it seems folly to be alive. No man of just his type and quality has ever before appeared upon the earth. He looked like a god. That wise, serene, inscrutable look was without a parallel in any human face I ever saw. Such an unimpeachable look! The subtle, half-defined smile was the reflection of the smile of his soul. It was not a propitiatory smile, or a smirk of acquiescence, but the reassuring smile of the doctor when he takes out his lancet. It was the sheath of that trenchant blade of his. Behind it lurked some

---

[1] Strange coincidence! Together in young manhood, Benton and Burroughs had first met Emerson, and together they sat talking of him when he breathed his last.

test question, or pregnant saying. It was the foil of his frank, un-
wounding wit, like Carlyle's laugh. It was an arch, winning, half-
playful look, the expression of a soul that did not want to wound
you, and yet that must speak the truth. And Emerson's frank
speech never did wound. It was so evident that it was not meant to
wound, and that it was so true to himself, that you treasured it as
rare wisdom.

April 30. Sunday. Today Emerson is to be buried, and I am
restless and full of self-reproach because I did not go to Concord. I
should have been there. Emerson was my spiritual father in the
strictest sense. It seems as if I owe nearly all, or whatever I am, to
him. I caught the contagion of writing and of authorship before I
knew his books, but I fell in with him just in time. His words were
like the sunlight to my pale and tender genius, which had fed on
Johnson and Addison and poor Whipple.
It is a bright, cool, clear day. . . . I must devote the day to meditating on Emerson.

To Benton a few days later:

My friends in N.Y. rather dissuaded me from going to the funeral
— thought there would be such a crowd that there would be little
satisfaction. Then it seemed uncertain whether it would be on
Sunday or Monday. . . . Still I shall always regret that I did not go
and look upon that wonderful face once more, even though it was the
face of death. The very land and climate of New England seem
impoverished by such a death.
Sunday I devoted to meditation upon our beloved master, the
outcome of which was a short piece which I sent to the Critic. If
they use it, and send me proof before I sail, I will send it to you. I
have also written a short contrast of Carlyle and Emerson which I
may send to the Critic.
I re-read Emerson's essay on Immortality last night. What a
noble chapter it is! What candor! He shaves as close to the main
point as perhaps it is possible to do in speech. There is more matter
in it than I thought.

Honest John Burroughs! A true disciple of Emerson, he
would speak what he thought to-day, and if to-morrow found
him thinking differently, he would be equally outspoken.
Excerpts from 'Emerson's Burial Day,' since it was never
reprinted, are quoted below. It is a flower of the spirit laid by
a son on the grave of his father. To read it is to know that,
however critical John Burroughs had been of Emerson —
however critical he was to be in the coming years — from first
to last he reverenced that serene, cloudless soul which had
shed such a beneficent influence upon his whole life.

It was undoubtedly Emerson's time to die. The gods were impatient of his long tarrying among us. His mind, like some rare essence that would no longer brook restraint, had cracked the phial in which it was held, and had begun to escape.

And now his work is done. The spell called living is broken. And does the real living now begin? We do not, and can never, know. We only know that the form of him who was so little of earth is placed away beyond our ken in the bosom of the great Mother on this April day. The door that opens and shuts but once to mortal man closes behind him, and we shall see him no more.

It is a rare privilege to have lived upon the earth at the same time with such a man as Emerson — to have seen the perfect flowering of the New England race and culture, after a century or more of preparation. As one of his younger contemporaries, my life has been most fortunate, and I owe him a debt that no words of mine can adequately measure....

He carried the typical New England traits and qualities — its shrewdness, its common sense, its thrift, its curiosity, its penetration, its conscience, its implacable good nature — into heights where they were never carried before, and probably will never be carried again. He scaled the empyrean in the guise of a quick and canny New England farmer. Not a flowing, opulent, luxurious soul, but a pure, penetrating, far-reaching one; the quality of his genius æolian, or like the sound of a horn amid the hills — single, far-heard, bewitching, and burdened with beauty and mystery....

It was fit that he should pass in April, the month of Shakespeare's birth and death, the month that opens the door of the more genial season. To what extent, and for how many of us has he opened the door of a brighter and more genial clime! He was an April man, an awakener, full of light, full of prophecy, full of vernal freshness and curiosity — hardy, tender, coy, genial, frank, elusive, simple, joyous, and with the fibre and the quality of the primal man. Peace to his great soul!

While Burroughs's second European trip was under consideration, the wistful Celt wrote Benton: 'My place here never held me so strongly as now that I am about to turn my back upon it.' And to his Journal he confided, May 4th:

The last night in my little hermitage before sailing. Every morning, if I have slept well, I am glad I am going, and every night I am sorry. Thus does the day make and unmake us. Tonight the old ties draw strongly, and I am sad.

He was not to go in peace on this journey overseas: Whitman's fortunes, which had been brightening, were suddenly overshadowed, as the accompanying letters to Gilder and Whitman show:

[J. B. to R. W. G.]

Whitman writes me that the District Attorney of Boston has threatened to prosecute Osgood and Co., for publishing obscene literature in 'Leaves of Grass,' and Osgood has dropped the book. So far as this is the wish of the city of Boston, I pray for the wrath of Sodom and Gomorrah to descend upon her. We shall try to head off the miserable idiot of a District Attorney by reaching the Att'y General in Wash'n. . . .

[J. B. to W. W.]

With your letter came one from O'Connor bursting with wrath. No doubt he will be a host there in W[ashington], and will reach that miserable Dis't. Att'y yet. 'Tis a pity Osgood has not got some pluck and so make a fight. No doubt we could beat them to tatters and make a big strike for the book. Write and ask him if he will fight, if he is well backed up. It is the last thing I ever dreamed of. If this is the wish of Boston, then I pray for her purification by a fire ten times bigger than the fire of a few years ago.

I enclose my check for the amount you ask for, $100. ['This was money in my possession belonging to Walt.' J. B. 1912.]

What a blank there in New England! To me Emerson filled nearly the whole horizon in that direction. But I suppose it is better so, though the very sunlight seems darkened. . . .

If our passage was not paid to England, I should not go. I am ashamed to go off at such a time. I have had no heart for the trip from the first, and now the death of Emerson (how those few words penetrate me!), and your troubles, make me want to stay at home more than ever.

If you have Mrs. Gilchrist's address, send it to me; also that of Mr. Carpenter.

I have written an essay on Carlyle which I think goes to the meaning of him more than anything I have seen.

Further word from O'Connor to Burroughs shows how he was rallying to the fray:

. . . I will see that you are advised of the progress of the war I mean to make to the death upon this scoundrel lawyer. I wonder whether Stedman has yet made up his mind whether Walt is persecuted. Mark now whether any member of our *litterati* takes up this infamous outrage — this revival of sixteenth century methods — this rehabilitation of Montfaucon and the Place de Grave — this suppression of a grand and honest book by an impoverished and illegal censorship — the tool of private spite, and bigotry, and club-house lust, anxious about its fig-leaves.

. . . I have never been so roused by anything as this. Harlan's action was a trifle — a mere bagatelle — in comparison. When I

think of it — when I think of its significance and consequences —
my blood seems to turn to lightning, and I feel my brain flashing. . . .

More fiery talk follows: O'Connor urges Burroughs to in-
spire every one abroad with the facts, and the dire consequences to Walt's book — to any man's book — if these contemptible censors and cowering publishers are not held up to
scorn. As he speaks of Emerson he softens:

Yes, Emerson's death darkens. I felt as if Monadnock had sunk
from the old horizon. There never was another place like Concord,
and now it melts away. . . . I could almost wish you were not going,
but you can greatly help Walt's book abroad, and fire the British
heart on this new infamy.

From Alloway, Scotland, to his brother Eden the traveler
sends tidings:

We had a smooth and prosperous voyage of eleven days across the
big ferry. . . . There was a death and a birth on board — a young
woman on her way back to Scotland to die of consumption, died the
second day out, and was buried at sea.

We spent a few days in Glasgow, and then came down here into
one of the richest farming districts in Scotland. The country is like
a garden, the fields are dotted with Ayrshire cattle. Such farming as
this is you have never seen. The land is not owned by the farmers,
but is all rented. The leases are all for ninety-nine years. The
farmers pay from $20 to $25 an acre per year, and expend about
the same amount for manures. The yield of wheat is from 50 to 60
bushels an acre.

The country is gently rolling and the soil is deep and smooth, like
Irve Tyler's flats. I have never seen such a fine farming country.
The cattle are in the pastures up to their eyes, and are all fat enough
for beef. The oats and wheat are several inches high, and the
potatoes are being cultivated and weeded. Yesterday I saw fifteen
women in a field on their knees pulling weeds after the cultivator.
They get about thirty-six cents a day. Certain kinds of field work
here is always done by women. They are rolling their oats, wheat,
and grass now. The horses are immense, weigh about 1500 pounds,
and are the Clydesdale breed. The best farm horses here sell for
three and four hundred dollars each.

Living here is higher than with us. The best beef is from 25 to 30
cents a pound. The butter is good and sells for about 26 or 28 cents.

We are stopping at a little hotel on the banks of the Doon, where
the poet Burns was born, and we pay about five dollars a day. We
have two rooms and live as privately as if in our own house.

The trees were all in full leaf when we landed, and the fields looked
like June. Julian keeps well and eats like a wolf.

We shall leave here this afternoon for a trip to the Highlands, and to the country of Walter Scott.

And to Benton:

I promised to drop you a line occasionally, and will do so now from this charming nook by Bonny Doon. . . .

We entered the mouth of the Clyde Wednesday morning, and the impression which the view made upon me I expect to carry with me into the other world, if I carry anything. The day was perfect, — bright, soft, dreamy, — and coming from the wilderness of the ocean into such a paradise of green shores, trees, birds, flowers, cattle, sheep, castles, villas, was a transition you can never appreciate till you have experienced it. We closed our eyes at night upon hell, and opened them in the morning upon heaven.

The scenery of the Clyde looks like the canvas of some master painter, only infinitely better. It looks as if it had all been passed through the mind and heart of man, and was still nature. There is no hint of the savage and the sublime, as with us, but a human tenderness and beauty and repose, and pictorial effect impossible to describe. Where the shores are distant and rocky, they seem covered with a tender green mould that you could wipe away with your hand.

The trees are in full leaf (except the ash); the grass and grain are several inches high; the larks are singing all about; the woods are full of strange flowers, the trees of strange birds; the Doon flows through the grounds of the little inn; and there is beauty and delight on every hand. We think and speak of you and Mrs. B. oftener than of anyone else, because the country about here is the ripened perfection of what one gets a hint of in your peaceful valley. Let your place and farm go on ripening and mellowing for two thousand years, and it will be like this — as far as it can be in our harsher climate.

The banks of the Doon here are about forty feet high and slope gently to the water. The bridges start from the brink of the bank and clear the water in one span of about fifty feet. The 'Auld Brig o' Doon,' over which Tam o' Shanter rode, bounds the grounds of the inn on the east, and the new bridge on the west. The sea is one and a half mile distant.

The other night, attracted by the report of a gun, I found my way into a wood that had grown up about the ruins of an old castle, and there met a young man who, in conversation about the birds, quoted my own name and words to me. Imagine his surprise when I told him who I was! He proves a valuable acquaintance, and has a brother and an uncle in Poughkeepsie, and had himself been within a mile and a half of my house. His name is Scoular, and the name of his uncle is MacDonald. I like his father much — a great admirer of Emerson and Carlyle — and we have had some delightful walks already. Tonight we are going there to tea.

The gloaming here is two or three hours long — wonderful. The beautiful Ayrshire cattle dot the fields. The roads are like a floor of rock. . . .

Of the subjoined letter, written from London in mid-June, Horace Traubel, printing it in 'With Walt Whitman in Camden,' reports Whitman as saying, 'It gives a little look into the Carlyle country — yes, and a big look into John's soul.'

DEAR WALT,
. . . My first taste of the country was at Alloway. . . . From there we went into the Highlands, where I did some mountain climbing; thence around to Edinburgh. From there we went down to Carlyle's country and spent a week at Ecclefechan. . . . I walked a good deal about Ecclefechan, and shall write something about it and weave in certain things I want to say of Carlyle. I enclose a daisy and a spray of speedwell that I gathered from Carlyle's grave.
I saw the graves of eight Thomas Carlyles. The 'Carls,' as the Scotch call them, were a very numerous race in this section. They were a stern savage set not to be trifled with. . . .
Mr. Carpenter has been up and spent a day and a night with me. . . . We have been out to Mrs. Gilchrist's twice to tea. She and Grace are alone, Herbert being off in Wales, painting. They chided me for not bringing you, and entertain hopes of seeing you yet. . . . I hope to hear yet that Osgood has not thrown up 'Leaves of Grass.' . . .

Until the travelers returned home no entries appeared in the Journal proper, but in a little note-book are many jottings, — notes on the birds, and notes contrasting European nature with ours. An undated entry follows:

One of the first impressions is that the cattle and sheep have all got in the meadows, and one's impulse is to go and drive them out. Then you look farther and see that there are no pastures as at home. It is all fresh and green and meadow-like, smooth and well-kept.

In an entry on May 27th he shows how impossible it is for him to forget old sorrows, however alluring the scene:

Again comes round the anniversary of dear Channy's death, and I am sitting here at 12 M on the top of Ben Venue, Loch Katrine at my feet, and a universe of mountains about me. On four peaks I can see snow, or miniature glaciers. Ben Lomond is eight or ten miles west of me, a little taller than this peak. If he were a little nearer I should knock his cap off yet.
The nakedness of these mountains, as regards trees, is what one is not prepared for. The wind whistles among the rocks and hums in

the heather, but at a distance they are silent. . . . A certain tameness in the view, after all, perhaps because of the smooth and grassy character of the mountains, not solemn and impressive like the tops of the granite mountains in Maine. These mountains are only very big knolls and sheep ranges — no sense of age or power. The rock crops out everywhere, but it shows no great faces or walls, no cleavage, nothing overhanging and precipitous. The pass called the Trossachs is far less impressive than the 'Long Woods' of my boyhood, at the head of the Pepacton.

His journeyings through the Carlyle country may be traced in 'Fresh Fields.'

There was no road in Scotland or England he would have been so glad to walk over as that from Edinburgh to Ecclefechan — the road Carlyle had traveled as a lad, and again in young manhood with Edward Irving; but as it was a distance of one hundred miles, he got what satisfaction he could from the fact that the engine which drew the train was named Thomas Carlyle.

Carlyle's grave was then unmarked, but the daisies and speedwells were growing there amid the grass. The old sexton told him that the 'Carls' all spoke as if against a stone wall. After telling a story illustrative of the contempt the 'Carls' could show, on occasion, he added, 'But a verra kind an' obliging family they waur — only ye must no cross them.'

Dr. J. H. Johnston and Mr. J. W. Wallace, British friends who visited Ecclefechan the year after Burroughs did, write that when the landlord of the inn spoke of the American author, and they inquired what John Burroughs was like, he replied, 'No verra big, an' no verra wee — joost a plain, ordinar' kin' o' mon, an' no like a writer ava'.'

[Note-book] June 8. Here I am walking through Wordsworth's country, from Ambleside to Grasmere. A cloudy day, threatening rain. As I scribble this beside the mossy stone wall, the call of the cuckoo comes over Rydal Water — a blithe sound, hardly birdlike. Have just seen Wordsworth's house, Rydal Mount, and looked long at it, and at the grove of noble beeches in front of it, and at the mountains back of it, and thought of Emerson's visit here near fifty years ago.

A fragment of cataloguing here transcribed shows what he saw in one of his walks:

June 26. Went down to Rochester with Herbert Gilchrist. The

old city, the surprising river, the doves and swallows, the flowers, white and pink on the top of the tower walls, the walk to Maidstone in the night and the wet; the victualless and bedless inns where we could not stay; the walk back next day by a new route; the old church; the path over the hill; the bumble-bees; the wilds of Kent; the victualless inn again; the wheat, barley, oats, hops, vetches, peas, beans, cherry orchards; the fields strewn with flint-like bones, all joints and processes; the larks, the hedgeless and fenceless highways in places; the vast army of windmills; the absence of sheep and cattle, all grain and garden.

The day following they journey toward Gravesend, the larks singing, the scarlet poppies blooming in the wheatfields, — the whole country a 'mellow, royal, motherly landscape.'

When the pedestrians go from Feversham to Canterbury there is more cataloguing — the straight long road, the poor milk, the many bicyclists, the climbing hop-vines, and suddenly the sight of Canterbury from Harbledown Hill, the point where the pilgrims used to behold it and kneel. On the chalk cliffs of Dover they stand and look down upon 'the wrinkled sea,' the coast of France dim in the distance; larks aloft, below the 'rattling pebbly beach,' and behind them the smooth rolling downs.[1]

In the haunts of Gilbert White, he spent two rainy days, visiting the grave, seeing the old yew tree and Wolmer Forest, and trying in vain to evoke the spirit of the nature-loving parson. In the Tennyson country he sought the nightingale, but saw neither the poet nor the bird, yet Emma Lazarus found his 'Hunt for the Nightingale' 'one of the most delicious pieces of prose poetry' that she knew; with 'the classic finish and elegance of Addison and Irving, and a breeziness and a grasp of natural fact, and a poetry all your own.'

From London the traveler wrote Benton:

. . . I went over to France for a couple of days, and cured myself of the fever for the continental tour. England and Scotland are enough for one year.

We have now been in and about London for over a month. The city has a strange fascination. It is a human Niagara, and the longer one lingers about it, the more it impresses and fascinates him. I really think I could live here. The feeling of home, and of living, and having a good time, pervades the very air.

[1] Parts of 'Nature in England' (*Fresh Fields*) are made up from these jottings.

I have made weekly excursions of two or three days to the country while Mrs. B. and Julian have stayed here. Yesterday I was at Winchester and Salisbury, and intended to walk to Stonehenge, but was not quite well enough to walk the nine miles and back.

I have seen a good many cathedrals, but St. Paul's is still the most impressive to me. There is not such gloom and grandeur about any of the purely Gothic structures, though great beauty and refinement.

. . . I tramped a good deal about the country and bagged a little game now and then. I expect to write about it, and about Carlyle. There are no hints of the points I want to make in anything I have yet seen about him. . . . An honest attempt to understand him and explain him, I have not seen. An old Scotchman, half tipsy, who took me up in his dog-cart on my way to Repentance Hill, said the 'Carls'. . . were a set of bullies. It seems to me Carlyle must have been almost totally lacking in amativeness, and this played the mischief with him, and accounts for his scorn and contempt. It made his heart barren and bitter.

We spent a few days in the Wordsworth country, and shall probably stop there on our return, as I did not get enough of those singular and beautiful mountains. You never imagined anything like them. Take your mountains, St. Riga and the rest, and shave them and rub them down smooth, cover them with green tapestry, and throw a large black rug over them, here and there, to represent the heather, make the vales at their feet smooth and lawn-like, with noble trees and quaint, picturesque, ivy-clad cottages and villages, and you have some idea of this scenery.

You will be surprised when I tell you that I have not seen any of the literary folk here. I have several letters (and offers of more) which I have not delivered. I did not come here to see the like of them, and I reckon they would not care for me. The only man in England I want to see is Tennyson, and of course I shall not see him. I thought to hunt up Richard Jefferies, but it is too late, as we expect to leave London tomorrow. . . .

We have kept pretty well. Mrs. B. has had some serious battles with the dirt of this country, but she keeps her courage up, and intends to fight it out on that line. J. is happy, and is much impressed with the animals in the zoölogical gardens.

Tell Joel the streets swarm with pretty girls here — such fresh rosy faces, full busts and — big feet!

I have not heard the voice of a frog or a toad since I landed in these islands. The nights in the country are as silent as the grave.

Why Mr. Burroughs did not let Anne Gilchrist arrange a meeting with Tennyson, with whom she was on the friendliest terms, is rather surprising. Reminding him in a letter, as he was leaving, that the human creature is not meant to live long on the wing, she added:

If you would only have chosen a perch to your mind, and settled down a bit, say at Hampstead or Haslemere, where you could have spent the rainy hours in writing, and those delicious, refreshing, fragrant hours that follow in our climate, in walking every day, and had thus, too, given yourself the opportunity for a little human intercourse that had time to grow friendly, my national vanity makes me think you would have taken back as cordial a liking for the people as you have for the land.

However, as he wrote Dowden, he went over mainly to see Mother England once more, and to steep himself in that benign nature. If he saw no literary folk, he scraped aquaintance with nearly all the song-birds.

He writes Benton of the Scotch lassie they brought from Glasgow and, concluding, says:

It is good to be back. . . . I am now, after a run out home, regularly ensconced in my little hermitage, chewing the succulent cud of my English and Scotch memories. That green land with its sweetness and repose will long haunt my memory.[1]

[1] Those English and Scottish memories yielded: 'Bird Songs, English and American' (*Century*, January, 1882, with fruit of his previous visit), 'Nature in England' (*Century*, November, 1883), 'In Wordsworth's Country' (*Century*, January, 1884), 'A Hunt for the Nightingale' (*Century*, March, 1884), 'Arnold, Emerson, and Carlyle' (*Century*, April, 1884), 'British Fertility' (*Century*, May, 1884), and 'British Wild Flowers' (*Century*, August, 1884).

CHAPTER IX

THE QUIET EIGHTEEN–EIGHTIES

1882–1884

What matter if I stand alone?
I wait with joy the coming years;
My heart shall reap where it hath sown,
And garner up its fruit of tears.

BURROUGHS

UNEVENTFUL, as men regard the lives of their fellows, is the life pictured in Journal and letters during this period — a life in which the breaking up of the ice on the river, the advent of the spring flowers, the tinge of yellow creeping on the willows, the discovery of a rare bird's nest, to name a few, are events of signal interest; when the finding of a goldfinch entangled in a web, and its release, make the day memorable; when more companionship is had with Plutarch and Sainte-Beuve than with men of his own day; when, for a time, that great Carlylean poem, 'Frederick the Great,' colors all his thoughts and days; when brief meetings with literary friends and an occasional lecture in New York are ripples in the tranquil stream. Echoes from the world of politics or from current events are but rarely heard, yet in the few that do occur the diarist is seen to be more a part of his times than the scarcity of such entries would indicate.

Wide as are his interests in books and nature and current events, he is most concerned in a few humble lives in the little village where he was born. As he said of Carlyle, so may it be said of him: 'The family stamp was never more strongly set upon a man. . . . He is his father and mother touched to finer issues. . . . A vague, yearning homesickness seemed ever to possess him.' Indeed, diverse as were their natures, I doubt if any two literary men, past or present, were ever so closely akin in reverence and affection for their kindred as were Thomas Carlyle and John Burroughs. The following passage which he quotes from Carlyle reveals the kinship between him and the mournful Scot: 'The Hill I first saw the sun rise over, when the Sun and I and all things were yet in their auroral hour — who can divorce me from it? Mystic, deep as the world's centre, are the roots I have struck into my Native Soil; no tree that grows is rooted so.'

The returned travelers were soon busy at the old tasks, he with vineyard and writing, and his wife with the fall campaign of housecleaning. The latter event was regarded with unwonted equanimity by the man, safe in his snuggery, his confidence reinforced by the Scotch lassie who came back with them. He soon began writing up his English impressions, finding in himself more on the subject than he anticipated.

In the light of later developments, it is amusing to read this passage from the Journal:

The writings of Emerson and Thoreau drew readers to seek them personally. My books do not bring readers to me [sic], but send them to Nature. I take credit to myself on this account. I seek always to hold the mirror of my mind up to Nature, that the reader may find her lineaments alone reflected there. I remember that this is one of the great merits of the 'gentle Shakespeare'; himself you see not, only the great world compacted and idealized as in a Claude Lorraine mirror. Shakespeare, I take it, was really a gentle spirit who never obtruded himself; who made little impression upon those who knew him; so that the memory of him was quickly lost; far less of an egotist, say, than Ben Jonson, and with a less striking personality — all his vast power working in a kind of impersonal way, just the contrary, say, of such a man as Carlyle.

As a matter of fact, during the last four decades of his life, John Burroughs was probably more sought after, had more of a personal following, more contacts with his readers, both through correspondence and in person, than any other American author has had, and, probably, more than any other author of modern times.

Oct. 4. Go out Home today with Wife and Julian, a bright, lovely day. At the crossing near Roxbury a first-class American railroad-crossing tragedy.[1]

[1] Here follows a graphic account of the terrible scene they, as passengers, witnessed when the train stopped. Both he and Mrs. Burroughs were called to court as witnesses. He used to tell what a good witness Mrs. Burroughs made, and what a poor one he made, she so positive and emphatic, he uncertain and hesitant. When it came to swearing just where they were when the train whistled, how long it whistled, how long it was after whistling before the train reached the crossing, he was unwilling to give positive testimony. 'She was probably no more certain than I was on these points, but she thought she was, and gave such positive testimony that she made what is called a good witness. If they had asked me what I saw *after* the accident, I could have told them accurately enough.'

One of his few comments on current politics occurs in an October letter to Gilder:

I should like to know the private thoughts of Arthur and his stalwart crew just now. That set is done for, thank the Lord! Perhaps the whole party is, but if so, it is legitimate and right. When the mountain and the valley change places, there is some deep principle or force at work.

In the subjoined letter, from one of the Concord Brahmins, one sees how transcendentally fruit from the Riverby vineyard was received in Concord

If the genuine Concord philosophy does not, as you intimate, flourish outside of Concord, its

'wine that never grew
In the belly of the grape,' —

fair clusters, sunned under wise eyes, ripened in vineyards by the fertile banks of the Hudson, do flourish there, and find way to gladden some of the host here dwelling by sluggish Concord stream.

The crate came safely to hand yesterday. And that your generous gift shall not be selfishly appropriated and enjoyed, our friends and yours — Channing, Sanborn, and Harris — are to partake thereof this evening at our fortnightly Symposium, our Mystic Club.

So if perchance we get heady,
'T will lighten us and steady,
Check our hilarious flight,
From soaring far from sight.

My thanks for your generous gift and your kind remembrance of me. Come yourself and see us.

Cordially yours

A. Bronson Alcott

To Whitman in late October:

I was much disturbed by your card. I had been thinking of you as probably enjoying these superb autumn days down in the country, and here you are wretched and sick at home. I trust you are better now. You need a change. I dearly wish that as soon as you are well enough you would come up here and spend a few weeks with us. We could have a good time here in my bark-covered shanty, and in knocking about the country. Let me know that you will come.

Specimen Days [and Collect] came all right. I do not like the last part of the title; it brings me up with such a short turn. I have read most of the new matter and like it. . . . I have just received an English book — Familiar Studies of Men and Books — by Stevenson, with an essay upon you in it, but it does not amount to much. He has the American vice of smartness and flippancy. . . .

I am bank-examining nowadays but shall be free again pretty soon.

O'Connor writes me that he is going to publish his Tribune letters in a pamphlet, with some other matter. I am glad to hear it. He draws blood every time.

I fear poor old Alcott will not rally; indeed, he may be dead now. I had a pleasant letter from him the other day. I had sent him a crate of Concord grapes.

I am very stupid today. For the past two weeks my brain has been ground between the upper and nether millstones of bank ledgers, and it is sore. . . .

To Edward Dowden, in mid-December, he writes:

Time, the broker, has discounted my locks at a usurious rate since I last saw your handwriting, but I manage to keep him away from my heart yet. In five years one is bound to pay some tribute to him. But he has touched Whitman much more lightly than his friends had any reason to hope. When I last saw him, not many months past, he looked better and moved better than he had for years. There appears to be a freshness and a youthfulness in his very physiology that is proof against the years.

You have touched off his book with delightful grace and ease. It is just the kind of notice that will please him. . . .

I was on your side of the Atlantic the past summer with wife and youngster; passed the coast of Ireland; smelled its peat hearth fires; thought of you, and wafted greetings in your direction. On our return in August I passed a day in the north of Ireland, walking over the hills and among the humble little farms. If it had not been for the distracted state of the country, I should have taken Dublin in our route, and made an attempt to look you up. . . .

It is quite an easy thing to do now — to cross the Atlantic, and I sincerely hope you may yet see your way to do it. I will agree to meet your steamer in New York anytime you will name, and will take you to Whitman and will show you the country in one man — the country as it is to be. If you cannot leave home, do as I did, bring your home with you.

I seem to see less from your pen in the current British periodical literature than formerly. I hope your routine work there in the College is not dulling your enthusiasm for the old pursuit. . . .

I am interested in your immersion in Goethe. I have always been skeptical about the heart of that monster of the deep, and now that you describe yourself as being quite within his belly, I hope you will look about you sharply for that piece of his anatomy. It is a task I have set for myself within the coming year, — to study him carefully once more, and see if my early impression of him was well-founded or not. He is a giant, no doubt; there is something almost impious in his insight into nature, but I doubt if I could ever come to love him. . . .

About this time the Authors' Club of New York, in process of organization, expressed itself at one of the preliminary meetings as unwilling to include Whitman. In high dudgeon, Burroughs wrote Stedman to strike his name from their list. Stedman's reply, with its intimation that he might sometime reconsider and join them, must have heightened his anger several degrees. He did not reconsider, but in later years occasionally attended special dinners of the Club.

Medical prognostications now began to cast a shadow over the spirit of our author. He wrote Benton he must go to New York to rub the moss and lichens off him, and let a medicine-man make some passes and grimaces over his painful shoulder. He went, but the medicine-man made an examination, and the patient made the grimaces. The diagnosis (hardening of the arteries) hung like a Damocletian sword for months to come over the impressionable patient; but, as he said later, he lived to see the grass grow green for a score of years, and more, upon the grave of his medical friend. New friendships and interests soon helped to dispel the forebodings occasioned by the disquieting diagnosis. Bird-students came to walk the woods with him; his son was developing finely; his essays were bringing interesting, sometimes racy, correspondents; he was writing on themes of absorbing interest, and reading Darwin with avidity — was, in fact, beginning to live a much less sequestered life than heretofore. That he would have liked to keep in closer touch with literary friends, the following letter to Stedman, written in early January, shows:

Your wistful glance toward the country in your note of 30th ulto. reminds me that here is where you ought to be, and that there is a good foot-hold here for you alongside of me — a home already made if you want such, and a suitable plot of ground if you want to do your own planning (or planting) and building. The Frothingham estate here could be bought for about $25,000; it would cut up into four homesteads. There is a fine large farm and immense fruit orchards. A friend of mine wants part of it, and I should be very glad to have some neighbors of my own choosing on the rest of it. Come up and found a literary colony here, and we will have an Authors' club meeting four times a week.

The West Shore RR will have a station close by. . . .

My leisure up here is like that of Nature herself. I have a drawer

full of articles since August, all weaned and dismissed, and several
more at the breast — or at the bottle, when the supply there gets
low. What a brood of poems and essays you would turn out if you
had my time!

Of his literary output from August to January he wrote
Benton:

The Atlantic has two, the Century one, the Critic four. The rest I
am still nursing. Longman's new magazine has written me for an
article, and makes the tempting offer of two pounds per page (of 500
words). You see I do not let my strawberries rot on the vines as you
do. I send them to market.

'Harper's Magazine' proposed that he and William Hamilton Gibson go South for the ensuing March, with a view to
preparing a series of illustrated magazine articles, later to be
incorporated in a handsome gift-book. The lucrative side of
the proposal, and a persuasive letter from Gibson, almost won
the hesitant home-body, but not quite — he always wanted
to choose his own subjects.

One reads with peculiar interest Burroughs's comments in
his Journal, after finishing the reading of Jane Carlyle's
letters:

Have hardly skipped a page. Why does one read them so entirely?
Probably because there is not a dull line in them — not a false note
in style or rhetoric. A more clear, incisive, telling way of putting
things would be hard to find. . . . It is the sprightly, charming gossip
of a life-long invalid to whom the great problem is how she is going to
live from day to day in this miserable world of nerves and kitchen-
maids, and be as a buffer between everything that might, could,
or would annoy him. Unless she can receive every blow upon herself, unless she can gather every shaft into her own bosom, she is
wretched. When she cannot aid him, she is more worried than he is.
When she hears him jump out of bed at night, over her head, because
the demon of sleeplessness possesses him, it brings her heart into her
throat, and she agonizes until she hears him return to his couch.
When he is on a journey she is made sick by her mental worry.
Most wives of authors are probably jealous of their husband's
tasks; they are rivals upon which they rarely look kindly. Mrs.
Carlyle was no exception to this rule. Frederick and Cromwell were
her enemies. She wanted a famous husband, but did not seem willing
to pay the price. She married for ambition, but was not contented
with the fruits. She pitched her tent upon the mountain-tops, and
then sighed for the cosey valley. Did she expect ambition would
breed love? that the cedars of Lebanon would bear roses? Carlyle

loved her, but it seems to have been a neuter-gender love. He was probably deficient in wholesome sexuality — not a woman-hater, or man-hater, properly speaking, but a despiser of all human weaknesses and frailties. He wanted just that kind of charity and sympathy, and just that tact and divination with women, and tenderness toward men, which the alloy of a softer metal with his splendid genius would have begotten. To the arts and instincts and insight of the sexes he was a stranger. 'Tis a pity he had not a little more of the Burns in his composition; he was Scotch in everything but in this very Scottish trait, while Mrs. Carlyle seems to have been eminently Scottish in this respect.

May 7. The fern, when it comes up, looks like a creature just born, still wrapped in the placental membranes. It looks as if it needed some maternal tongue to lick it into shape. Discovered yesterday that the hickory with its swelling buds gives out a pleasing gummy odor at a few rods' distance. What perfume a forest of them would emit! No peach blossoms yet. Cool; good grass weather.

May 11. . . . Johnson [Robert Underwood] and his boy [Owen] came today. Feel like a boy again. The face of nature has an added charm. So much for this brief feeling of companionship!

May 12. Brilliant day with drifts of cherry blossoms against the fresh green. We lounge about, listen, and talk and admire, absorbing the May beauty at every pore. Johnson says the sugar-maple blooms — clusters of delicate, yellowish-green fringe, depending from little canopies of just-hatched leaves — in some way suggest oriental decorations. There is much more of grace and delicacy in the bloom of our maple than in that of the European. The soft-maples are loaded with bunches of scarlet keys, a lovely mass of color against mingled larches, spruces and hard-maples. . . .

And so on, page after page of May loveliness to which he had responded so many seasons, and on which he was then beginning to look

> 'With eyes that have grown sad in growing wise,
> Through Mays that manhood ne'er forgets.'

With June came many bird-students, their coming, and that of pogonia and the lady's-slippers, and the finding of the domed nest of the golden-crowned thrush all duly chronicled. One of his visitors, a city girl, on being shown a nest of young chipping sparrows in the downy stage, drew back with aversion, exclaiming, 'Why, they are all mouldy!' Now he records having to eat his own words because of his hasty generalizations:

A girl in Ohio sent me a blue wild flower, fragrant, she said. It was *Polemonium reptans*, nearly related to phlox. I had said in 'Signs and Seasons' that we had no blue flower that was fragrant — a timely blow. Early yellow flowers, too, I had said were not fragrant, when along come yellow violets from California, fragrant; and yellow jasmine from Georgia — all from women. Hit him again!

After commenting upon Carlyle's 'Cromwell,' which he had just finished reading, he adds:

Here I sit and see the summer days go by, playing the old game with nature and life, and making few new points, hardly any, I may say. The same old story; but the air tastes sweet, and I love to be here. It is a good place to loiter and see the procession pass. Read a little every day, walk a little, work a little, doze a little, and half think and half dream a good deal. [How little does one know him who could assert, with the assurance of perhaps a half-dozen meetings with him, as had one critic, that 'he loved much, observed and interpreted much, *speculated a little, and dreamed not all*'![1] That he loved, observed, and interpreted much, goes without saying, but acquaintance with his books alone should convince one that he speculated much, while even those who knew him only cursorily, know that he dreamed a good deal.]

Nature is in her juiciest mood just now — all sap and leaf. The days are idyllic. I lie on my back on the grass, in the shade of the house, and look up to the soft and slowly moving clouds and to the swallows (chimney) disporting themselves up there in the breezy depths. Not always happy — who is? So much of life at best is mere vegetative happiness, a neutral ground. Only at rare intervals are we positively happy.

As we grow old life becomes more and more background or middle ground; the foreground dwindles; the present moment has less and less power to absorb us and hold us, alas! alas!

As did Emerson for his lectures, so, sometimes, did Burroughs for his essays, levy on his Journal, though hardly with as little concern as to sequence as Emerson was said to show. Burroughs often got his start for an essay by confiding something to his Journal — the seed-corn for the crop he gathered later. In the Journal for June 16 he writes, 'Cut out here and sent to the Critic a little essay on Carlyle and Emerson.'

With Richard Watson Gilder he went to Cambridge for the Commencement exercises.

[Journal] June 27. . . . . Hear some of the graduating class discourse — not so pertinent, nor so alive as those I heard a few days ago at Vassar.

[1] Italics mine.

A long walk by Longfellow's house, then by Lowell's — stately, mellow, and homelike. [From Cambridge they go to Concord]. . . . Some fine views here and there — *New* England, truly. . . . At Sanborn's in the evening. Much talk. Then to Dr. Emerson's. A worthy son of his father, stamped mentally and physically with the Emersonian stamp — eye, voice, mouth, all Emersonian. Talked well about Thoreau. Said Channing drove away his family, then drove away his dog. This last act angered Thoreau much.

28. A pleasant breakfast at Sanborn's. His new house the most courageously plain, and therefore the most pleasing, of any recent house in Concord. No aiming at architecture. A combination of brick and wood. A great success.

Gilder and I walk to Walden Pond, much talk and loitering by the way. Walden a clean bright pond, not very wild. Look in vain for the site of Thoreau's hut. Two boys in a boat row up and ask us the questions we have on our tongues to ask them. We sit in the woods and try to talk about immortality, but do not get very near together — like ships at sea, we soon part company.

In afternoon call on Mrs. Emerson and Ellen. Mrs. E. a fine, stately old lady. Eye clear, face shapely, mouth good. Would have taken her for the wife of Emerson anywhere, looks distinguished, and very spiritual. Talked well, no signs of age but in her snow-white hair. Emerson's mark was upon her, too. It seemed as if she had been embalmed in his mind and influence, though she by no means shares his way of thinking.

Something fine about Ellen Emerson, a kind of Emersonian Amazon, brow classical, dress loose and shapeless, form tall. Mrs. Forbes more like her brother, the Doctor, in looks. Her children, four of them, conduct us to the cemetery. I correct the boy's ornithology in one or two points as we pass alone — a bright lad of ten or eleven.

At Emerson's grave amid the pines we linger long. Then walked to the old Manse, then to Sanborn's to tea.

I saw nothing in Concord that recalled Thoreau, except that his ripe culture and tone might well date from such a place. On the whole, Concord is the most pleasing country village I ever saw. Nothing like it in England, where only the poor live in villages. It impressed me much. Its amplitude, its mellowness, its homelike air, its great trees, its broad avenues, its good houses. Emerson and Hawthorne are its best expressions in literature. It seems fit that they should come from this place.

In July, Mr. Aaron Johns came on from Washington, and the friends camped for a week on Furlow Lake, Aaron's departure, as usual, leaving his comrade forlorn.

The reading of Darwin gives rise to this entry:

July 19. People laugh and scoff at the Darwinian theory of the descent of man, but the fact that each of us sprang from a little wriggling animalcula — a little fish that wriggled itself into a little cell, and was thence developed, or evolved, is just as incredible to me as Darwin's theory. No doubt at all but that back in the womb of Time man was equally low and rudimentary; and that he has been developed through the ages as every child is developed today from the ovum of its mother.

No more did God create man than he created you and me. He created us slowly, from very simple beginnings, and he created man in the same way. . . .

When, on August 6th, he finished Darwin's 'Descent of Man,' he comments as follows:[1]

A model of patient, tireless, sincere inquiry. Such candor, such love of truth, such keen insight into the methods of nature, such singleness of purpose, and such nobility of mind, could not be easily matched. The book convinces like Nature herself. I have no more doubt of its main conclusions than I have of my own existence.

Following some incompetent observer, he makes a curious mistake about our native grouse, namely, that the sound it makes in drumming is produced by the bird striking its wings together above its back. If Darwin could ever have *heard* the sound, he would have known better than that.

Darwin's tone and habit of mind is always that of the master.

Among the friendly letters of this period is one from his old chief in the Treasury Department, Hugh McCulloch — a cordial appreciation, and an invitation to 'Holly Hills.' On the envelope is penciled the impression made upon Burroughs by the old Maryland homestead:

None of the smart and restless architecture — orchards, forests; in some way it makes me think of Sir Walter Scott — on such a generous scale — a royal munificence everywhere; a country for great halls and homes, for hospitality; primitive forests carpeted with the tenderest grass.

Although his peach-crop was a failure, the husbandman garnered two short articles that autumn for the 'Century' — 'Birds' Eggs,' and 'A Glance at British Wild Flowers.' Pictures of the autumn days are mingled in the Journal with speculations on religious and philosophical questions.

---

[1] Since this book was published in 1871, it seems incredible, with his interests, that he had not read it before, yet no mention of it occurs in Journal or correspondence until this year.

1. A Salt Breeze

At Ocean Grove, late September finds the journalist wondering why he is so averse to making casual acquaintances. Amusingly he describes a table-mate — 'a woman who eats a pound of beefsteak at a meal' — and wonders why he has not spoken to her. No detail of her behavior was lost on him. To Elberon and back, on the beach he walks, his shoes in his hand; he looks upon the house where Garfield died; notes the rose gerardia; and finds the ticking insect — a large green grasshopper, like a katydid — which has been puzzling him. Of those saunterings:

Long walks on the embroidered marge of the sea; broad, scalloped borders, vanishing and returning; frills of lace, sea-foam mantillas thrown on the sand perpetually. . . .

While there, finishing Darwin's 'Origin of Species,' he comments:

A true wonderbook. Few pages in modern scientific literature so noble as those last few pages of the book. Everything about Darwin indicates the master. In reading him you breathe the air of the largest and most serene mind. Every naturalist before him and with him he lays under contribution, every competent observer in any field. Only the greatest minds can do this as he does it. He furnishes the key to every man's knowledge. Those that oppose his theory unwittingly bring some fact or observation that fits into his scheme. His theory has such a range, accounts for such a multitude of facts, easily underruns and outruns the views of all other naturalists.

He is in his way as great and as remarkable as Shakespeare, and utilizes the knowledge of mankind in the same way. His power of organization is prodigious. He has the candor, the tranquillity, the sincerity, the singleness of purpose that go with and are a promise of the highest achievement.

He is the father of a new generation of naturalists. He is the first to open the door into Nature's secret senate chambers. His theory confronts and even demands the incalculable geological ages. It is as ample as the earth, and as deep as time. It mates with and matches, and is as grand as, the nebular hypothesis, and is in the same line of creative energy.

Sept. 27. Walt Whitman came yesterday and his presence and companionship act like a cordial upon me that nearly turns my head. The great bard on my right hand, and the sea upon my left — the thoughts of the one equally grand with the suggestions and elemental heave of the other. From any point of view, W. W. is impressive.

The slope of the back of his head and shoulders and back — how suggestive! You would know that he was an extraordinary man.

Sept. 29. Long autumn days by the sea with Whitman. Much and copious talk. His presence loosens my tongue, that has been so tied since I came here.

I feel as if under the effects of some rare tonic or cordial all the time.

There is something grainy and saline in him, as in the voice of the sea. Sometimes his talk is choppy and confused, or elliptical and unfinished; again there comes a long splendid roll of thought that bathes one from head to foot, or swings you quite from your moorings.

I leave him and make long loops off down the coast, or back inland, while he moves slowly along the beach, or sits, often with bare head, in some nook sheltered from the wind and sun.

The grainy, saline voice of the sea. Shoveller of sands, moulder and carver of coasts, grinder of shells and of rocks, beating them up with a pestle and mortar, washer and screener of soils, hoarder of silt, covering the sunken floors deep with the earth-pollen, reservoir of the rivers, fountain of rains, purifier of climes, — the everlasting, insatiable, omnivorous, remorseless sea.

The crescent-shaped waves, reaping and reaping only shells and sand, yet I seem to hear the hiss of steel as of some giant cradler fronting waving fields, the rustle of sheaves, the pounding of flails, or whirr of cylinders, the shovelling and screening of grain.

The farm-boy, the scientist, the poet all speak here. Again, September 30th:

Perfect days by the sea with W. W. A sort of realization of Homer to me. No man I have ever seen cuts such a figure on the beach as W. W. He looks at home there; is ample for such a setting.

When Whitman spoke to Horace Traubel of those days, he said: 'A rare experience! John himself was in extra good feather.'

Still one more record of those days:

Oct. 1. A last look at the sea with W. W. In the early gray light we stood upon the windy verge and saw the 'foamy wreck of the stranded waves cover the shore.'

Looking down the beach, the scene recalled November frosts and snows — the waves churned into foam and spume blown by the winds — the rime of the sea. Great fluffy masses of sea-foam blew like wool far up the sands. The swells not large, but grand and full of fury. . . . Return home at 2 pm. The crinkling and dimpling river looks tame enough. The sea is the place for large types. . . .

In a week's time Burroughs wrote Whitman:

I hope you are still mending, Walt. I am almost certain you eat
too heartily and make too much blood and fat; at least, that you eat
too hearty food. As I told you, I was profoundly impressed by a
couple of articles in the Fortnightly Review by Sir William Thompson, on Diet with relation to Age and Activity. He shows very con-
vincingly that as our activities fail by the advance of age, we must
cut down in our food. If not, the engine makes too much steam,
things become clogged and congested, and the whole economy of the
system deranged. He says a little meat once a day is enough, and
recommends the cereals and fruits. I think you make too much
blood. The congested condition of your organs at times, shows it.
Then you looked to me too fat; and fat at your age clogs and hinders
the circulation. . . . If I were you, I would adopt such a diet as would
. . . lessen the arterial strain. This is common sense and, I believe,
good science. In the best health we grow lean, Sir William says, like
a man training for the ring. I gained much flesh this summer, and
am dull and spiritless this fall as a consequence. I must work it off
some way.

Whitman told Horace Traubel that he was much touched by
'John's' solicitude, and that, though he pushed the invitation
to Riverby away, he did it 'gently, gently.'

When Burroughs wrote Charles Eldridge of being with
Whitman at Ocean Grove, and told of the benefit he himself
had received from the hot sea baths, he commented on
O'Connor's failing health, and added, sadly, 'The night is
probably not far off for some of us; it is quite certain it is not
far off for me; but 'tis the common lot. So be it.' For how
many years before the shadows really closed round him, and
them, did he brace himself to meet this 'night' for himself, his
kindred, and his friends!

Out of those joyous days by the sea Burroughs wrote 'A
Salt Breeze' ('Signs and Seasons'); and Whitman, while
there, wrote at least one poem — 'With husky-haughty lips,
O Sea!'

2. A CRITIC CRITICIZED

Burroughs describes his first meeting with Matthew
Arnold, in his Journal, October 29th:

Go to N.Y. in the rain to meet Matthew Arnold at Gilder's. Was
cordially met by him; found he knew me and was glad to see me.
Liked him better than I expected to. A large tall man with nearly
black hair, closely-cut side whiskers, prominent nose, large, coarse,

but pure, mouth, and muscular neck. In fact, a much coarser man than you would expect to see, and stronger-looking. A good specimen of the best English stock.

Further personal description is found in his essay 'Arnold's View of Emerson and Carlyle' ('Indoor Studies'). This observation, omitted from the essay, is found in the Journal:

But what is that look I see, or think I see, at times, about his nose and upper lip? Just a faint suspicion of scorn. I was looking for this in his face. It is not in his brow, it is here, if anywhere — the nose sniffs a bad smell, or an affront, and there hovers about it a little contempt.

He then describes Arnold's way of looking at one — throwing his head back, looking out from under his eyelids, and sighting one down his long nose, drawing off, as it were, and giving his *vis-à-vis* his chin — the critical, and not the sympathetic attitude; yet adds that Arnold did not impress him as cold or haughty, quite the contrary.

That Burroughs was then absorbing and assimilating his Darwin, so many years before he was to write about him, the Journal now gives continual proof:

In the light of Darwin's theory, it is almost appalling to think of one's self, of what he represents, of what he has come through. It almost makes one afraid of one's self. Think of what there is inherent in his germ! think of the beings that lived — the savage lower forms — that he might move here, a reasonable being! At what a cost he has been purchased! a million years of unreason for his moment of reason! a million years of gross selfishness, that he might have a benevolent throb!

'Bought by the blood of Christ' is the hyperbole of the Church, but every child that is born today is bought by the blood of countless ages of barbarism, or countless lives of beings; and this not figuratively, but literally. Out of an ocean of darkness and savagery is distilled this drop of human blood, with all its possibilities.

One sees in the above the same comprehensive acceptance and application of scientific truths that came out in 1909 in his essay in the 'Atlantic,' 'The Long Road' ('Time and Change') — a masterly literary exposition of evolution.

After a visit that autumn from his uncle, Edmund Kelly, he makes a long entry about his ancestry, with special data about a great-uncle, John Kelly, 'a monstrous queer man,' as his Uncle Edmund had said, who lived in a hut in the woods, and was kept from starving by neighbors who carried food to him. He was accustomed to talk to himself, and had a way, when on the road, of stopping and standing still a long time and gazing all around. His analytical kinsman adds, 'I feel the same trait in myself.' It was a trait which those who knew John Burroughs well must often have observed — a slow, regardful, comprehensive glance in which he seemed to be absorbing the scene, the face of the day, or the mood of the hour, making it a part of his very being. Where others begin the day with morning devotions, he began it with this attentive, absorbing consideration: Here is a new day. What of her protean forms will Nature show to-day? It was the devotion of his spirit to the ever-recurring miracle, so indifferently regarded by the most of us. Evolution had brought him far in advance of that point on the Long Road where, pausing, that hermit uncle of two generations back, had been wont to regard the face of Nature in mute wonder, with aimless, unseeing eyes.

[Journal] Nov. 19. A soft, mild, Indian summer day; sunlight weak, many times diluted with autumn shadows, but tender and dreamy. No thoughts in me, only a vague longing and unrest.

My best and truest friend among womankind, Mrs. Fannie Meade, is dead, since October 25. Nearly all night, November 15, I lay awake thinking of her. In many ways the noblest, most loving, most discerning, most charitable woman I have ever known. She visited me here the latter part of August, 1880. Her death nearly blots out the West.

To Benton:

Your visit was the one tree in the midst of the desert of my autumn. Let not the dreary sands of time stretch so far between us again. . . . Julian says he will send you a picture of a 'sail-ship' next week. Mrs. B. is struggling with carpets and the dust of ages. . . .

Arnold's lecture on Emerson, of which Burroughs heard reports before hearing the lecture itself, exercised him and Benton much, as is seen in a letter to Benton:

I shall probably write something about it when I see or hear the whole lecture. We have all felt and spoken of the friendly character of Emerson, and have seen and felt his value to the spirit, and that he was much more than a mere man of letters, but to say that he has written the most important prose work of the 19th century, and yet that he is not a great writer, ... and is less even than Addison, is absurd.

If he is not a great man of letters, he is a great man speaking through letters, which is perhaps quite as important. He had no literary faculty which he carried about with him on his finger like a falcon, and with which he hawked all manner of game from mice to pheasant, like Voltaire and Swift; but he had a power and at times a largeness of utterance that these wretches never approached.

You may say Bacon was not a great essayist, and yet the wisdom and learning of a great mind are revealed in his essays.

But I must save all this powder for an essay.

The truth about Arnold is, he is a great critic-pedagogue — the outcome in literature of the best type of the English schoolmaster (here I am burning my powder again) — very clear, very cool and self-possessed, and very valuable; he is the best disciplinarian at large at the present time, and always throws his ruler at the right boy, but — supply the 'but' yourself — my dinner bell rings. ...

Both Burroughs and Benton felt that Arnold was a bit inclined to give our American pride in Emerson a severe shaking-up, if not a fall. In their further exchange of views they remind one of clannish boys who will uphold, through thick and thin, the fellows in their part of the town, whenever boys from across the river assail them. Among themselves they may have many a lively tussle, but let boys of another clique cast so much as a threatening glance at one of their 'bunch,' and mightily will they rally to his defense. So when Arnold came across the water, and in his urbane, yet trenchant critique, sought out the weak places in Emerson's armor, John Burroughs quickly took up the cudgels for Emerson; but in no provincial way; in fact, in a way no less urbane and searching than Arnold's own. And yet, when occasion offered, Burroughs as promptly rallied to the defense of Carlyle as of Emerson. The truth is, he was keen to discern heroic qualities, and ready to give allegiance to either near or distant champions of the ideals he cherished.

Horace Traubel records Whitman as saying of the subjoined letter: 'John is extra fine at that sort of work [criticism], especially in letters, where he qualifies nothing — just lets himself go on free wing. Read the letter. It's better than a good apple.' The letter was written to Whitman from Riverby, in January, 1884:

That piece of writing of yours in the last Critic is very impressive. It is seldom you have fallen into such a noble and lofty strain. As I am myself trying to write a little these days, it makes me sad. It is like a great ship that comes to windward of me and takes the breeze out of the sail of my little shallop. I shall have to lay by today and let the impression wear off. I think you have hit it exactly with that word 'physiological.' It lets in a flood of light. The whole essay is one to be long conned over.

I went down to New York to hear Arnold on Emerson Friday night. Curtis — the pensive Curtis — introduced the lecturer. I wonder if you have heard Curtis speak. 'Tis a pity he is not a little more robust and manly. . . .

Arnold looked hearty and strong, and spoke in a foggy, misty English voice, that left the outlines of his sentences pretty obscure, but which had a certain charm after all. The lecture contained nothing new. The Tribune report you sent me is an admirable summary. . . . He does not do full justice to Emerson, as I hope to show in my essay. At least Emerson can be shorn of these things, and left a more impressive figure than Arnold leaves him. He had much to say about Carlyle, too, but would not place him with the great writers. Because he was *more* than a literary man, he denied him literary honors.

Drop me a line when you feel like it. Winter is in full blast up here and the river snores and groans like a weary sleeper.

After glancing again at the letter, Whitman said fervently, 'When John is wholly John, he can't be beat.'

Further impressions of Arnold are given in the Journal:

A large fine audience, lecturer introduced by Curtis in a neat little speech — Curtis is the cosset of the elocutionary graces. He fondly leans and sighs and languishes upon their bosoms. . . .

Arnold put his MS. high on a rack beside him, turned to his audience, let off a sharp glance in my direction through his eye-glass, straightened himself up, and, after a delay that was a little too long, lifted up his voice and spoke his piece. Voice too thick and foggy — has none of the charm and grace of his literary style; hence his lecture is better in the reading than in the hearing. There is something almost like pudding in an Englishman's throat when he speaks from the stage.

3. Orphaned

From criticism of critics, and all other questions, our author was soon to turn with utter indifference. Almost at the beginning of the new year came a telegram forewarning him of his father's death, and the cry that went up from his heart, before he could take a train home, shows how futile had been his attempts to prepare himself for the blow. As to a comrade, he turns to his Journal. A more touching filial portrayal, not excepting Carlyle's of his father, was perhaps never written than is found in the Journal of John Burroughs with his loss fresh upon him — homely pictures of farm-life, inseparable from his parents, early and late reminiscences, vivid portrayals of character, and a love that embraces and sanctifies all. Some excerpts follow:

Jan. 8. . . . In a few hours I shall know the worst. It is his time to die, and he has long been looking and waiting for the end. It is best so, but, oh! how can I lose him from the world, my Father! . . .

How many times, sitting alone in my Study, during the bleak winter nights, have I said over the names of my dead, his name always hovering near, as if so soon to be added to the list! How many times, while Mother was still living, have I at night felt suddenly drawn towards them, as if I must at once be with them! They were there now, but would soon be gone. Why did I tarry here? And I would start from my chair and pace the floor. How many times while home with them did I look at them, and listen to them, as if with the eyes and ears of the future years, when they would be gone; as if to anticipate the crying want I should then feel to see and hear them, and store up memories of them that would appease my aching heart! 'Oh, listen!' I would say, when I heard their voices at night in their bed, 'so soon you will want to hear their voices, and they will be forever still.' Now hers is still, and maybe his, too. . . .

After this, there is no record till January 21st:

Stern rugged winter days, and the snows cover a new grave beside Mother's. At rest at last, after 81 years of life.

Then he reviews his home-going on the 9th:

How lonely and bleak the old place looked in the winter landscape by moonlight — beleaguering winter without, and death within. . . . How the wind howled and buffeted that night, and the steady roar of the mountain, like that of the sea, came to me in my sleepless chamber. How often in youth I had heard that roar, but with what different ears as I snuggled down in my bed while Mother tucked me in!

Early in the morning I went quietly and with composure and looked upon my father's face. Never had I looked upon his face before in the morning, before he had arisen, without speaking his name; and I could not refrain from speaking his name now, and speaking it again and again.

The marble face of death! What unspeakable repose and silence there is in it!

I saw more clearly than ever before how much my own features are like his — the nose the same, only, in his case, cut away more at the

nostrils. The forehead, too, precisely the same. Head nearly as large
as mine, feet and hands smaller.

It was his time to die; it is better so; and the reason said yes, but,
oh! the heart! the time for its loved ones to die never comes. . . .

Everything preceding and following the 'stroke' is recorded in the Journal. Closely he questioned every one,
hungry for every detail. The homeliest things are put in,
some even unprintable — so eager was he for every moment of
those swiftly fleeting hours.

Of the thorough-going Old School Baptist sermon which
Elder Hewitt preached, with its arguing about election and
foreordination, he says:

Such a sermon as Father delighted in and would, no doubt, have
preferred should be preached at his funeral.

And continues:

Father was so much to me, not perhaps in reality — for he cared
nothing for the things I did, and knew me not; but from the force of
filial instinct and home-feeling in me. He knew me not, I say. All
my aims and aspirations were a sealed book to him, as much as his
peculiar religious experiences were to me. Yet I reckon it was the
same leaven working in us both. The delight he had in his Bible, in
his hymn-book, in his church, in his creed, I have in literature, in the
poets, in nature. His was related to his soul's salvation hereafter,
mine to my soul's salvation here. . . .

Father laid claim to few of the virtues and graces; delighted to tell
a good story against himself as well as against another. He owned he
was a coward, and would make a poor soldier. When the *posse* came,
in the anti-rent times, he ran under the bed and left his feet sticking
out! He always laughed when the story was told. No hypocrisy or
pretension about Father. He had more virtues than he laid claim to.

Well, we shall meet again: our dust in the earth, and the forces
that make up our spirits in the eternity of force. Shall we know each
other then? Ah! shall we? As like knows like in nature. I dare not
say farther than that.

When he wrote of his father's death, he told Benton that
his grief over the death of friends was like his sea-sickness —
not so severe as with some, but likely to last the whole voyage.
His recurring comments throughout the years prove how well
he understood himself in this respect. At the home-going in
April — with no father to open the door to him — he faces a
new sorrow: Little Channy, the nephew of his dearly-loved
'Channy B.,' is dying, 'a child of rare sweetness and intelli-

gence.' The death of an obscure child in a Catskill mountain village is not the significant fact here, but how it affected John Burroughs. Always his descriptions of the suffering he witnesses are painfully graphic. One understands why it is that he cannot long look upon suffering — it is too terribly real to him; he takes in the slightest shade; his imagination relentlessly pictures the end. 'I stay but a little while,' he writes — 'cannot bear to be near the suffering child.' Yet in his Journal he lives over the scene, agonizing with the parents:

Can I ever forget that look of utter despair upon Emma's tear-drenched face as she came and threw herself upon me! 'Oh, Uncle John, he is gone, he is gone, my darling, and I was all alone with him when he died!'

What words had I to comfort her, or to comfort him, when he came towards me, as if for succor? None. I could only pour out my tears with their own.

I loved the boy dearly, and never so much as when I saw his lifeless form lying there in his crib, and when all love was vain. It was enough to break my heart to look upon him, he was so beautiful. Asleep, but, oh, such sleep! such repose, with that pensive, heart-breaking look about the closed eyes that Death alone can give. Oh, that look! — who can describe it — the look of a sweet, innocent boy who has met a speedy death! It defies all words — the memory of it is a sorrowful, yet beautiful possession forever.

Curtis and I go down to the grave-yard and select the spot for his grave beside his uncle, Channy B., whose death, ten years ago, come May, was my first great sorrow. By Father's new-made grave I pause with such thoughts as few may know, and by Mother's, and by the graves of all my dead.

Curtis says to me, 'Here, I suppose, we will all lay one of these days.'

'Yes,' I reply, 'here is to be our last bed,' — each trying to talk carelessly and hiding any emotion. Whose place will be next to Father's, I mentally asked, and had my own thoughts.

As he thinks of the bereaved parents of little Channy, he writes:

I know well when the loss will be felt most keenly by Smith and Emma — if there can be degrees in such agony — when they wake in the morning after the blessed forgetfulness of sleep. Oh! what a pang the first waking moment will bring! Abigail said she heard them weeping and moaning about 4 o'clock. My God! how my heart bleeds for them!

But the bloodroots are starring the ground in bushy places, and soon he is walking the April woods with bird-students, and noting the old friends that spring up in the paths. 'The flower of the blood-root enclosed, or partly enclosed, by the leaf, is strikingly beautiful,' he writes. More poetically, on another April, he illustrates his apprehension of the mere fact with his ability to adorn the fact with a pretty conceit, yet without any lessening of its value as a fact:

Plucked my first bloodroot this morning — a full-blown flower with a young one folded up in a leaf beneath it, only the bud emerging, like the head of a papoose protruding from its mother's blanket.

Again he speaks of the leaf shielding the flower-bud, as one shields the flame of a candle in the open air, with his hand half-closed about it.

On the train to the tiresome banks he comes upon Mary Hallock Foote and her family, *en route* for Idaho:

A woman with rare charm — full of genius and full of womanliness. Said my 'British Fertility' made her sad. She quoted Holmes' remark that 'grass makes girls'; thought instead of troubling ourselves about Woman's Rights, we had better look to woman's health, and study physiology and the laws of life a little more; all other questions were premature.

What self-knowledge and what engaging candor are disclosed in the accompanying entry:

As a writer, especially on literary themes, I suffer much from want of a certain manly or masculine quality, — the quality of self-assertion — strength and firmness of outline. I am not easy and steady in my shoes. The common and vulgar form of the quality I speak of is 'cheek.' But in the master writer it is firmness, dignity, composure — a steady, unconscious assertion of his own personality.

When I try to assert myself, I waver and am painfully self-conscious, and fall into curious delusions. I think I have a certain strength and positiveness of character, but lack egoism. It is a family weakness; all my brothers are weak as men; do not make themselves felt for good or bad in the community.

But this weakness of the *I* in me is probably a great help to me as a writer upon nature. I do not stand in my own light. I am pure spirit, pure feeling, and get very close to bird and beast. My thin skin lets the shy and delicate influences pass. I can surrender myself to Nature without effort. I am like her. That which hinders me with men, and makes me weak and ill at ease in their presence, makes me strong with impersonal Nature, and admits me to her influences.

I lack the firm moral fibre of such men as Emerson and Carlyle.

I am more tender and sympathetic than either, perhaps because there is a plebeian streak in me not in them. This again helps me with Nature, but hinders with men.

And the very next entry proves, in a way, what he had just written:

A green snake in the grass in front of my Study, disposed carelessly across the tops of the bending spears, all but invisible. By mere chance I see him as I lift my eyes from my book — first think it is some plant. After a while he slowly, very slowly, like the hand of a clock, draws himself down into the finer grass of the bottom. After he has reached the ground with the forward part of his body, he still keeps his tail upright, which slowly sinks into the grass like a green stalk going into the ground. All this for protection, I suppose. He was practically invisible.

That one with interests so keen and varied in outdoor nature should also have had, as had Burroughs, such penetrative insight into the world of books, often surprises one, though why should it, since books are but nature revealed in the mind of man? As one comes upon his books of literary criticism after long familiarity with his outdoor writings, it is like finding in the midst of a limitless garden a roomy dwelling with open door through which one may pass and sit by the study fire in quiet converse with a host, honest, wise, and companionable; for we cannot always wander with impersonal nature; and to find, combined in a single author, besides his interpretations of nature, his engaging discourse about the books one loves, and guidance and counsel in the realm of the spirit, is deeply satisfying.

Of the ascent of the Wittenberg he writes Benton in August:

We set out for Slide, but contented ourselves with his near neighbor, the Wittenberg, 3825 feet high. The last thousand feet we pulled ourselves mainly by our hands up the rocks.

The view from the top, where we passed the night, was the finest mountain scenery I ever beheld. Ingersoll said the climb was rougher and harder than any he ever had in the Rockies.

[Journal] Sept. 26. A day of great beauty. All the forenoon upon the hills bee-hunting. Find a swarm in a large maple on the side of the mountain. . . . The day not merely bright, but radiant, full of glory. . . . In the afternoon go a-fishing, Ed, Julian and I, down the winding, loitering river, for bass and suckers. Take a fine lot, with a few trout that did not know the law was up on trout.

What a day! still, restful, the very air luminous. I have to pause and regard the day as one presses a rose to his nose. All the maple trees in the valley burning.

Despite the golden days, to his Journal he turns and writes of the 'days that are no more,' rehearsing the laborious lives of his parents almost as an act of penance:

How slight my toils and troubles, and my little essay-writing seem, compared with such lives! The blue devils never found them idle and vacant as they find me. There is no panoply, no shield, like utter absorption in work. A large family, too, shields and fends one, and to be a part and parcel of your neighborhood, of your town, to belong there, to have grown there, to have been put there by destiny, is a great matter.

What comfort they had in their church, in their 'yearly meetings,' and their 'associations'! what comfort in the intercourse with their friends!

They lived on a low plane, as it were, and the ambitions, the doubts, the yearnings, the disappointments — all the most far-reaching shafts of evil fortune, passed over their heads.

How gladly would I, too, have filled my house with children! how gladly would I have surrounded myself with troops of friends! how gladly would I take root and become one of my fellows!

When sorrow visits his friend Benton, he writes in understanding sympathy:

I am grieved to know that another grave has opened in your pathway, and this time the grave of a brother. Alas! I, too, have lost in Orville a valued friend.

I know well how such a loss, next to that of father and mother, lets in the cold and the desolation — takes down and removes the precious barriers that one tries to fend himself with, against the great chilling Unknown and Unknowable. Piece by piece the roof is taken from over one's head, till the vast and mysterious void descends wholly upon him. Or, a family is like a flock that warms and cheers one another against the night; one by one the flock dwindles, till some one of the number is alone on the mountains.

CHAPTER X

A COMMON GRAYNESS

1884–1887

A common grayness silvers everything.

BROWNING

DESPITE much of variety in his life for the next few years, retrospection is still the prevailing mood. Everything is viewed in the light of the afternoon sun, a little faded and diluted by the vapors, and with a pensive tinge.

Let us hope [he writes] that the land of old age, when we have once really arrived there, will have its own compensations and charm. When the sun really begins to shade the hills, there is a new charm in nature — more color in the sky, more privacy and illusion on the earth. Let us hope it will be so in life.

I am trying to write a little [he says in a letter to Benton], but my ink flows badly. Proof of the new book ['Fresh Fields'] nearly finished.

One finds him in an October entry unconsciously hitting upon the quality which insures the permanence and charm that characterize his own writing:

Must write an essay on the value of the sense of reality to the literary man. Indeed, only those in whom this sense is strong, whether poets or prose writers, ever achieve any lasting work. A lively and intimate sense of things, and to convey this sense in words, so that the reader shares it with you, is at the bottom of all literary success. Think of this sense in Dante! To be real, to have real impressions and emotions, and not feigned ones! It is closely allied to being sincere.

Nov. 4. Election day.
    Rain, rain,
    To the defeat of Blaine!

Vote for Cleveland. Ah, me! a pretty bitter pill. Never before voted for a Democratic candidate for president, but shall do so again, if I live and the Democrats take the stand on a tariff for revenue only. High protection has had its day. Let our manufacturers sink or swim now; the people should be no longer taxed to buoy them up.[1]

[1] He came to have great admiration for Cleveland, and twice voted for him, and many times thereafter voted the Democratic ticket; in fact, was henceforth an Independent in politics.

Nov. 22. Indian summer again in the sky, but winter upon the ground. Sold some honey to Dick Atkins, and Julian and I put it on a sled this morning and ran across the fields over the crust with it to his house. It was a pretty little idyl — a sled loaded with clover honey, and we running with it through the soft sunshine over the hard snow.

The following characterizations appear in the Journal after a few days in New Haven:

... [Dr. Newman Smyth], a man of solid and clear talent. Met Prof. Beers and Lounsbury, both fine fellows. Beers a slight man with a big voice, — a slight incongruity here. Lounsbury a larger man with a smaller, higher-keyed voice, but more in keeping with his look and quality. Prof. Eaton a large hearty fellow, with rather a fine tone to him; on his knees examining the mosses, sometimes on his belly, his eye-glasses falling from his nose just as he gets ready to look.

The mosses are a world by themselves — a Lilliputian world, yet very ancient — the second step, probably, in the vegetable life of the globe. Eaton knows them all, and brought home many specimens.

He said Torrey and Drummond were one day walking in the woods by West Point when Torrey said, 'I have never seen so and so.' 'Never seen so and so!' said Drummond with scorn, and stooped and plucked the moss at their very feet. ...

Dec. 4. To Philadelphia. Found Walt and Dr. Bucke at Green's Hotel. Walt looks well, as usual, and seems to be so. The grain of him yet seems sound and good, though perhaps a little more inclined to a purplish tint. ...

Pass the night, all of us, at Mrs. Smith's — a Quaker family in Germantown. ...

Walt is writing a long preface for his poems. Has many ups and downs about it. One day thinks it a good idea, and the next thinks it is too much like a concession — that his poems should be taken as they are, without any argument or explanation, like the works of nature.

He seemed anxious to hear what I had to say about it. I told him it was a secondary matter: that the poems would have to stand or fall on their own merits. As time went on, his Preface would be dropped if it had nothing important in it, but if it is necessary to the poems, it would be retained. I said, 'Write it, if you feel you have something valuable to say, and let it take its chances; it can neither make nor break.'

It is noteworthy how much more assured is the tone of the younger man now. He speaks to Whitman, no longer as disciple to master, but as one candid friend to another.

Of Holmes's 'Emerson' he comments to Benton thus:

I have dipped into it and find it poor — unworthy of Holmes, and unworthy of Emerson. Holmes is no critic, and is perpetually liable to slump into bad taste. Think of talking of Emerson's mouth as 'a port of entry'! He will sacrifice anything for a witticism. He has sold Emerson's birthright for a mess of Holmes' pottage.

What nonsense to talk of the difference between prose and poetry as the difference between full dress and undress! Does the man mean that there are not poetical ideas, and prose ideas?

In the Journal a few months later he writes of Holmes:

He is like a stove that always draws well; the fire is very bright and lively, and the combustion is complete; but then, the heat is not very great — often no more than the heat of rushes or straw. If his profundity and seriousness were equal to his wit and brightness, he would take rank among the great ones. No smoke in our genial Doctor, no smouldering embers, but always the clearest and quickest of flames.

When his sister Jane and her husband visit him that winter, they sit in his Study, in the firelight, and talk of the past. 'Jane said old folks look very good to her. That is my feeling, too. I turn and look fondly after every old woman I see on the street.'

From this period one traces in the Journal, in the comments on literary and religious topics, a deepening and broadening of his mind; his abiding love of nature bearing fruit in a keener insight into spiritual laws; a harmonizing, as it were, of the body and soul of things — the evolution of the same trend evinced in young manhood, in his studies in analogy. His spontaneous comments upon the books he is reading are from no point of view but his own.

Emerson said that his body seemed never to have broken the umbilical cord that held him to Boston. John Burroughs was likewise held by a prenatal tether to the Old Home cradled amid the Roxbury hills. An early January entry emphasizes this:

Every few days, especially in the winter evenings, the feeling comes strongly upon me that I am away from home; that I am only detained here; and that I must go back to the old place and slacken my thirst at the old home-fountains once more. While Father and Mother were living the feeling was especially strong at times, but I thought that after they were gone it would cease; but it does not. It still seems at times as if I must go back there to live; as if I should find shelter there; as if I should find the old contentment and satisfaction in the circle of those hills; but I know I should not. The soul's thirst can never be slaked. Mine is a hunger of the imagination. Bring all my dead back again and place me amid them in the Old Home, and a vague longing and regret would still possess me.

Jan. 26. To N.Y. today to attend the breakfast given to Edmund Gosse. Gosse is a charming fellow, and easily the superior man present. I fell quite in love with him. He spoke admirably.

The unexpected always happens, and, to my dismay, the chairman, Colonel Waring, called me up. Of course I had nothing to say, hence my melancholy and dissatisfaction with myself today. Yet it is so easy to speak on such occasions after all. So little counts for so much! A farthing's worth of wit will carry a man through; but I had not even a farthing's worth. I shall have a contempt for myself for at least a week to come. . . .

Feb. 2. . . . The ice-harvesting just opening. The broad white plains before my window dotted with moving horses and men. . . . The canal is being opened this morning and runs a straight broad black band directly out from the north end of the ice-house. I see the men whip their hands to warm them up. Sun dazzlingly bright. . . .

Am still writing on Arnold — have my canal fairly opened, and am about ready to stow away my scattered leaves in their final shape.

One gets a picture of the heroic winters of pioneer days, in this brief account of his ride over the Roxbury hills in a whirl of snow:

How the great oxen wallow and plunge through the drifts, rising and falling like old Neptune's steeds, though rather slower of foot. Indeed, we are at sea on a bob-sled; over fences, through fields, we go, the Herculean oxen stopping at nothing.

At the Old Home he finds Hiram absent-minded, — much occupied with thoughts of his father:

Emma said that every day he went and looked at Father's clothes, and then at his picture. At night we went together and looked at them, and into his chest, and handled over many of his things. How the unshed tears choked my throat!

All the while I was there it seemed as if presently some one must come out of the rooms, or in from out-doors — that the family were not all at the table . . . and that the rest of them would appear presently. . . .

Such a vision of snow and winter as one gets in this country. . . . You see the whole landscape at a glance, and see nothing but a snowy desolation.

To Benton in mid-March:

I plead guilty to gross remissness in not writing to you before.
Here I have sat daily in my bark wigwam, and covered half a ream
of paper with ink, and not a leaf for you! but if any of it gets born
into print, then it will be for you, and for all clear heads like
yours.

Across or over what a solid wall of winter I look back to your
visit! . . . The ice in front where we skated is still like a rock, and the
ice-boatmen are having it all their own way. If you would like a
taste of that sport, come over and you shall have your fill. It is
perpetual riding down hill: you ride down, and then turn, and ride
back again, with equal speed. . . .

I have had one letter from Joel and judge he is reaping honors in
the western world, to say nothing of the tender hearts of the maidens.

Yes, I went to the Gosse breakfast. It was quite a swell affair. I
liked Gosse immensely, and was very sorry I had let pass so many
chances to see more of him. He is the most captivating Englishman
I ever met.

I was actually called on for a speech, and was utterly humiliated
because I had nothing to say. . . . I am nothing if not loaded, and it
takes me a good while to load — in public. Johnson [Robert Under-
wood] had assured me there would be no speech-making, so I had
eaten my breakfast with a feeling of perfect security. Next time I
will have my revenge by going with a speech in my pocket half a
mile long.

We all keep well, and are the victims of the same petty cares and
troubles. . . .

April 3. My forty-eighth birthday. How rapidly they come and
go!

Health pretty good; legs nearly normal, more in harmony than one
year ago, no lameness. Occasionally numbness in ends of toes. Right
arm lame for some weeks past; left a little lame. Heart flutters
occasionally, but not so often as during the winter. Not troubled
with sensation of cold in arms and legs as formerly.[1] . . .

The thought uppermost in all minds is the death of General Grant,
a brave, resolute, patriotic, unimpeachable, common-sense man; not
shrewd or sharp in a worldly way; often victimized, but a noble,
solid character. He held together, and kept his head, under circumstances which broke or scattered more brilliant men. Much of pure
adamant in him. How free from brag and bluster! how taciturn! I
have seen him many times in Washington, between 1868 and 1872,
but I shall see him no more. . . .

[1] This is almost the beginning of the self-scrutiny which was to occupy him
increasingly as the years advanced. He was too close an observer of everything
not to regard himself and his symptoms with equal closeness. Ever instantly
aware of the least film over his health, he was keen to discover its cause, and, if
possible, to correct it.

April 25. At Stony Hollow six Kingston girls got on the train with
bundles and baskets of arbutus. Such a lot of arbutus I never before
saw brought out of the woods. They had enough to fill a clothes
basket; it perfumed the whole car. They must have made a clean
sweep; in fact, they were hoggish. I asked some of them if they were
going to deck a public hall with it. In the vicinity of all the large
towns the wild flowers are exterminated by this senseless greed. . . .

The girls probably did not detect his sarcasm, for, strongly
as he felt the desecration, he could not have looked his severity
in the presence of those bright eyes and laughing faces.

To Benton, in June, goes this persuasive missive:

I feel budding within me an expedition to Slide mountain, and to
some of those trout streams. How do you feel? I should like to go
this week — before strawberries bribe me to stay at home, and
before my clover crop compels me. The summer-boarder will soon
be on hand, too, profaning the mountain-tops with his Alpine-stock.
Is there any expedition in you? . . .

In 'The Heart of the Southern Catskills' ('Riverby') Burroughs writes of this expedition to Slide with Myron Benton
and the van Benschotens. It was of Myron that he wrote,
who danced all night to keep warm. Climbing Slide on June
7th, they overtook the fleeing Spring, bedecked with April
flowers. They heard a new thrush (Bicknell's) — 'a thrush's
song, plain enough, but in a minor key — attenuated, like a
fine wire, and singularly resonant.' Delectable days in Woodland Valley followed; many trout were taken; wild strawberries added the idyllic touch to their meals. Then back to
Riverby, to the plain bread and butter of living.

In a letter to Mr. E. P. Bicknell, undated, but probably
written the previous year, he speaks of the new thrush, revealing at the same time his limitation in failing to see the
need for scientific nomenclature:

I ought sooner to have acknowledged your review of the birds of
the Catskills, which I have read with much interest. It is a very
thorough and timely piece of work. I must try and visit those
mountains myself next year and see and hear that new thrush. I
regret to see that you have been re-baptizing some of our familiar
birds in that muddy fount of scientific nomenclature, or else following the lead of some one who has — perhaps that feather-splitter,
Dr. Coues. I see the wood thrush is no longer *Turdus melodus* but
has had a new layer of the barbarous Romish jargon put upon him.
I do not sympathize at all with this practice. It is worse than use-

less. Doubtless if every specimen of a wood thrush were examined minutely enough, no two would be found exactly alike; hence every individual should have a name of its own. The aim of science should be to simplify things, to show us unity under diversity, but ornithology of late years seems bent on making the surface confusion worse confounded. The common names of birds are alone permanent and reliable, the so-called scientific are in perpetual tilt and mutation. I expect that one of these days some one will have the courage to write a treatise on our birds and banish to the devil's rubbish-hole, where they belong, all the Romish names of our pretty and innocent songsters.

I do not expect that you will take this spleen of mine to heart, but that is the way I feel about it. Accept my thanks for your treatise. I can paste slips of paper over the outlandish names.

In this entry, and in much that follows, is seen how completely Burroughs shared his son's interests:

October 12. Julian's first day at school. I went up with him — a great event to him, and to me. What long, long thoughts it set going! My first day at school was more than forty years ago. . . . Julian said he would not mind going to school, if he were not so dumb about his book. He knows so much about other things, that he seems to think it a disgrace to know so little about his book. If he lives to look back to this day, forty years from now, how strange and far-off and incredible it will seem to him!

Oct. 22. A still, overcast motionless day, after the heavy rain of yesterday. The brilliant foliage of the maples covering the ground beneath them almost takes the place of sunshine. They indeed shed a sort of mild radiance or glory that tempers the heavy shadow of the day in their presence.

Mrs. B. advises me to give up writing and do something else for a living. She advises me in the same spirit that the wife of a cobbler, or a carpenter, might advise her husband to give up his trade and try some other.

Nov. 8. Last night Julian said to me, 'Papa, which is the best business — to be a finder-out about the earth and stars, or to be an artist?' I had told him how much the artist, Herkomer, was said to have made during the few months he spent in this country ($25,000), which seemed to impress him much. . . .

There are those who will concede that the little questioner's father was a finder-out about the earth and stars, and an artist too.

[Journal] Dec. 18. Read today in the Academy of the death of Mrs. Gilchrist. Many a sad thought has it caused me. Just now I

can see or think of no one in England but her. She is the principal
fact over there, and she is gone. The only woman I ever met to
whose mind and character I instinctively bowed. She was a rare
person, a person of rare intelligence.

A few days later comes this from Whitman:

The death of Mrs. Gilchrist is indeed a gloomy fact. . . . Seems to
me mortality never enclosed a more beautiful spirit.

It was to Anne Gilchrist, whom he called his noblest
woman friend, that Whitman wrote the poem, 'Going Somewhere'; and, grouping her with William D. O'Connor, Dr.
Maurice Bucke, and John Burroughs, in 'Specimen Days,' he
calls them his dearest friends — 'friends of my soul —
staunchest friends of my other soul — my poems.'

In 1886, after the termination of the bank-examining, Burroughs employed his extra leisure in writing, chiefly about
science and theology. A significant entry reads:

I look upon that man as lucky who feels a want the Church can
supply. It puts him in relation with the world, gives him an interest
with communities far outside of his own neighborhood that is wholesome and desirable. The name of his Church and his heart throb
with the home feeling, wherever he is. It doubtless awakens a more
personal feeling in him than that of patriotism. . . . We do not like to
feel isolated and alone. A common race, a common country, is not
enough; there are those who belong peculiarly to us, who think and
feel as we do; let us in some way unite ourselves to them; let us find
our bretheren, put all our hearts together, and see if we cannot warm
one little spot in this cold universe.

What comfort my father had in his Church, and in its organ, The
Signs of the Times! These were the voices of his bretheren and
sisters who spoke here, though they lived in Oregon or in Texas.
Their words warmed him. That they had had the same experiences
that he had had, the same struggles and doubts and despairs,
touched him in a way peculiarly close and precious.

None of his degenerate sons belong to the church, and none of
them are as worthy as he — none of them stand so well in the community as he did. I do not speak so much of myself; I know I am
Father's superior in some ways, and his inferior in others. I have not
his self-reliance, nor his innocence. He was as unsophisticated as a
child. I cannot accept my place and lot in the world as cheerfully as
he did, and I doubt much if I could have fought the same battle as he
did, under the same conditions, with the same success. I look back
at the work he did — he and Mother — the farm they improved and
paid for, the family they reared, with unspeakable longing. How
idle and trivial seem my own days!

After five days in New York comes this entry:

Feb. 13. . . . Visited the Morgan collection of pictures, saw a picture by Jules Breton, 'The Communicants,' that pleased me much. I'm convinced that Millet ran his theory into the ground at times. In the Woodsplitter you cannot tell whether the background is woods, or tied up branches of corn-stalks, or sugar-cane. His figures are great because of their seriousness, and the force of nature they hold or express.

At the Water Color Exhibition saw little that took me, though I am no judge of pictures. . . .

J. W. Alexander makes a sketch of me for the Century — a good picture, I should say, but not a good likeness. . . .

On the advent of 'Signs and Seasons' he announces, 'Probably the least valuable of my books.' (He usually felt this way just after a book was done.) Whitman's commendation, which follows, must have been gratifying:

Your book has come so nice and fresh, like a new pot-cheese in a clean napkin. — I have read the first piece — 'Look Out' ['A Sharp Lookout'] — all through and thought it fully equal to anything in the past, and looked over the rest of the pages — doesn't seem to me to deserve the depreciatory tone in which you speak of it.

Sarah Orne Jewett wrote heartily about the new book, especially envious of the experiences that had gone into 'A Taste of Maine Birch.'

Though complaining to his Journal that his days are blank, his entries on life and literature belie his words. As he sits by the boiling sap-pan, out on the brow of the hill, in the crystalline March days, he reads fitfully, and fitfully comments upon what he reads:

Lowell is not a healing or helpful writer; he does not touch the spirit, the soul, but reaches only the wit, the fancy, the intelligence. He has no religion, none of that subtle piety and goodness and loving kindness that mark the great teachers and founders.

Writers and poets might well be divided into two classes: those who rest with the mind, and those who penetrate to the spirit. Poets like Pope and his school, men of quick and keen intelligence, and prose writers like Lowell, belong to the former class; while Wordsworth, Emerson, Carlyle, and men of this stamp, belong to the latter, and address the soul.

The *Westminster Review* praises my style, says language in my hands is like a violin in the hands of a master. But really I have no dexterity as a writer. I can only walk along a straight, smooth path. Of the many nice and difficult things I see done in prose, by dozens of

writers, I am utterly incapable. What I see and feel, I can express,
but it must be all plain sailing. I do not know how to utter platitudes, if I wanted to, and the other things come only at rare intervals.

[Journal] March 19. Finished Gibbon's 'Decline and Fall' this
morning, begun last summer — my principal reading during all
these months. Not easy reading to me. Gibbon's sentences are like
spheres — there is only a smooth curved surface for the mind to
grasp. Carlyle groaned over Frederick, but how much more reason
had Gibbon to groan over his task! and yet he says 'it only amused
and exercised twenty years' of his life.

His work is like a piece of masonry of dressed stone: every sentence
fits in its place; there is not a jagged line or an unfinished spot anywhere. And it is plain to see that he tore his material from the rocks
and mountains, as it were, and set it in this smooth, compact order.
A splendid bridge, as Carlyle said to Emerson, leading from the old
world to the new.

J. W. Alexander was painting Whitman at this time. Burroughs was hopeful of the result, but, years later, said the
artist had failed to get Whitman's power and ruggedness:

A likeness, yes, many an artist gets the likeness — the thing is to
get *the man*. An artist can paint no bigger picture than himself.
That is why ——, with all his attempts, can't get Yours Truly —
it isn't in him; but I like him too well to tell him so. There is where
my cowardice comes in. Alexander made a kind of Bostonese Whitman.

In early April, to Benton:

What a dissolving time we have had! This last downpour almost
liquefied our very hills. I was afraid my ten acres would all slide into
the river, but part of it seems to have stuck. The river looks as if
there is at least one part mud to two parts water. If your farm had
the fertilizing matter it now holds in solution, what crops you could
grow for the next fifty years! . . .
The blizzard gave us the epizoötic. . . . We are all well now, but
the kitchen divinities are not as serene as they might be — a new
girl, and a stupid one.
We expect in May to go off to Kentucky and the West. . . . The
first week in May I have agreed to go up to Smith College to help a
class of young women 'name all the birds without a gun.'
I see you would fain shut my 'Open Door,' or look upon it as no
door at all, but only a crack in the wall; but the paper seems to have
made quite a hit. The Philadelphia Press wrote me that they had
published nothing in a long time that had called forth so many
communications and remarks. They sent me two letters, one of

which I enclose. Neither writer had ever heard my name before. So you see there is a new field there for me all unreapt. I might get the following of two classes of readers, neither of which knew the other.

. . . I should like to see my things in the Atlantic, but I shall send nothing more there unless I am asked. I told you that they returned my 'Bird Enemies.' They also returned the Arnold-Emerson article, though I greatly improved it before it went to the Century. The chapter in 'Fresh Fields' called 'British Fertility,' they also rejected.

Scribners, I hear, will start a new magazine soon. The first number is set up and will be printed as soon as the time is up agreed upon with the Century.[1]

I do not write much, and probably shall write less in the future. My harvest is about gathered.[2] . . .

[Journal] April 16. The fair days continue — tranquil, peaceful, brooding April days, the most delicious of the year. Soft, vapory moonlight nights, too. In the morning the long-drawn call of the highhole comes up, then the tender rapid trill of the little bush or russet sparrow; then the piercing, sword-like note of the meadow starling.

I am content to sit about all day and dream and muse, and let my eye roam over the landscape, lingering long on the emerald spots.

On the same date is a beautiful passage on the power of the Past which, a little changed and abridged, he wove into his essay 'The Spell of the Past' ('Literary Values'). Down the *Rue du Temps Perdu* our Celt is ever turning a yearning backward glance. There was, however, none of this mournfulness in the bird walks with the college girls which began that spring, the continuance of which was to be of mutual pleasure for years to come.

[Journal] April 27. . . . Reach Northampton at 2 pm. Beautiful country; the heart of New England, a ripe mellow country. The meadows a great feature. So many colleges all about seem to give an air of culture which our state lacks.

Great enthusiasm among the college girls. I led great packs of them to fields and woods and helped them identify the birds by their calls and songs. Two or three times a day we go forth, once to the top of Mt. Tom. On Wednesday the President drives me to Amherst, a beautiful place, a sort of high island in a great rolling plain.

Joel Benton, a cousin of Myron, susceptible, and vain of his resemblance to Tennyson, dressed the part to perfection.

---

[1] After October, 1881, the old *Scribner's Monthly* became the *Century Magazine.* The present *Scribner's* started in 1886.

[2] His *Last Harvest* was gathered five and thirty years later.

Burroughs took a mischievous delight in dangling before his imagination the betwitching college girls he met on his travels:

My walks and talks with the Smith College girls would set every old bachelor like you fairly wild. Twice a day I walked with fifty of them, and every night I was surrounded by them; never was a wolf so overwhelmed by the lambs before. One of the lambs gave up her room to me, and I am not certain but a lamb blacked my shoes in the morning. It was all very pretty and charming, and I have half promised to go again.

I was glad to hear from you, and know of the many things you have been writing and 'placing.' . . . Your industry shames my idleness, though I have just written a long essay on Drummond's 'Natural Law in the Spiritual World.' The book is a fraud and I have tried to put my pen through it in a good many places.[1]

The only thing I have that would do for the Cosmopolitan is a short essay which I might call 'Science and the Poets,' and which I will let him have for thirty dollars. It is mainly occupied with Emerson's use of science. It is the tail-end of an essay which I published in Macmillan's Magazine for July, on 'The Literary Value of Science.' The Wide Awake has just asked me for a series of bird articles. . . .

From Frankfort, Kentucky, to his wife in Cleveland, he writes:

Mr. Proctor and I returned last night from a four days' drive over the country. I got a good taste of blue grass. It is the finest country I have yet seen. We passed a day and night at Ashland, Henry Clay's old home. Tomorrow I go out twelve miles to a large farm, Mr. Alexander's, to loaf a couple of days and see what I can absorb of the country.

Then I go down to the Mammoth Cave, and then through western Kentucky. The Governor of the state has invited me to come and spend some time with him, but probably I shall not go.

I shall not get to Chicago before the first of June. . . . I do not mean to hurry. . . . I enclose check. . . . Tell Julian that Barnum's circus is here. . . .

Writing Myron Benton of his two days at the Mammoth Cave, he said that three hours in the Cave itself satisfied him, and that he was chiefly astonished at his want of astonishment:

I am always more or less bored when I am toted about to see things which I am expected to admire. I would have done much better in Kentucky had I gone alone, as I did about England, and

---

[1] 'I was too hard on Drummond,' he said, years later; '"fraud" is not the right word; but it was a transparent piece of sophistry, an attempt to prove that Scotch Presbyterianism is scientifically true; the book would not hold water.'

not been, as it were, everywhere introduced to things. I like best to
scrape acquaintance with Nature and with men. . . . I do not know
yet that I shall get anything out of the trip, I fear not much.[1] I am
glad I went — that is disposed of and will haunt me no more. It is
not for me to go gadding about seeking wonders. I do better along
my old cow-paths.

Some of his literary activities are traced in the Journal for
September 25th:

Have written three articles since first of July: on myself ['Egotistical Chapter,' first printed as 'Mere Egotism' in 'Lippincott's,'
later in 'Indoor Studies']; on Science and Theology ['Light of
Day']; and on my Kentucky trip ['Riverby']; besides working a
good deal over two other articles.

Evidently a little concerned as to how his discussions on
religious questions would be received, he sends the following
letter to Benton:

Before the Wiggins earthquake, which is due today, shakes the
roof down upon me, I make haste to get off my hands a certain
questionable production which goes to you by this mail. If it reaches
you at all, it will not be till after the catastrophe is over, so that you
will not be found by the avenging powers harboring such a treason-
able article.

What I send you is an essay on 'Science and Theology.' I want
your criticism of it, and let your criticism be for reproof and edifica-
tion. You will see what it is all anent of. The North American
Review writes me that they will accept it after January, but in the
meantime I think of sending it to the Nineteenth Century, or the
Fortnightly Review.

Put your finger on the weak places; also tell me if you think it
would produce a commotion among my readers in this country, if
published here. *Is it offensive?* If you can read it, and let me have it
back next week, I shall be much obliged. Let Joel read it also. . . .

Many thanks for Charlie's [Charles E. Benton] account of the
Battle of Gettysburg. . . . The Century, with all its famous war
papers, has not had so vivid and good an account of a battle. I
believe Charley could throw us all in the shade with his pen, if he
were to devote himself to it. Stir him up to do more — he astonishes
me. . . .

Benton thought a commotion among Burroughs's feminine
readers was inevitable if 'Science and Theology' were cast into
the midst of them, but that, if it were a matter of conscience,
that should not disturb the author. Evidently it did not, for
Burroughs replied that he had tried the essay on several ortho-

[1] He got 'A Taste of Kentucky Blue Grass' and 'In Mammoth Cave' (*Riverby*).

dox persons, and that they liked it almost too well. After telling what he is reading he adds:

> I want to get the points of view of other honest minds. Have just read Dr. James' study of 'Primitive Christianity,' a book written nearly from my own point of view; and Dr. Bruce's 'Miraculous Elements in the Gospel,' — a Scotch Free Church view — a book which shows marvellous changes in the past twenty-five years. These men are in earnest now about trimming themselves to the gale. The way they are shifting their sails to catch, or to withstand this strong wind of Science is very interesting.
> . . . Have also been reading Mulford's 'Republic of God,' a book which repels at first, on account of [its] current religious jargon, . . . but which has a noble music, and very lofty thought. . . . I am now reading Lecky's History of Rationalism, a work which astonishes me by its learning, its eloquence, and its broad philosophic spirit. I ought to have read it long ago. . . . I shall get his History of European Morals.
> I took three articles to the Century in November — Arnold, the Southern Catskills, and Kentucky Blue Grass. They paid me $450. for them — too much. I told them so. Appleton paid me $90.00 for the Science and Theology article.

The long-standing comradeship with Mr. Aaron Johns is again glimpsed in this brief entry:

> His coming brings other days, brings our camp life beside the delicious trout-brooks, and all that goes with a free life in the woods. It brings twenty years of the past. My Comrade, my soldier! I have a kind of attachment for him that I have for no other man.

> October 16. At Lake Mohonk for past three days, invited to be present at the Indian Conference, an enjoyable time. Meet President Gates of Rutgers College; like him much; a genuine fellow; has a quality which only those born and bred in the country ever have. President Gilman, also, of Johns Hopkins; like him. Met Elaine Goodale, a very sweet, attractive face; serious, thoughtful, genuine. Expect great things from that girl.

Still discussing religious books in his Journal, he tells of sending off 'A Lay Sermon' to the 'Forum.' He retracts somewhat his former opinion of Mulford's book:

> Mulford's 'Republic of God' — a book that seems as if written in a kind of dream, nothing clearly logical or wide awake about it. One fancies him mumbling these things in his sleep.
> Blackie's 'History of Criticism' — the style of the book suggests a man rushing through the house and slamming the doors. It is cer-

tainly a noisy style, a good deal of life in it, occasionally coarse, with something of the air of a smart, flippant advocate.

Dec. 19. Julian said this morning, soon after waking, that he felt as if a great change was coming — 'as if a great joy was passing away.' He is beginning to doubt the existence of Santa Claus. Poor boy! Such a discovery does leave a void.

How much deeper and more painful a void would have been left in the minds of our fathers if they had suddenly made the discovery which their children have gradually made, that *their* Santa Claus, the great Dispenser of the gift of life, was a delusion, a fiction, and that natural law brought all these things to pass! What a chill, what desolation, would have possessed their credulous souls! What! no God with whom I can commune, to whom I can pray, whose presence I have so often felt near me, upon whose mercy and love I can throw myself in trials, in sickness, in death! Fancy the state of orphanage which such a discovery would bring about in the hearts of our fathers! Yet this discovery has come to many of us, and we are not seriously disturbed. We go on with the game of life with quite the old zest, and perhaps have less quaking at the thought of the termination of it than our fathers did. Our minds, our spiritual wants, adjust themselves to new conditions.

The great Santa Claus is gone, but the good things still come, only they come through unexpected channels; through means that are perfectly comprehensible, — much nearer to us; and much more constant in our daily lives than we had supposed. They come naturally, not miraculously. God no longer sends the rain or the snow; but they come by the operation of laws as regular in their workings as that which makes the clock strike, or the pendulum swing.

The discovery that events so fall out may shock us at first; it takes away the charm of the personal element, the direct benefaction to us, and the charm of mystery. The imagination and the emotions are left cold and unresponsive. But the rain would fall, and the spring return, just the same, if man were not here.

It is a terrible shock to our childish pride and egotism, to the filial and family feeling in man, which elects God into a father, solicitous about the good of each member.

The truth is, the beneficence of God so far transcends our conception of it under the symbol of fatherhood, that it seems quite the opposite.

The same evening Julian remarked, with a sadness that went to my heart, 'The world has told a great many lies, if there is no Santa Claus — making pictures about him, and telling so much about him in books.'

Dec. 25. Bright and sharp; ground covered with snow. A gloomy Christmas, a domestic earthquake — shock after shock, threatens to bring the roof down.

Dec. 29. Earthquake shocks still continue, now mild, now severe.
. . . A fine skate on the river, ice like glass; quite invisible, it is so
smooth and clear. The sensation is like that of flying over the
surface of the water. Julian with me on his first skates.

January 11. Three years ago this day Father was buried. How
the thought comes to me here in my solitude. Today Wife and
Julian leave me to board in Poughkeepsie. It may be the end of our
housekeeping. It certainly is on the old terms. . . .

In February, tired of the solitary life at Riverby, he spends
some time with his family, before going on to Washington.
There meeting again Hugh McCulloch, his old chief in the
Treasury Department, who had given him his position in
those dark days of seeking work, he says: 'Old age is really
upon him, and the end of his life's journey not far off. A
large, noble, and lovable man — no public man to whom I
feel so drawn.' He roams in his old haunts on Piney Branch
and Rock Creek with Mr. Robert Underwood Johnson:

How the old scenes touched my heart! The voice of the little
brook fills all the valley with its soft murmur. We look for hepaticas,
and after we have given up finding any, lo! a single flower upon the
dry leaves. . . .

The March Journal furnishes a vivid picture of Whitman:

Find Walt sitting in a chair with a long gray-bearded goat-skin
behind him, a shawl pinned about him, and a chaos of papers, letters,
books, MSS, and so on, at his feet and reaching far out into the
room. Never saw such confusion and litter — bundles of letters,
bundles of newspapers, cuttings, magazines, a cushion or two, foot-
rests, books opened and turned down, dust, and above all the grand,
serene face of the poet.

He is more alert and vivacious than when I saw him in May;
inquires anxiously about O'Connor. . . . We have much talk, and it
does me good to be with him again. He talks affectionately about
Beecher just dead and says many things in his praise. The word
'miscellaneous,' he says, describes him. . . . We sit by the firelight
till 9, when I go back to Philadelphia.

Some days later the journalist himself talks of Beecher:

. . . A man of the times, large, coarse, multitudinous, copious,
eloquent, versatile, touching our common American humanity at
more points, perhaps, than any other preacher of his time.

He gave forth no divine light and no divine warmth, yet he amused
and warmed and swayed the multitude. He was peculiarly American

in his freedom, his audacity, his breadth, and his secularization of the
pulpit.

The great source of his popularity was that, after all, he represented us so well, represented our better tendencies and possibilities.
. . . Expansive, quick-witted, every leading and formative idea of the
times found lodgement and reinforcement in his mind. He was as the
sea, and could, on occasion, exhibit the might and vehemence of the
great natural forces.

March 23. Mrs. B. and Julian came back today. Gone since
Jan. 10. Most of that time have lived here alone in the house. Glad
to have Wife back, and hope things will go better in the future. . . .

April 3. Sunday. A sun day, indeed, the fairest of the spring days
so far — warm, bright, delicious. I sit and pen this amid a hum of
bees like June. How robin answered robin, and bluebird called to
bluebird, and sparrow challenged sparrow this morning!

My 50th birthday. Half a century of life, and so little done!

A beautiful box of flowers last night from a class in rhetoric at
Fulton, N.Y. . . .

'Half a century of life and so little done'! Surely here he
could not see the woods for the trees. That very year a movement was on foot, started by Mary E. Burt, that was to spread
far and wide the results of this half-century of his life. Miss
Burt knew the needs of children. Her vision, enthusiasm, and
practicality were enlisted in their behalf — to put before them,
simultaneously, nature lore and good literature. Thousands
who never heard her name have reaped the benefit of her work.
Believing that children would eagerly read the unadulterated
Burroughs, she began by asking the Board of Education in one
of the Chicago schools for thirty-six copies of 'Pepacton' for
regular reading-books. Most gratifying were the results. Mr.
Oscar Houghton, of the firm of Houghton, Mifflin & Company,
went on to Chicago to see what had happened there — such a
thing never having occurred before among modern authors —
and, on witnessing the enthusiasm of Miss Burt's pupils,
asked her to edit a small volume of stories from Burroughs.
'Birds and Bees' was the outcome — a little candle which has
thrown its beams a long way, for this was practically the beginning of the movement of the study of nature in home and
school.

At this period Mr. Burroughs was passing through a crisis
of which a hint (which must suffice) is given in an April letter
to Benton:

Your truly paternal letter came while I was in Washington.... You have, as I always knew you had, much of the spirit of Him who said, 'Neither do I condemn thee'; and I am grateful to you for showing it to me at this time. It is easy to condemn; the Pharisee could do that; but it requires quite a different nature to forgive, and to judge a man by his best....

This is my fiftieth birthday, and a lovelier one I never had. If the brightness within were only equal to the brightness and promise without!

Mrs. B. wants me to sell the place and go to Poughkeepsie to live. But I cannot live there, and I can live here. I am as much dependent upon the country for my income as you are for yours.

Out at the Old Home in April, the following transaction is recorded:

Go down to the village with Hiram and he gives me a mortgage on the farm for the $1100 I have signed with him (paid $600). The looking over the old deeds calls up such thoughts of the past, and of Father and Mother. How my heart yearns for them!

April 12. Go to N.Y. to see Walt and be at the lecture. In the Century office run upon Lowell and Charles Eliot Norton. Johnson introduces me to Lowell. He greets me heartily....

Lowell is a pretty strong-looking man, more than a mere scholar; a man of affairs and of the world, and able to hold his own in places that test men's mettle. Of his kind, he easily ranks first of the New England writers....[1]

Norton I found a sweet, gentle nature, a man to make fast friends with.... He spoke warmly of the pleasure my books had given him. ... We met again at the lecture, and I sat in the box with him and Lowell.

Found Walt at the Westminster Hotel, fresh and rosy and sweet as ever. The lecture went off finely, a distinguished audience, and much sympathy with him....

Walt looked grand and distinguished as he sat in his chair and received the callers. His is easily the grandest face and form in America. He stood it well; the little excitement was just what he needed, — a wholesome human breeze that quickened his circulation and made his face brighter.

At 12, John Fiske and some one else came in and began to discuss the immortality of the soul. Walt said he would have given anything to have got away to his room and to bed, and as some one else caught on to the discussion, he did so.

In the morning at 8 I found him dressed and resting from his bath, and as fresh and rosy as ever. At 10 he went to the photographer's with Jennie Gilder, and then to the studio of Miss Wheeler [Dora]

---

[1] It is interesting to note how a charming personality could cause him temporarily to modify his criticism.

for a sitting. Think Miss Wheeler will make a strong picture of him.

Whitman's lecture on Lincoln, a benefit lecture, was held in Steinway Hall. 'We all sat together in a box. Stedman's little granddaughter, looking like a fairy, went on the stage with a bouquet of lilacs for Walt. He took her in his arms and kissed her. They received several hundred dollars, I think.'

One spring day as he and his son were gathering wintergreen berries, he seemed for the first time to see the real beauty of the adder's-tongue, *alias* dog-tooth violet — both misnomers. One wishes that trout lily, or fawn lily, names he has suggested, might become the accepted common name!

As we stood there beyond the bridge, discovered two by the roadside, just opened. The sunshine was falling full upon them, and with their recurved petals or perianths, and long purple anthers, they looked so brisk, fresh, lively and delicate, that they gave me an impression I had never before had. They were not drooping, but looked the sun fairly in the face, and apparently laughing all over. Then a little later we discovered one that had come up protected by a large, lichen-covered stone. The flower with its fresh canary yellow, and new spotted leaves, was set squarely against the face of the stone, and we paused and admired it, and commented upon it. Under some hemlocks where the old snow-banks yet lingered, the adder's-tongues were piercing the leaves like awls. They did not raise the leaves, but pushed up through them, making a smooth round hole.

Although he thought his days were leaving no trace, they were, in fact, leaving imperishable pictures, on the pages of his books, in his Journal. Many of those 'less tangible things' that he sought and found in the woods have become permanent possessions of his readers. That gay little company of adder's-tongues will flash upon the inward eye as vividly as do Wordsworth's daffodils.

[Journal] April 25. April is doing her best now, — clear, warm, wooing days that affect one like music.

Since July I have written the following papers:

A Taste of Kentucky Blue Grass, In Mammoth Cave, Science and Theology, The Modern Skeptic, The Natural and the Supernatural, Mere Egotism, Spring Jottings, Observations of Nature, (two last in Chautauquan), Early Spring Sounds, The Ethics of War, A Hint from Franklin, Reason and Predisposition,— besides other short papers not yet ready for printing. Yes, and a short paper on Beecher for the Memorial volume.

May 11.... Just now the leaves and branches of the young hickories are being born. They come into the world like young birds, or young puppies. The great hickory buds grow and swell and color up till they are often two inches long, when the fleshy sheath parts and the young branch, leaves and all, emerge. The leaves are folded up and pressed together, like hands in prayer. The great flesh-colored, membranous scales or wraps, how curious they look! They turn back and surround the tender branch like a purple or crimson ruffle, and then, after a few days, drop off and perish. I do not know of any other tree whose branches spring from the parent bud so fully developed.

June 8. Julian and I go down to West Point and spend the day. Meet young Ed Denton, a school boy of mine 24 years ago, and spend most of the day with him. A fine hearty man, and a capital botanist. The mock battle of the cadets takes Julian much, and tickles me, too.

Mrs. B. still in the dismal dumps. No thoughts these days, and no zest for life; seems as if my intellectual life never was at so low an ebb, no interest in anything....

June 16. A visit from Mr. Denton.... Spent the day in the woods. The showy cypripedium in bloom. A great treat to Denton who is a fine botanist and a genuine lover of the plants, and of the wild. A visit from such a man, — serious, earnest, and genuine, does me good. He gives me a watch, in his enthusiasm over the flowers there in the swamp, and I give him a set of my books. In afternoon I take him another way, and we find the whorled pogonia, another new orchid to him, but blossom fallen.

A letter from Whitman tells of Herbert Gilchrist painting his portrait, and Sidney Morse making a bust of him. Burroughs said of these efforts:

Gilchrist tried to paint Walt, but it was a failure.... Morse made a big shaggy, Homeric bust which had power, but he overdid it. He didn't show the womanliness there was in him — there was something so fine and delicate in Walt!

Burroughs's own pen-pictures of the poet, often as they recur, are welcome. This, after a midsummer visit, gives more than a picture of Whitman:

...He came slowly down the stairs... looking better than last year. With his light gray suit and white hair, and fresh, florid face, he made a fine picture.

Among other things we talked of the Swinburne attack. Walt did not show the least feeling on the subject — was absolutely undisturbed by the article. I think he looks upon Swinburne, as I do, as a sort of abnormal creature, full of wind and gas, but not worth attending to. I abhor his poetry, and I know that Walt has no stomach for it. He is a mere puff of mephitic gas. I told Walt I had always been more disturbed by Swinburne's admiration for him than I was now disturbed by his condemnation. I was heartily glad that his true character had at last come out.

By and by Walt had his horse hitched up, and we drove down to Glendale to see young Gilchrist, — a fine drive through a level farming and gardening country.

Walt drives briskly and salutes every person he meets . . . he said as he grew older the old Long Island custom of speaking to every one on the road was strong upon him. . . .

We talked of many things. I recall this remark of Walt's: that it was difficult to see what the feudal world would have come to without Christianity to check and curb it.

. . . The cherry-lipped young Englishman was well and brisk, and apparently enjoying himself in a very flat, uninteresting country, and an uninteresting household. Walt drove back before dark. . . .

From the Catskills he writes Benton in early September:

All this blessed summer has passed, dear Myron, and I have not written you a word, and I have no excuse but my besetting sin of indifference and lethargy.

We rented our house in June, and came up here to my brother's the latter part of the month. . . . I expected to have gone to Colorado the first of July with Mr. Turner, but he did not get ready, so the trip is put off. . . . I do not like the thought of it, but I will never be any younger, and I believe I ought to see that wonderful country before I die.

My life has been sluggish and uneventful since I last wrote you. I have read but little, and thought less. This country up here with its great stretches of smooth rolling grassy farms is very restful, but it does not seem to stimulate my mental life.

Wyatt Eaton, the artist, is stopping at Roxbury, and I occasionally spend a day with him. He is painting my portrait.

The people to whom I rented the house want to buy it. I am half a mind to sell it and be homeless the rest of my life. If it were not for Julian, I should not hesitate a moment.

[Journal] Sept. 10. Just finished 'Katia' by Tolstoi, a simple, pleasant little story, the moral: Don't try to repeat life; each stage of life has its happiness. And don't expect to be always young, or to be always madly in love with the man or the woman you marry. The flower of love, like every other flower, is bound to fall, and to be succeeded by something different, but equally good and desirable.

. . . Wish I could write up my holiday here in this pastoral country and call it 'Out to Grass.'

The Journalist is finding John Fiske difficult reading:

His style is so much like an apparatus, and a cumbrous one at that, instead of the deftness of his own hands. It is like a patent reaper — there is little or nothing personal, or that savors of fresh, individual genius.

Presently we find him voicing this complaint:

The fall does not bring the relish for life and for Nature that I hoped it would. Can it be that henceforth I am only to have skimmed milk?

However, he soon sounds a new note and writes Benton of interests and activities which have put to flight his *ennui:*

I have been busy — not with my pen, but with the spade and hoe — resetting my vineyards. Have put out about 2000 grape-vines, and expect to put out more, all choice kinds from which I expect some profitable returns. I have enjoyed the occupation much. What a blessed thing is work — something one can do with a will! Your house-building has undoubtedly been a god-send to you — it sets new currents going — and my vine-planting has been the same to me. I was fast losing my hold upon my bit of land here, so that the $12,500 I was offered for it was a sore temptation; but now I seem to have renewed my title to it, and can easily put the offer by. . . .

Mrs. B. has been more than busy in the house, and has purged it from basement to garret. . . . She has a new girl, but will soon be alone again. . . .

Do you know a worthy man and his wife in want of a place? . . . I must look up such a couple before spring.

My outlook for the winter is not very cheering — a low bank account, a low coal-bin, and almost a dry ink-horn.

CHAPTER XI

THE FRUIT OF THE VINE
1888–1892

*See, the smell of my son is as the smell of a field which the Lord hath blessed:
Therefore, God give thee of the dew of heaven, and the fatness of the earth.*

Genesis

WITH the advent of the year of the triple-eights which, Mr.
Burroughs used to say, would not come again in a thousand
years, came a real epoch in his life. He bought nine additional
acres and began the vineyard work which was to absorb much
of his time for the next decade and more — an enterprise
which led Stedman to name him 'The Vine-Dresser of Esopus.'

In the work of clearing and draining the land and setting
out vines he found new delight; his health improved; his sleep
was sweeter, and his days lost their somber tinge. Passages
in 'The Secret of Happiness' ('Literary Values') tell of the
magic change wrought by yielding to the demand of his
yeoman ancestry.

In underdraining the moist places in the land, he said he
seemed to be underdraining his own life and carrying off the
stagnant water there also. The work was arduous: posts to
set out, wire to string, ploughing, planting, fertilizing, spray-
ing, trimming, tying up, and harvesting. When he gathered
his first harvest of grapes, he must have rejoiced as much as
did Thoreau when he had made the land say 'beans.' Thoreau's venture had had somewhat of brag in it. He crowed over
his beans to his neighbors; but Burroughs tended his vineyard,
intent on making it pay; on gathering the choicest grapes that
could be raised, and on supplementing the scanty income from
his books, in order to support his family in greater comfort,
send his son to college, and be free to write as the spirit moved.
In all of this he succeeded.

Walter H. Page, in writing of this phase of the life of Burroughs, called attention to the fact that while he had given
himself to the study and interpretation of Nature, he had
regularly sold his grapes at the highest market-price; and that,
however much he was an organic part of his garden and vineyard, he was equally a part of human society — an observa-

tion which recalls a comment of Mr. Bliss Perry's on Emerson: that, though he could muse on the over-soul, he could raise the best Baldwin apples and Bartlett pears in Concord, and get the highest current prices for them. In getting the best current prices for his grapes, peaches, raspberries, and other fruit, Burroughs found his purchase of more land to be one of the best investments he ever made. For vineyard and garden contributed to, rather than detracted from, the cultivation of the 'other garden,' whose harvests cannot be reckoned in dollars and cents. The fruit of the vine, gathered in Concords, Campbell's Earlies, Niagaras, Delawares, and Gaertners, was tallied by the observations and meditations that simultaneously grew into essays, and in the essays that grew into volumes, during those busy, fruitful years.

How completely he planted himself in his vineyard is seen in that, long after he had ceased to take an active part in it, he still went to it for the title of one of his volumes ('Leaf and Tendril'), drawing from his long years of husbandry apt figures for the preface — one of the most felicitous among his many felicitous prefaces. For the blind, sensitive, outreaching tendrils of his thoughts on the great questions as they groped their way in the world-vineyard, he found a symbol in the tendrils of the vines growing near his Study. There, as he sat and wrote, and heard the sharp 'Click, click' of 'Hud's' (Hudson Covert, his faithful helper in the vineyard) shears, trimming and pruning, he prayed the divinities that preside over growing things both indoors and out to help him trim his own vines as heroically as 'Hud' trimmed his — to get rid of as much old wood as possible, and leave only the young, vigorous shoots; and he who tastes the 'grapes,' knows that the prayer of the Vine-Dresser was answered.

At the beginning of this eventful year, the husbandman was busy also in his 'other vineyard,' pruning away at his essay on Arnold, before transplanting it to his new book ('Indoor Studies'); or, shall one say, he was trimming here, guiding there, and relentlessly lopping off superfluities, intent only upon a choice yield.

The following June letter to Hamilton Wright Mabie shows how the essay on Arnold had impressed a brother author:[1]

[1] For the loan of this and other letters, I am indebted to Mrs. Mabie; and to her and Mr. Edwin W. Morse, and Dodd, Mead & Co., for permission to quote from letters published in Mr. Morse's *Life and Letters of Hamilton W. Mabie.*

IN THE SUMMER-HOUSE AT RIVERBY

I do not take too seriously your generous appreciation of my Arnold essay, though among the younger writers of the country there is no one whose good opinion I value more. I remember your own work in this field, especially that noble essay of yours in the Princeton Review on some characteristics of modern literature as distinguished from the ancient. This was a serious, penetrating, and conclusive piece of work, and I ought ere now to have sent you my congratulations.

My criticism is far less satisfying to myself, and I believe it is to the public, than my out-of-door papers. It is not my proper field, but I cannot always get my fresh salt on the tails of the birds; but one can catch an author almost any time. But I can say this for myself: I always make a serious study of the man I write about, and work away at it till my thought on the subject runs clear.

I hope you and your wife are well and *in the country*. The world is very beautiful now. Indeed, it has been so to me all the spring, for I have been a day-laborer in the field since the first of April. Life has a new zest. I am just beginning to know the sweetness of real labor. I believe it cures the soul as well as the body. How good the earth tastes to my hoe! Every drop of sweat I shed in the soil seems to come back to me in flowers and perfume.

Indoor interests never blinded him to those without. One morning early in January, as he sat at breakfast, he was thrilled to see a fox running over the snow, a few rods below the house. It trotted through the currant-patch and disappeared in the lane beyond. 'I love to think of that wild cunning creature,' he writes, 'passing over my lawn and amid my currant bushes, just as if . . . it were a remote mountain lot.'

The following letter to one of his unknown readers is characteristic of his friendly replies to correspondents. It was written to Mr. W. W. Christman in January.

That a young farmer, trapper and wood-chopper, is also an appreciative reader of my books, is an interesting fact to me. The books must at least contain some flavor of reality to appeal to a mind so constantly conversant with real things.

That the nests of wild birds are sometimes attacked by vermin is a new fact to me. . . . I have no doubt the essence of the skunk has some rare medicinal properties, if one has the courage to use it.

Stick to the Whitman; he can do you good. The book of Thoreau that will please you most is 'Walden, or Life in the Woods.' It is the best book of the kind in English literature.

Other letters to the same young man followed, exchanging natural history observations; offering to read his articles, some of which he placed for him. Some of the observations of this correspondent are quoted in 'Riverby,' and in 'Far and Near'; and Burroughs wrote an Introduction to his article on foxes, printed in 'Forest and Stream' (1907).

It is always pleasant to come upon his generous appreciation of fellow-writers; for example, this to Gilder:

> I feel like thanking you for your noble sonnet on Emma Lazarus. It is one of your best. It has the rare merit in a sonnet of being easy and flexible — makes no desperate effort to cover the space and fill the sonnetic conditions. Most sonnets affect me like those trees we often see cut into some arbitrary and artificial shape; they pain me; but this sonnet of yours ... seems to have flowed naturally into shape. And that last line — it is worthy of Milton, or any other master.

During a severe bronchitis at this season he consoled himself with Lewes's 'Life of Goethe,' and Boswell's 'Johnson,' and with some tentative writing of his own on style and poetry. When commenting on a Whitman letter of that period, which speaks of a second bust being made of him by Sidney Morse, Mr. Burroughs said:

> Morse made two busts of Walt. We all paid five dollars apiece towards one. I broke mine up. It made Walt look smart, American, and wide-awake, but had nothing of his repose and grandeur. I think the Herald did it as an act of charity. . . .

In January he writes Benton:

> . . . Most of my time has been vacant and dull. Probably this is why I have not written sooner. When one's mind is active, and his time full, I find that letters get attended to with other things.
>
> When winter shut down upon me so suddenly in December, it brought me no congenial task to take the place of my grape-planting. I have nibbled away at my pen, but have accomplished nothing, and have about made up my mind that my days of the pen are over. At any rate, I shall in future look out for something else to fill up my time.
>
> We have been living here since I last wrote you. We are now talking of going to Poughkeepsie to board awhile. . . . Julian goes to school at West Park and does not want to leave. . . . I have taught him to play chess, and he pushes me hard when we have a game. At checkers he easily beats me. He has a great thirst for knowledge, but is rather backward with his book.
>
> I have not read Darwin's biography. . . . I suppose his experience about the poets is not exceptional. I fear we shall all come to it. Can you still read the great poets? I cannot. I have not looked in Shakespeare for years, and do not care to. I know what he is, and

have no desire to taste him more. At least, the plays. The sonnets I read occasionally. I read Wordsworth a little, and Tennyson, but expect by and by I shall read none of the old poets. . . .

Anent the comment as to his probable loss of appetite for poetry, it is good to know that his hunger for certain poets did not fail him. True he did not read Shakespeare, Tennyson, and many another any more, but he did not need to read them — many of their lines were fast in his memory. He quoted them often.

A passage from the Journal, which follows, is as good as any characterization of Johnson to be found in his essay on Johnson and Carlyle:

Johnson's bearishness, his temper, his arguing for victory, his love of applause, were not traits of greatness — all these things are deductions. No great thought or view ever escapes him. How contemptible his hatred for America! His views of most foreign countries are narrow. He had a narrow mind anyhow. But his conversation was remarkable. His mind was wonderfully discriminating, and was so instantly — quick as a flash. His sentences are like level deadly rifles; they do not go off vaguely in the air; they are aimed at the subject and hit it squarely.

He seems to have been pious mainly from fear; just as he wrote mainly from want. Fear narrowed and darkened his mind. He believed God to be another touchy and acrimonious Doctor Johnson. Yet one comes in Boswell's pages heartily to love the old bear.

He bowed very low and elaborately before all kinds of dignitaries.

There was not a spark of poetry in him that I can see. He did not make one verse or line that still lives.

He said he had lived so long in London that he could not remember the difference of the seasons.

What a barren life such would have been for John Burroughs, to whom the seasons, and all that they bring, were his very life! The eclipse of the moon described in the next entry, of such signal interest to Mr. Burroughs, would doubtless have been regarded with indifference, if not scorn, by the learned Johnson. With a heave of his great chest, a snort, and a terrific 'Sir,' one imagines the worthy Doctor announcing sententiously: 'There be blockheads enough in London to stand and gape at yonder apparition. Let us go within and drink our tea, and engage in agreeable converse, undisturbed by the profitless phenomenon.'

A total eclipse of the moon tonight. The first I ever saw. The moon seemed to be covered by a piece of smoked glass. It hung there in the western sky, a dim coppery ball that gave no light. . . . There was not a cloud in the sky. The shadow on its face seemed thickest and darkest toward the top. By and by the lower edge or limb began to shine out. Then it was very interesting to watch it slough off this dark, opaque skin, like a bursting, swelling, developing process.

The bright clean limb of the moon, how it protruded from this confining shell! It seemed to swell out till the impression was precisely as if the luminous part was confined by a copper case, like a cork by a bottle, and was slowly getting free.

How surely an ignorant people would have said that the moon was passing through some crisis, was being confined and held by some dark object which yet was unable to keep it! It was like a bud in spring bursting out of its scales. For this swelling, protruding effect I was not prepared.

When the eclipse was half off, the moon looked elongated, and as if the freed part was much larger than the confined part. By and by the shadow was only a little round cap that sat upon the head of our round-faced friend like the cap on an English soldier. One half expected to see the cap burst, and the expanding edges of the moon to show at the edges, but it did not. It was slowly crowded off; and the large free moon again rode the heavens in triumph.

While the house at Riverby was closed for the winter, the family boarding in Poughkeepsie, the author frequently walked across the river on the ice to look at his new possessions. On one such trip sad news awaited him:

[Journal] March 12. On Monday, my little dog, Laddie, my fourth dog, met his end, murdered, like Lark, by Dick Atkins's vicious brute. I went up home on the 10 am train. George was at the depot and told me Laddie was killed a few moments before. He was following George when he fell in with a small dog near Atkins', between whom and himself, it seems, there was a standing feud. Whenever and wherever they met, they fought.

George went on and left them fighting, thinking no harm would come of it. Presently the old dog heard the fracas and came out and pitched into the smallest dog, as is his custom, and in a few minutes Laddie was left for dead.

When I came to him, about an hour afterward, I saw he was still alive. I lifted him up and laid him on the dry grass where the sun shone warm upon him, and protected him from the wind with some boards. He breathed and winked, but did not recognize me. Three hours later I came to him, and seeing him still alive, I spoke to him as of old. He made no sign, but instantly all his wounds, which had dried up in the sun, began to bleed afresh. My voice quickened his pulse, and the bloody drops began to trickle down all over his poor bruised body. It cut me to the heart. They were like bloody tears appealing to me for help. Shortly afterward he breathed his last.

I loved him much, how much I did not know till he was gone, as is always the case; and his love for me was unmeasured. . . .

Many a time, in the years to come, as he told of the blood starting afresh at the sound of his voice, his eyes would fill with tears and his voice was infinitely sad as he murmured, 'Oh, Laddie, Laddie!'

The great blizzard occupies much space in the Journal — 'such a storm as comes but once or twice in a century.' He mentions a similar one having occurred in January, 1857.

Now he is sitting to Miss Dora Wheeler for his portrait, and seeing much of Mrs. Candace Wheeler, of Gilder, and of Edith Thomas. Of the latter he wrote, 'A thin, nervous girl with dark hair and eyes — talks in a curious feminine bass, — the voice of country solitude.'

As the ice moves out of the river, on the last day of March, he begins work on his new land, first blowing up the old apple-trees with dynamite, exclaiming boyishly, 'My! how the old trees do jump!'

[Journal] April 3. My 51st birthday. A bright lovely day, full of spring signs and sounds. The sparrows, robins, and bluebirds fairly scream for joy. I am joyful, too — as happy, probably, as I ever shall be. Something to do! A bit of land to redeem and work up into a vineyard. The sparkling river, the strong sunshine, the calling and singing birds, and my occupation on the side of the hill — how alive it all is, and how real! Mrs. B. comes home today.

Despite the busy days, religious and philosophical entries are frequent in the Journal; likewise such glimpses as the following:

This labor in the field gives me a keener relish for Nature. I get such glances from her — stolen glances. One may have too much leisure. But the laboring man does not get sated with Nature. He has not time. To him she is like a mistress who never fully indulges him.

Soon a shadow falls across his days:

The death of Matthew Arnold, which came without warning the other day, has been constantly in my thoughts since. Does it give a sad tinge to this April, or does April beautify and render more significant his death? It does really seem to put a seal upon him as I think of him as I go about my work and hear the happy birds, and see the grass springing. April can make even death beautiful.

I look upon Arnold as the greatest critic of English literature.
Such steadiness, directness, sureness of aim and elevation, we have
not before seen. He had the best qualities of the French, and he had
something the French have not. He was not at all a miscellaneous
man; he stood for certain definite things; he was like a through train,
always on time, and only fetching up at important points. His
poetry is wonderfully good, only, for some reason, it does not melt
into one, and stick to his mind, as it ought to. As with all first class
men, his death leaves a vacancy that no one else can fill.

As spring advances, work and joy go hand in hand. The
week of apple-bloom comes and goes; the petals fall; the world
is like fairy-land; he revels in its beauty. The spring work
over, he goes to Roxbury, carrying with him a shad from the
river — a luxury to the inland dwellers. Up there spring
comes lingeringly; again he sees the apple-bloom; again hears
the bobolinks in the meadows, and the hermit thrush on the
mountain. He follows the trout-streams of his boyhood, attended by a throng of memories; and at night writes in his
Journal:

I fish a little and dream a good deal. Take three fine trout, which
are as well as three hundred. . . . I am tempted to go up to the spring
[near the old school-house] . . . but I do not go. The spring is doubtless there, but where are the childish faces it used to mirror? Dead,
many of them, and scattered far and wide. . . .

I have been hard at work [he writes Benton], and have got my
body so disciplined I can hoe potatoes all day without flinching. We
put out an acre of early potatoes in April, and are now hoeing them.
We have put out 2400 grape-vines, 2000 currant bushes, and 2000
hills of raspberries. . . . I have not spent so happy an April for years.
. . . The hoe-handle is better for me now than the pen, and I mean to
stick to it.
Wife is pretty well, or would be, if she would not try to keep her
floors like those in the Celestial city. . . .

[J. B. to W. W.]

. . . I want to find time soon to come down and see you, if company
does not bore you. . . . The world has not been so beautiful to me for
a long time as this spring; probably because I have been at work like
an honest man. I had, in my years of loafing, forgotten how sweet
toil was. I suppose those generations of farmers back of me have
had something to do with it. They all seem to have come to life
again in me and are happy since I have taken to the hoe and crowbar.
I had quite lost my interest in literature, and was fast losing my
interest in life itself, but these two months of work have sharpened

my appetite for all things. I write you amid the fragrance of clover and the hum of bees. The air is full these days of all sweet meadow and woodland smells. The earth seems good enough to eat.

How I wish you were here, or somewhere else in the country, where all the sweet influences of the season could minister to you. Your reluctance to move is just what ought to be overcome. It is like the lethargy of a man beginning to freeze. . . .

Traubel quotes Whitman as saying of the foregoing:

It is a June letter — worthy of June — written in John's best out-of-doors mood. Why, it gets into your blood and makes you feel worth while. I sit here, helpless as I am, and breathe it in like fresh air. . . . You see John writes letters — real letters. He does not strike you as a maker of phrases. . . . John has the real art — the art of succeeding by not trying to succeed; he is the farmer first — the man before he is the writer; that is the key . . . of his success.

Traubel also quotes him as saying:

You must never write him without sending him my love. And, Horace, do not forget the wife, Mrs. Burroughs — for she, too, has been kind and noble to me and I want her to know that I think of her. Then, [after a pause] John is one of the true hearts — one of the true hearts — warm, sure, firm — I feel that he has never wavered in his friendship for me; never doubted or gone off — that I can count on him in all exigencies; and I think affection plays a great part in John's regard for me, as it does in mine for him. John is making an impression on his age — has come to stay — has veritable, indisputable, dynamic gifts.

[Journal] June 20. Go down to West Point with Denton and others and make an excursion to tamarack swamps. The great purple-fringed orchis in bloom in the swamps. Am taken with a bad headache. Go home with E. P. Roe, who keeps me over night and treats me very kindly.

Whitman's failing health was now weighing heavily upon his friend's heart:

Trying to taste the bitter cup in advance, so as to be used to it when it really comes. How life will seem to me with Whitman gone, I cannot imagine. He is my larger, greater, earlier self. No man alive seems quite so near to me. . . .

However, from Whitman himself soon comes a letter to revive his spirits — a pathetic letter, with its many erasures, showing his difficulty in getting the right words, but showing also his abiding affection and unconquerable optimism.

In the summer of 1888, when Walt Whitman was critically ill, Dr. R. M. Bucke and Horace Traubel, when trying to pre-arrange the funeral services, were woefully disappointed because John Burroughs refused to be one of the speakers. Dr. Bucke's letter to O'Connor implied a criticism that Burroughs would not consent to do this last office for his friend; but O'Connor's reply to Dr. Bucke (July 19, 1888) shows how perfectly he understood the refusal:

Poor John Burroughs! I can sympathize with him in his declination. He *could* not speak. It would split his heart in two. I feel now as if the effort would break mine; but if I can, I must make it.[1]

Journal excerpts, here given, reveal Burroughs's activities, his whimsical comments on his crops, his hopes and fears, and yearnings.

July 24. Digging our potatoes for market, price high ($3.75) but yield poor, owing to dry weather. May get back the expense and a little more, in which case the fun of the thing will not have cost me anything. All my hoeing, watering, killing of bugs, on Sundays and nights, will not cost me a cent.

July 25. Whitman still improving. A great load is lifted from my spirits.
Think of the myriads of people that fill the past, the great ocean! There in that sea of faces I see Father and Mother. How precious they look to me! Oh, if they could only draw near and speak!
The little mouse I saw swimming in Balsam Lake did not get as wet as a domestic animal would have. It was quite dry, save on its legs and belly. Its fur shed water like a duck's feathers.[2]

July 26. The July days go by and bring me little pleasure or interest. I pull weeds by spurts, read a little, and look after the farm work. I crave and need above all some one to talk to, some comrade, and quite a different home life from what I have; . . . Julian is still too young to meet the requirement.

Dr. John C. Burroughs, one-time President of Chicago University, visited Riverby in August. 'Immensely tickled to see him,' writes the Journalist, 'a man to love and follow — of all my relatives, he it is whom I love most.'
In September he writes his vineyard news to Mrs. Burroughs, then at Hobart:

[1] O'Connor, whose condition even then, was critical, passed on before the good gray poet did, his death, May 9, 1889, being reported to John Burroughs by Whitman himself.
[2] *See* 'Talks with Young Observers' (*Riverby*).

I shall plant largely Niagaras. Van Benschoten's Niagaras have done so well, and yield so enormously, that I shall try more of them. He got 14 cents a pound. He must have cleared over $2000.

I am more encouraged than ever. I see no reason why I cannot do as well and have an income by and by of $3000 from my fruit. I have demonstrated this season that it will pay to take care of Concords. We shall have ours all off before other people about here begin to cut much. . . . We cut and shipped over a ton on Sunday — 50 crates for $105 — will net me about $75. We keep it red hot about here. There's about one ton left on the vines. . . .

I work hard and feel good, and all is serene in the kitchen. . . . You better not come home yet. Maybe I will come up when the grapes are off.

Have J. read some to you every day. You will have to find a boarding-place in Poughkeepsie, as I am not willing to go to housekeeping again. We must try a new plan of life. 'I-Know' [his dog] is fat and happy, but thinks the Cook stingy. So she is — for one whole day there was no bread in the house, but plenty of clams. Write soon. With much love.

To Julian:

. . . The cabbages have headed finely, and the sun-flowers are doing well; but they are very modest — they all hang down their heads. Maybe they are mourning for you. . . . You must explore the cave and write me about it. . . . Tell me all about your playing, and if there are any trout in the stream where we placed them last summer. I want to see you, but you must not get homesick. With much love,

Your affectionate Papa.

[J. B. to U. B. September 15, 1888]

. . . I must go to Camden next week. Horace Traubel writes me there is no chance of Walt's being any better than he is now, and that if I want to see him, I better come at once. So that if we go to the seashore, it must be early next week. . . .

. . . Tell J. his letter came all right and pleased me much. 'I-Know' and the cat are happy. We are blasting rocks and plowing under the buckwheat. . . .

The Journal (September 19th) gives other glimpses of Whitman:

. . . To Camden. Walt is lying on his bed when I enter the room. He looks and speaks as usual. I stand by his bedside a few moments, his hand in mine, and then help him up and to his chair, where he sits amid a chaos of books, letters and papers, as usual. . . . I note his hearing is poorer than when we met a year ago. I stay an hour, then, for fear of tiring him, go over to Philadelphia. Come back at night and find Walt bright and ready to talk. . . .

20. This was one of Walt's poor days and I do not see him, though call twice. Go to the grave of Franklin and gaze at it long through the iron fence. How much it calls up and suggests! Visit the Old State House and Independence Hall.

In the evening see Walt for a moment. He presses my hand long and tenderly; we kiss and part, probably for the last time. I think he has in his own mind given up the fight, and awaits the end.

To Benton in late September goes news of the vineyard's yield, and prices:

I find when I take hold of my farm myself, I can make it pay. . . . It agrees with me, and I see that in a couple of years I can be pretty sure of a good income from my fruit. . . .

Literature is quite neglected these days. All requests for articles go quickly into the waste-basket. If my appetite for magazine-writing ever returns, then I may hang up my hoe for a season, but I propose to let my intellectual domain lie fallow for awhile.

Come over and let's have a talk. I expect a basket of many kinds of choice grapes from Rochester. Come and help me decide upon the best kinds. . . .

Henceforth, the letters from Whitman show more and more the ravages of disease, yet a surprising mental grasp, and always loving remembrances to friends. In an excerpt given below he speaks of his physician:

Dr. Osler [William] (very 'cute — a natural physician, rather optimistic, but best so) thinks I am either on a very good way, or substantially cured of this last attack — I only wish I could feel so, or even approximate it — But anyhow, thank God, so far my thoughts and mental power are entirely within my control. I have written a short letter to the Critic (by their request) on the 'poet' question.

To Mr. Asa K. McIlhaney, a teacher in Bath, Pennsylvania, Burroughs sent this painstaking reply concerning tree-planting:

I am glad to hear that your pupils are going to keep Arbor Day. If you can teach them to love and cherish trees, and the proper way to plant them, you will teach them a very valuable lesson.

Boys, give the tree plenty of room, and a soft, deep bed to rest in; tuck it up very carefully in its bed with your hands. The roots of a tree are much more soft and tender than its branches, and cannot be handled too gently.

It is as important to know how to take up a tree as how to plant it. A friend of mine brings quite large hemlocks from the woods, and plants them on his grounds, and has no trouble to make them live.

He does much of the work with his hands, follows the roots along and lifts them gently from the soil, and never allows them to dry. The real feeders of a tree are very small, mere threads; the bulky muscular roots are for strength; its life is in the rootlets that fringe these, and to let these delicate feeders dry, even by an hour's exposure to a drying air, is to endanger the vitality of the tree.

By the way, in your planting, do not forget the hemlock. It is a clean, healthy, hardy, handsome tree. Do not forget the ash either, if only for its beautiful, plum-colored foliage in Autumn. Above all, do not forget the linden, or basswood, a tree generally overlooked by our arborists. It is as pleasing as the maple in form and foliage, and then is such a friend of the honey-bee. What a harvest they get from it, and just when the sources of honey supply begin to fail.

I have somewhere said that when you bait your hook with your heart, the fish always bite, and I will now say that when you plant a tree with love, it always lives. You do it with such care and thoughtfulness. . . .

I think the maple is my favorite tree because it is my home tree — it was the prevailing tree in my home woods. . . . To try to name one's favorite flower is like trying to name one's favorite friend, or favorite child. . . . I suppose the flower that I am most eager to see in the spring is the arbutus, though it was not a flower of my boyhood. The flower along mountain streams that I like best to see is the bee-balm, or Oswego tea. The swamp flower that I go farthest to see is the showy lady's slipper, *Cypripedium spectabile*.

Myron Benton comes in November. This joyous entry marks the event:

Suddenly the world and life look different to me, so glad am I to see him. For a moment the atmosphere of long-gone days is over things again, and the old joy in life comes back.

In the Journal he writes of his son's first composition:

Go up to school to hear the speaking, compositions, etc. Julian anxious I should be on hand to hear him. He is quite embarrassed when his turn comes, but he does well, decidedly the best of all of them. . . . His essay . . . was the second one he has written. His other described his tramp from Highland home two winters ago. . . . I am glad to see his mind takes this turn. He does not look far off for a theme, like the other boys, but writes about something near at hand, that he actually knows about. His essay was in my own vein, and vastly more promising than anything I ever did at his age. It was a real piece of writing about my dogs.

How curious it was to me to see him stand up there and read an original essay.

Dec. 27. . . . Reading 'Tom Brown' to Julian these nights, and get very much excited over it myself.

Anxiety over the weather and losses in the vineyard and elsewhere had their cumulative effect during the ensuing year, but the Vine-Dresser kept his relish for work. He continued writing on theology, and made short sallies into other literary fields; still, as yet, the hoe was mightier than the pen.

In time the snow drove the solitary one to Poughkeepsie, and, although the cramped quarters of a boarding-house were not conducive to writing, he wrote a second essay on science and theology, one on 'Lovers of Nature,' and 'some miscellaneous stuff.'

In March, with Gilder and Mr. R. U. Johnson, he met Mrs. Grover Cleveland, Arlo Bates, Theodore Roosevelt, George Kennan, and Mrs. Elizabeth Custer, on none of whom does he comment in his Journal except on Mrs. Custer, — 'a bright charming woman.' It was at this meeting with Roosevelt (probably the first) that Roosevelt told him of first coming upon his books when in England, and how homesick they made him because they were so thoroughly American.

[Journal] April 3. My birthdays come and go just like any other days. Nature seems to take no note of it! but what long sad thoughts are awakened in my mind! How inevitably my heart goes back to the old spot, and to the memory of those I shall see no more! . . .

I work part of the day under the hill. . . . The light of the world seems surely gone out for me. The fox sparrow sings, but it hardly wakens the old response. Health pretty good; no unusual symptoms; should probably sleep well if Mrs. B. and Julian were well and did not cough at night. The liverwort in bloom down by the river.

April 7. . . . Julian and I go to the woods; no flowers yet; ants just out languidly patrolling their mounds. Frog-spawn in the pools. We sit a long time on a rock in the woods and enjoy the genial warmth and the clean open woods, with the creek glancing and murmuring below us. . . .

Pretty sad these days, probably some physical cause. My mind is turned to the past — the present seems thin and cold. Is this age?

To Benton he writes of sending a couple of articles on his theological heresies to the 'Christian Union,' which, to his surprise, they published, after which he sent them one on his old themes. The 'Chautauquan' also has an article of his, and has asked for another — on Thoreau; but want of sleep, the farm-work, and kitchen worry, he says, make the writing of that doubtful. He asks Benton for the data for a biographical sketch which he is soon to undertake about him (for the 'Magazine of Poetry'), and closes with the glad news: 'Spring is really with us — the hepatica is out!'

Proof-reading of 'Indoor Studies,' setting out vines and raspberries, and excursions to the woods, fill the April days. He finds the bloodroot, with its head emerging 'like the head of a papoose from its mother's blanket,' 'the little anemone, trembling and blushing like a delicate, high-bred school-girl,' and arbutus, 'the breath of April.' Soon the maples are shaking out their tassels; the peach and cherry trees bloom; the stone house is rented; Mrs. Burroughs returns to Poughkeepsie to board, and he and Julian and 'I-Know' are keeping house in the gardener's cottage, well content.

On hearing of the death of William O'Connor:

A man of extraordinary parts, but lacking the sanity of modera-tion of the greatest men. I cannot write about him now — it is too great a subject. [He seriously considered writing a biographical sketch of O'Connor, but never compassed it.]

The arrival of the new book ('Indoor Studies'), in June, elicits the customary indifference from its author.

When Mrs. Burroughs and Julian start for the Catskills, the father immediately begins to feel forlorn without his boy: 'I hate to see him go. I shall be very lonely. He is all I have. He often tires me with his endless questions, but I find much companionship with him.'

The July entries are rain-drenched; 'the damp, mildewy weather' soon causes the Vine-Dresser to flee to the moun-tains also, there working in the haying, reading Amiel's 'Journal,' and trouting.

[Journal] July 30. The hell of rain continues. A heavy shower yesterday, and a down-pour this morning that set the whole ground afloat. Washed my new vineyards badly — almost a cloud-burst. No wind here, but probably a cyclone back of the hills somewhere, as, in the midst of the rain, shingles and leaves and small branches of trees and vines fell swiftly down from the clouds. It was a curious sight. How long, O Devil, is this to last?

Aug. 3. Still the rain comes down. Three tremendous showers this week, and innumerable lesser ones. The earth oozes water at every pore. Never saw my land so overflowing.... Flood and devastation throughout the country. This season will be as memo-rable as that of the great snow-storm in March 1888....

The husbandman's pride comes out in a letter to his wife, in which he says that in a recent drive through the fruit region, he saw no vineyards to compare with his own.

Tell Julian I will send him my reel. I have a little wild rabbit for him. He is so small he can sit in the hollow of my hand. He eats milk, sweet apples, and grapes, and grows finely. I caught him under the hill. I have much fun with him. If I come up I will bring him. Love to you both. . . .

How much he was suffering from the weather in his avocation as Vine-Dresser, is gathered from the Journal, August 14th:

Again the damnable rains are upon us. After nearly a week's respite, and after we had all predicted fair and dry weather at hand, the rain began last night with such thunder, and is still (9 a.m.) pouring. I am nearly ready to believe in a *malignant* Providence, at any rate. Looks like a deliberate purpose on the part of the weather gods to destroy all the crops of the country.

He was evidently not accepting the universe very whole-heartedly at this time; but a more accustomed mood is seen in the entry which follows:

Dry, dreamy August days at last, no rain for ten days. Warm and tranquil. The time of excursions at hand. Nearly every day boat-loads of happy persons go by with music and laughter. I work part of the time, and sit and dream or read in the summer-house, the rest. Pick a few peaches each day. Mrs. B. and Julian at Stamford yet. Pretty lonely times, but not unhappy. . . . Van cutting weeds, Lute plowing the grapes.

Sept. 28. Up early and off to Camden to see Walt. . . . Find him eating his breakfast of toast and tea, and looking remarkably well, much better than a year ago. He stands a fair chance of out-living us all yet. Sit three hours with him and have much talk. He sits amid the chaos of books, papers, etc, so serene and clean and calm, and such wild confusion about him! Even the window papers were partly torn from their places and hung down, as if to heighten the effect.

In a few days, from Whitman comes the following note:

So you didn't come back. I expected you, and Tom Harned and Horace too were here looking for you, and were disappointed. The 9th volume of the big American Literature from Stedman came this morning. I see you appear in it with a good portrait and ten pages of text. . . . I see you are extracted from and biographized in Harper's Fifth Reader, too. . . .

In October Burroughs writes Joel Benton:

You may see me in the N. A. Review, if you look, taking up the cudgels for Huxley against Dr. Abbott — a hasty article, not very well digested — written in July when my thoughts are usually soft and in the velvet. I should have waited till frost.

A heavy shadow, lowering for many a month, is hinted at in the Journal, November 3d:

Went to Roxbury last Monday to look after Hiram's matters. Spent two days in the village; very wretched; did not go up to the old place — too painful. . . . Hiram's outlook very black. He must give up the old place. I shall probably lose heavily by him. Well, I did what I thought was my duty. I wanted to see him keep the Old Home, but clearly he is not competent to manage the farm. It will be almost like losing Father and Mother over again to see the Old Home go into strange hands, but I fear I am powerless to avert it.

Nov. 25. A mild but wet November. . . . Spent part of time in Poughkeepsie with Wife and Julian, but begin to see I cannot stand it there. . . . I will live alone with my dog and cat. . . . I moved down from the old house [gardener's cottage] last week, and am again in the big house. . . . I doubt if my father ever stayed alone a single night in his house. Probably none of my family, unless it be Abigail, have passed so much time alone in a house.
Am reading Carlyle's letters (from 1814–1836), wonderful letters. A wonderful man, — so mature, so firm, and sure upon his feet from the first! hardly any of his opinions or criticisms during his twenties did he ever need to revise.

Nov. 26. A bright day. Spent the afternoon up by the creek screening gravel. I had real enjoyment, almost happiness. The bright sun, the full bounding stream hastening along within a few feet of me, the trees and rocks, the wild, secluded place, my dog, 'I-Know,' capering about, the brisk exercise — it all went to the right spot. It dispelled my gloom and almost made me cheery. The walk home, too, near sundown — how it called up my many many walks along this road in happier days! I came back to a deserted house, but have eaten my supper with comparative satisfaction. . . .

One night in early December, as he and his dog sat by the kitchen stove, the wind roaring about the lonely house, a dispatch came summoning him to Roxbury on Hiram's affairs. He started the next morning. Hiram failed to keep his appointment at the village lawyer's, and, heavy-hearted, the younger brother walked across the hills to the Old Home, only to learn that Hiram had gone, no one knew where. Too well he understood. The poor soul had gone away to avoid him.

In the old south bedroom he slept but little that night; his heart ached for the fugitive, knowing the steps that must be taken. Divining that Hiram had gone to Eden's, he sought him there. His suffering and sympathy are revealed in this poignant entry:

. . . As I reach the house I see Hiram through the window. I felt ashamed and humiliated for him. I go in and greet them all, barely speaking to Hiram. He looks confused and guilty. I quickly open on him and tell him the sheriff is in possession, and that he is to be sold out. Much talk and discussion follow. I try to show him how utterly hopeless it is for him to go on with the farm without ruining me. Then to bed. Poor, fitful sleep.

Up early, Hiram in a hurry now to get back home. We walk across the mountain through wind and snow. As we toil up the mountain, I note how troubled and careworn he looks. He stoops as if bearing a great burden. My heart bleeds for him. I know how he is weighed down, but nothing can be done. He has lost the battle; the old farm and home he cannot keep. I am powerless to help him more. The roof over my own head is threatened.

We reach home before noon. After dinner we go to the village. Hiram goes reluctantly. He will walk behind me, as if I were leading him with a rope — leading him to the slaughter. I could fly to get away from the painful business.

At the lawyer's office Hiram deeds the farm to me, and turns over all his personal property — signs away everything he has in the world. Poor boy! and he does it so readily, like a child. Then we go back to the Old Home. I sleep near him in the old chamber, or try to sleep, as he does; but neither of us sleep much.

I spent a week in Roxbury trying to sell or rent the place and let Hiram stay there. One afternoon, walk five miles and back through the mud, to see a man who wants to buy a farm.

I chop wood and work about the place. No man stands to his offer to buy. I shall have to rent it. Much trouble and sorrow. Have about $3000 at stake in it. Must keep a home there for Hiram, if possible.

In a week's time he returns to Roxbury:

Spend four days at the Old Home. . . . Today rent it [the farm] to G—— B——. Will this plunge me deeper in the sea of trouble? . . . The burden of the farm seems off my shoulders for a moment, though the thought of Hiram sends a pang through my heart.

Another sorrow comes:

[Journal] Dec. 23. . . . My dog 'I-Know' is dead — killed Friday night by the gravel-train, as he tried to pass under it. It sends a deep pang through me — my faithful dog, my sole companion these days and nights. I sit here in my deserted house tonight without him. Every now and then, half forgetting, I turn to see where he is, or to wonder why he does not come.

'I-Know's' only fault was his excessive good nature, and his cowardice in the presence of other dogs, or of any form of supposed danger. Very intelligent and handsome, and gentle as a lamb. Even the cats imposed upon him, and made a rug of him — fit mate of his weak and sensitive master.

I am less grieved than when my other dogs have died, because I have had experience and will not be caught that way again — will not again allow a dog to take such a deep hold upon my affections. After a time, I suppose, I can lose dogs without emotion. But how I shall miss the faithful creature from my solitary life; and how long will his memory be fresh in my heart! I brought a basket of bones for him, as usual, which now the cats will have to gnaw. . . .

The Journal mentions but two essays as fruit of the following year. The chronicles are chiefly of seasonal events and vineyard vicissitudes. A brief visit in January from his old camp-mate Aaron Johns gladdens his heart. A few days later he is mingling housework and work in the vineyard — cleaning the kitchen floor and setting posts. He gives a little bulletin of his health on January 4th:

At the beginning of the new year I find myself apparently stronger and better than in many years. No more dizziness, rarely any heart fluttering, and able to stand long walks without fatigue. The worst symptoms are melancholy, loneliness, and a sense of it being late in the day with me. . . . If I could be here and have all inside as it should be, I should be fairly happy; but I am growing old; this incessant retrospection is one sign, if I needed any evidence besides my mirror.

8 p.m. A dispatch from Eden saying that Hiram is at his house, and has had a light stroke of apoplexy. How quickly the gloom thickens round me, and how all my feeling against Hiram suddenly changes! This, then, is what his weak and foolish conduct means — this thing has been coming upon him a long time; his brain has been slowly giving way. Alas, alas! what shall I do? Cannot go tonight, and what could I do, anyhow?

Poor brother! has the giving up of the old farm indeed broken your heart? Alas, alas! it was inevitable. I could do no more. What a burden the whole subject has been to me! and maybe the heaviest burden of all is yet to come. Suddenly the thought of Hiram, and my love for him, overtops everything else. We shall all go that way, probably — apoplexy. Hiram first, and not yet 63! No doubt his work is done, if his life is yet spared.

I sit long and long in the silent and darkened room, thinking of him, and of all he is and has been to me.

5. Sunday. . . . Julian and I walk up to the asylum and sit long on the pine needles under the trees, looking out over the fine landscape to the north. We talk of many things, but my heart cries incessantly, 'Hiram, Hiram!'

The blow is, however, averted. An engaging entry, March 27th, at eleven in the forenoon, reads:

Sitting in my vineyard, waiting for my part in putting up wire. Zeke is at other end of row putting in staples. When he gets back here I rush in with nippers and tongs, cut the wire and stretch it, while Zeke drives home the staples. Day bright and lovely, wind fitful and capricious; sparrows sing all about me. What a variety of songs they have! Robins call and sing; phœbe calls; clucking frogs. Find first liverwort a few moments ago, sweet-scented. A little red butterfly dances past. River looks very muddy. Am happy sitting here and drinking in the beauty of the day. Storm due tomorrow.

The storm came, and while it raged he sat before his Study fire and wrote 'Country Notes,' an essay which he pronounced 'of little worth — a mere pot-boiler.'

The following Sunday, an event worth recording! — he goes to church in Poughkeepsie with his wife! It is a 'rather commonplace Methodist sermon' that he hears. A few days more and arbutus calls him to the woods:

The soil calls for the plough; the garden calls for the spade; the vineyard calls for the hoe. From all about the farm voices call, Come, do this; do that. We obey the call and set out the vines. . . . How the peepers pile up the sound at night! . . . the toads trill their long-drawn *tr-r-r-r-r-r-* all day long.

One of his letters with the soil and the sun in it went in mid-April to Hamilton W. Mabie:

These lovely April days find me pawing the soil up here at a lively rate. I am fairly besmirched with new earth from my head to my heels. Last night I slept eight hours without a break. How is that for an insomniast? You should see how fresh and tender the earth is here when we open it with our plow. After all these ages it still has the look and smell of youth. The new furrow, how it delights me!

You ask me for a piece. I will give it you if possible. This feast of the soil will soon be over with me and then I will remember your request.

[Journal] April 28. Tonight is soft moonlight, a young moon, air motionless. I hear the shouts and songs of the fishermen on the river, and see the lights of their lanterns scattered up and down — a delicious night.

The days that follow are so lovely he longs to stop the clock of time. On May 1st one comes upon the germ of that simile of which he was so fond, and which, several years later, he elaborated in his Introduction to a new edition of 'Wake-Robin.' Farther along in the year he developed the thought still more, its final form being the passage with which his readers are familiar. Below is the original passage:

It is not honey which the bee gathers from the flowers, but sweet water or cane sugar. The bee takes this, digests it, adds something to it, and makes honey. In red clover and in columbine you can taste the sweet, but it is not honey. Those who read my books think I get my honey direct from nature, but I do not; I get the crude material there, but the product I try to give forth is as much mine as Nature's. Unless what I see and observe has passed through my heart and imagination, and becomes my product, it is of little interest or value.

May 14. . . . Heard my white-crown sing this morning. He sat in one of Atkins's cherry trees. *Fee-u, fee-u, fiddy, fiddy, fee* — with a pathos and tenderness about the long notes that no other sparrow song equals. Not so brilliant and loud as the fox sparrow's, but oh! so plaintive and far away! A song in keeping with the rare beauty of the bird.

Despite his anxiety because the June winds and rains are ruthlessly breaking off the tender arms of the grapevines just as they have begun to bloom, he gathers a little fruit from his 'other vineyard,' in the form of 'Faith and Credulity,' which he considers 'rather feeble,' and marvels that the 'North American' accepted it.

[Journal] July 24. A visit from Dr. John Johnston,[1] of Bolton, England, a modest, quiet, interesting man, 36 years old, born at Annan; went to school in the Academy where Carlyle once taught. A canny young Scot. Like him first rate. . . . A great lover of Whitman, whom he had just visited.

[1] Author, in collaboration with Mr. J. W. Wallace, of a unique little book, *Visits to Whitman in 1890–91.*

Some months later, acknowledging Dr. Johnston's account of his visit to Whitman, Burroughs wrote:

You certainly have a wonderful gift to catch the flying moment. Whitman has never before been so vividly and realistically sketched. . . . If you lived near him, or if you had my opportunity, you would make a book better than Boswell's. Do come again and complete your sketch. . . . I am hibernating now, only I am sucking the paws of the great authors instead of my own. . . .

In the autumn Burroughs found to his relief that the tenant on the home farm could actually pay his rent. He gladly renewed the lease for another year. As he and Hiram climbed the mountains in search of basswood for fruit-crates, he rejoiced in the contrast to the preceding year's saddening experiences. To Benton he writes his vineyard news and adds:

I do no literary work, though I have plenty of calls. An article in the October N. A. Review on 'Faith and Credulity' was written last spring, in P——. It is not much. I shall try to get back on my old lines this winter, but doubt if I succeed. The theological seems to be the last state of man — after that, barrenness.

I have a dog now [Dan], and Julian has doves, so that we can do our own barking, and grow our own squabs. I am trying to read 'Lux Mundi,' but find it hard reading. It does not antagonize me enough. I agree with so much of it. I shall switch off on the Ice Age in the N. A. . . .

In December, however, the fruit-grower turns to his pen, and as he sits in his Bark Study and watches the river closing in, he again begins writing on his theme of twenty years before — Analogy.

Strenuous and absorbing as the vineyard work continued to be, the fruit of his pen was more abundant in 1891 than for several previous years, despite the following:

Jan. 5. Snow all night and nearly all day from the north. . . . I sit all day in my Study and labor, and do not even bring forth a mouse. Indeed, a mouse would be very encouraging.

Trying to read Martineau's 'Basis of Authority in Religion,' a ponderous tome, very tiresome. M—— is a deep thinker and a strong effective writer, but he is tiresome — a fatal fault.

His invitations were always persuasive, irresistible, and one sees him bubbling over with anticipation in this note to Benton:

Mrs. B. says Come, the spirit says Come, we all say Come. Wife has two excellent girls in Julian and me, and a third one in the new range. She will not allow me to say that she sits with folded hands all the time, but all the same, she says Come! . . . It is perfectly safe walking over the river at Hyde Park now, and that road has more trains than this. . . .

And after Benton leaves, to the Journal:

Myron and I have our old talks again. Every moment he was here gave me pleasure. How much more life would be to me if I could often have visits from such men as Myron.

In a few touches he makes one a sharer of the winter scene upon which he looks, and of his own emotions:

Feb. 7. Overcast this pm. Thawing. Ice-boats all waiting for a breeze, which will not come.

I look out on the ice and see a little black speck over towards Hyde Park. It is Julian going for the 2.40 train. I hear the train coming; the black speck seems to move faster, but when the train passes it, and stops at the station, there is a wide strip of ice yet between it and the shore. Then the black speck creeps back.

His adverse criticism of his friends, in occasional letters to them, is no less interesting than his praise; witness this of February 1st to Gilder:

I am going to give you the benefit of a criticism I have heard of the Century magazine, and which I think applies particularly to this number. I feel the force of it myself fully. It has ugly pictures of ugly objects. A picture should be, or should suggest something pleasing. Why should the eye be greeted with something ugly in an illustrated magazine, any more than the nose should be greeted by a bad odor in a house, or the ear by a discordant sound? These Georgia crackers are hideous. Think what their effect might be upon a sensitive, imaginative pregnant woman who might be fascinated by their very ugliness! If I were a woman I think they would make me miscarry.

I think this Kemble is the worst realist who has yet turned up. What a contrast to Wiles' beautiful drawings! You probably will not thank me for this criticism, but when one sees a defect in a great public institution like the Century, why should he not point it out? That these pictures are true to life is no justification. All the more need that the artist should mix in a little of the ideal, if he has any. If he has not, let him go to sweeping the street crossings. . . .

I liked that poem in St Nicholas on Leo — 'Over the roofs of the houses I hear the barking of Leo' — There was something delightful in it. Julian and I often repeat it. Your Atlantic poem was a little difficult, but it was a fine poem and a deep one. . . .

[Journal] Feb. 15. Down to zero this morning. . . . Bluebirds in the air. General Sherman is dead — the last of our great generals of the War.

March 3. . . . Read 'Liza' by Tourguenieff. A real experience to read a novel by this great romancer. The taste of his books is always sweet and good to me. No hair-splitting here, no tiresome analysis; all is large, simple, fresh. Sad, but perhaps no sadder than life.

March 12. Presto! what a change! The river a great smooth mirror this morning. The ice slipped away in the night as quickly as the Arab. It began to move a little yesterday afternoon. First sparrow song this morning, how delicious! To my delight and surprise heard over by the station this morning my little sparrow of last year — him with the long silver loop of sound! What would I not give to know just where he passed the winter! and what adventures by flood and field he has had since last fall! but here he is, safe and sound. Of course it is the same bird. I have never before heard a sparrow with that song.

March 14. . . .
Since December I have written the following pieces:

3 for Youths' Companion	paid	$120
1 for McClure Syndicate	"	40
1 on Wild Flowers for St Nicholas	"	50
1 for Independent	"	15
1 " " 'A Hard Nut'	"	15
1 for Ch. Union, 'Popular Errors and Delusions'	"	20
1 'Analogy'		50
1 'Points of View'		20
1 'Eloquence and Poetry'		25
Finished 'The Spell of the Past'		50
		405

March 17. Clear and sharp. A day like cut-glass — hardly a film in the sky. Helped Zeke haul lumber for crates. . . . Highland burned up last night. . . .

April 3. My 54th birthday. . . . Worked most of the day in the horse-stable with DuBois. . . . A sad and gloomy day to me. . . . Health good, or would be, if I could be allowed to eat my food in peace. . . . Saw an angle-worm this morning, crawling on top of the snow.

April 6. Much shocked this morning to find our new station and Post Office burned to ashes. A great calamity in the neighborhood. . . .

About this time acquaintance with Miss Ludella L. Peck, Professor of Elocution at Smith College, ripened into one of the most beautiful and satisfying friendships of his later years.[1] The following is from one of his early letters to Miss Peck:

That you find some touch of the joy of life in my books is of course a pleasure to me, and even a greater pleasure to know you find it in Whitman, because so few women can master this poet and get at the real power and inspiration there is in him. So few men either, for that matter. His later writings and poems I do not care for, but there is a lift in his earlier work that is tremendous.

In the subjoined Journal excerpts one glimpses both his indoor excursions and his outdoor delights:

22. . . . Finished Dr. Nansen's 'The First Crossing of Greenland' — an honest, vivid, delightful work. A real bit of experience, even to read it. The book is pervaded by an admirable spirit; a book of travel I shall long remember. That inland ice — the last great remnant of the old Ice Age, cannot easily be forgotten. Such pictures of the Esquimaux are also novel and refreshing.

27. Enchanting April days. Cherry and plum trees in bloom . . . a mist of yellow-green over all the trees. A drive to Sherwoods yesterday p.m. Very beautiful. S—— had a lot of young lambs. How good they looked to me! The swamps and water courses along the way yellow with marsh-marigolds. Now, at 11 am, a fitful wind starts up from the SW and comes to my nostrils laden with the perfume of cherry-blossoms, a delicious bitter-sweet, or almond scent. I never remember it so noticeable. Standing under the tree it pours down upon you. . . .

May 1. A warm, soft, smoky, almost voluptuous day, clad in the white and pink of the fruit blossoms, and the tender green of the young leaves. A day like a dream. Cat bird, wood thrush, orchard starling, and cuckoos here, and several warblers.

A visit from Douglas Sladen, a hearty, modest, handsome young English author and poet — an Oxford man. Looks like Gilder, an English Gilder. Has lived in Australia, and been to China and Japan. We have a long talk, and then a walk to the woods and gather many wild flowers. We ate our dinner alone, but ate it in peace. His visit did me good. . . .

At this point in the Journal is a passage about the Lamp Rock in Central Asia, a rock which the natives believed to be

[1] Through the kindness of Miss Mary Jordan, the literary executor of Miss Peck, I am permitted to use such letters as serve my purpose.

inhabited by a fierce dragon, until an investigating English traveler found that the cave was a tunnel; that the mysterious light came through from the other side; and that the striking glow which it made at the mouth of the dark cavern was but the light of common day. 'Nearly all our providences and mysteries will clear up in the same way,' adds the Journalist, 'if explored. There is no light more mysterious than the light of common day.'

The passage is of special significance in that some years later, when gathering into a volume his essays on theological subjects, he introduced the figure of the Lamp Rock in his preface, felicitously naming the book 'The Light of Day.'

[Journal] July 23. Go to Onteora Park today.... Johnson [R. U.] came in afternoon. Very pleasant life in the camp of Mrs. Wheeler. J. and I sleep in a big tent.... I meet here many people whom I shall not soon forget.... Saturday we drive to Platterkill Clove. Monday to the Mountain House. The scene here is a great surprise: You drive swiftly along a good road up an easy grade till you alight in the rear of a great hotel. You walk straight through the hall and there lies the world below you as if seen from a balloon.... On Thursday we went to the top of Round Top, over 4000 feet. It was like a view from the clouds.

His reactions at the passing of Lowell are seen in the Journal, August 16th:

Lowell died a few days ago. His death gives me a pang. I owe him little, yet he was one of the men who helped adorn life. He had no message for me, yet he spoke brave and stirring words for the country, and for the higher life. The first and only time I ever saw him was in N.Y. in April 1887, I think;— first in the Century office, where he was very cordial and complimentary, and then at Walt Whitman's lecture in the evening.... The only service I ever did him was to hand him his hat on that occasion.

[Journal] Oct. 15. A big break in the record of my days. Very busy with the grapes till September 20. A fine season for shipping, for the most part.... Shipped 21 tons.... Brought $2100. Shipped mostly to Boston. Am convinced that small baskets pay best. In future keep clear of N.Y. market....

[J. B. to M. B.]

The grape campaign was rather a trying one. We had over twenty tons, and we bent all our energies to getting them off early. One day we shipped 4700 pounds and for ten days about 1½ tons a day....

My grapes were fine, and were soon in demand in Boston, so that at the end of the season I have a very respectable bank balance. At last year's prices, I would have made a nice thing, indeed. Some of my new grapes are disappointing, others are very promising. I think highly of the Winchell and shall plant it next year. . . .

I am going to put my brother [Curtis] on the old farm. He has a family of three boys and two girls, and so is strong-handed enough to put the work through, and as they all seem really in earnest, I am going to give them a chance.

I am doing but little reading and no writing. 'Life on an Ostrich Farm' I brought with me, and Goldwin Smith's 'Trip to England.' . . .

Journal and letters in November reveal a return of the *ennui* of which he complained so much before undertaking his grape-culture. 'It seems to me that life never had fewer attractions for me than it has now,' he writes. A letter to Gilder reveals the same sense of emptiness:

Many thanks for the little white-winged volume which brought me many messages from the fair land of poesy. Its voice is as pure and clear as that of a bird. Some of the religious poems, like that of The Passing of Christ, and Credo, mean a good deal more than appears on the surface. Be careful or the heresy hunters will be on your track.

My days are empty and profitless. I know yours are full of work and pleasure, I congratulate you.

[Journal] Nov. 6. . . . Walk up to Terpenning's for butter in afternoon. Paus[e] in the cemetery on my return. Already the names of so many people there whom I know, quite a throng of them. I linger long about their graves. Consider whether or not I want to be buried here. The old Baptist burying-ground at Home is offensive to me. Had rather be buried beside my dogs; or else in one of the old fields at home.

27. . . . Quite a streak of mental activity a few days ago, but nothing valuable came of it, as it was mainly misdirected; but it revives my hopes.

Yesterday, Thanksgiving, I went to NY with Anthony Gill to see a foot-ball match between Princeton–Yale. The spectacle fills my mind's eye yet: the great well-dressed, well-behaved crowd — 35,000 people, mostly young; the flutter of flags and colors; the cheering and horning; and a glamor of romance in some way about the college youths struggling there against each other. Alas! that I have no college associations.

In late December, at the word that Whitman is sick unto death, he hastens to Camden.

[Journal.] Walt on the bed with closed eyes, but he knows me and speaks my name as of old and kisses me. He asks me to sit beside him awhile. I do so, holding his hand. He coughs feebly. . . . Asks about my family and sends his 'best' love to Wife and Julian. Gives me two copies of his complete poems just out. He tells me where to find them. After a while I go out for fear of fatiguing him. He says, 'It is all right, John,' evidently referring to his approaching end. He said his brother George had just been in and it had quite unnerved him for the first time.

Xmas. . . . Walt . . . rallied considerable during the day. . . . He speaks of Mrs. O'Connor, of Eldridge, and his wife, his voice natural and strong. . . . I dined at Harned's and spent evening there. . . .

26. . . . Doctors think he may live a day or two yet, or may go any hour. I go up and look at him long and long, but do not speak. His face has steadily refined; no decrepitude or breaking down; never saw the nose so beautiful. He looks pathetic, but how beautiful! At eleven I take a silent farewell. Reach home at night. How green the patches of winter grain were in New Jersey!

This sudden transition from his sorrow to some observation in nature is so characteristic. Marked improvement in the poet lifted for a time the lowering shadow.

In the ensuing year the Vine-Dresser had more intercourse with his kind than in preceding years; mingled more with cultivated persons, and saw much more of metropolitan life.

On the first day of the new year he wrote 'A Life of Fear' ('Riverby'); on the next, discussed in his Journal how rare a thing is the religious nature. It is a curious list he offers — present-day and earlier characters commingled. Among those named, whom he regarded as truly religious, were Abbott [Lyman?], Mulford, Father Taylor, Elias Hicks, and John Knox. Considering those he had known in his native town, he dismissed all but Elder Hewitt and Gran'ther Kelly. His father, he said, had a streak of religion; but he found few who were spontaneously religious, seven days in the week, without thought of reward or punishment, here or hereafter. Continuing:

True religion and undefiled is just as rare as true poetry. As the poet hungers for the beautiful, so the religious nature hungers for the divine — that which Jesus exemplified more fully than any other man — the humanization of the eternal power of the universe, or the fatherhood and brotherhood of God.

An interesting bit of self-analysis is found under date of January 10th:

My moral nature is not fruitful, as was that of Emerson and Carlyle, if I may compare myself with these illustrious men. It is not the source of my ideas, as was theirs. The source of my ideas is rather my rational and intellectual nature, or [and?] my emotional nature.

I have few reflections to offer upon life, on man, on society. I would make a poor preacher. I am interested in things, in laws, in growths, in nature, more than I am in man. The platitudes of the moralist and the preacher are tools I can never get the hang of.

Again:

M—— C—— [a young devotee of astrology and of character de-lineation, who had sent him some decidedly candid readings of his character] says I have a standard, but no principles. She says it is my ideality and naturalness that have led me into free paths, rather than any evil trait. She says I am lazy, and lack self-esteem; that when I do think well of myself, then I am conceited.

She says I have natural or instinctive justice, but not as much intellectual justice as I should have. Justice, she says, is the mother of principles. My reverence and ideality, she says, would give me a standard, but not principles. . . .

I said I had no will. She says I have — she sees it in my Roman nose. . . . She says I am mouldable and very progressive, and certain in some things; but that I am stuck like a snail to its shell to Emerson and Carlyle, and the rest. She says I would not know what to do without them; that I must put away standards for principles. . . . She is a very penetrating girl.

His new correspondent, who had, for some months past, piqued his interest and curiosity, elicited this reply:

Your letter affords me a good deal of entertainment. I have been trying to realize you to myself. You are only a voice. I should like to materialize you. You would make a better mark to shoot at. Shall I give you black hair and black eyes and make you weigh about 110, of nervous temperament, health pretty good, not a very good sleeper? Or maybe you can help me by sending me your photo. . . .

I think our differences are mainly disputes about words. You certainly would admit that the charm and value of a new writer is in the new quality he brings — that which is peculiar to him. I do not mean oddity or eccentricity. I mean newness, freshness. It is the Wordsworthian element in Wordsworth, and the Emersonian element in Emerson that we prize. They do not so much give us new truths as they give us a new medium through which to view the old truths — a new personality.

It is true that love and friendship and sympathy are facts, but what kind of facts? to what sphere do they belong? There are mathematical facts and scientific facts and social facts; there is truth of poetry, and truth of logic. Some of these truths belong to the reason and understanding, and others to the conscience, the taste, the emotions, that is, they are sentiments.

You want me to advise you. My first advice to a young lady would be to fall in love with a suitable young man and marry him. My second advice would be, make yourself beautiful, interesting, kind, sympathetic, cheerful, and by all means, keep well. Your temperament is intense; therefore avoid tea and coffee and stimulating foods, and spend your time in the open air; work with your hands at gardening. You must have a career, an ambition — something to do, as well as to think and to know.

I cultivate fruit in summer and read and lounge under the big trees, and in winter write out what the summer has brought me.

I do not know any Russian or Italian poems, but you should read Tolstoi and Tourguenieff. Dante will do for Italian poetry. You must read Wordsworth, and do you know Walt Whitman? His poems are immense, if you are robust enough to stand them. Do you know Amiel's Journal? Do you know Matthew Arnold's books? They cannot be skipped by one in quest of the best there is in the world. Do you know Goethe's books? He is the great doctor and critic of the modern world. 'Knowledge comes, but Wisdom lingers' — you may read and read and not be wise. Wisdom comes from life. I have been greatly aided by Carlyle. . . .

And later, after another outspoken analysis:

I love to be torn apart, but have mercy! have mercy!

Nothing in me but charcoal — I don't feel the diamonds. You only think you see diamonds. Would to God there were!

Do you think I am a selfish man? Wife says I am intensely selfish, and I dispute it — no more selfish than man inevitably is as the positive, agressive, dominant nature. One of my weaknesses is that I yield too easily to others, and do not stand up for my own rights. I cannot say no, and I cannot give pain, and I always take a back seat, or else stand, and let others sit; or, may all this go with selfishness? I love to serve others. My wife does not. She must have the best and the first, yet she is the unselfish one, she claims. May there not be a noble and an ignoble selfishness? Tell me, O, doctor of all laws! . . .

You always put your finger on the weak spot. You are right, but I did not believe I should be detected. I wrote the latter half of the book [What book?] in a different mood. It was less gentle. You have found me out . . . . I always try to keep back the ugly and give my best.

I think Hawthorne was king of all our literary fellows. He has helped me more than your beloved Thoreau; but since you love that

old bachelor, here is his photograph and a bit of his writing when he
bade good-bye to a friend.

More of his self-criticism in the January records shows the
ability of the trained observer to turn his scrutiny upon himself:

How much force I waste whenever I write upon literary subjects!
I have to undergo a sort of apprenticeship to every subject I write
upon — do a great deal of futile and preparatory work; write and
destroy; write and destroy; leave behind tomorrow what I do today.
It is like opening a quarry. Oh, the rubbish that has to be removed,
and then, often, to find there is nothing but rubbish there!
In my writing, other than my out-door, natural history papers —
I find, if I do not look out, I am talking in the air. How much I see in
my essays that are merely shots fired in the air! One must feel the
resistance of something real and tangible — not aim to round his
periods, but to pierce the subject and draw blood.

Jan. 16. Cardinal Manning died yesterday. A good man and
worthy of remembrance. His last conscious hours of life were spent
in imploring God to have mercy upon him. He was firmly possessed
with the Christian idea that he was about to go from a place where
God was not, to a place where God is and abides. And that there
was great danger that his God would be displeased with him, and
would punish him. How curious, how curious! Poor Man! why
could he not have died in peace? . . .

The following letter, written in February, is one of a few
which passed between the Hoosier poet and the Vine-Dresser
of Esopus:[1]

DEAR JOHN BURROUGHS:
When you tell me that you take my — *my* — poems Sunday
nights over the apples and the nuts, the unconscious poetry of your
tribute is, in my liking, a peg higher than 'Across the walnuts and
the wine' of England's laureate.
Aye!

> *'Across the walnuts and the wine'* —
> Granting the verse so all divine,
> In sooth, my fancy fondlier shuts
> Over the apples and the nuts.

Gratefully and faithfully yours
JAMES WHITCOMB RILEY

To Benton, in February, Mr. Burroughs gives his views as
to prophylaxis in *la grippe:*

[1] Permission to quote the letter is given by Bobbs-Merrill Company.

We have been steadily here since you last heard from us. . . . The Grip has not touched us. This is the way to ward off the Grip: keep up the general health; keep the house cool, especially sleeping-rooms; and *eat plenty of raw onions*, and meat only once a day. The Grip germ cannot stand raw onions.

I have been unusually well, and have had considerable literary activity. . . .

Early in March he writes of having worked too steadily on his Whitman essays, which he finds 'not very satisfactory,' though his appetite for literary work is keener than for several years past.

On March 23d a long entry on General Grant discusses the two men in Grant, the ordinary man and the hero — the War bringing the hero to the surface, the Presidency submerging him, but the hero shining clearly forth in the 'Memoirs.'

The month which had begun with the laughter of the robins ends with the news he has long been dreading: Whitman died March 25th. The brief Journal entries, probably written many days later, as was often his custom, but poorly express his real feelings. He was for a time benumbed. We must read between the lines.

March 29. Black crêpe on Walt's door-bell, shutters closed. I find Bucke, Harned, and Traubel there. Look upon Walt's face long and long. Cannot be satisfied — it is not Walt — a beautiful, serene old man, but not Walt. After awhile I have to accept it as him — his 'excrementitious body,' as he called it. Pass the night with Traubel.[1]

On the funeral day, he went to the house and there saw the crowd filing in and out. His Journal continues:

M. C. [the character analyst already referred to] came — tall, thin, and homely. At one, Conway and I, and others, go out for some oysters. As we eat our stew before the counter, the oyster man shows us Walt's book with his autograph in it, presented by Walt.

[1] A letter by Higginson which appeared in the New York *Evening Post*, March 28th, with unfair and insinuating charges against Whitman caused J. B. to reply in a paper written on the 30th, one paragraph of which follows: 'I have known Whitman for nearly thirty years, and a cleaner, saner, more wholesome man in word and deed, I have never known. If my life depended upon it, I could not convict him of one unclean word, or one immoral act.'

J. B.'s reply to Higginson's article, called 'Walt Whitman After Death,' was refused publication by the *Post*, but was printed by the *Critic*, April 9th. Two other articles by J. B. about Whitman had previously been published by the *Critic*, one on February 6th, 'Mr. Howells's Agreement with Walt Whitman,' and 'Walt Whitman,' April 2d. The Higginson article just referred to was reprinted by the *Nation*, on April 7, 1892.

At the cemetery. . . . A great crowd. The scene very impressive; the great tent perfumed with flowers. . . . [Robert G.] Ingersoll speaks, — an eloquent, impressive oration. Shall always love him for it. Some passages in it will last. As he was speaking, I heard a bluebird warble over the tent most joyously. The tomb is grand, and will endure as long as time.

At night twelve of us go to Philadelphia and have dinner and much talk.

March 31. Warry [Whitman's nurse] and I and Horace Traubel go out to Walt's tomb. Very glad to be there again with the crowd gone. An overcast, chilly day. At noon am taken with one of my bad headaches. A bad night.

April 1. Start for N.Y. Get proof from Forum and N. A. Review. Lunch with Gilder at Players' Club; meet Woodberry, the poet; have a two hours' talk with him and rub Whitman into him with a vengeance. But I am sure he is already lost — nothing in him but 'art' and 'art' and 'art.' . . . Pass the night again with Ingersoll.

April 3. My 55th birthday. . . . Work all day on proof. A strange excitement upon me. My heart seems running away. No sleep last night. Yet I am well and mind more active than it has been for years!

How the birds do sing and call! and the swamps are vocal with the little frogs.

To Mabie, on April 3d, goes this fervent letter:

I seem to be a good deal broken up since I came home last night, and can hardly hold my pen, but I cannot wait longer to thank you for your magnificent editorial on Whitman. From the depths of my heart I thank you. I shall love you always for these brave and manly words. . . .

There is great hope for literature when the younger men like you show such a spirit. More and more I see that the Christian Union is rising into the great currents that are to shape the future. I never want to see you take in sail, but to throw yourselves more and more to the free winds of God's open sea.

In two April letters to Miss Peck are found more of his real feelings than the Journal is as yet revealing:

I am just back from the funeral of my great friend and am a good deal broken up. And, too, I am under a strange excitement which I do not clearly comprehend. My heart beats so loud and strong it disturbs me when I try to sleep. I have had but little sleep during the week, and strangely enough do not feel the need of more.

Your serious and sympathetic face and kind letter cheer me much.

I thank you for them. This is my birthday, my 55th, and I walk about, listening to the happy birds, and looking out upon the placid river in a curious kind of a dream. But one thought fills me — the thought of the 'large sweet soul that has gone.' . . .

I have written much this winter about Whitman. In December the Critic asked me to write about him. This set me going, and I kept on. I shall have an article in the May Forum, and in the May N. A. Review. The past week's Critic and Christian Union each had articles by me. I have one more paper to write — on Whitman the Man.

My little book on him of 1867, you cannot get. I send you a copy, the only one I have, which you may return sometime. . . .

[*J. B. to L. L. P.*]

The April days have a pathos to me they never had before. I have been in such close communion with Whitman's spirit during the last few months in writing these articles, that his loss takes deeper hold on me than it otherwise would.

I have not his faith in immortality and cannot have. Some people are born with faith, some achieve faith, and some have faith thrust upon them. What faith I have, I must earn by the sweat of my brow, and that is very little. In some moods I lean strongly upon my great friend, and find comfort in his unconquerable belief in immortality. In other moods, death seems a great blank. We are simply sponged off the blackboard of existence, and the great Demonstrator goes on with new figures and new problems. We exist in his thought — is that enough?

One year ago last fall I passed through Northampton and thought of you. When I pass through again the thought of you may make the train stop.

[Journal] April 5. Still more-than-summer heat. Burn brush and gaze and gaze out upon the beautiful, spring-touched world. [Is the merciful benumbing beginning to pass off?]

April 6. Again, dear Master, I have bitten into this great apple of an earth with my plow and find it as sweet and appetizing as ever — the same old delicious smell; the same old fresh look; yet the new furrow is more eloquent and pathetic to me than ever before. Again the swelling buds and the sprouting grass; again the robin racket in the twilight; again the long-drawn *tr-r-r-r-r-r-r-r* of the toad in the gloaming; again the tender ditty of the sparrow; again the waterfowl streaming northward; again the 'fields all busy with labor '— but thou, thou, in thy tomb!

In the Journal entries that follow, rehearsing the familiar spring tokens, he sighs, 'The world so sweet, so benignant these days, yet my thoughts are away in that Camden cemetery where the great one lies.' In the exaltation born of sorrow, he adds, 'W. W. is the Christ of the modern world — he alone redeems it; justifies it; shows it divine; floods and saturates it with human-divine love.' Again, April 15th:

I am fairly well these days, but sad, sad. Walt constantly in mind. I think I see more plainly how Jesus came to be deified — his followers loved him; love transforms everything. I must still continue my writing about him till I have fully expressed myself.

Writing to Benton at this time, he says, in part:

I liked your O'Connor letter very much. . . . It was the only adequate word that has yet been spoken on that eloquent and chivalrous soul. I heard it highly spoken of in Camden and in N.Y. The critics seem to pass by O'Connor on the other side, as if they were still afraid of him.

You should read his pamphlet on Donnelly's Reviewers, if you have not. It is rare fun to see him gore and toss certain reviewers. I do not accept his conclusions on the Bacon-Shakespeare craze any more than you do, but I enjoy his marvellous forensic abilities.

I was told that Ball before he died wrote a letter to O'Connor, or to his wife, acknowledging the fraud he tried to perpetrate on Mrs. Akers.[1] I think I must write something on O'Connor some day.

In December the Critic asked me to write them an article on Walt. I declined at first, but after my return from Camden went at it, and then could not stop; and kept writing on him nearly all winter. . . . I also had one in the Chicago Interocean (requested). The two May articles I like best. I have one or two more on the stocks.

The article in the Nation was by Higginson, and was a dastardly attack. Have you seen Higginson's last book — 'The New World and the New Man'? Higginson turns out about the best literary veneering that can be had in this country. If my life is spared, I will make his ears burn some day. He is so thin — a mere elegance, with no solid backing at all.

Whitman's loyal disciples everywhere were naturally incensed at the gratuitously abusive article by Higginson. From San Francisco, Charles W. Eldridge wrote feelingly to Burroughs:

I want to thank you for your reply to Higginson's 'malignant' article in the N.Y. Nation on Walt. It was well done. Frank Sanborn also, in the Boston Advertiser of the 14th instant has a quiet but very effective rejoinder in which he turns his literary points on

---

[1] Claiming that he, Ball, wrote 'Backward, turn backward, O Time.' O'Connor had exposed the fraud when many were crediting the claims of Ball.

him in a very satisfactory manner. Besides, he brings out the fact that the article is the offspring of a deep-seated prejudice against Walt and his work. I have personal knowledge that this is true:

When we were about publishing the 1860 edition of 'Leaves of Grass' in Boston, Higginson occasionally came into our place. On one occasion he saw a copy of 'Leaves of Grass' on my desk and said that the book always made him sea-sick, having first become acquainted with it on a voyage to the West Indies, when he was just recovering from *mal-de-mer*. He further showed his disgust by saying that if Walt's book represented health, then he (Hig.) was diseased.

Since that time he has not failed, when opportunity offered, to say spiteful things about Walt and his book; notably in an article in the Woman's Journal, in which he twitted Walt with the fact that, being of lawful age when the War broke out, he did not enlist; and to which William O'Connor made a stinging retort in his letter to Dr. Bucke. . . .

A Journal entry late in April has something to say of other writers who were taking occasion to disparage Whitman in the face of the recognition his death was calling forth:

. . . There is no hate or bitterness toward Whitman like that of many of our minor poets. They fly at him like a whiffet dog at a mastiff. The same set, if they happen to be story writers, like the Crawfordsville poet, also snap and snarl at the heels of Tolstoy, one of the most heroic and powerful characters of history. How I ache to lift them with my boot!

When replying to Dr. Johnston and a band of Whitman-appreciators in Lancashire, England, Burroughs wrote, on April 22d:

The opinion of Whitman held by your countrymen is much more interesting to me than the opinion held by my own, because it shows so much more insight and appreciation. There have been a few good notices here, some flippant ones, and many atrocious ones. One has just been sent me from a Maryland paper that makes me ashamed of my kind. . . .

I am still writing on him. Indeed, I am only just beginning to see his real greatness. I don't think any of us fully realized how great he really was. . . . I don't suppose any of us knew how much we loved him till since his death. . . .

Buchanan's poem is very beautiful. It made me weep. Indeed, it does not take a great deal to make me weep when Walt Whitman's name is mentioned. I trust you keep well, and that your band of Whitman brothers has lost none of your love for him or for one another. . . .

[Journal] April 24. . . . Today is buried in distant Chicago a man

I loved — J. C. Burroughs, son of my father's Uncle Curtis. He was one of the few men I have known of whom I felt, 'He has walked with Christ' — so simple, sincere, gentle, charitable and brotherly. A man of great activity and endurance, tall, thin, homely. His life was one of toil — wasted his best strength on the [old] Chicago University as its president — latterly was school superintendent. Visited me in the year of the triple-eights. A man whom all persons liked or loved.

May 1. . . . Dr. Bucke came this morning. Very glad to see him. He reminds me strongly of Walt — large; long gray beard, and walks with a cane.

We have a day full of talk and communion. How true it is that you must love a man ere he seem worthy of your love! I did not use to like Dr. B., but since the death of W. my heart has softened towards him, and I begin to feel a strong attachment towards him. I see more and more in him to love and admire. A little inclined to run off with a single idea and make too much of it. His idea now is that there is such a thing as Cosmic Consciousness; that it is a new sense or power developing in the race; and that Walt had it in a pre-eminent degree — Paul had it, Buddha, and Mahomet. I fear he will ride the idea too hard. In pm we drive to the woods and get arbutus.

The pensive tone in a letter, dated May 16th, to Miss Peck, expresses the prevailing mood in Journal and letters — Spring, and his Comrade gone from the 'rich apple-blossomed earth':

. . . How beautiful the world is these days, all bloom and perfume. I walk through the orchards and springing meadows, as I suppose everyone does at my age, with sad happy thoughts. I suppose the wave of apple-bloom with its sad sweet reminiscences passes over you too. I have just had some rare visitors in the shape of several white-crowned sparrows. They lingered about my place in full song for nearly a week. So plaintive and touching is their song — the song of memory, of the days that are no more. . . .

I am a farmer these days and treat my correspondents shabbily, but my vineyard has no reason to complain.

When June comes, Burroughs and his son go a-jaunting in New England — to Boston, to Smith College, and to the Rangeley Lakes, returning for the raspberry and currant campaign at Riverby; but even while that progresses, he finds time to read Pierre Loti's 'Into Morocco,' which he pronounces 'graphic — just enough of everything':

Pride of style in writing is just as bad as pride of style in dress, or equipage. The best style is the absence of style, or of all conscious style. You must not think or know how well-dressed the man or woman is. Loti's style does not court your attention at all. It is a mirror.

Aug. 26. Just as we began to praise the weather and say, How fine, how seasonable! it took a turn, and the rains began again. . . . The weather gods are the most exasperating of all the gods. Nine times out of ten they will turn a blessing into a curse. They are nearly always on a debauch. They will push the dry weather till we are parched and burnt up, and the rain till it becomes a deluge. Finished the Champions today in the rain, and many vines of the Moore's Early.

P.M. Rain very heavy; sets all the drains running and the grapes cracking; I mutter my anathemas, but the sulky divinities only raise the gates of the clouds higher.

Sept. 11. The war on the grapes has been hotly pursued the past ten days. Shipped eleven tons last week. Never more favorable weather to work. Looks as if my crop might bring me $3000.

Dear old Whittier died a few days ago — more of a real countryman than any of the rest of our poets. Curtis, too, has passed — the soul of gentleness and grace, and, I may add, of honor.

20. . . . On the 17th the bottom went out of the grape-market, leaving me with two or three tons of Concords on the vines. These we are sending off slowly and getting low prices. For the first time in nearly a month I can sit at my ease and look up at the serene sky. Have lost near ten pounds in flesh during the grape-campaign, but am well, and stronger than one year ago. . . .

Vineyard matters, however exacting, could not make him oblivious to a rare little visitant of whom he writes to Miss Peck:

All these lovely September days I have been struggling with my grapes — over 30 tons of them — to get them to market in good shape and in good time. I have hardly taken time to look up at the 'splendid silent sun.' A Carolina wren — the only one I ever heard this side of Maryland — took up his position on the edge of the vineyard when we were packing the grapes, and kept up his calls and warblings day after day, as if to mock me with the remembrance of my free and happy life years ago in Washington. One morning I dropped my work for five minutes and went out to interview him. After peeping slyly at me a few moments from a bush, he flew to the top of a grape-post and sang and called his best. He brought all that past, and all that Southern country back to me in a flash.

Well, we have got the grapes off — only a driblet of a ton or two left — and I am beginning to look up at the sky again and to dream day-dreams in my big chair in the summer-house.

Later he camps with Gilder and his sons in Woodland Valley, then journeys to an obscure place on Long Island to visit Herbert Gilchrist, of whom he writes entertainingly in his Journal:

Gilchrist drives me to his hermitage through the dusk, over the sandy, gravelly roads. . . . An old farm house in a little trough on the shore, shut in by low woods, a picturesque spot, but secluded and lonely. Here this young Englishman lives all alone, year in and year out, cooks his own food, and works at his picture (Cleopatra). . . .We sat up till midnight by the open fire and talked. . . . In the morning we made clam fritters for breakfast.

We talked much of Tennyson whose death is near. G. knew him well. Said he was much less gentle and guarded in speech than Walt Whitman; would say rather blunt, rude things before ladies. G. said such men as Whitman and Tennyson strike us as poets and artists all through — they are born such, while such men as Browning strike us as only poets at times, or in part. The lives of W. and T. were the lives of poets, pure and simple — the lives of children — unworldly and unconventional. They were not men of current society, or of current affairs at all. G. feels that Whitman was a great artist from the start, but regrets a crude, uncultured streak in him at times.

How H. G. can stand this solitude is a mystery to me. Came from London to try to find himself in this humble, secluded place. Probably a marked reaction against over-populated England which Englishmen so often show — Nature trying to remedy her own excesses. . . .

Oct. 10. Golden October days continue. I spend the days looking into Tennyson and musing on various matters — a mellow, poetic spirit, like that of the dead poet, seems to pervade the air. All the woods and groves stand in their richest autumn livery.

Is there more reverie than contemplation in Tennyson, and is he, to that extent, weakening and dissipating? Does he sap the will? Longing, retrospection, regret — these largely make the atmosphere of his poems. . . .

He was the poet of the old world, not of the new — of a rich, deep, ripe, refined civilization — not of a new, fermenting, democratic era and land, like America. We enjoy him, but he is not of us. He is not always manly. He is much less, as a personality, than Whitman — much more of a polished, conventional, orthodox poet. It is rarely that he gives one the impression of mass, of power, or makes you a partaker in the universal brotherhood of man. Ripe and mellow always, but tonic and uplifting rarely.

Noting a visit from Miss Mary Burt, he characterizes her as 'a woman of rare sense and intelligence, who is destined to

work a revolution in methods of teaching.' He is now trying
to mingle more in neighborhood affairs; he attends the dedication of the little Baptist church where he lives, but finds the
sermon 'like hard water in which one tries to wash' — it does
not take hold. On Thanksgiving he goes to his brother
Eden's for the family reunion, at which time he sells his brother
Curtis the Homestead farm.

[Journal] Dec. 5. Go to N.Y. with Wife. Spend week in city, much
of time with Miss Burt. Visit Berkeley school and hear the boys
read from my books. Attend a literary reunion in Brooklyn. Hear
Marion Crawford read — a strong, fine voice, but no life or flexibility
in it. . . .

11th. . . . At Stedman's in evening. To Boston on Tuesday with
Miss Burt and Mrs. Ben Ali Haggin — a pretty, black-eyed widow.
. . . Spend the week in Boston. Am interviewed and dined and put
through generally. Twice on my feet trying to speak before gather-
ings of teachers. Meet Bradford Torrey, a fine-souled fellow — suggests a bird with his bright eyes and shy ways and sensitiveness.
Meet E. E. Hale. Call on Prof. Norton at Cambridge, a fine man
and gentleman.

A passage in the Journal, later elaborated as 'Talks with
Young Observers' ('Riverby'), gives the incident of coming
upon the track of an otter — an animal rare in the Hudson
River Valley — the strange imprints in the snow challenging
his attention and leading him to trace the course, even to read
the mind of the creature, although some of its tracks were
writ in water. Shortly after occurs a Journal record which appears to be but the putting upon paper of a train of thought
he had been silently pursuing. Like the otter, the journalist
many a time dips in the pool, and one sees no trace; again, as
it were, he emerges upon the bank, and one sees such traces as
these:

. . . It is all the more pathetic and difficult to deal with because all
her faults are virtues perverted or pushed too far. Her terrible clean-
liness, her ceaseless war upon dust and dirt — what a virtue lies back
of it! Her thrift — wearing out herself and others to save her things
— what a virtue is perverted here! Her brutal frankness springs
from a trait we all admire — truthfulness, sincerity; but when she
calls you a liar without provocation, or because you differ from her,
it is too much of a good thing. She hates deception to the point of
discarding all the disguises and half-tones of life — nothing but the
bare, ugly prose left — no charm, no illusion, no romance.

The spirit in which she condemns evil is worse than the evil itself.
She always fires on a flag of truce — 'Want to parley and apologize,
do you? I thought you would eat your own words — but you shall
eat them red-hot!' ...

A fragment in the same vein, found among his papers, reveals how poorly the early efforts at adjustment had succeeded
throughout the years; and shows an earnest attempt to ap-
praise the irreconcilable qualities of mind and character in
two persons whose attachment to each other was unquestion-
able, despite all that each endured from the other:

It is the oft-told story. A crude, undeveloped young man marries a
girl older and more experienced than himself. He develops, she simply hardens, and their interests diverge. In middle life they are far
apart: she knows him not at all, does not share his real life, only his
kitchen life. The things he lives for are nothing to her; she has no
mental or intellectual or social wants; hardly any religious wants.
One supreme want she has, to which she sacrifices everything —
health, hospitality, friends, husband, child — the want to be free
from dirt and disorder. She is one of those terrible housekeepers
with whom there is no living — a housekeeper, but not a home-
maker.

You couldn't find a book of my writing in that house. They are
never mentioned there. She has no pride in them. She refuses to see
people who come to see me — the people whom my writings draw.
She looks upon my writing as a kind of self-indulgence which she
ought to frown upon. She is jealous of everybody, man and woman
alike. No doubt she loves me; but she would have me play second
fiddle to her. I had to build a study outside. She literally cleaned me
out; and now she is mad because I will not spend my evenings with
her in the kitchen. She has not spoken to me today.

She has many noble traits, but the ordinary friction of life makes a
fury of her. She has a strong will, and must have her way. I have a
weak will, and find it hard to say No, or to stand up for my rights,
and that irritates her. All my habits and disposition irritate her. I
am easy and indulgent, and think anything is good enough for me
and her. She is particular, exacting, proud, and very conventional.
She opposes me at every point. We can have no conversation whatever. I sit meal after meal and hardly say a word, year in and year
out.

She was rude and uncivil to a friend of mine who came here last
week with his novel to read to me. She visits in but one house, here
and there — hardly once a year. No one comes here. She has no
correspondents. She gives herself, body and soul, to the drudgery of
house-keeping. She will not keep a girl, because she cannot get an
angel.

I am not blameless. I have my own sins to answer for — sins she

has driven me into . . . but she has not been true to any of my higher
wants and needs — has trampled them all under foot, though igno-
rantly and blindly, I admit. She has no self-knowledge at all — I
never saw her like in this respect. She thinks herself a model wife.
. . . I don't see how I can live here much longer. I should like a year
or two of real peace and sunshine before I die. . . . Oh, what a boon
is good nature! like sunshine, like a genial climate.

In at least three books about Burroughs, published since
his passing, these domestic infelicities have been so conspicuously set forth (and in two of them from very imperfect understanding of facts) that it seems incumbent upon the authori-
tative biographer to attempt a fairer presentation of both
sides of the picture — as fair as may be and still observe
reticences due the living.

The wives of geniuses have ever had a hard time of it, but
when evidence from both sides is in, it is sometimes found that
the geniuses themselves have not slept on beds of roses. The
domestic infelicities of Socrates, Shakespeare, Milton, Byron,
Burns, Carlyle, Coleridge, even John Wesley and Lincoln —
to name a few — have been pitilessly exposed to the public
gaze. Indeed, so commonly does one come upon such incompatibility, one sometimes wonders whether greatness is in-
consistent with domestic felicity, or whether domestic in-
felicity tends to produce greatness. Again one recalls certain
notably happy unions among geniuses — the Samuel John-
sons, the Brownings, the George Macdonalds, the Emersons,
the Hawthornes, the Lowells, come quickly to mind. Still,
the learned Johnson, who wrote so fondly of his 'Tetty,' declared she was like so many ladies with a reverence for cleanli-
ness — 'slaves to their own besoms, and only sigh for the
hour of sweeping their husbands out of the house as dirt and
useless lumber.'

If the marital maladjustments of common mortals were as
cruelly exposed to the public eye as are those of geniuses,
doubtless the impression of the preponderance of such difficulties in marriages with geniuses would be far less apparent.
In many unhappy unions the fault may be due to neither
husband nor wife, but to the fatal mismating constantly occurring between persons of all ranks and callings. To blame
one or the other, unqualifiedly, is short-sighted and unjust.
It is fairer to try to understand the conditions, when, as al-

ways, the fuller the comprehension, the freer the forgiveness.

Happily, in the case in question, compensation was ever at work; and it may be fairly concluded that toward the more obviously enduring work of the author, the thrift and prosaic industry of his wife contributed more than might appear on the surface; while the very conditions of incompatibility which made a happy home life impossible for either, and which sent him persistently out of doors, resulted both in his own peace and contentment and in the books born of his intimate and sympathetic intercourse with Nature.

In an essay of this period — 'A Plea for a Quiet Life' — Burroughs speaks feelingly of housewives worn by the 'mania of owning things'; and advises them to follow Thoreau's example and pitch their belongings out of doors to escape the eternal dusting of them. He lamented that women would wear themselves out scouring things. 'They may have kept their mop-pail " ten years and as good as new,"' he said, 'but they have not kept themselves as good as new. We are so many of us like Jeanie Deans, who carried her shoes in her hand and went barefoot, to save them.'

About this time, when speaking before a women's club in Massachusetts, he complained that women were poor observers chiefly because they were not enough interested in the outdoors. He hoped to provoke his hearers into disproving his statements:

American women need a wider field of interest. I tell my own wife so — whenever I dare. 'Come out,' I say, 'and see the vineyard — see what a fine lot of grapes we have got! . . . see how we have mended the highway!' . . . To hold her own with men; to be man's mate, woman must have something like his interest in science, in politics, in economics.

Commonplaces now, but far from such when he uttered them. Woman has moved far since the eighteen-nineties, though she still has far to go. It seems not unlikely that, even as the influence of John Burroughs began in the eighteen-eighties to be strongly felt in the schools, so also, in women's clubs all over the land, since the eighteen-nineties, have his nature books had no inconsiderable share in enlarging the horizons of women (as well as those of men) by taking them out of doors. Certain it is that in the last three decades of his

life women students of nature, women's clubs all over the
States, and women correspondents and visitors continually
appealed to him for help in their studies, and for papers and
addresses that would contribute to their knowledge of nature.
Their getting out of doors and their emancipation have gone
hand in hand.

CHAPTER XII

SPECIMEN DAYS AND THOUGHTS
1893–1895

To me the converging objects of the universe perpetually flow,
All are written to me, and I must guess what the writing means.

WHITMAN

WHEN one has at command such self-revealing passages as the Journal entries, already and hereinafter quoted, comments not really necessary seem intrusive; hence, chiefly through such the story is carried along. As already shown, these quiet days, so far removed from the men and events that were more obviously stirring and influencing the world, were in reality subtly influencing the lives of his fellows. The plain, homely, unostentatious man in that little hamlet by the Hudson first lived the days for themselves alone, and later drew from them the material for the books which have opened the eyes and delighted the minds of two generations of readers. As he went about his tasks in garden and vineyard, and sauntered in field and wood, he unconsciously exemplified his conviction that all of us have the wealth of the universe at our doors — ours for the mere stretching forth of our hands.

Alone with his cat at Riverby, in January, he writes to Benton:

Winter bears down hard, but I manage to keep him at bay.... There is little new with me. The solitude of life increases, as I suppose it does with you; the shadows are a little deeper and longer as the sun creeps down the sky.

... My seventeen acres brought me $4000 — expenses $1500, which leaves a good margin of profit. And then we are free from it from October till April. ... The old farm out at Roxbury has prospered also. My brother and his family are doing well. Indeed, I have sold it to them, and they have made a good payment. We spent part of July and August out there, and had a good time. ...

I have read Thoreau's 'Autumn,' which is dull — only now and then a passage worth printing. That man Blake is not the man to edit those Journals. It needs some one who knows a crisp turnip from a pithy one. In his Journals Thoreau describes everything. He experimented endlessly; tried to transmute everything to gold, and only now and then succeeded.

Renan's last book, 'Letters and Recollections,' is delightful. It is curious that so many men who repudiate the creed of Christianity have its spirit. When Renan was smitten upon one cheek, he actually did turn the other. . . .

A paper of mine on 'The Decadence of Theology' will probably be in the next N. A. Review.

[Journal] Feb. 14. . . . Symonds's mind has not the clear, strong stamp of Arnold's. He will not leave so definite and indelible a mark upon literature. In power of appreciation he is greater than Arnold — has wider sympathies, but has not his singleness and directness. Arnold's thoughts are more typical and spinal.

In a few days he goes to New York, and, after attending a dinner at the Authors' Club, makes this naïve entry:

. . . Spoke for the first time and did fairly well. Papers say my speech and J. Jefferson's were the speeches of the evening. With practice I think I could beat any of them — too much chaff in their speeches — no serious word.

On March 2d, in Washington, he writes:

Walk up to my old house on V Street in morning and stand as long as I dare at the gate looking in. Place much neglected and in need of repairs. The brick walk I laid is still in good condition, as is part of the fence I built. What a host of thoughts and memories crowd in upon me!

March 4. Snow and cold; a villainous day for the inauguration of Cleveland. We start at 11 in a covered wagon. See C. and Harrison pass up the avenue in a carriage. Throngs of shivering people; slush on the streets; snow in the air. At the Capitol, after long waiting, we witness the ceremonies in front, jumping and slapping to keep warm. Then Cleveland steps forward and speaks his piece, with uncovered head. 'Grover, put on your hat!' we all feel like shouting. I only hear his strong, manly voice buffeted by the wind.

The record tells of dining with Major Saxton; [1] of looking up his old friends in the Treasury; of dining with Roosevelt; of the Bakers holding two receptions for him; and of his speaking about the birds before a class of young women at the Normal School, later walking with them through the fields at Chevy Chase; and of visiting the grave of William O'Connor.

[1] Major Willard E. Saxton, a friend of Whitman, Burroughs, and that group in the sixties, is (1925) the sole surviving member of the Brook Farm Colony. He went there as a boy of fifteen, as compositor on *The Harbinger*.

[Journal] March 25. Made my second after-dinner speech last night at a dinner given by the Aldine Club to Mr. Aldrich. Did not do so well as at the Authors' Club dinner — ate too much, and drank too much champagne — fancied I would not be called upon. Yet I was the only speaker who repeated any of Mr. A.'s poetry, and I did not learn it for the occasion.

[J. B. to L. L. P.]

I am going to take a bit of this birthday to write to you. I think I should have done it had I not received your delightful letter, as I was thinking of you this morning. I always think of all the pleasant things I can on my birthday, and the thought of you is always pleasant and cheering. The sad thoughts will steal in too, but I make them keep pleasant company.

Yes, indeed, we have waste places here, vast stretches of them. I do the best I can to fill them or to cover them up, and yet they eat up a great deal of one's life.

Most of the winter my family has been in Poughkeepsie, and I have been there part of the time. Every week or two I would have to flee back to my solitude here, and to the spirits that fill it. I would open the house, and the cat and I revel in the bliss of being let alone for a few days. If I had had wings or snow-shoes, I should have come your way. I came many times in spirit as it was, but spirits are greatly hampered, and are very helpless. I wish we might carry our bodies with us into the next world.

In March I spent two weeks in Washington, but the air was full of ghosts to me — ghosts of departed friends and departed days. . . .

I have material for a book on W. W. which I shall have put in type before long. I have too much, and am holding on to see how much it will shrink.

. . . I think you will be interested in Professor Trigg's book on Whitman and Browning, lately published by Macmillan & Co. It is not very wonderful, but it shows that Whitman's soul is marching on.

I am so glad that you and Miss Jordan are coming to Poughkeepsie. If the weather is fair you shall come up here and we will picnic in the woods.

Many self-delineating passages from the Journal must be omitted, not because they are 'pithy turnips,' but because, however crisp and good, they are so numerous. One cannot, however, omit an April entry — the embryo of his delightful verses 'The Song of the Toad.' ('Bird and Bough.') With each returning spring this insistent, persistent, pervasive call appeals to him:

Warm and bright, real vernal warmth. Currants showing the fruit stems. These days the song of the toad — *tr-r-r-r-r-r-r-r-* — is heard in the land. At nearly all hours I hear it, and it is as welcome as any bird song. She is in the pools and puddles now depositing that long chain or ravelling of eggs. Her dapper little mate rides upon her broad back and fertilizes the eggs as they are laid.

Yet the April twilights were to come and go for many a year before he was to celebrate in verse that solo of the blinking toad, that 'tender monotone of song' rising from the ponds and pools, which to him symbolized the knell of winter.

A characteristic passage from the Journal, April 29, blends his present with his past:

May Atlantic came this morning and recalled a May Atlantic that came thirty-two years ago, on such a morning, when I was living at Marlboro. It had an essay in it by David A. Wasson, on 'Rest and Motion,' and I remember well how eagerly I sat down outside the door to dip into it before school-time. The hills across the river were green with the young rye, or red with the new furrow, and life to me was full of joy and eagerness.

Oh, if I could take up this Atlantic with the same zest and expectation! Yet the day is sweet to me. The call of the highhole as it comes up from a distant field has the old suggestiveness. Even the wheezy cackle of the crow-blackbird is pleasing. Why do all the bird voices call up my youth and the Old Home? It is something of those long-gone days that makes them linger in my ear.

I have just been out digging rocks with the boys, and satisfying a sort of craving for rocks and soil that comes upon me in the spring. Father was a great rock-digger and rock-breaker. Every spring, till he got too old, he used to build a piece of wall with stone from a meadow or pasture, and thus make many spears of grass grow where none grew before. It is a keen satisfaction. In a few days now we have made room for several more grape-vines by digging out the place-rock where it came to the surface. We broke the sleep of long ages of those rocks, sometimes with bars and wedges, sometimes with dynamite. Where the sun has not shone in some millions of years, we let it in. In seams all but invisible, we find fibres of roots, and now and then a lichenous growth merely discoloring the stone. How life will squeeze into the narrowest quarters!

Now he and Julian take a long tramp through Bear Fly; the woods are flooded with sunlight; they start up a bittern; they scale the rocky crests and scramble through sunken valleys. Halted by the swift waters of Black Creek, they build a bridge of stones, and push on. Presently they meet a family group of hepaticas — blue, pink, white, purple — 'like bevies of happy-faced girls on their way to a picnic'; now they come upon dicentra — 'fairy clothes-lines strung along the faces of the rocks, and hung with yellow-white breeches, or, were they strung to the hoisting-poles?' Now they reach an abandoned farm, where they have an adventure with a black snake; they flush a grouse; they struggle through a swamp, winding in and out of the bushes, and finally mount Sherwood's Hill, where, looking down from its summit, they shout to Sherwood that they have scaled his works from the rear, and demand instant surrender. Out comes the family, waving a welcome; and down the winding stairway of rocks the travelers make their way, while the bleating sheep and lambs crowd about. Then home by another route, finding arbutus hiding under the leaves. Truly, 'a day long to be remembered.' Blest was the boy who had that April walk, and blest is he who may have that, and other walks, even by proxy! How many such days Burroughs gathered into his heart — April, May, and June days, and on through the calendar! Minot Savage once said that John Burroughs got a little more of June than the rest of us get, because, through years of consecration to all that June offers, he had earned the right to take June into brain and heart and life. What month has he not taken into his heart and life? April most, perhaps, June next, but it is almost equally true of the whole round year.

May 10. Rare May days, perfect. Every hour a new delight. A tender green awakening over all the trees. How the river sparkles in the soft morning light! Nearly all the birds here except cuckoo. The white-crowned sparrows sing — *Oh, feu, fee-u, fee fee* — with indescribable plaintiveness and sweetness. Promises of a tremendous currant crop.

Such days in my youth on the old farm I would be spreading dung, or knocking 'Juno's cushions,' and looking wistfully towards the horizon. Oh, that I could go back into that enchanted land! But we never know it is enchanted when we are in it.

Over those hills now the plow is turning the furrow as I saw it in youth; the woods and fields look the same. Yet how all is changed! because the eye that sees it is changed; it is getting old and sated. Bobolinks yesterday and today in song as they pass overhead.

May 11. The delicious May days continue. Not a cloud by day or night. Sun warm, melting, wooing. Cherry trees a mass of white bloom. The air fairly shaken with bird voices. The cuckoo and orchard starling here this morning. Maple leaves like tiny, half-opened parasols. River like a mirror, dotted with the shad fishers. What a racket the orioles make! The kinglets silent for two days past. White-crowned sparrow in song. The song of the toad is still heard.

As I sit here in the summer-house at 8.30, a soft, moist, cool haze shuts down and veils all distant objects. Beyond the [Crum] Elbow all is a white obscurity.

Why do I think of Father and Mother so often such days? Just such days came to them. How busy and eager they were about their work! I see the cows hurried off to the pasture, the teams started for the fields, or to haul out manure. I see Father striding across the ploughed field with a bag partly filled with oats slung across his breast, from which he clutches a handful of seed and scatters at every step. The mountains begin to show signs of foliage near their bases, but on the summits the trees are still naked, or maybe a little snow gleams out here and there amid the trees.

12. . . . This day Symonds' book on Whitman came to me, and I nearly finished it at odd intervals, sitting in the summer-house and looking out into the lovely world.

It is a strong book and will play its part in settling W.'s fame. I see in it little to except to. The hearty endorsement of the sexual poems quite surprised me. Symonds acknowledges his own debt to Whitman in strong, eloquent words. I suppose the very first order of men never owe so great a debt as this to a book. They get it at first hand from God, from Nature, from the soul. Men of the stamp of Symonds, and of myself, get it from our masters.

I could have wept over the book, thinking of Symonds just dead, and his words ringing so clear and eloquent; and of Walt, whom my soul so loved.

[Journal] May 24. To Mount Auburn Cemetery, to the graves of Lowell, Longfellow, and Phillips Brooks. A lovely spot, ideal. At the foot of the grave of Brooks, in one of the iron gate-posts, find the nest of a chickadee.

To Wellesley College in p.m. A place of great natural beauty, probably the finest college grounds in the country. In evening speak to the students, four or five hundred in the hall. Talk too long — over an hour — rather better than at Norton.

Having acquired the habit of going, he attends a Greek play at Vassar, and the Whitman birthday dinner in New York, saying of his speech at the latter that he did not speak to his own satisfaction — did not say the best things he had in mind. On June 1st, he meets John Muir — 'an interesting man with the Western look upon him. Not quite enough penetration in his eyes.' On return home, he and Julian and young Ben Ali Haggin camp out in Snyder Hollow (Wood- land Valley). Of this he writes a friend, 'I am just back from camping in the Catskills and the fragrance of the hemlock boughs is yet in my clothes, and the songs of the brooks yet in my ears.'

That summer there came the first letter he ever received from Theodore Roosevelt, written from Washington, D.C., on black-bordered paper, its juvenile chirography so at variance with its contents. Roosevelt wrote that he was sending him his 'Wilderness Hunter.' He called attention to his having quoted Whitman in it, and alluded to Burroughs. He wrote of his particular admiration for Burroughs's two essays, 'Before Beauty,' and 'Before Genius,' and wished the ideas in them could be drilled into our people, and especially our literary people, and confessed that he had with difficulty refrained from urging Burroughs's writings, not merely upon the lover of nature, but upon lovers of manliness and right doing, and of their country.

To Myron Benton, on June 27th, Burroughs writes:

Your letter finds me with a sort of spring torpor upon me. I want to doze in my chair and do a good part of the time. I hope I am making new wood — arms for next year's fruit, like my vines, — but I doubt it . . .

He must have done something besides doze in his chair the next few weeks, since his Journal mentions shipping 2100 and 2300 pounds of currants a day, in addition to which he is keeping house for himself and Julian, canning cherries, and fighting grape-rot and leaf-mildew; with the strenuous raspberry campaign following close upon the currants. In mid-July, he and Julian drive to Lake Mohonk with Mr. W. S. Kennedy. The grandeur of the rocks and the unique beauty of Mohonk impress him afresh on each visit. Some days later he makes his first ascent of Slide Mountain, the highest peak of the Catskills.

[Journal] 22. Tramp up Big Indian valley today with my roll of blankets on my back. . . . Reach the summit about two and pass the night there. A good time all alone with that sublime view. Porcupines very plenty and annoying at night. I make a nest under the ledge of rocks on the summit and sleep fairly well. A grand view of a storm from 7 to 8. Look straight out into its heart of fire. . . .

The next day he wrote that he had tramped the twenty-six miles more easily than he ever did a like distance, and added:

'What a vivid sense of the presence of those mountains I brought back with me!'

After the strenuous 'grape racket' in September, during which time he shipped more than thirty-six tons of grapes, and still had several tons on the vines, the market suddenly went flat, so he sat down and wrote an article on Poe.

A November letter to Benton gives his reactions to recent experiences:

I thought we would be at one in our opinions about Poe. E. E. Hale, Jr., of Iowa State University, has a letter in this week's Dial by way of rejoinder. The letter is good, in admirable style, and I agree with it. It only says, in effect, that while what I say may be true enough, yet style, form, art, must be insisted upon, too, especially in this country where the tendency is too strong the other way. Mr. [Francis Fisher] Browne (he asked me for the article) says the paper has provoked a good deal of discussion, which was what he wanted. . . .

I felt little enthusiasm over the [Chicago] Fair. It was rather a perfunctory matter with me. I reckon I have about lost my appetite for seeing things. The group of buildings was superb, like an architect's boldest and grandest dream, and the things inside them were all one could expect, and more. The world belongs to the young. The Fair is for the young; I was impressed more and more with the fact that the world is full of young people. You and I, Myron, will soon be 'old coves.' How empty the world seems to get as one grows older — that is, empty of interesting and important things. I find I do not cut half the leaves of the magazines any more. I have no fears lest I miss some important thing; and the days, too, are beginning to pass with me, with uncut leaves. I suppose it is a tendency we should struggle against. I do occasionally try to get up an interest in a walk, and when Julian can go with me I do very well. The other day I forced myself into the woods with a gun, and was rewarded with a partridge — the first for fifteen years; and yet I was sorry the moment I saw the poor bird fall. It is harder and harder to kill things — even a chicken. Ah, me! if we should live to be as old as some of your ancestors and relatives, what would become of us! My enjoyment of the world and of life has been very keen, hence, I suppose, this approaching satiety.

I went out to the Old Home after you were here. I get thirsty for those fountains of youth, but I find it is an unquenchable thirst. 'Gone, gone!' is written upon every field and object there. . . .

It is noteworthy that this mournful letter was written in the evening of the same day on which he had tramped the woods with his mattock, and spent several strenuous hours, handling a ton of earth over two or three times, full of eagerness and curiosity, to find the banqueting-hall in a weasel's den.[1] It illustrates the truth of what he so often said, 'I am an optimist by day, a pessimist at night.' Alone in his Study that evening, weary from the long tramp and the arduous work, his brooding thoughts found him out, and he wrote sadly to his friend; but the next morning, as the Journal shows, armed with shovel and mattock, he returned to the investigations; and, doubtless any one who could have seen him working there, would have found it difficult to believe that the hand that wielded the heavy tools was the same that had penned that doleful letter.[2]

[Journal] Dec. 5. . . . Read some chapters in one or two of my books, sitting alone here by the fire the other night. I could have wept over them — they were so fresh and joyous, so untouched by the fret and fever of the world. Where is the paradise I lived in when I wrote these books? Here, right here where I now live. A kind of perennial youth breathes in those books. No merit of mine. I could not help it.

One of his infrequent comments on political topics is here transcribed:

In the Garfield-Conkling controversy, as related by Senator Dawes in the last Century, there are the elements of a great tragedy, like the Greek plays. Here was this haughty, imperious, eloquent Conkling refusing to take the magnanimous part, refusing to believe in it at all; refusing to credit the people with any love of magnanimity; believing in nothing but party and in crushing your rival; incapable of taking a large, disinterested view of the situation; full of hate, jealousy, selfishness — to rule and triumph with him being more than country, or duty, or truth; seeing everything through the passion of personal pride. Here was this man, at last a victim of his own selfishness and conceit — crushed by the popular feeling of magnanimity, which he refused to believe in; utterly humiliated and rejected by the party he had placed before country or duty! What bitterness was his! Did the Furies ever before so blind a man for his own destruction? One of the proudest men that ever walked, brought to the deepest humiliation by his own deliberate folly!
Every politician in this country who has presumed upon the narrowness and the meanness of the people has come to grief. Conkling did. Blaine did. Hill did. No clap-trap, nothing theatrical, or

---

[1] 'Eye-Beams' (*Riverby*).
[2] Once, when going over these letters to elucidate them, on my exclaiming at the pathos of that line, — 'The days, too, are beginning to pass with me, with uncut leaves,' — it sounded so much sadder than his prevailing mood, he laughed almost sheepishly, and said, 'You see my weakness — that habit of retrospection — and besides, I was older then than I am now, I guess.'

that has the air of self-seeking, is a success. Honors and victory come to the disinterested man.

Then, out of the spirit which Conkling stirred up, and of which he was the arch-fiend, came the murder of the President. Think of that long suspense and agony — the Nation sitting by the bedside of this dying man! The elements of an immortal tragedy, unsurpassed by anything in history!

Conkling was great only as a party boss and leader. Dawes says his speech before the Committee of Conciliation was the greatest of his life — his theme was himself, and his own political grievances. These inspired him. Any great cause or principle outside of himself never so inspired him. His country never made him so eloquent. He had no self-forgetfulness, no magnanimity, no true greatness. Theme for a lecture — 'The People's Rebuke to the Politicians.'

Feb. 26. Took down Carlyle's 'Past and Present' last night and leafed it over for half an hour, tasting it here and there. I was glad I did not feel obliged to read it again. It is hard reading. I confess I did not want to be bruised and bumped about by a ride over this rough road. Run the eye over the page and see how rough and thorny it looks, and it feels no less so to the mind. The great classical turn-pikes, how different!

In Carlyle's prose at its worst, as in Browning's poetry, the difficulties are mechanical; it is not in the thought, it is in the expression. There is fire and intensity about it. But a blow with a club will make you see stars, or a sudden jolt give you a vivid sense of real things....

Carlyle will never be forgotten. He is one of the few monumental writers, but probably he will be named and referred to oftener than he is read.... A man's private storms and whirlpools and despairs and indigestion ought to appear in his work only as power, or light, or richness of tone. It is near 50 years since 'Past and Present' was written, and none of its dire prophecies have yet come true. Yet I love this Scotch Jeremiah as I love few men.

Feb. 29.... Milton's poetry, for the most part, is to me a kind of London Tower filled with old armor, stuffed knights, wooden chargers, and the emblems and bedizzlements of the past. Interesting for a moment, but dead, hollow, moth-eaten. Not a live thing in one of his poems that I can find. Yes, there is a nightingale, and there are a few flowers, and a human touch here and there; but half a dozen pages would hold all that any man need read.

The 'Samson' is said to be in the Greek spirit, but what business had he, a Puritan of Cromwell's time, writing in the Greek spirit? Why did he not write in his own spirit, or in the Puritan spirit? the 17th century spirit? What business had he masquerading in this old armor? He put no real life under these ribs of death. His 'Paradise Lost' is a huge puppet-show, so grotesque and preposterous that it is quite insufferable.

Milton seems to have been a real man, but he stands there in

English literature like a great museum of literary archæology. He seems to have had no experiences of his own, and rarely to have seen the earth and sky, or men and women, with his own natural eyes. He saw everything through the classic eyes of the dead past. Who reads him? Professors of literature, I suppose. He was a great craftsman, no doubt, but he has been of no service to mankind, except a literary service; he has helped us to realize the classic spirit of letters, and the absurdity of the old theological dramiturgy. He spoke no word to any man's real moral or spiritual wants.

March 18. . . . Standing after night-fall now anywhere on the lawn, one hears a slow stirring or rustling in the leaves and dry grass. It is made by large earth-worms coming up out of their burrows and rushing out over the ground, whether for feeding or breeding, I know not. J[ulian] calls them 'night walkers.' In summer he hunts them at night to make bobs of. They are very sly and jerk swiftly back in their holes on the slightest sound. I suppose they feel your footstep on the ground.

March 22. . . . A passage omitted, on second thought, from my essay in last Critic on the Sapphic Secret:
Discursive and experimental writers, like Mr. Thompson and my-self, — the mere nibbling mice of criticism — should temper their wrath when they sit in judgment upon the great ones — the lions who make the paths through the jungles of the world. It is no fault of theirs that they are not mice, but is it not a fault of ours that we do not see them to be lions?

March 31. Wonderful aurora last night, beyond any I have ever before seen. Once while a boy I saw something approaching it.
The wonder of this display was that it made a complete circle all around the horizon. We stood in the midst of a great tent of stream-ing aurora. The ghostly flame shot up from north, east, south, west, and came to a focus just a few degrees south of our meridian. Never before have I seen it rise up from the south.
The apex of this tent was the scene of constantly shifting and vanishing forms of light. It was fairly apocryphal. At times it seemed as if the heavens opened at this point, and troops of angels and wingèd horses came straight toward us. A pencil like Doré's would have caught many suggestions. Sometimes the electric clouds would gather at this point like foam over the point of an escaping fluid, and whirl about. Sometimes there would be curious openings through it where the black sky and the stars would appear. A deep crimson flush would appear here and there near the horizon, and spread upwards to the zenith. . . .
Never was anything more spectral and unearthly. It was a wild dance of many-colored, sheeted, ghostly forms. What an impression such a phenomenon must have made upon rude primitive man! I myself could hardly keep down an emotion of superstitious fear.

[J. B. to L. L. P.]

... Do you mind my passage at arms with Maurice Thompson in the Critic? I may touch him up again, as he beats the air so wildly. I am not in any of those places where he plants his blows, and the issue between us is not there. He is always snarling and snapping at the heels of Whitman and Tolstoy like a whiffet dog at the heels of a bear, and I thought that for once I would shy a pebble at him.

[J. B. to Mrs. B. A. H.]

April 21. I was disappointed that you and your party did not come yesterday. So I walked to the woods alone and plucked the first arbutus — only a spray or two here and there. Such a perfect day and yet you did not come! And your letter did not give me much cheer. I so dislike to make this public exhibition of myself. Can this bitter cup not be passed by? Must I drink it in order to see you? I have nothing to say to those people. I cannot tell them how to teach Nature in the schools. Nature cannot be taught, and I cannot bring the country with me to give you all a whiff of it. I might come with some hay-seed in my hair, and some road-dust on my shoes — and then you would be ashamed of me. Seriously, I fear you will not get much talk out of me, tho' I might answer questions about my crops and the state of the market, or tell you of the gossip about my hives, and the flirtations in my trees. Well, we will see. Do not make your occasion hinge entirely upon me and then it will be easier for me. ...

Ploughing, writing, concerned over a brood of possums, converting the wagon-house into a fruit-house, reminiscing, dreaming — so go the days.

[Journal] April 27. ... A few days ago the air was filled with a delicious wild perfume, a pungent, stimulating, bitter-sweet odor. I could not trace it to its source. It seemed to be general, and to fill all the air. Was it from the just-bursting buds of the sugar maples? I know of no other likely source.

Tops of trees over in Langdon's woods just faintly etched in opening leaf-buds. Currants blooming.

On the night of the 24th went up to Kingston to hear and see Ingersoll [Robert G.]. Much stouter and redder than when I saw him last May. Can drink whiskey, he says, but not wine. Wine makes him throb and throb. He ate his supper in his room after the lecture; drank iced-milk and iced-water freely.

Lecture full of telling points, much sound argument, and many eloquent passages.

April 28. A lovely day, a feminine day, veiled, tranquil, almost voluptuous. ...

Had a glimpse of Father the other night in my dreams. We were at the table, and a plate of trout was passed around, and I saw Father pick out the big one, as I have so often seen him do. I smiled in my sleep.

May steals in, warm and soft; the wood thrush arrives; he notes the first run of shad; the apple trees are leaping into bloom; he dips into Edmund Gosse's 'Notes on Walt Whitman,' and confides to his Journal that he regards Gosse, though clever, as a very small critic, a man who has spent his days in overhauling and sorting the small potatoes of English literature, and who knows much about said literature that is not worth knowing, and that would be a weariness to know. Continuing:

He sees nothing but a barbarous, unregenerated poetic nature in W. W. . . . He thinks the secret of Whitman's attraction for certain minds is that they see themselves in him. Well, a poet in whom such men as Stevenson, Symonds, Emerson, Thoreau, and others, see themselves must be something or somebody. . . . In Mr. Gosse's poems we see only little Mr. Gosse. When we can all see ourselves in him, he will have increased immensely in size and importance.

One recalls how well the now caustic critic of Mr. Gosse liked him on meeting him a few years before, but let any one tread on Whitman's toes, and John Burroughs was there to chastise vigorously.

After a midsummer visit to the Old Home, reflections on the style of Walter Pater are mingled in the Journal with accounts of raids on the woodchucks, some of the latter of which are here transcribed:

In my woodchuck-shooting I lingered much about Grandfather's old place over the hill — killed 5 or 6 'chucks there, two that lived in the cellar of the old house. Think of shooting wild creatures peering out from the ruins of your grandfather's house! I dug out the spring and drank there — the spring where my ancestors slaked their thirst one hundred years ago. Father had played here as a child, and here Mother did her first washing after her marriage. A little sparrow had its nest amid the weeds and briars where stood the old house, and sang so sweetly but plaintively to my ear — a bird song amid graves.

To Mabie, that autumn, he wrote appreciatively:

You have again placed me so largely in your debt that I fear I shall never be able to balance the account. Your editorial is the most penetrating and appreciative piece of writing I have yet seen upon my little books. I thank you with all my heart.

You have one invaluable trait of a critic, or [of] any writer — one of the prime essentials of all greatness — generosity. You can be generous without flattery — the generosity of a broad, open, affirmative mind. I am always refreshed by the large and generous appreciation of your Outlook essays. I speak of this one feature especially, because it seems to me it is very rare in current criticism.

My hasty talk as it appears there spread out over your pages seems very choppy, or sort of bob-tailed to me. I wonder that you made room for so much of it.

I have been wanting for years to have a visit from you, but the domestic divinities or furies, or both, have always been unfavorable. The question of help in the kitchen threatens to wreck us. An acquaintance once met Emerson in the train on the way to Boston. 'Where are you going?' he inquired. 'To get an angel to do the cooking,' replied the sage. When angels are willing to cook, I think the kitchen problems in this country will be solved. . . .

This glimpse of Charles Dudley Warner in his Hartford home:

Warner meets me at the station and we are soon at his house — a charming place surrounded by noble trees with long vistas. Like W. very much — a man to love, — gentle, mellow, human, with droll surprises in his talk as in his writings. Reminds me of Myron Benton. Wish I could see him daily. His house full of books and inviting chairs and nooks — the ideal scholar's house, pictures, too, and curios — a house like the man.

October 9th. Just heard of the death of Holmes — no news of warning sickness had reached me. Even his cheer and vivacity have at last yielded. . . . The last star of that remarkable constellation of New England authors. I owe him entertainment and more or less stimulus, but probably no deep service. A brilliant talker; in letters gifted with both wit and humor, and the poetic temperament — an open fire to warm your hands by. He had the gift that makes literature — something direct and intimate — his mind touched yours. One of the best of our discursive writers.

Again and again his mind dwells upon the hope of organizing a community of congenial literary friends. One such attempt is seen in excerpts from a letter to Miss Ludella Peck:

Mr. and Mrs. [Percival] Chubb are charming people, and I am the richer for their acquaintance. He is a modest, thoughtful, genuine fellow, and she is one of the best types of the coming American woman. I hope to see more of them. They are talking about getting a lodge up in the Catskills. Could not you be induced to build a hut

up there also? A few of us might form a little community up there
and get some satisfaction out of our summer vacations in a simple
and rational way. There is health and long life amid those mountains. The Adirondacks are too far and too expensive.

Nothing very eventful has happened to me since I wrote you on
my birthday last April. I have had a few bright days, many gray
ones and a few dark ones. I fear I have not grown much in grace nor
much in wisdom. I have sent to market twenty tons of grapes, and
about two ounces of manuscript.

[Journal] 13. Never a morning does Julian start off for school but
I long to go with him, to be his mate and equal; to share his en-
thusiasms, his anticipations; his games, his fun. Oh, to see life
through his eyes again! How young the world is to him, how un-
tried, how enticing! How he enjoys his holidays! On his last holiday,
as he sat eating his breakfast, he said, 'How glad I am it is this
morning, and not tonight!' The whole day with all its possibilities
was before him. When he came back at night after his long tramp,
without any game, he was still excited and happy over what he
might have seen, or might have got, had there not been any *if* in the
way. Ah! the happy boy!

29. New book ['Riverby'] came today. Doubtless the last of my
out-door series [*sic*]. I look it over with a sigh. For a quarter of a
century I have been writing these books — living them first, and
then writing them out. What serene joy I have had in gathering this
honey! And now I begin to feel that it is about over with me. My
interest, my curiosity, are getting blunted.

In 'The Halcyon in Canada' ('Locusts and Wild Honey'),
he said that the French Canadians call the white-throat *la
siffleur;* but on being set right by Dr. van Dyke (who wrote
him that that term is used for the hawk, the white-throat being
called *le rossignol*), he replied as follows: [1]

You could not please me better than by saying my books are true;
their truthfulness is the one quality I am sure of. That you love
them, and can read them in the woods, is good evidence that they
have other qualities also. You know what literature is, and have
made the article yourself and I trust will make much more.

I am glad to hear you have climbed Slide. I wish you had been
with me there last July. I passed a night alone on the summit — had
the whole universe to myself. A big storm came up and I could look
squarely into the thunder-cloud and see the bo[l]ts forged. . . .

Thank you for setting me right about the white-throat. I should
have asked more persons about it. It is very pleasant to hear the
Canadians have bestowed so fond a title upon it. Two years ago I

---

[1] This and other letters from J. B. to H. v. D. are kindly lent by Dr. van Dyke.

found the bird in full song in the Catskills near Onteora Park in the month of July. Of course it breeds there. Just now I see the fox sparrow on the snow in front of my window. It is a wonderful songster, and more of a whistler than the white-throat.

Sir Arthur (then Mr.) Conan Doyle is thus characterized after he meets him in New York:

A large, hearty John Bull, plain features, but a good healthy, fresh, boyish nature. Liked him much. Mr. Mabie presided with his usual skill. Of the speakers I was most drawn to Mr. Frost, president of some college in Kentucky — plain, earnest, native, good — no vanity, no attempt at oratory, excellent.

Early in the new year, chiding himself for not having attended the Stevenson Memorial meeting, the journalist thus comments on R. L. S.:

His death fills quite a space in my thoughts. He seems nearer to me than any other contemporary British man of letters — of the younger school.

Some one has said, 'Be an artist, or prepare for oblivion.' Stevenson was an artist, and he is safe from oblivion, for a time at least. Yet he is not one of the great ones. His literary equipment surpasses his more solid native human equipment, as with so many of the late school of writers. He was not a man of mass and power, any more than I am. We are all light-weights, and try to make up in cleverness what we lack in scope and power.

Stevenson is not one of the men we *must* read. We can pass him by; but he is one of the men who fills the hour and relieves the tedium of life. He inspires love, and the thought of him as gone from life, and sleeping there in far-off Samoa on a mountain-peak, fills me with sadness.

[J. B. to L. L. P.] April 7

Your birthday greeting warmed and cheered my heart. Your golden thoughts and wishes brought me a golden day — all sun and sky, and part of it was passed at my old home. That you were thinking of me that bright morning and wishing in my behalf, is something I like to dwell upon. It blends in with the thoughtful yearning mood that possessed me all that day. Nothing else came to me so precious as your greeting. What does life yield, anyway, to be compared with love, sympathy, appreciation? all else is dust and ashes. I reciprocate your affection and good wishes most sincerely. You are a true, tender, noble woman and I love you much. I wish and wish that I could see you oftener; that you lived near me. You would be a great comfort and help to me, and maybe I might add a ray of sunshine to your life also. I do hope our paths will intersect somewhere this summer. What fun if the Chubbs and you and I could pitch a tent together somewhere in the Catskills in July or August! . . . I am hoping to hear that they want me to find them a house up here for the summer. Then surely you will come? If you do not, and I can get away, I shall come to Northampton. So swift the years fly, so soon the end comes!

. . . I found the robins piping and laughing here on my return, the sparrows singing, the phœbe calling, and the river free of ice. Every spring the river is born again. Its youth is immortal. The hills grow old and perish, but the river is ever renewed. I have not heard the highhole yet, nor the turtle-dove, but the fox-sparrow sang this morning, and yesterday I heard the first warbler over in the woods. I am eager to go forth with the bees and gather the first spring pollen, April pollen. How one hungers for the new bread of Nature at this time. I trust you find some of it in your walks. I am sure if I were there we could find a little of it. The pussy willows yield pollen to me before they do to the bees, and I am sure I find it in the air where they do not.

On Friday I heard the first piping frog in the wood. I think it had just woke up. In a few days now the whole clan will be gathered in the marshes, and my ear will again hear the chorus it so loves.

Well, my dear friend, spring has come again. I hope it may come to our hearts and make them bud afresh — make our friendship put out new shoots and flowers. I trust it may lighten your cares and brighten your days. I shall cherish the thought of you, and waft you good wishes from the April hill-tops.

Oh, do not wait till my birthday to write again! Every April day is my birthday.

CHAPTER XIII

THE RETREAT TO THE WOODS

1895-1899

I will arise and go now, and go to Innisfree,
  And a small cabin build there, of clay and wattles made;
Nine bean rows will I have there, a hive for the honey-bee,
  And live alone in the bee-loud glade.

And I shall have some peace there, for peace comes dropping slow,
  Dropping from the veils of the morning to where the cricket sings;
There midnight's all a-glimmer, and noon a purple glow,
  And evening full of the linnet's wings.

W. B. YEATS

WITH the spring of 1895 a vague hope, long held by John Burroughs, began to shape toward realization. For years he had roamed the wild region in the hills a mile and more from his river home, skated the woodland pools, tracked the walkers in the snow, sought the cypripediums in the swamps and the arbutus under the hoary hemlocks, and had sighed for a lodge in that wilderness; and yet the first steps which he took toward it were seemingly foreign to the lodge — were chiefly concerned in reclaiming the wild swamp-land roundabout. He knew the rich black soil would grow superior garden produce, and when Amasa Martin, a young farmer, grew enthusiastic over the project, Burroughs advanced him the money to buy a hundred acres of the wild land, reserving for himself twenty acres of cliff and swamp, in part payment. They made a road through the woods, drained the swamp, dug out stumps, and literally skinned the land to get down to the rich black muck.

The first mention of the undertaking in the Journal appears on May 1st, when he writes of blasting out rocks in the muckswamp; and on the morrow:

All day at the swamp with George and Charley. Break through the rocky barrier today and let the water out. I lay a long time on the rocks. Shad-blow just out; little leaves the size of mouse-ears all about me. How lovely the world looks! Even Popple Town hill from my perch on the rocks looks classical. As I come home the perfume of the sugar-maple by the roadside falls upon me, sweet as apple-bloom.

On return from a visit in New York he writes characteristically to his hostess:

I am again deep in my beloved muck-swamp, but the thing fights back with poisoned sumac, so that if I were with you now, I should be compelled to look at you with only one eye, which I can assure you would be a great privation. I had rather look at you with half a dozen eyes, and even then my vision would not keep pace with my admiration. You know I like you better than a muck-swamp. I know you have no venom. You are like one of the splendid white cypripediums that often bloom above the peaty soil.

He could no more resist making a pretty speech to a pretty woman than he could withhold homage from the woodland flowers along his path.

[Journal] June 14. I do not seem to be getting much out of these June days. Every day I go to the muck-swamp; every day I listen to the birds; every day I sit in the summer-house and look long and wistfully upon the river and the landscape beyond; every day I think of Father and Mother and the Old Home; every day I wish and wish for I know not what; every day I try to read in books, but feel only a languid interest.

I think in living here I have always had the feeling of an exile. I am away from my own, though I hardly know what my own is. As nearly as I can define it, it is my family, and the Old Home. The Past, oh, the Past!

A dour stroke of fortune came to him in July when a storm of rain and hail destroyed nearly all his grapes:

[Journal.] Probably three inches of water fell in less than one half-hour. Two clouds or storms met and fought it out just over my vineyard. Each cloud apparently gutted the other, and one came down as hail, the other as rain, all in a heap. No damage done over the river, or north or west of us.

One seems to accompany him on the walk recorded August 12th:

Nearly every day I walk over to my muck-swamp for a taste of the wild. . . . The walk through the woods, the glimpses, the vistas, the sudden revelation of the bit of prairie surrounded by gray rocky arms; Amasa swinging his bogging-hoe in the solitude; the fat, marrowy soil; the sitting on a fern hassock, and the talk and gossip; then the spring, and the long, delicious draught repeated again and again; then the Scotch-caps and black-berries; then the slow loitering and browsing about — how sweet it all is! I look away to the west and north, and there is the distant landscape with farms and woodlands; and beyond all the blue curve of the Catskills. Then I come back refreshed.

At this point, Hiram, homeless and poor, came to Riverby hoping to settle down there; but his presence, as obnoxious to Mrs. Burroughs as it was welcome to his brother, caused the latter to cast about as to how he could provide a home for Hiram, and also indulge his ingrained hospitality toward other friends without burdening his wife with the cares which such hospitality would entail. Thus the rustic retreat began to take shape in his thoughts, and, not long after, by the swamp itself.

The first mention of the cabin in the Journal is on November 25th, when, after a jaunt to New York, he records, 'Home today and at work on the house in the woods.'

His frank pleasure at his success in speaking in public is seen in a preceding entry:

This day I speak to the girls at Packer Institute — a large hall, a large audience. I speak on the Art of Seeing Things with marked success. My first real success on the platform. I am tickled with myself. I find the large audience, the large hall, like swimming in deep water; 'tis very easy. Had I been told beforehand what was before me, I should never have dared to undertake it. Mr. Proctor was enthusiastic; said no speaker since Curtis had so pleased a Brooklyn audience. We were just the opposite, he said: Curtis's was Art, mine was Nature. I told him I was a green-horn. 'Then remain a green-horn all your life,' said he.

In the morning I go with Chubb to the High school and speak to the boys, in the evening to a Whitman dinner, where I speak again, but not with much fulness or go — am not well prepared. . . .

Saturday. Stayed with Proctor last night and heard the nightingale. It sang well, he said, but did not fully let itself out like the wild bird. Its song is a brilliant medley, no theme that I could detect, like the lark's song. All the notes of the field and forest the gift of this bird; but I cannot judge its song till I hear it in nature where it belongs.

Sunday. . . . Go to Plymouth church and hear [Lyman] Abbott. Eloquence a little perfunctory, a little of the sin of which most preachers have so much, and whereof 'a little more than a little is by much too much.' Why not speak naturally and just as you feel? Why be moved until your theme moves you? Let a man be eloquent when he can't help it. Yet Abbott is a fine preacher, and a liberal, growing man.

Before the Women's University Club also he speaks, but a few days later he is absorbed in rapidly pushing up the stone

THE BARK STUDY AT RIVERBY

SLABSIDES NEAR WEST-PARK-ON-THE-HUDSON

chimney of his cabin, with the help of a stone-mason, and is
'happy all the day long.' They finished the chimney the day
before Christmas. The next day 'the boys' from Poughkeepsie picnicked with him in the cabin, 'the boys' being a group
of friends, of which Mr. Edmund Platt was one, who came
often thereafter to the woodland retreat.

The little bark-covered cabin had not yet received its ex-
pressive name, but Slab Rest, Foot Cliffs, Crag's Foot, Rock
Haven, Whippoorwill's Nest, Coon Hollow, and Echo Lodge
were, in turn, tried out as the shelter neared completion.
While the various names were being tested, he sent this bit of
fooling to a metropolitan friend:

I have been building me a retreat over by the muck-swamp, to be
called Echo Castle. My plan was to kidnap you and fetch you here
of a dark stormy night and imprison you, and keep you from New
York for a whole year, and make you well again with love and
tenderness, and so lay the foundation of a beautiful legend that
would in time greatly enhance the value of my wild possessions; but
now you have relented and written to me, and asked me down, I
shall postpone the execution of my audacious plan awhile. Maybe
I can inveigle you up here without resort to force.

I am sorry you are not well, and I shall not easily forgive you. I
keep pretty well, and expect to till the end.

A neighbor, Mrs. William van Benschoten, suggested the
name 'Slabsides,' and on January 28th it is first called by that
name in the Journal.

The muck-swamp and the rustic cabin lie in a depression
of the hills behind West-Park-on-the-Hudson. The place is
reached by going west from the railway station for perhaps
half a mile along the country road, then turning to the left
into the woods for a mile more. Traversing the rough, winding
road through the woods, one comes rather unexpectedly upon
the little slab-covered house — a bit of human handiwork
tucked away in that rock-girt basin. There it nestles in the
clearing, vine-covered, rude and substantial without, snug
and comfortable within.

Celery and lettuce in the black soil give a welcome touch
of domesticity to savage nature roundabout!

Visitors to the cabin may recall these lines of Charles
Cotton, which the Seer of Slabsides was wont to quote con-
tentedly:

Good God! how sweet are all things here!
How beautiful the fields appear!
　How cleanly do we feed and lie!
Lord! what good hours do we keep!
How quietly we sleep!
　What peace, what unanimity!
How innocent from the lewd fashion
Is all our business, all our recreation!
　·　·　·　·　·　·　·　·

How calm and quiet a delight
　Is it, alone,
To read and meditate and write,
　By none offended, and offending none!
To walk, ride, sit, or sleep at one's own ease;
And, pleasing a man's self, none other to displease.

The roomy veranda, with rustic railing and shaggy cedar posts, the sloping roof, the great chimney, the climbing vines, the wide rustic door with latch-string out, and a curiously twisted knurl for a door-knob, all fit into the picture. The cabin is a story and a half. The seams of the plain boards of the interior are covered with split-birch saplings. Originally the rafters had the bark on, but they have been denuded by wood-borers, which have left a delicate tracery instead. A satiny yellow birch partition separates the living-room and bedroom on the lower floor. Stairs lead to the loft, which has a guest-room, and a roomy attic, with extra cots. The bedsteads are made of satiny birch. The furniture is home-made. The legs of tables, stands, window-seat, and mantel-trimming, of sumac limbs, have a spiral twist, from the imprint of the climbing bitter-sweet. A smoky iron tea-kettle hangs from the swinging crane in the wide stone fireplace; on the hearth are old-time andirons and tongs. The built-in book-shelves overflow with books and magazines. The writing-table, near the window-seat in one corner, is a plain board table, supported by tripods of sumac. In a niche under the stairs stands the dining-table. At the right of the fireplace is the kitchen corner, and the dish-cupboard, with rustic loops for handles.

A few 'needments' sufficed the hermit for his simple house-keeping. His treasures: the blue and white coverlids, the wool of which grew on the backs of Roxbury sheep; patchwork quilts his mother made; a few of her mulberry-pattern dishes; a woolen holder, on which a girl-visitor had appropriately outlined an oven-bird; birds' nests, and other trophies from the woods; books, and the photographs of friends.

Early in the year the builder of the little cabin allowed himself to be inveigled into speaking before various organizations — the Teachers' Training School in Brooklyn (on 'Observations of Nature'); the Phi Beta Kappa Society at Yale, on Whitman; a Woman's Club in Lowell, Massachusetts, and one at Stamford, Connecticut, on natural-history topics. Writing Mrs. Percival Chubb [1] of these engagements, he said:

I seem like a man who in some unguarded moment has been caught by the skirts in some piece of machinery which is slowly but surely drawing him in, maybe to his destruction, certainly to the destruction of his peace of mind.

To his Journal he confides the quakings he experienced before confronting his Yale audience:

Am dreadfully scared and worried as I sit in my room at the hotel. It seems utterly impossible for me to read that lecture. I could fly to the moon easier; but when the hour strikes, and I find myself face to face with the enemy, my courage and confidence mount, and I acquit myself entirely to my satisfaction. I speak about one third of it and read the rest. A fine audience. . . .

One is amused to read in a letter of March 2d, to Mrs. Chubb, his explanation of the success of his Yale lecture:

My little journey in the world has at last brought me around to my own fireside. . . . You will be glad to know I had a real success at Yale, and much of it was owing to that wonderful Fellows Compound you gave me. It set me up a good many notches so that I did not need the champagne. It made my mind so active that I rewrote, or rethought, all the first part of my lecture that day I left you, on the way to the train. . . . The effect of the Compound upon me is so instant and marked, that I am a little afraid of it, and shall use it sparingly. . . .

Of Helen Keller he wrote:

A visible soul. Am strangely affected by her; can hardly keep from tears. She repeats my poem, 'Waiting.' Says she believes it all. So happy, almost ecstatic, all soul and feeling. Quite handsome, except her eyes.

About this time, Stedman, writing of Burroughs's paper in the current 'Conservator,' — 'Two Critics of Whitman,' — makes an observation of biographic interest [2]:

[1] Letters from J. B. to Mr. and Mrs. Chubb are kindly lent by Mr. Chubb.
[2] Permission to quote from Stedman's letters is kindly given by Mrs. Laura Stedman Gould, who also lent many letters from J. B. to E. C. S.

You show a difficulty in escaping from first impressions . . . [Italics mine]. I have often thought of trying to disabuse you of it, but have had a feeling that it would be of no use — that you are sweet, and strong, and true, but lack a certain flexibility. Now, as the scientists tell us, even the ice-glaciers and the granite mountains do *flow.*

[Journal] Feb. 29. Met at a lunch given by Dr. Eggleston to Dr. Billings, at the Century Club, Messrs Stedman, Howells, Warner, van Dyke, Matthews, Morse — ten of us. Stedman is a lovable man. . . . He is like a good, frank, brave bright boy. A fine talker who tells you you are a fool in a way that does not hurt. Eggleston, with his iron-gray mane, makes a fine figure; a wonderful talker, too. I am not quite at home with these men — have no wit or repartee or anecdotes. My mind is too serious, and my life has been too secluded. I cannot talk out of the air and make the sparks fly, as they can.

The first overnight guest at Slabsides was Professor Oscar Lovell Triggs, of whom the journalist says, 'He came for two days and we have a feast of Whitman and a flow of soul.' Of a subsequent visit he writes:

We have had a day and night in the Whitman land and much talk and real intellectual intercourse. I think Triggs will yet strike out something new and valuable in the way of criticism — maybe formulate the principles of the new democratic criticism. . . .

Henceforth, new friends, young and old, learning how approachable he was, began to invade his solitude. He was soon to find those lines in 'Waiting' coming true:

> Asleep, awake, by night or day,
> The friends I seek are seeking me.

The loneliness of which he had spoken so much in his Journal was ever after relieved by individual callers, by small groups and crowds, who came for a tramp in the woods, a picnic at the cabin, or a talk by the fireside. The Journal speaks of early visits from Mr. Ernest Ingersoll, and Professor van Ingen; of brief flittings to Albany and Binghamton to lecture, then back to the sweet solitude.

In mid-May, he writes of Hiram's advent at Riverby with his bees and bee-traps:

He sleeps in my Study and eats in the fruit-shop. I prepare his food and wash his dishes. It is a great comfort to see him around. . . . It does me good every hour to have him here.

This arrangement, however, soon proved intolerable. His own food choked him when he had to hand his brother his food on a plate, as if he were a tramp, and see him eating it on a bench outside the kitchen door. 'What was too good for Hiram was too good for me — it was impossible to go on that way.' So the brothers soon regularly set up housekeeping at Slabsides. The Journal for May 26th says:

> . . . I feel like a toad when he escapes from under the harrow. I look about me and find life worth living after all. Hiram is a great help, just by his presence — alleviates my chronic homesickness amazingly. . . . Celery begins to grow rapidly.

One of the first letters to be written from his new retreat went to Benton:

> . . . Now for two weeks I have been living at Slabsides. . . . My brother Hiram is with me, and we are quite comfortable and happy. I like it so well that I may stay most of the summer. The quiet, the seclusion, the wildness, and the freedom from domestic tyranny are like balm to my spirit. . . .
>
> We have out 30,000 celery plants, and shall put out many more. . . .
>
> [Ernest] Ingersoll is building a house near me, and is stopping with me for a few days. When can you come over and taste the hospitality of Slabsides? I can give you a good bed and plenty to eat, and a hearty welcome. Come and stay several days.
>
> A Women's Natural History Society of Albany [the Dana Natural History Society] — 30 or 40 of them — threaten to descend upon me in June for two days. I should like to have you here then to help stem the tide.

This Dana Society, which received its *entrée* to Slabsides through Miss Mary B. Church, of St. Agnes' School, Albany, made an annual pilgrimage there for years, usually in the time of the cypripediums. He had innocently asked them there for overnight, but on learning the size of the body, nothing daunted, stirred himself to find lodgment for them — Slabsides could be made elastic enough to accommodate a good many, the near-by rocks would lodge many more, and, if necessary, the houses of his neighbors along the road could be commandeered. It is pleasant to note that he who had been the recipient of so much hospitality, showed so hospitable a spirit as soon as he had a place wherein to welcome his friends.

Now the Journal is full of bird gossip and flower gossip, and the ever-absorbing topic, the weather; of visits from Dr. Maurice Bucke, Mr. Frank M. Chapman, and others. In late June, John Muir's visit is noted:

I met him at Hyde Park. A very interesting man, a little prolix at times. You must not be in a hurry, or have any pressing duty, when you start his stream of talk and adventure. Ask him to tell you his famous dog story (almost equal to 'Rab and his Friends'), and you get the whole theory of glaciation thrown in.

He is a poet and almost a Seer. Something ancient and far-away in the look of his eyes. He could not sit down in a corner of the landscape, as Thoreau did; he must have a continent for his playground. . . . Probably the truest lover of Nature as she appears in woods, mountains, and glaciers, we have yet had.

July First. Miss [Florence] Merriam and Miss Eaton came today. Two pleasant women. We saw a green warbler feeding a cowbunting.

13. A hot wave. . . . Celery outlook very dubious. Have about finished the Whitman book ['Whitman: A Study'].

In July he went to Onteora Park to attend the dedication of a monument to the early artists of the Catskills — Cole, Gifford, Church, McEntee, and others. Daily, during September, he and Hiram go down to Riverby and help pack and ship the grapes; then, climbing to Slabsides, sit in congenial silence in the dusk.

To Benton, Burroughs comments at length on the political situation, concluding:

Have you read 'Wealth against Commonwealth'? [By Henry Demarest Lloyd.] If not, get the book. It is a great book of the kind. It makes me so mad that I can't read it long at a time. It tells how the people are robbed by the trusts and combines. Get it. Price $1.00. Come and see me.

Excerpts of letters to Gilder also show how Burroughs was stirred by the questions of the day:

I have pondered over your letter and find but little in it that I take exception to. I have always known that as a man your sympathies were with the poor and the unfortunate. You would not be a poet were this not true. You would probably part with your last dollar to help a distressed case sooner than I would. Your splendid work on that Tenement House Committee shows the stuff you are made of. But as an editor you are far less outspoken on the wrongs of the people, the greed of monopolies, the insolence and tyranny of rail-

JOHN BURROUGHS AND HIS BROTHER HIRAM AT SLABSIDES

HOUSEKEEPING AT SLABSIDES

roads and other corporations than I should be. I would pour hot shot into them all the time. . . . The officers of all the great trunk lines of railroads have done things, and still do them, that I or you would not be guilty of any sooner than we would be guilty of robbing a hen-roost. . . .

The public must fight these corporations and all other monopolies. I would show them up just as Kennan showed up the Russian despots. I would give the people a true history of the oil trust, and the sugar trust — 'nothing extenuate, nor set down aught in malice.' I believe any magazine would make its fortune that dare to do it. It would boom it as your War articles did the Century. . . .

I am glad to hear what the wealth of New York is doing and proposing to do for the poor there — if only the wealth of N.Y. and of other places would not make them poor in the first place! The instinct of self-preservation is strong in wealth, too.

You refer to Washington and the Revolution. You must remember that, as a rule, the wealthy, educated, aristocratic class at that time was on the side of King George. Nearly every Tory was a man of means. Of course there were exceptions, and Washington was one of them.

The wealth, the learning, the conservative [persons] of a country are nearly always on the side of the oppressor. It has been so from Christ down. I hesitate to act with the Republican party at this time because it is on the side of Dives, and scoffs at Lazarus; it is doing what every trust and combine and millionaire in the country wants it to do; it is on the side of the oppressor.

I shall read the pamphlet on 'Cheap Money' you send me. I am seeking light on these subjects. . . . I am protected by a barrier of neither silver nor gold, but of good gray rocks. Let party strife rage.

After speaking at Doylestown, Pennsylvania, to an audience of eleven hundred persons, the journalist writes dispiritedly:

Do not speak easily and smoothly, and the audience not very sympathetic — jaded, I suspect, from the daily and nightly lectures of the three preceding days. Room too close. My undershirt is wet with perspiration when I have finished.

A few days later this still disturbs him.

I saw persons asleep in my audience for the first time. It had a depressing effect upon me; and that orchestra in front with their stolid, indifferent faces — that depressed me — a wet blanket the first thing. Was more nervous than ever before, and felt yesterday like cancelling all my engagements. I am no doubt shortening my life by this foolish lecturing business.

Nevertheless, he was soon speaking before another Pennsylvania audience:

Am not in good form. Can't see the faces of the people, nor see my notes — footlights glaring in my face. Once the audience tittered — in derision, I think. I can't recall at what, probably at my awkwardness and failure to see my notes.

Don't think these Pennsylvania audiences care for me, or what I have to say. I am much cast down. I find I *must* have the sympathy of my audience, and if I fail to get it, the wind is taken out of my sails at once. I am a poor machine — never run twice alike — too sensitive. Am apt to do extremely well, or very poorly, according to circumstances. . . .

This last experience so unnerved him that he broke his engagement to a Brooklyn audience; and for years to come one hears little or nothing of his lecturing. Despite his difficulty in saying 'no,' he did say it very decidedly to many requests, his peace of mind being worth more to him than the substantial honorariums they dangled before him.

[Journal] Nov. 23. . . . Hiram and I have only a few more days at S.S. [Slabsides].

The Whitman book came Saturday — think it has reality — that the reader will on the whole have the sense of having come in contact with real ideas and distinctions, and not with mere words. Could have made it much better if I had given another year to it.

The grace with which he could tender a book is seen in this letter to Miss Peck:

. . . To make partial amends for my seeming neglect I come now with a book in my hand, which I suppose I have written for you as much as for anybody, or, rather *from* you, from the sympathy which I knew you and others like you would feel in my undertaking. The book has been upon my hands for three or four years, and has caused me to neglect many other things. It ought to be a riper fruit than it is. I made it better each year, and at each re-writing, and probably could have kept on doing so; and one of these days I expect I shall regret that I did not wait a little longer; but life is short and art is long. So I have taken the irrevocable step of publication.

I shall welcome any criticism you may be moved to make of it. I always profit by any frank opinion of my friends. A sincere judgment never wounds, however adverse.

I hope you are well, and find the compensations in life that a spirit like yours is pretty sure to find.

I have spent the season in the wilderness, in a rustic house I built last fall. I am writing you from this Whitman land, but the cold will soon drive me out. . . . I am much more happy here than in my house on the river. I came in here for seclusion and solitude, and I have had more company than in any other year of my life; but I have

enjoyed it all. Solitude in the morning, and company in the afternoon, I find, is about the thing.

[Journal] 26. Thanksgiving. Warm as September. Play croquet
with the Gordon girls. Hiram leaves me today to be gone several
months — thus closing a curious and interesting chapter in my life.
He leaves me pensive and vacant.

Hiram never looked into one of my books lying here on the table
while here. When the Whitman book came I said to him, with the
book in my hand, 'Hiram, here is the book you have heard me speak
about as having cost me near four years' work, and which I re-wrote
about four times.' 'That's the book, is it?' said Hiram, but never
showed any curiosity about it. . . .

28. I shall never be able to tell how much I am warped or biased
in Whitman's favor, so that I am barred from taking an independent
view of him. I would give anything to be sure that I see him as he
is; to be his judge, and not his attorney. I early fell into the way of
defending him, and it may be, *may be*, that I can take only an
ex parte view of him. The moment I begin writing about him I
become his advocate. My mind slides into the old rut at once. I
must think further about this.

He writes as follows to R. G. Ingersoll: [1]

I have never thanked you for your splendid letter about my
Whitman book, which really warmed my heart. I was so proud of
the letter that when I was in New York I showed it to my publishers,
and they at once wanted to print a sentence from it in an advertisement of the book; of course I said no; but they extracted from me a
promise to ask your permission to do so. . . .

I have found a wonderful brain and nerve restorer in Fellows'
Compound of Hypophosphite. Whitman told me that he thought it
saved his life a few years ago. It seems as if civilized man sometimes gets to the point when he needs some deadly poison. It seems
to surprise and tickle his whole nature.

A wonderful food, too, to restore nerve exhaustion is Concentrated
Clam Juice — comes in bottles — all grocers have it. I can see
clearer two hours after taking it. [His friends used to tell him that
he ought to get a commission from the manufacturers of the various
foods and nourishing drinks that he recommended so enthusiastically.]

Early in the new year this picture of the winter days occurs:

I wonder if there is another so-called literary man who spends his
time as I do — in the solitude of the country, amid the common
people.

[1] For the loan of the letters to Colonel Ingersoll, I am indebted to Mrs. R. Brown.

Here I sit, night after night, year after year, alone in my little Study perched upon a broad slope of the Hudson, my light visible from afar; reading an hour or two each evening, and then to bed at 9. No callers, no society, no proper family or home life. Not in years has a person dropped in to spend the evening with me. Occasionally Julian comes in after his return from school, and we talk awhile. (Julian is developing a very quick, keen and eager intelligence.)

Up in the morning before daylight and lend a hand in getting breakfast, and then the furnace and a few chores; then fifteen minutes' walk to the PO and back; building a fire in the Study; a little reading, and then at 9 to work with my pen till noon.

Then dinner and a few chores; then sawing and splitting the wood for the next 24 hours; then a walk to Slabsides or elsewhere; a little reading or dozing in my Study; then supper and darkness again.

Every day and every day in winter the same. What long, long thoughts I have! What constant retrospection! what longings for the old days and people! The world goes by me afar off. I hear its roar and hubbub, but care little to mingle in it. It is mostly vanity and vexation of spirit.

His letters of sympathy to his friends always went straight to their hearts. This to Miss Peck, in early April, reads:

What can I say to you that will assuage the pain of this new and keener grief? Nothing, but that you have my deepest sympathy and my truest affection. . . . I know what it is to look upon the graves of father and mother, and how in a sense I look upon them daily, and always expect to as long as I live. That shadow becomes lighter, but it is never lifted from one's life. If one can only see the sunshine through it!

Well, it is certain that we shall join them, but whether as dust to dust, or soul to soul, we can only hope. Here in my solitude I think so often of my parents and of the Old Home. As I grow older I seem to be nearing them, at least they are more in my thoughts. My oldest brother is with me, and we sit by our open fire at night and talk of the old days, and repeat over and over the names of those we knew so well who are now no more. I never tire of hearing about everything connected with our youth. Even the dogs, the oxen, the horses, the hired men my father had — we dwell fondly upon them all. . . . I cook my own food, keep my own house, have sweet solitude and quiet, and plenty of time for working and walking, and for doing neither. . . .

I appreciate your criticism of it [the Whitman book]. I feel much the same about it, I could make it better now — at least get rid of some of the repetition. Mr. [Gerald Stanley] Lee's review of it in the Bookman interested me much. It seemed to me a little obscure or equivocal in places. I had to read some parts of it over two or three times. He writes well, but he must not be seduced by his own brilliant talent. . . .

I did a little writing this winter before my sickness — two papers for the Century (one on Bird Songs, to appear in June, and a paper for the Atlantic to come out in May), besides some other work not yet quite in shape. I am now deep in economic studies and may write something in that field.

In early May the bird-students begin to come. Of the first group that year he makes this comment:

Mrs. H—— and her friends come — two very interesting women. The New Woman is a great improvement on the old. She loves the open air like a man, and is nearly as unconventional. There seems to be more poetry in her soul than in man's.

The arrival of warblers and other birds, of floral visitors, and of many a human guest is chronicled, but no arrival that season set up quite such a ripple in his mind as the one chronicled on May the seventh:

Yesterday morning when we first got up at 5, Hiram called my attention to some large black object about mid-way of a tree near the top of the ridge back of Ingersoll's. It seemed as large as a turkey. Hiram said he bet it was a 'coon. I felt sure it was an eagle. We kept an eye on it for near an hour, then we saw it move. Presently I saw a gleam of white as the bird bent forward to preen its plumage; then it stood up and lifted its plumage and wings, and shook itself — a bald eagle and no mistake!

Had he passed the night there? I hope so. By and by, having fixed himself for the day, he launched into the air and flew directly over the house. The thought of him lingered all day.

What attracted him here, attracts me — the wildness and seclusion, the precipitous gulf. Noble lodger! I hope you will come nightly to my craggy retreat.

In accepting the vice-presidency of the Audubon Society in Washington, that spring, Burroughs wrote his friend Mrs. J. M. Patten:

I know your society will frown upon the milliner's use of bird skins. I hope it will also discourage the senseless collecting of eggs and nests which so many young people take up as a mere fad, and which results in the destruction of so many of our rarer birds. The thing to cultivate is a love for the birds, and the habit of close observation of them and their habits. . . .

With the passing of September a momentous event occurs in the life at Riverby:

Sept. 27. . . . Julian starts for Harvard.

He goes off cheerfully, but my cheerfulness is only put on. I wheel his big trunk over on the wheel-barrow. Thus he starts for College, I serving as porter.

The dear boy: How youthful he looked! Oh, if I could go with him and be his chum! Well, he is come into the Promised Land for which I longed, but of which I never got a glimpse.

How late in the day it seems to me, but not to him. It is early morning with him. Had I gone to College, it would have been forty years ago. I shall see him again, yet how sad the autumn fields look! Think of all the Harvard boys who had that life so long ago! and soon my experience, and his, will be of the long ago.

Early in October, longing to see their boy, Mr. and Mrs. Burroughs go to Cambridge. He attends lectures with Julian, and a football game between Harvard and Dartmouth, and listens to a 'flat, insipid sermon.' Then reluctantly they return home:

[Journal] Oct. 14. Julian goes with us to the street car on Harvard square, in the clear, crisp morning light. He stands there on the pavement as we move off, and waves his hand. I look back and see him run quickly across the street toward his hall. I dare say my heart is much the heaviest. It is the October of my life, the May of his. We rode all day through the sunlit land.

Now he has a new subject to yearn about. His boy is seldom out of his mind. 'Distance *does* contain a little of the bitterness of death,' he says.

After a visit to Mr. Mabie he records:

. . . Mabie and I walk in the morning. A pleasant family — new house, excellent taste, books by the thousand. In p.m. Whittridge, the artist, comes in. Like him much — the plainness and simplicity of a country farmer. We take to each other.

[Journal] Nov. 7. How much more valuable to a man is an instinct for the truth than any special gift . . . If he craves the truth alone, he will not be disturbed if his theories and systems fall in ruins about his head. Then I must find a larger and deeper truth, he says. What an instinct for truth had Darwin! when facts appeared to be against him, how he welcomed them! they became his friends. . . . A man with a system to uphold is handicapped, unless he has an instinct for the truth. . . . Taine's criticism is less valuable than it would be had he no system to uphold. They are free indeed whom the Truth makes free, because the Truth finds them free.

The wistful Celt laments to his Journal that he and his son

could not have climbed and descended the hill of life nearer together. When Julian comes for the first vacation, the father's joy is pathetically keen:

Julian home from Harvard! I met him at Esopus and we walked down the track. How delighted we are to see him! He looks well, and a little more manly than three months ago. How he blots out everything else for the time being!

How I pity those who have no boy to come home from College at the holidays! He is full of the life there. How poetic and romantic it all seems to me! Today he is off hunting with Jimmy Acker.

28. Julian goes up the river in his boat after ducks. At 3 p.m. I go down to the river and am alarmed at the condition of the ice; vast masses of it grinding on the shore. Seems impossible for a boat to live in it. So I start up the river-bank hoping to see him coming back.

The ice roars louder and louder and jams and grinds harder and harder, and I become more and more alarmed. The farther I go, the more anxious about the boy I become. My imagination begins to work and I am soon wretched indeed.

At last I reach Esopus dock, but no Julian in sight. A man there tells me he saw him go up about 2 p.m. It is now 4. The man, who is an old river-man and duck-hunter, says the ice makes it dangerous. Darkness will surely come on, and the boy with his canvas boat will be ground to pieces, or frozen fast in the ice.

I tear up the river and reach Pell's dock, a mile further up. Then I fancy I see him in an open canal of water near the quarry dock. He does not seem to be rowing, and the ice is shutting up the opening south of us, faster and faster.

Bill O'Brien joins me and we look and speculate, and try to put in his boat and go to the rescue; but it is too heavy. Then I tear along the shore again, and when within a quarter of a mile of what seems to be his boat, I shout to him. Just then his gun goes off, and I see he has been stalking a duck, and is not alarmed, and is in no hurry. I shout to him and he rows along, much amazed to see me. No danger, he says, and laughs at my anxiety.

The sun is down and the tide nearly slack. I try to persuade him to put the boat ashore at Pell's and come home with me on foot, but he refuses, and says he can beat me home; that there is open water all along shore, as, indeed, he found.

Nip and I take the road home. The good level walking is such a change from our scrambling along the river-bank that I am less tired than I thought. . . . At ten minutes to six we are at home, and a few minutes later, Julian reaches the dock. . . .

The Journal for the year closes with an extract from a correspondent's letter concerning his essay 'On the Re-reading of Books' in the November 'Century.' The pathos of the paper, she said, was enough to break one's heart — as if the author had tried everything in life and found it only dust and ashes. 'I knew there was a plaintive tinge in the essay,' he wrote, 'but did not dream it was really sad. . . .'

[Journal] March, 1898. My outdoor papers could only have been written by a countryman and a dweller in the country. But probably my literary criticism and [other] essays suffer from this very cause. They should have been written by a dweller in cities, a mover among the throngs of books and men. This would have helped to give them snap, decision, brevity, point. The intellect, the judgment, are sharpened in the city; the heart, the emotions, the intuitions, the religious sense are fostered in the country.

A letter to Gilder acknowledging a poem about the vireo rehearses the vernal delights:

I pity you dwellers in town nowadays. Think what you miss in not hearing the evening song of the toad, . . . the chorus of the peepers, the sunset challenge of the robin, the warble of the bluebird, the trill of the song sparrow, the piercing plaint of the meadowlark. Even to see a bit of dry road again in March pleases more than all the pavements in the world. My thoughts go and scratch with the hens, they nip the new grass with the geese, they follow the wild ducks northward. Already there are little rills of vivid green in the fields, already the birds begin to swarm in the elm tops like bees, already the hazel nuts have shaken out their long yellow catkins beneath the little crimson blossoms — a great display of masculinity, and a feeble display of femininity. So don't you wish you were a countryman? It is such a March as we had when you were here in '78.

In April he and Hiram move over to Slabsides, whence he writes his son of his much-boasted oil-stove there:

I had quite a circus with the stove one day. I could not make the gas light. I used a dozen matches, burned alcohol four times, and danced a war-dance around it, and was about to pitch it down the rocks when I discovered there was no oil in it! A stove that won't go once in a while without oil is a contrary thing.

With the help of a nephew, Edward Burroughs, the guest-room at Slabsides was 'done off' that April.

[Journal, August 20.] No echo of the War in my Journal, yet what an absorbed spectator of it I have been! and now that it is ended, I feel a great strain taken off me. I no longer rush for the newspaper in the morning, nor tarry impatiently at the station for it at night. I shared the popular feeling about it, and wanted to see Spain kicked out of the Western Hemisphere. The Spanish blight and mildew have rested upon these fair islands long enough. If the races there are not worthy of liberty and self-government, we will put a race there that is.

What a brilliant spot the War has made in our recent hum-drum history! Out of a corrupt Mammonish time emerge these heroes, plenty of them, vying with one another, courting Death as a bride. How their example has electrified the whole country, and fused us, and made us more completely one! It makes us realize that we are a country. It has begotten an enthusiasm of nationality. Henceforth we are a worthier and a nobler people. This heroism at Santiago is enough to leaven the whole lump. . . .

After Julian returns to college:

Again I wheel his trunk to the station, filled with the old sad thoughts. . . . He is not very well, and this, too, troubles me.

How well it is that children think less of their parents than parents of their children! If it were not so, sons and daughters would never leave home; families would never break up and scatter, as Nature meant they should. The old cry to the young, 'Oh, do not leave me!' But the young are full of hope and courage, and the future, not the past, sways them. Not until they have become parents themselves and tasted the pathos of life, do children know how their parents suffer.

And to his son:

I knew you would be blue and homesick. I confess I am not sorry that you were. I like to see the same traits and emotions in you that I detect in myself.

Capacity to feel deeply and keenly means capacity to suffer deeply, as well as to enjoy deeply; and without this capacity, what is man? I like any proof of heart in you, because I have feared at times that you were deficient here.

A week by the sea with Mrs. Burroughs, then he and Hiram again repair to Slabsides, where, before many weeks, he sustains a new loss:

I make my last entry this month to record the death of my beloved dog, Nip, which occurred yesterday afternoon, by falling through the high railroad bridge over Black Creek. We went on a walk up the track, as we have done a hundred times. I stopped at this end of the bridge to look down upon the creek. Nip passed over. I heard a train coming down the track and called him back. He came to near the end, when he paused, and in some way his hind feet slipped off the tie and he fell through before my eyes. He struck heavily on soft ground, got up and ran, crying, a few yards, and fell in his death agony. When I got to him he had ceased to breathe.

It was one of the worst shocks I ever had, and quite stunned me. For a moment the whole universe seemed bereft, and my whole outlook upon life changed.

I laid his limp body beside the abutment of the bridge and came home in the twilight and passed a sleepless night. When I was not thinking of him, I was dreaming of him. I dreamed of sending two girls for his body with a pole to which they were to tie it. I got the strings and pole for them. Then I dreamed that the railroad men had buried him, and had shot him before doing so; and Mrs. B. guided me to the spot in the road, and I dug him up.

This morning I brought him over here in a basket and laid him down once more beside the fire, that my eyes might behold him again in his old place. What a counterfeit of sleep!

I did not know I loved the dog so. Now Hiram is gone, he was my only companion. I shall bury him here, near Slabsides — almost a part of myself.

[Journal] Nov. 1. A bright, mild day. I spend part of it at Slabsides trying to write, the thought of Nip constantly hovering about my mind. Men of my temperament make much of their griefs. It is another form of our self-indulgence. We roll the bitter morsel under our tongues, and extract the last drop of bitterness. It is probable that I make the death of Nip the occasion to gloat over the past, and of that which can never return. This is my disease; it is in my system, and the loss of the dog brings it out afresh. It gives it an acute form. But I was deeply attached to him, and the thought of him will always be precious to me.

Nov. 2. Alone at Slabsides.

Of all the domestic animals, none calls forth so much love, solicitude, and sorrow as the dog. He occupies the middle place between the other animals and man. Our love for him is below that for our fellows, and above that we have for any other dumb creature. How many men there are now in the world, millions of them, whose love for their dogs is next to that they have for friends and families; and their grief at their loss next to a domestic bereavement!

My grief for Nip has lost the acuteness of the first day and night, but I carry in my heart a constant heavy sorrow. I rather wish I had buried him in some secluded spot near by (instead of here in front of the house), where I could have gone on occasion, withdrawn from other thoughts and things. I fear I shall cease to notice the humble grave constantly before me.

The letters which he wrote to his son during his years in college (and which Mr. Julian Burroughs has kindly permitted me to use) [1] show the most complete entering into the activities and problems of the college youth — his studies, his collateral reading, his future aims, deportment, fads and hobbies. His diet, and even his *affaires de cœur* received sympathetic attention. In a letter in which he discusses his son's choice of a wife, he offers:

The best wife for an intellectual man is a wholesome, comely, natural girl, with good instincts, and a big heart, and not especially intellectual, and of temperament opposite to his own.

Of Mr. Israel Zangwill, whom he hears at Cambridge toward the close of the year, he writes:

A discourse full of point, wit, and sense. A hatchet-faced man with hair that suggests a wig; it seems to sit upon his head rather than to grow out of it. Voice not big or strong, but agreeable. One of the coming leaders of literature.

The atmosphere of the University so stimulated him that after finishing his essay 'Wild Life About My Cabin,' which he wrote in the Harvard reading-room, he noted in his Journal, 'Must begin another.' He mentions visiting Trowbridge, lunching with Drs. Cleghorn and Bowditch, with Scudder and Higginson; and dining with Shaler and James, at the latter's home meeting Professor Harris of Andover. After the acerbity he had expressed toward Higginson in earlier years (because of his attitude toward Whitman), it is pleasant to read his comment made on further acquaintance:

Higginson very agreeable and complimentary — a fine, scholarly, accomplished talker and diner-out; looks ruddy and well, though his voice begins to show his seventy-five years.

He writes a friend in Poughkeepsie of the damper put upon his last days in Cambridge by an attack of influenza:

I wish now I had stayed at home. The simple, honest country microbes I can stand, but these subtle, sophisticated city germs get the best of me every time.

Of his trip to Salem he writes:

We go to Salem. I stand for some time on Gallows Hill where the

---

[1] Excerpts from certain letters written by J. B. to his son and published in Julian Burroughs's *My Boyhood*, are reprinted through the courtesy of Julian Burroughs and Doubleday, Page & Co.

witches were hung, among them an ancestor of mine, Rev. George Burroughs, over 200 years ago.

A typical New England landscape, barren and rugged, low broken rocky waves [?] with a ragged covering of turf — a body of rock with a tattered and torn covering of soil. Nothing to mark the site of the hanging. If I had the means, I would put up a monument there. Walked about the streets and into the Roger Williams house. . . . Thought of Hawthorne and many other things.

At Gilder's, in New York, he meets Zangwill, Howells, Stockton, Edith Thomas, and Helen Gray Cone, and visits among many friends, saying unwontedly:

Never saw New York more beautiful — the long vistas of those streets, the fine weather, the slight haze, the beautiful women, all filled the eye.

On reaching home, however, he wrote his son: ' It seems good to be in my little Study again — if I only had Nip or Hiram!' Excerpts from letters to his son follow:

. . . I am glad you are beginning to wake up and find yourself — that is, to get hold of your bent and your real wants. I was a long time in finding myself. I had few aids compared with what you have had. A good book, a great author helps a man command his own resources. I doubt if your college courses do much in this way — they are too technical. You will find your real teachers and help in the college library.

You do well to read Howells and Thoreau. Howells is the most artistic writer we have; his handling of his matter is exquisite, and Thoreau is a capital moral and intellectual tonic. He is like a clear frosty morning. Read his Maine Woods and Cape Cod and Excursions. Some day try Emerson — his Essays. He was my teacher and university. When I was your age, and a little older, how I revelled in him!

Your use of the word 'hell' in your letters grates upon my ears. Discard the word. Only extraordinary occasions call for such a terrible word. We are both well and longing to see you.

. . . Your views of life, and of the things worth having, agree with my own. . . . It is becoming very plain to me that you are cut out for a man of letters. This is as I would have it. Throw your whole soul into it, and do not mind the discouragements of your Mother. Her ideals, you know, do not get beyond wealth and respectability.

I shall be greatly disappointed, though, if you do not, in due time, make up your mind to marry. It is the proper thing to do, and is the way to rivet yourself to the world and to life. It is the order of nature. Love some sweet, gentle girl and make her your wife before you are twenty-four. It will make you a broader, more tender, more effective man and writer.

The farm, with my income from the books, and my pen will keep us all nicely till you can earn money yourself. You must have a career of your own, and I know you have enough push and ambition to carve out one.

I think you better drop Howells for a time. You do not want to get under his dominion. He is not a big enough man. Read Tolstoy, Hawthorne, Thackeray, and the French novelists, and then aim to see things for yourself, as they do. . . .

With much love and deep solicitude for your well-being
                    Your affectionate father
                                                    J. B.

The spring finds him writing on 'The Art of Seeing Things,' and characteristically recording on a certain date, 'I finish my paper'; and a few days later, 'Finished my paper'; and, quite a while later, 'Putting the finishing touches on my paper.' When possessed by a subject, he was never done with it; so long as he kept the paper by him, he would return to it, making it better and better.

[Journal] April 1. . . . Write to Julian and return his story. Poor boy! how he is yet to toil and sweat before he can shine in print!

An April entry records his literary achievements since the preceding November, with the proceeds from his magazine-writing:

$100	'The Vital Touch in Literature' (Atlantic)
75	'Recent Phases of Literary Criticism' (N. A. Review)
25	'Nature With Closed Doors' (Breeder's Gazette)
25	'Nature Study' (Outlook)
50	'Winter Bird Life' (Youths' Companion)
80	'Bird Talk' (St. Nicholas)
175	'Wild Life About My Cabin' (Century)
80	'Criticism and the Man' (Atlantic)
125	'Literary Values' (Century)
150	'The Art of Seeing Things' (On hand)
25	'A Walk in the Fields' (Independent)
75	'Thou Shalt Not Preach' (On hand)
985	

15 Bright lovely days. . . . Hiram comes today and we go over to Slabsides and begin life there again. Remnants of snow yet in the woods.

Mr. Bruce Horsfall came to Slabslides in April, there making a portrait of Burroughs which was reproduced in the 'Century Magazine' that year.

Of the happiness of the Vassar students, whose visits to Slabsides are so frequently mentioned in the Journal, Mr. Burroughs used to say, 'They were happy, and so was I. Their happiness was contagious.'

'When we were about to leave,' wrote Mrs. George L. Naught, concerning one of these visits, 'Mr. Burroughs would call out: "Girls, have you all registered? Have you got all your handkerchiefs, and gloves, and hairpins?" And he would go about helping gather up our belongings.' The same correspondent related a story told her by Miss Mary E. Adkins, a teacher at Vassar:

She had gone with a party of girls to visit the Sage of Slabsides, and the two walked to the spring for a bucket of water. On the way back, he put the bucket down to look over the surrounding scene. A collie dog came and drank out of the bucket. Mr. Burroughs chided him a little, poured a little water over the edge, saying, 'I guess the rascal didn't hurt it,' and carried what was left along the path to the cabin.

On May 21st the Journal tells of his return from a visit to the Old Home; of the coming of more and yet more visitors; with which entry the life at Slabsides ends for many months to come.

CHAPTER XIV

IN GREEN ALASKA

1899

> On Unalaska's emerald lea,
> On lonely isles in Bering Sea,
> On far Siberia's barren shore,
> On north Alaska's tundra floor;
> At morn, at noon, in pallid night,
> We heard thy song, and saw thy flight,
> And I, while sighing, could but think
> Of my boyhood's bobolink.
>
> *To the Lapland Longspur*

WHILE chewing the cud of sweet content at Slabsides, keeping an eye on the vineyards, and nibbling the while at his pen, there came to Burroughs, in the spring of 1899, a disturbing proposition — an invitation to join the Harriman Expedition to Alaska. Two strongly opposed desires tossed him back and forth — curiosity about new lands, and love of his own haunts; but curiosity won the day, and, turning the key in the door of Slabsides, he fared forth. His Journal for May 23d shows his mingled feelings:

Join the Harriman expedition to Alaska today in New York. Pass my place on the Hudson at 4 p.m. Look long and fondly from the car window upon the scenes I am about to be absent from till August. The sun is shining warmly. I see the new green of the vineyards. Wife is waving her white apron from the summer-house. I sit alone in my room in the Pullman car and am sad. Have I made a mistake in joining this crowd for so long a trip? Can I see Nature under such conditions? But I am in for it.

The railway magnate E. H. Harriman and his family were joined on this expedition by some forty scientists, authors, mining experts, and archæologists — John Muir, authority on glaciers and mountains; Dr. B. E. Fernow, on trees; Dr. George Bird Grinnell, on the Indians; Mr. Louis Agassiz Fuertes, the bird-portrait painter; Mr. Frederick Dellenbaugh, the explorer; Mr. R. Swain Gifford, the landscape-painter; and many others eminent in various fields.

As historian of the expedition, Burroughs's impressions were written from day to day.[1]

[1] First published as *The Harriman Alaska Expedition*, by Doubleday, Page & Co., later, somewhat altered, as 'In Green Alaska' (*Far and Near*).

He said of the narrative:

A thing has to stay in my consciousness for a while and develop
there before I can reproduce it satisfactorily. If I could have waited
six months or more — until I felt moved to write, I might have
brought forth something more creditable. But they made me go
about it deliberately, before I had carried it long enough. That is not
my way of writing — I go to Nature for love of her, and the book
follows, or not, as the case may be.

If, in this case, one misses something of the author's interpretive quality, he is still held by the graphic account of the
observer. As the chronicler looked out upon the country west
of the Mississippi, he knew those endless vistas of prairie land
were not for him, whose need was always to nestle in the lap of
Mother Nature, and feel about him the arms of the near horizon. Yet as the liquid song of the Western meadowlark filtered
through the roar of the rushing train, he longed to roam over
the treeless plains.

Like a moving panorama is his note-book of the scenes:
Now he glimpses the summits of the Rockies, ghostly and
dim. 'We are crossing them without seeing them — they duck
down and slip beneath us.' Along the Green River, Nature
dreams of canyons, before her wish is fulfilled in the Grand
Canyon. In the Bad Lands of Utah he finds the earth presenting a gashed, quivering look; and he finds Multnomah
Falls 'the most thrillingly beautiful bit of natural scenery' he
ever beheld.

From Boise City, Idaho, he wrote to a friend in Poughkeepsie:

I am already over 3000 miles from you and probably not yet half
way to the end of our journey. . . . It is a feast of beauty and sub-
limity, sometimes almost a debauch. . . . Our train is made up of
seven coaches. . . . Over forty persons in our party — a fine lot of
men. I like them all. My roommate is B. E. Fernow from Cornell.
He is a forester, and a good fellow. . . . I like Mr. Harriman and his
family of six children — two of them grown girls. . . .

To one of his young friends at Vassar, in late May, he writes
engagingly:

Wonders are cheap in this land. On Saturday we drove sixty
miles in stages over the great sage-brush plains to visit the famous
Shoshone Falls, a rival of Niagara. Two Niagaras here, one of rock,
and one of water. Take down your map and look up the Shoshone

Falls on the Snake River, and see me standing there on top of a volcanic table-land, looking down 1000 feet on the falls, and wishing you and my boy were with me. Can you see my rapt gaze? Can you see me peering over the fathomless but fascinating brink of the awful chasm? Can you see me plucking wild flowers of strange beauty, then turning quickly to see or hear the strange new birds? As we roll over the plain white capped mountain peaks from 60 to 160 miles off play hide-and-go-seek with us. The day is bright and cool, the air exhilarating, the company enthusiastic. Some are on horse-back, some in coaches, some in buggies, all are full of fun and frolic. I sit on the top of a coach with three young women, daughter and friends of Mr. Harriman — how happy they are, I fancy you as one of them. Well it was a great day in a series of great days. Yesterday we came down the Columbia from the Falls and again my soul was captured by a waterfall. Oh, the siren, how she sang and came near detaining me when the waiting train summoned us aboard. Not water but the spirit of water, of a clear mountain brook playing with the wind and with gravity on the face of a cliff 600 ft. high. The rock covered with a greenish golden moss; the pool at the base hidden from view by rocky walls. How shy, how withdrawn, how delicate! How inconceivably beautiful it all was! It warmed me like a great symphony. How I longed to go back there and spend a day, or a life. Such a combination of rock, and color and water I never again expect to see.

I have kept well and fairly happy but there have come times, as I knew there would, when I wished myself home again. The company is a fine one but I do not mix easily with a lot of men; women like me better than men do, and understand me better. Men are worldly and seldom dreamers, as I am. I like Gifford, the artist, and two or three others, best; we affiliate; we love things. . . .

To Mrs. Burroughs, on June 1st:

This morning we found ourselves at Victoria, on Vancouver's Island. . . . We have a fine steamer [the *George W. Elder*] and it swarms with life like an Atlantic liner. We took aboard sheep, steers, cows, hens, chickens, turkeys, and a vast lot of supplies of all kinds. We have cherries and strawberries as long as they will keep. . . . My old trunk looks just as it did when I started. I put on my thick underwear this morning. I will write again the next stop.

[*J. B. to M. S.*]

We are waiting here [Victoria] for a telegram from Washington, allowing us to land on Seal Island in Behring Sea.

I have a fine large state-room all to myself on the upper deck. John Muir is next door. This is a British city about the size of Poughkeepsie, but is finer and solider built. It rains here most of the time, as it does in England, but no snow to speak of.

Here we leave civilization and plunge off into the Pacific. . . .

While I have tickled the back of the Continent; have rubbed and chafed its very backbone, now we shall scratch its flippers in the Pacific and maybe its long proboscis in the Aleutian.

I think I am the most untraveled man in the crowd. Many of them know all this Alaskan and Western world as well as I know Julian's Rock. And they are fearfully and wonderfully learned. The Botanists and Zoologists talk in Latin most of the time, and the Geologists have a jargon of their own. I keep mum lest I show my ignorance. Oh, these specialists, who cannot see the flower for its petals and stamens, or the mountain for its stratification!

Throughout the voyage, jocose rhymes, posted anonymously in the smoking-room, or read of an evening in the social hall, contributed much to the enlivenment of the voyagers. 'Westward Ho!' written by Burroughs, shows with what good spirits he embarked, though bound to make propitiatory overtures to the ship:

Bow westward, faithful steamer,
  And show the East your heels —
New conquests lie before you
  In far Aleutian fields.
Kick high, if high you must,
  But don't do so at meals!
  Oh, don't do so at meals!
Your swinging may be graceful,
  But I do dislike your reels.
    .   .   .   .   .

We're bound for Arctic waters,
  And for the midnight sun;
So quicken your propeller,
  And your pace into a run.
Just touch on lone Siberia,
  To take a Polar bear,
Then hie away through Bering Strait,
  And frigid regions dare;
But in waltzing with the sea-gods,
  Oh, don't forget our prayer!
    .   .   .   .   .

Dr. Frederick V. Coville gives this incident of one of their evenings in the ship's saloon:

The Captain had sent to the saloon a stoker and a deck-hand who could do stunts. One of them sang a troubadour's song, the other gave a lively dance on a hatch-cover, brought in for the purpose. Not to be outdone by any one from the forecastle, members of the scientific staff volunteered stunts. John Muir did a neat double-shuffle, immediately followed by Mr. Burroughs, who, to the astonishment of everybody, stepped forward to the hatch-cover and gave an admirable clog-dance, evidently a hang-over from boyhood days — an astonishing exhibition of agility in an old man with white hair and beard.

In 1921, when Dr. H. H. Laughlin, interested in studying John Burroughs from a biological point of view, after a brief interview, wrote a scientific paper about him, he made one assertion which he could hardly have made had he been familiar with the author's work; namely, that Burroughs was 'strangely indifferent,' if not 'insensitive,' to color — was, 'perhaps, even color blind'! The erroneous inference must have grown out of the fact that Mr. Burroughs told Dr. Laughlin he felt but little interest in the brilliant sunsets of La Jolla, California, where the interview took place — a remark accounted for by his illness and depression at the time.

One doubting the susceptibility of John Burroughs to color should read 'In Green Alaska'; read his description of the phenomenal sunsets there; of the sapphire icebergs, the brilliant flowers, the purple mountains. A passage or two, taken at random, will suffice to refute the notion that he was insensitive to color:

I have often seen as much color and brilliancy . . . but never before such depth and richness of blue and purple upon the mountains and upon the water. When the sun went down the horizon was low, and but a slender black line of forest separated the sky from the water. All above was crimson and orange and gold, and all below, to the right and left, purple laid upon purple, until the whole body of the air between us and the mountains in the distance seemed turned to color.

Nothing had prepared us for the color of the ice . . . of the bergs that rose from beneath the water — its deep indigo blue. Huge bergs were floating about that suggested masses of blue vitriol.

Green, white, and blue are the three prevailing hues, all the way from Cook Inlet to Unalaska; blue of the sea and sky, green of the shores and lower slopes, and white of the lofty peaks and volcanic cones — mingled and contrasted all the way.

His sensitiveness to sound was equally marked. He said that the roar made at the Treadwell mines, on Douglas Island, by the crushing of quartz rock, tore the air to tatters, and stunned and overwhelmed the ear — that Niagara would be a soft hum beside it.

The Muir Glacier he thought the most impressive spectacle to be found on this continent. It held him with strange fascination; and with John Muir at his elbow, permitting no one else to express an opinion about glaciers, but discoursing continuously about them, Burroughs's scientific imagination was greatly stimulated. Amid those scenes of elemental grandeur, the plaint of the golden-crowned sparrow, the rich warble of Townsend's fox sparrow, the sweet strain of the dwarf hermit thrush, and the ditty of the pipit were inexpressibly welcome. Had Alaska yielded him nothing but the three bird poems ('To the Oregon Robin,' 'To the Golden-Crowned Sparrow in Alaska,' and 'To the Lapland Longspur'), it would have been enough. The homesick note creeps into all three, especially into the last two. He described the appealing song of the golden-crown: 'Only three piercing notes — *dear, de-ar, dee-ar* — they almost broke my heart — they seemed to come from the depths of the bird's soul.'

Mr. Frederick Dellenbaugh furnishes these incidents:

Gifford and I had been out trying to get up close to the front of the Muir Glacier on the land. We met Burroughs and Gannett, who had been fortunate enough to witness the same giant break that we had seen. . . . I had on rubber hip-boots, but J. B. had only 'goloshes,' so could not wade the stream and keep dry. It was a long way around by land. I offered to take him over on my back, and he accepted. It was a ticklish operation, for the force of the current for a few steps was very great, and had I slipped we should both have had an icy bath in very muddy water.

As they ran through Clarence Strait, a sight most impressive met their eyes, which those who had lingered in the cabin to sing hymns missed — long, jagged, snowy ranges to the north, lit up by the alpen-glow, with dark gloomy mountains in the foreground. Dall, exultant, exclaimed, '*This* is Alaskan scenery! what you have seen before was only British Columbia scenery!'

From the bridge, Burroughs called to Muir on the deck below, 'Muir, you ought to have been out here fifteen minutes ago, instead of singing hymns in the cabin.' 'Aye,' responded Muir, 'and you, Johnny, ought to have been up here three years ago, instead of slumbering down there on the Hudson!'

While in Prince William Sound, Burroughs wrote to his young friend (M. S.) at Vassar:

I wonder if my little girl thinks at all these days of poor old Ulysses and his wanderings, exiled from home and friends and summer, a-chill on the Northern seas, beleaguered by icebergs, frowned

upon by glaciers, and held as by enchantment in a vast circle of
snow-capped mountains? He has not been warm for a month, except
when mountain-climbing, or hugging a hot-water bag; and one of his
chief delights is recalling the days when he sweltered in an atmosphere of 90° at home. Have you really had warm hands and feet all
these June days, and is it a fact that there is not snow on the mountains? I am sitting now in my stateroom in my heaviest winter
clothing and an extra flannel shirt and overcoat, with a blanket over
my knees, and yet I am not warm. At intervals I take a rapid turn
around the deck, or go up and hug the smoke-stack, then come back
and write until my hands and feet are numb again. The strange and
grand scenery warms my spirit, but the air is the air of March. At
one time when we coquetted a whole week with the Muir glacier I got
neuralgia in my face. . . . I have gained in weight and flesh, and, I
hope, in grace, for all the cold. . . .

　I can have all the solitude I want — can sulk all day in my room
and no one will concern themselves about me. I can jump on shore,
or stick to the ship, as best suits my mood. I like some of the men,
am indifferent to others, and cleave to none. I do not smoke nor tell
stories, and find it hard to be hale [*sic*] fellow, well met, with everyone.

　Kadiak, July 3. At last we have a touch of summer; flowers everywhere. How I am reveling in it all, happier than a boy. This little
forget-me-not covers the hillsides — it is bluer than your eyes.

Small wonder that on reaching grass-carpeted Kadiak, the
country-dweller babbled of green fields. 'Bewitching Kadiak!'
he exclaimed, months later, 'the spell of thy summer freshness
and placidity is still upon me.'

At Unalaska he had his belongings carried ashore, intending
to tarry there till the ship came back from Siberia; but Muir,
getting wind of it, slipped ashore and stole his bag, bringing it
back just as Burroughs was about to disembark. The ship
was clearing away; Burroughs was forced to remain on board.

'I did so want to get familiar with Nature in that new
region — it would have meant so much to me,' he said regretfully, years later. He had his revenge in the following lines:

> Snapping, snarling Bering Sea,
> Hissing, spitting as we flee —
> Spiteful sea!
> Where thou art's no clime for me;
> Climbing hills that sink and flee
> Into vales that bitter be —
> Treacherous sea!
> Still our course is over thee.

Full of anger, full of spite,
Strong in bluster, weak in might,
Draped in fog both night and day,
Barren sea!
Only murres abide with thee.
Had not John Muir put in his lip,
Thou hadst not found me in this ship,
Groaning on my narrow bed,
Heaping curses on thy head,
Wishing *he* were here instead —
On green hills my feet would be,
'Yond the reach of Muir and thee.

Another contribution, though anonymous, was traced to
Burroughs:

Publish it in the smoking-room —
Put it up and let it bloom
All in type in the smoking-room.
Be it a sermon, or be it a joke,
Be it on dredging, or be it on smoke,
Be it a pæan, or be it a croak.
  Pin it up and give it a boom,
  All in type in the smoking-room.
  Dall and Fernow,
  Burroughs and Johns,
  Muir and Kipling (?)
  Each responds,
On all occasions, great and small,
  With rhyme or jingle,
  Double or single,
In verse iambic, dythrambic, trochaic and all
  Tickling each other,
  Chafing a brother,
  Or making a great pother
  About nothing at all.
From 'Westward Ho' to sylvan Fernow,
Or Dall with his pipe, pensive and ripe,
From Muir a-dream o'er his glacier-stream,
Or Johns a-fuss o'er his octopus,
To B—— bowing down to a sparrow's crown,
Or in high glee o'er Bering Sea.
Whatever the theme, with wit a-gleam,
Or full of fog as our Captain's log,
  Post it up and give it a boom
  In the filmy air of the smoking-room.

While in Bering Sea, Tuesday, July 11th, the party passed
St. Lawrence Island a little before noon. A little after noon
they crossed the 'date-line,' which there coincides with the
Alaska–Siberian boundary. They were then in Wednesday,
June 30th.[1] After leaving Plover Bay and steaming to Indian

[1] Russian calendar.

Point, where they halted, midnight and a new day overtook
them, Thursday, July 1st. Then, steaming east, in a few hours,
a little after sunrise, again they crossed the 'date-line,' and
ran into Wednesday, July 12th. Thus, in less than twenty-
four hours, they changed their day of week and day of month
three times, and their month twice. Writing these facts to
Burroughs, Mr. G. K. Gilbert said:

It is not often that even the circumnavigator crosses the 'date-
line,' and passes from the jurisdiction of the Gregorian calendar to
that of the Julian at the same time; and our quick return, with an
intervening midnight, made a rare combination of paradoxes.

Burroughs said that he traveled two hours in Asia and was
tempted to write a book about it.

The little people at Plover Bay reminded him of dolls
stuffed with sawdust, while their babies looked like scare-
crows. There the forget-me-nots, of a deep, ultramarine
blue, grew scarce an inch high. He was amazed to see flowers
on the tundra at Port Clarence, within sixty miles of the
Arctic Circle. The song of the golden plover, with its under-
tone of entreaty, was to him the voice of the tundra — soft,
alluring, plaintive. With birds about him, he felt at home in
any clime. Even on shipboard, almost his last entry tells of
the songs of birds drifting to him through the open windows.
Verily,

> Nor time, nor space, nor deep, nor high,
> Can keep my own away from me.

As they anchored at sundown in Safety Cove, July 28th,
Burroughs contributed the subjoined verses to the evening's
jollification:

> Homeward bound, homeward bound!
> Adventurous ship, we've been the round
> Of fiord and strait, sea and ground,
> From Plover Bay to Puget Sound.
> Now face about and eastward run,
> Pursue no more the setting sun;
> Cut down the seas with haughty prow,
> Toss them back with gracious bow;
> Nor tarry long upon the way,
> By gulf or inlet, isle or bay,
> Till thy propeller be at ease,
> Home at last from alien seas.

New worlds we've seen from off thy deck —
Alaska's wonders at our beck;
Polished slopes of heights sublime —
Record large of elder time;
  .   .   .   .   .   .

The awful fronts of glaciers wide,
That smite the sea with thundering tide;
A thousand hills of sombre woods,
A thousand peaks with snowy hoods;
A thousand isles that bask and dream,
A thousand bays that dance and gleam;
Volcanic cones with veilèd face,
Elias, grand in lunar space;
Emerald steeps of tenderest hue,
Tundra vast beyond the view;
The cruel Czar's Siberian shore,
Where Arctic seas forever roar;
Peoples strange of tented race,
Of habits wild, with dusky face —
All these and more, far more besides,
We've seen from 'bove thy iron sides.
  .   .   .   .

On August 9th he wrote in his Journal:

Returned from the Alaska trip in much better condition than
when I left. . . . Have written up my impressions from day to day in
the Harriman book, and in the three poems.

What joy to be back again and once more at my ease! No news
from home till I reached Portland, August 1. All is well.

To John Muir he writes in September: [1]

. . . Yours was the first word I had had from any member of the
H.A.E. . . .

I found . . . that the bottom had not fallen out of things in my
absence. Indeed, I am beginning to suspect that the sun would rise
and set just the same, and grapes would continue to ripen, if I were
to vanish for good and all. . . .

I see there has been an earthquake up there recently. I fear it has
given your sheep a terrible shaking-up. Your old bell-wether is
probably in a sad plight. I should like to have stood upon St. Elias,
but not upon the Muir Glacier, during the event. I fear our Indian
friends at Yakutat suffered seriously.

My thoughts go back most frequently and most fondly to Kadiak.
That place really touched my heart. I almost wish I lived there. I
think I must see it again.

We had a lucky trip across the continent, no heat, no dust, and

---

[1] This and other letters, written by J. B. to J. M., are lent by Dr. W. F. Badè,
literary executor of J. M., who also kindly gives permission to quote from Mr.
Muir's letters.

only one delay — a day and a half in the Badlands in Utah, from a washout. . . .

The Century will print my bird poems. Fuertes has been asked to make the bird pictures. . . .

November finds him and his brother resuming their quiet life at Slabslides, after he returns from a visit to the Harrimans at Arden and a jaunt to New England. Of his frequent flittings from home he writes:

After a while the fires of life begin to smoulder; the ashes accumulate. Then some mild excitement is needed, some social stimulus, something to fan the coals a little. I suspect this is my case now. I need more things to enliven me.

An event memorable in the annals of Slabslides is chronicled in the Journal on the last day of November — one of the three visits which Mrs. Burroughs ever made to the little cabin in the woods.

Mild, still days with gleams of sunshine. Spend the day at Slabsides with Wife and Hud[1] and his family. Eat our dinner there and walk about.

To Miss Clara Reed at Vassar College, goes this cheery December letter:

I have just come over to Slabsides, have built a big fire, and am writing you in front of the leaping flame. . . . You have never seen my open fire. It is a spirited affair, and puts a new face on things in a twinkling. Then, you know, I cut my own wood, and so have relations with it from the stump. I built the chimney also, and that improves the draught. I bake my potatoes in the ashes, and broil my chops over the coals, and that makes us still better acquainted. An open wood fire ventilates the mind as well as the room. All my blue devils go up the chimney with the smoke; and what sparkling spirits come down and dance and hover about the glowing embers! Just here I got up and put on some green hickory branches, and they are already beginning to sing like winter wrens. Now there comes a fine, intense, long-drawn note, like that of the English robin. There is more music in green hickory than in any other wood; but if you want fire-crackers and rockets, put on dry butternut. One wants about the same virtues in an open fire that he does in his friend — warmth, glow, music, but not too much pyrotechnic. I dislike the butternut people who, under the heat of conversation, snap and bang all the time. I trust your room-mate is birch or hickory — quiet, glowing, lasting. But how I am running on about this fire!

[1] Hudson Covert, for twenty-three years his faithful vineyard man at Riverby.

I do not stay much at Slabsides now, but come over and spend part of each day here and do some of my writing. . . . I am glad you like the Century article. Did you see my poem in the November Century? My first magazine poem! Of course I am proud of it. There will be one or two more. . . .

The closing year has this characteristic entry:

To be remembered in art or literature, or in almost anything else, you must do something unique, and that no one else could do. The secret of your power lies in the breadth of your relation to mankind and to common nature; in the richness and fullness of your human endowment. But immortality is the result of something above and beyond all this; something which is your own, and must suffuse and color and shape all the rest. The universal and the special, the general and the particular, must be blended and harmonized.

CHAPTER XV

'RING OUT THE OLD'

1900

What the light of your mind, which is the direct inspiration of the Almighty, pronounces incredible—that, in God's name, leave uncredited; at your peril do not try believing that.

CARLYLE

MORE than six of the eight decades in the life of John Burroughs were lived in the nineteenth century. On January 1st of the closing year of the century, he bids farewell to the fleeing years:

Good bye 1800 and all thy progeny! We have grown old together. Thy end has come, but I stay a little longer. I have looked upon thy face all my life. My father looked upon it all his life, my grandfather more than half of his. Now the door is shut and we shall see thee no more.

Welcome to thy successor! But he is a stranger, a new-comer, and it is hard for the old to make new friends; we become acquainted, but not wedded. The new days can never be to us what the old were. In our youth the days become a part of us; they mingle with our blood; they take on the very color of our souls; but in age they hardly touch us; they come and go like strangers. Only youth can live in the present and the future. In youth we constantly pay tribute to the future, and, to make the account even, in age we constantly pay tribute to the past.

In afternoon, walk over to the woods and to Slabsides, while Julian and Hud drive up after the boat.

January 19. In my walk in the woods saw where a small flock of quail had passed, six of them. They crossed over from Brookman's swamp to mine. What a pretty trail they made in the thin snow! In places where the woods are densest, they seemed to huddle close together like scared children. I could almost fancy them taking hold of hands — real babes in the woods. How alert and watchful they have been! Owls, foxes, minks, cats, hunters — all had to be looked out for. In the more open places they scattered more, no doubt looking for food. In the fall there were 12 or 15 of them, now only 6.

January 29. The British reverses in South Africa make me gloomy. I am more than willing that British arrogance and superciliousness should get a good slap, but my final interest is in the higher type of civilization and the better race. The Boer was a Boer

200 years ago, and he is a Boer still; he will never be anything else. He is a kind of human woodchuck. He fights well; so will a wood-chuck. There is no fear in his prototype of the fields.

England will have to take my advice and treble her force — invade their territory with an army of 100,000 men while Buller holds Joubert. This will save bloodshed and end the war.

January 30. I suppose that one reason why, during my Alaskan trip, there was all the time an undercurrent of protest and dissatisfac-tion, is the fact that I have passed from the positive to the negative side of life, when we begin to take in sail; when we want less and not more; when the hunger for new scenes and new worlds to conquer is diminishing; when the inclination not to stir beyond one's own chimney corner is fast growing upon us. The positive side of life lasts till fifty or sixty — differs in different men — then there is a neutral belt when we don't care whether we go or not; then the ground begins to slope the other way, and we begin the great retreat.

There were no apparent signs of retreat in February as he went about New York meeting friends, on one occasion ad-dressing the Wellesley College women in their club-room. March found him at home, reading the proof of 'The Light of Day,' and having many misgivings about it. On finishing the last batch of proof, he wrote disconsolately, 'Sick enough of the whole business.' To duck-hunting on the Shattega with his son he gladly turned and to sugar-making at the Old Home. Every few days he went over to Slabsides to watch Amasa plant potatoes and celery; to plant his own peas; and sometimes to accompany groups of students from Vassar, from the Quincy school, teachers from Atlantic City, Dr. Chapman, Mr. Rudolf Binder, and many another.

As he saw and heard April, so we see it, as we read:

A typical, moist April morning, warmth and humidity reign. Sit some time in my summer-house. A meadow-lark on the top of the sugar-maple over my head gives forth her [sic] clear, piercing, memory-stirring note. Then a highhole strikes up under the hill — a call to all things to awake and be stirring. He flies from point to point and repeats his call. It is not a song, but a summons and a declaration. It is a voice out of the heart of April — not a sweet voice, but, oh, such a suggestive and pleasing one! It means the new furrow, and the seed, and the first planting; it means the springing grass, and the early flowers; the budding trees; and the chorus in the marshes. It is warm and moist with the breath of mid-April. *Wick, wick, wick, wick, wick,* he says — *Come, be up and doing! Air your house! Burn your rubbish! Scatter your compost! Start your plow! The soft-maples are blooming, the bees are humming, the robins*

*are nesting, the chickens are hatching, the ants are stirring, and I am
here to call the hour! Wick, wick, wick, wick, wick!* Then the bush-
sparrow sang her plaintive, delicious strain beyond the currant-
patch, while the robins laughed and tee-heed all about. Oh, April,
month of my heart!

The soil never looked so inviting as in April; one could almost eat
it; it is the staff of life; it lusts for the seed. Later one wants it covered with verdure and protected from the too fierce sun. Now his
rays seem to vivify it; by and by they will bake it. Go and dig up
some horse-radish now, and bring in some crisp spinach, and the
sweet and melting roots of the parsnips. Let us taste the flavor of the
soil once more — the pungent, the crisp, and the sugary.

Beware of the angle-worms this morning as you walk in the yard
and on the roadside; they are crawling abroad now. Beware of the
newts, too, where they cross the road from the woods to the marshes
— you may tread upon them.

In the twilight now the long-drawn trill of the toad may be heard
— *tr-r-r-r-r-r-r-r-r-r-* — a long row of vocal dots on the dusky page
of the twilight. It is one of the soothing, quieting sounds — a chain
of bubbles, like its chain of eggs — a bell reduced to an even, quieting
monotone. These are the only jewels she has about her, these jewels
of sound.[1]

To Miss Clara Reed he sends news from Slabsides:

You were lucky to find the water-thrush's nest. I rarely find them,
though I look for them every season. There is one now that haunts
the little stream that passes my door, and I am hoping it will nest
here. Last night my cat [Silly Sally] gave it a scare and herself a
partial ducking. She saw the bird disappear between the banks of the
ditch and, calculating as nearly as she could where it had alighted, she
made the leap at a venture. She missed the bird and plunged into
the mud and water. A more disgusted cat I never saw. She came
back flirting the wet off her and looking at herself with shame and
anger. I reproved her sharply, but could not help laughing.

There's a wren's nest near the stream, and two nests of turtle-
doves close by. The scarlet tanager has a nest near here, I think, but
the secret is well kept so far.

The other day my old eagle came and sat for two hours on one of
the dead hemlocks above me. It was a noble sight. . . .

I had young Teddy Roosevelt with me three days, two weeks ago.
What a chase he led me! We had some fine adventures. He is only
twelve, but has the real stuff in him. He is like his father in minia-

---

[1] Still more strongly than a previously quoted entry, does this suggest his poem,
as yet unwritten, on the song of the toad:

A linkèd chain of bubbling notes,
　When birds have ceased their calling,
That lulls the ear with soothing sound
　Like voice of water falling.

ture. He climbed trees and rocks so recklessly that I expected he
would break his limbs or his neck, but he did not.[1]

'The Light of Day' was published in July. Its separate
essays had been growing under the author's hand for a dozen
or fifteen years, stimulated by the steady onward march of
science. The last hour, as it were, before the dawn of the new
century was a fitting time to launch a book so eminently sane,
vigorous, and candid — a book which urges the sufficiency
and universality of natural law; and which shows that the
mysterious light which our fears and superstitions have
thrown around the subject of religion will, when brought to
the test of reason, either vanish entirely or give place to con-
victions that can withstand the common light of day.

Standing apart from all creeds, its author sympathizes with
whatever, in any religion, answers to human needs; his aim
being to try to disentangle the eternal truths from the mere
trappings of religion. For the spiritual truths underlying the
myths and wonder-tales and parables, he had abiding reverence; but he believed that, with the intellectual progress the
masses had then attained, the time was ripe for substituting
the strong meat of open-minded reason for the milk of superstition; that it was time to ring out credulity, and ring in
honest-minded investigations.

He believed that the earnest seeker after truth is the seeker
after God; and that to follow Christ is to try to live as disin-
terestedly as he lived, in meekness, unselfishness, and brother-
liness — not for the purpose of gaining redemption hereafter,
but because the divinity within each soul so urges it to strive.

A Methodist clergyman, after reading 'The Light of Day,'
wrote its author that the book 'begins in twilight, and ends in
darkness' — a verdict over which the author always chuckled,
and supplemented with the statement that one reviewer
dubbed the book 'the light that failed.'

Burroughs found on publishing the book that he had
reckoned too little with the type of mind that must hold to its
beliefs in the miraculous, a type which, like the poor, we have
always with us. Just as surely as the child-mind loves its
fairy-tales, so surely will there always be certain adults who
will think as a child, speak as a child, and refuse to put away

[1] See 'Babes in the Woods' (*Far and Near*).

childish things; and until such immature thinkers reach for
maturer things, it were useless, perhaps cruel, to wrest from
them their mental playthings.

Burroughs was careful at the outset to explain that his contention was not with religion, but with theology — the whole
drift of the book being to discredit dogma, but to exalt religion as a sentiment, a comforter, a guide.

While the articles which make up the book were appearing
in the 'Popular Science Monthly,' and other magazines of advanced thought, a Congregational clergyman in Illinois
wrote, thanking the author in behalf of both science and
religion.

> While I cannot indorse all you say in them [he said], I am heartily
> in sympathy with your main ideas; and, knowing, as I do, the charac-
> ter of the young preachers who are filling our pulpits, I want to tell
> you that they are coming more and more into harmony with your
> ideas.
>
> I had heard that you are an infidel, a skeptic, and all that; and so I
> was overjoyed when I read the two articles above referred to. Yours
> is the religion of humanity, of nature, of God, and of the near future.
> *I cannot say it just that way to the world, but I can say it to you*, for you
> can appreciate it and understand it. . . . Go on with your good
> work. . . .   A. J. B.

The above italics are mine. Therein lies a hint of the
striking difference between the writer of the letter and John
Burroughs. The latter *could* say it to the world; in fact, could
do no other. Free from the bias of creeds and from associations with any church, he was free to seek the truth, and free
fearlessly to set forth his apprehension of it.

Burroughs confided to Benton:

> I do not hear much from my last book, and did not expect to.
> Those papers sort of haunted me till I overhauled them and bound
> them up in a book. Now they rest in peace, buried, probably, but of
> no more trouble to me.
>
> It is an honest book, but of course unsatisfactory, as all such books
> are. No doubt I often think I have touched the bottom of the great
> questions, when I have only reached the length of my plummet-line.
>
> As literature I feel that the book is all right. Some of the best work
> I have done is in its pages, I think. . . .

It is doubtless true that, while being a stickler for tolerance,
Burroughs was a bit intolerant himself when commenting on

the hide-bound dogmatists; and that in stripping away the husks from the various creeds, he seemed sometimes to over-look the kernels of truth they contained. He sometimes seemed to fail duly to credit the churches with their practical religion and their value in the community. Nevertheless, he realized keenly what the church was to his parents, and what it stands for in any community as a civilizing, sustaining, and uplifting force. He was, too, keenly alive to what the great historical religions have, each in its day and place, been to mankind. If, in trying to divest orthodox theology of its out-worn garments, he sometimes showed a regrettable impa-tience, he was, on the other hand, never flippant concerning anything sacred. In an unpublished fragment he thus com-ments on his father's utter faith in the literal interpretation of the Bible:

With what faith and contentment my father sat there in his pew in the old yellow meeting-house, and here I am a wanderer in the great unsectarian fields of nature!

I would gladly have sat in the pew, too, if I could; but forces be-yond my control turned me out into the great out of doors of the universe. I have partaken of the fruit of the forbidden tree of scientific knowledge, and know the truth from error. Hence I am driven forth from that paradise to earn my spiritual bread by the sweat of my brow.

I certainly have not my father's faith, but I often think that I have more than his contentment. I am not tormented by the fears that beset our fathers — the fear of hell and an offended God.

John Burroughs an irreligious soul! Only to one who insists on the sign for the thing signified; on the letter, instead of the spirit, of the law. He was irreligious only as Emerson was ir-religious, who would not extinguish the divine light in his own soul for the obscurity in which the theologians of his day would have enveloped him. Is this excerpt from 'The Light of Day' the utterance of an irreligious man?

Convince me that the historical part of the Bible is not true . . . yet the vital, essential truth of the Bible is untouched. Its morals, its ethics, its poetry are forever true. Its cosmogony may be entirely unscientific, probably it is so, but its power over the human heart and soul remains. Indeed, the Bible is the great deep of the religious sentiment, the primordial ocean. . . . Verily the spirit of the Eternal moves upon it.

Whether there be a personal God or not, whether our aspirations after immortality are well founded or not, yet the Bible is such an expression of the awe, and the reverence, and the yearning of the human soul in the presence of the facts of life and death, and of the power and mystery of the world, as pales all other expressions of these things; not a cool, calculated expression of it, but an emotional, religious expression of it. To demonstrate its divergence from science is nothing; from the religious aspirations of the soul it does not diverge.

. . . We are conscious of emotions and promptings that are of deeper birth than the reason; we are capable of a satisfaction in the universe quite apart from our exact knowledge of it; and the religious sentiment belongs to this order of truths.

From the fortunes of 'The Light of Day' its author turned abruptly in late August, and joined a party of campers in the Adirondacks, on Ampersand Creek.   His opinion, which follows, differed considerably from that held in 1881 when, after a disappointing experiment, he wrote: 'Leave the women at home next time. The camp is for men alone.'

Here I stay till the last day of August with real enjoyment. A jolly lot of people, mostly graduates of Cornell. I fish and tramp and loaf.

On Sunday, the 25th, we climb Mt. Seward, reach the summit at 9 a.m., a hard climb, but a grand view — six women and ten or a dozen men. I stand it well. I gain in hardiness every day and can make long tramps without much fatigue. Spend a day and night at Ampersand Lake — unforgettable — the gem of all the Adirondack lakes. Some of the company spend the night on Ampersand mountain and have a glorious time. Tim, the Guide, Peter, the Cook, the beds of boughs, and all the rest, call for special mention. Maybe some day I can write it all up as an illustration of the pluck and hardiness of the new woman. She could tramp and climb with the best of us.

To one of the 'new women,' on return to Riverby, he wrote:

MY DEAR WINIFRED [Ball],

I had a prosperous journey yesterday and this morning at 6.30 was safely at W.P. [West Park]. . . .

The grape-racket is in full blast here, but they were not anxious to see me, and I wish I had not practiced such heroic self-denial, but stayed for the venison, and, maybe, another slice of Seward or Ampersand. I was ridiculously happy and contented at that camp for an old gray-beard, and I see I am going to find it hard work to get down to the prosy realities of even Slabsides. For weeks to come I shall be walking about in a pleasant kind of a dream.

You were all more than good to me. Give my love to them all. I owe this rare treat to you, and I thank you over and over. Do let me try to repay you at Slabsides, or at least to show my willingness to repay.

If I could only shower upon you some of the fruit that is all about me!

That autumn, noting that he does not feel his accustomed melancholy, — even Julian's departure for Harvard affecting him less than usual, — he attributes his exemption to having abstained from eating grapes. In later years he used to say that he ate grapes for years before learning that the grapes made him as blue as they were themselves.

[Journal] October 18. When I cut and pass Hiram a piece of bread at the table, I think of how many times I have seen Father and Mother do the same in the old days, and my heart is tender. Here I am, at this late day, passing Hiram bread in more senses than one. Poor boy! It is a joy for me to do so.

October 21. Mild, bright day. Hiram leaves me again in the afternoon. I watch him through a crack in the door till he disappears behind the bushes, and say to myself, 'We may never meet again.' A little nubbin of a man, with a very small mental horizon, but very dear to me. . . . Almost every moment while in the house, he was drumming with his fingers on the chair or table, and whistling a low tune to himself — in a sort of brown study. His drumming and whistling became quite a nuisance at times. [But he never let Hiram know it.]

[*J. B. to L. L. P.*]

Your beautiful letter has been here on my desk all these weeks unanswered, while so many letters not beautiful have been promptly replied to. Strangers write and I answer, old friends write and I make them wait. I hardly know why it is so unless it be that one replies to the multitude with his hand, and to his friend with his heart; and the heart is not always in the mood, but is disposed to wait for the golden moment. I fear the golden moment has not yet come with me. I shall be happy if it turns out to be silvern. The gold of life is less and less abundant with me, and the lead and the pewter more and more common. Just now I am a little off in my health, which always enhances this feeling. . . .

[He rehearses his Adirondack experiences with Professor Burr, Mr. John Elliot of the Felix Adler School, and others.] I found I could tramp and climb mountains with the best of them, and catch more trout, ten times over, than all the rest put together.

The first of October I went to Atlantic City. . . . There I spent a week touching the hem of old Ocean's garment, and drawing from it health and strength. Now I am here again in my rustic cabin, seeing my days go by, and little more than an idle spectator of the brawling, blundering world of men and things.

I hope to write some again by and by, but I may not. I always try to wait for the cream to rise, but I may find out that there is nothing left to me but the old, oft-skimmed milk. . . .

The death of [Charles Dudley] Warner has touched me deeply. We were apples on one bough, and he has fallen. I had not seen him for three or four years, but had thought of him as unchanged. He was a very genial, lovable man, and his works will live after him.

Mention of Yale and West Point football game, and of voting for Bryan precede the mournful entry:

The world seems strangely empty and deserted. The show is about over for me. My curiosity and enthusiasm are about spent.

At the behest of McClure, Phillips and Company, in November he engaged in a new enterprise which was to have a larger reach than the thing itself. He began compiling an anthology of nature poems which should be representative of his own tastes and preferences. For three months he browsed among the nature poetry in the Boston and Cambridge libraries, tasting here and there, accepting, rejecting — according as the poems agreed with his own observations. In poetry about birds he wanted the real bird as a basis, and then as much poetry as could be evoked from it; unless, as in Keats's 'Nightingale' (which contains no natural history at all, but embodies the poet's sensuous impressions translated into his longings and waking dreams), the poet gives himself; in which case, he said, we could well afford to miss the bird. Poems in which Nature is treated fancifully or allegorically; those void of genuine emotion; also those in which the form is difficult, he avoided. Some, too, were omitted because of copyright restrictions. One hundred and twenty British and American writers of verse are represented in the anthology ('Songs of Nature'). His comments as the work progressed are found from time to time in his Journal:

In hunting for nature poetry, I do not find one poem in twenty that I can use. As soon as I strike a piece of Wordsworth's, or Tennyson's, or Bryant's, or Emerson's, what a difference! I can use but little of Lowell's. His verse is dry — is too much *made*. Longfellow is better.

I cannot read Swinburne without a kind of mental nausea. If I strike one of his poems without knowing the author, the nausea comes before I have read ten lines. Why is this? Swinburne seems to me abnormal; his is a diseased mind. His metrical felicities seem a mere trick.

, November 20. Every day I plunge into the sea of poetry, nature poetry, but only now and then bring back a pearl. It is all good and respectable, but it is not alive. Much of the real stuff in the Southern poet, Cawein, but his form is so difficult; his language is so knotted and tangled that I cannot use any of it. Reading his rhymes is like riding a lean, lame horse, bare-backed. He seems to affect a studied roughness and brokenness.

This immersion in poetry was the theme of most of his letters at that time, this to Miss Clara Reed being an example:

Outside of the well-known poets I find but few pearls — at best a little mother of pearl now and then. An enormous amount of nature poetry has been printed in the last twenty years but I can use but one poem out of a hundred. Here is a collection by Oscar Fay Adams of twelve volumes, one for each month, but I do well if I get two poems from each book by our minor poets. So many of them are more in love with their art than they are with the things they describe.

It will not do merely to paint nature, the poet must, in a measure, recreate her. I do not want a description of an April day, I want the day mirrored in the heart and life of the poet, as it is in Wordsworth, and in all the greater poets. The fanciful treatment of Nature is nearly always distasteful to me, but the imaginative treatment, like Keats' Nightingale, or Wordsworth's Cuckoo, is what I crave. If in your reading you find such poems, call my attention to them, please. . . .

This atmosphere of poetry proved contagious. After a few weeks' incubation, he himself succumbed to an attack of rhyming fever. Having looked in vain among the poets for the celebration of certain things he loved, he set about to see what he could do with such subjects. Aside from a few poems written in early manhood, his well-known 'Waiting' remained his only poetical undertaking until, on the Alaskan voyage, he had written the three bird poems already referred to. (One does not, of course, reckon here the various facetious verses he wrote, on occasion, all his life; for mere rhyming was easy for him, and he often amused himself and others by trivial excursions in this field.) On December 24th occurs a record of his more ambitious adventures into the land of Poesy:

All this month of December I have been in exceptional health and spirits, and have had unusual mental activity, stimulated, no doubt, by the rhyming-fever that seized me shortly after I came to Cambridge — a delight in work such as I used to have twenty years ago, and that I thought would never come back.

I have finished poems on the following subjects, some of them long — too long — namely: Snow Birds, Phœbe, The Hermit Thrush, Trailing Arbutus, Hepatica, The Song of the Toad, Columbine, The Barn on the Hill, and the Cardinal Flower. And there are others in sight.

Julian went home on the 22. I stay because I do not like to let the ink dry on my pen.

Despite his dining with friends on Christmas Day, and spending the evening with a gay company of young people, he confides to the Journal, 'I am sad as usual on this day — such a throng of memories as it brings up!' And on the last day of the year, and of the century, he writes of being 'blue,' and 'poking about' an old cemetery in the afternoon, where he found a stone with the date 1625; but he found something else there, too, for on the following day he wrote of finishing his bluebird poem, begun the day before. Thus was the old century linked to the new by this beloved bird of his boyhood — the bird 'with the earth tinge on its breast, and the sky tinge on its back' — the bird of hope and promise.

END OF VOLUME I